THE WRITINGS

OF

GEORGE WASHINGTON.

VOL. II.

Painted by G. Stuart. Engraved by A. B. Durand.

WASHINGTON.

From the original picture in the possession of the Athenæum,
Boston

THE

WRITINGS

OF

GEORGE WASHINGTON;

BEING HIS

CORRESPONDENCE, ADDRESSES, MESSAGES, AND OTHER PAPERS, OFFICIAL AND PRIVATE,

SELECTED AND PUBLISHED FROM THE ORIGINAL MANUSCRIPTS;

WITH

A LIFE OF THE AUTHOR,

NOTES, AND ILLUSTRATIONS.

By JARED SPARKS.

VOLUME II.

BOSTON:
LITTLE, BROWN, AND COMPANY.
1855.

PART FIRST;

COMPRISING

OFFICIAL LETTERS

RELATING TO THE FRENCH WAR,

AND

PRIVATE LETTERS

BEFORE THE AMERICAN REVOLUTION.

INTRODUCTION

TO THE FIRST PART.

In the method, which has been adopted for the present publication, the First Part consists of letters and papers written before the American Revolution. They relate chiefly to the French War, in which Washington was actively engaged for five years. During a large portion of that time he was commander-in-chief of the Virginia forces, and his correspondence in that capacity, both as furnishing historical materials and manifesting the characteristics and resources of his own mind, is curious and valuable. The importance attached to this correspondence by himself may be understood from the fact, that, many years after the letters were written, he revised the first drafts, and caused them to be carefully recorded in volumes. They have been preserved in this condition. Several of the originals still exist in his own handwriting. The same letter-books also contain military orders and reports of courts-martial, with connecting and explanatory remarks, which appear to have been added at a later date. These records form a complete narrative of the events in which Washington was concerned, from the time he joined General Braddock till he retired from the army.

At Braddock's defeat, Washington, in common with the commander-in-chief and the other officers, lost all his papers, which were taken by the French, sent first to Canada, and thence to France. Among these were contained his official correspondence of the preceding year, and a private journal of the campaign, important as developing the particulars of his military movements, of the death of Jumonville, and of the affair at the Great Meadows. Fortunately this loss has been in a good measure repaired from other sources. By the courtesy and favor of the British Ministry, I was allowed free access to the archives of the public offices in London, where I found, particularly among the manuscripts in the office of the Board of Trade, several valuable documents illustrative of these events. Through the politeness of Mr. Lockhart, I was also made acquainted with the existence of Governor Dinwiddie's letter-books, and a collection of Washington's early letters, in the possession of Mr. Hamilton of London, who very obligingly permitted them to be copied for my use. The file of Washington's letters contained the originals written to Governor Dinwiddie, describing all his military transactions previous to Braddock's defeat, and of course filled up the chasm occasioned by the loss of his papers in that disastrous battle.

In the library of the War Department at Paris I had, moreover, the good fortune to find some original papers respecting the operations of the French, on the frontiers of Virginia, during the time of Washington's first campaigns, copies of which were freely granted to me.

Many particulars, in addition to these materials, have been derived from the military and other letters, official and private, which were received by Washington in the time of the war, and were preserved at Mount Vernon. These have served to shed much light upon his own writings, by contributing matter for brief notes, and more full explanations in the Appendix. For this object I have likewise consulted such other manuscript authorities as could be obtained, relating to the period in question, and the best printed records and documents, such as the journals of assemblies, statutes at large, proclamations, governors' messages, and the correspondence of officers high in rank, both military and civil, English and French. It has in all cases been my endeavour to establish facts, as far as possible, by original testimony, and to take nothing at second hand where the means existed of ascending to a more authentic source. As this aim has been pursued with a scrupulous care and persevering diligence, it is believed, that as much accuracy has been attained, as the nature of such inquiries will admit, and that nothing has been passed over, which would serve to illustrate the character of Washington, or explain the transactions in which he took an important part.

After he resigned his commission in the army, and retired to his plantation at Mount Vernon, he devoted himself for fifteen years almost exclusively to his private affairs. He was usually a member of the Virginia House of Burgesses, but few traces remain of his public acts in that body. A list of the voters at his several elections, denoting the persons for whom they voted, has been preserved, from which it appears, that he was uniformly chosen by a large majority over all his competitors.

Two manuscript volumes contain the copies of letters, which were written between the time of his leaving the army and the beginning of the revolution. They are copied out with peculiar neatness in his own handwriting. As these letters were directed chiefly to his mercantile agents in London, employed to sell his tobacco and the other produce of his plantations, and to purchase such articles as he wanted from that market, they have little in them of public or permanent interest. They show the exactness of method, the unceasing industry, the minuteness of detail, and rigid economy, with which he managed all his affairs, and prosecuted every kind of business he undertook. Political reflections, general remarks, and opinions on higher topics, are occasionally introduced, but these are incidental, few, and brief. From this part of the correspondence such selections have been made, as were suited to the objects of the present work.

For many years previous to the revolution, it was Washington's custom to keep a diary of some of the principal incidents, that occurred within his observation. For this purpose he commonly used an almanac, interleaved with blank paper, and bound in a small volume. He made daily entrances under three heads, namely, first, "*Where, how, or with whom, my time is spent;*" secondly, "*Account of the Weather;*" thirdly, "*Remarks and Observations.*" He was a careful observer of the weather, and almost every night recorded the aspect of the heavens during the preceding day, whether cloudy or fair, the direction of the winds, and temperature. Whenever he left home he carried the interleaved almanac in his pocket, as also another little book, in which he entered daily the amount of money paid out by him, and the specific objects for which it was paid. This habit ceased during the revolution, but was renewed afterwards. The contents of his diary turned chiefly on agricultural operations and other business concerns. These volumes, kept for a series of years, afford some biographical materials not destitute of interest.

It has been a task of some difficulty to determine what general principles should be adopted, in selecting the parts for publication from the whole body of papers left by Washington. In the first place, the mass of manuscripts, which extends to eighty volumes, consisting chiefly of letters, is so large as to preclude the idea of publishing more than a comparatively small portion. Again, from the nature of the correspondence, being mostly official, and many of the letters having been written to different persons on the same subject, there are necessarily frequent repetitions, and numerous particulars constantly intervening, which, though essential at the time in the transactions to which they relate, have no longer any interest or moment. Of this description are the innumerable details incident to the subordinate arrangements of an army, such as supplies, provisions, clothing, camp equipage, arms, ammunition, and other points of minor consideration, which engaged the incessant care of the commander-in-chief, and entered largely into his correspondence even with Congress and the highest officers both civil and military. To print all the materials of this kind would not only be useless in itself, but would add so much to the size and expense of the work, as, at the same time to make it cumbersome and unattractive to readers, and raise its cost above the means of many individuals, who may wish to possess these personal records and authentic memorials of the acts, opinions, and character of the father of his country.

Under these circumstances I have endeavoured to pursue such a course, as would the most effectually attain the object to be desired, in bringing these papers before the public; namely, to exhibit the writings of Washington in a manner, that will render strict justice to the imperishable name of their author, and contribute the greatest advantage to his countrymen, both at the present time and in future ages. For this purpose I have laid down two rules, which I have labored to follow with as much discrimination as possible; first, to select such parts, as have a permanent value on account of the historical facts which they contain, whether in relation to actual events, or to the political designs and operations in which Washington was a leading or conspicuous agent; secondly, to comprise such other parts, as contain the views, opinions, counsels, and reflections of the writer on all kinds of topics, showing thereby the structure of his mind, its powers and resources, and the strong and varied points of his character. Upon this plan it has been my study to go carefully through the manuscripts, without regard to what has heretofore been made public, and gather from the whole, and combine into one body, the portions most important for their intrinsic value and historical characteristics; so that the work, in its complete form, may be a depository of all the writings of Washington, which it is essential to preserve, either as illustrating his political and private life, or the history of his country during the long and brilliant period of his public career.

According to this plan, when a letter throughout bears the features above described, it will be printed entire, as will in every case the addresses, speeches, messages, circulars, and other state papers, issued by him from time to time. But many of the letters, both in the public and private correspondence, for the reasons already assigned, will necessarily be printed with omissions of unimportant passages, relating chiefly to topics or facts evanescent in their nature, and temporary in their design. Special care will be taken, nevertheless, in all such omissions, that the sense shall not be marred, nor the meaning of the writer in any manner perverted or obscured. Nor is this difficult, because the omitted passages usually treat upon separate and distinct subjects, and may be removed without injury to the remaining portions of the letter.

It ought to be premised here, that, in preparing the manuscripts for the press, I have been obliged sometimes to use a latitude of discretion, rendered unavoidable by the mode in which the papers have been preserved. They are uniformly copied into volumes, and this task appears to have been performed, except in the revolutionary correspondence, by incompetent or very careless transcribers. Gross blunders constantly occur, which not unfrequently destroy the sense, and which never could have existed in the original drafts. In these cases I have of course considered it a duty, appertaining to the function of a faithful editor, to hazard such corrections as the construction of the sentence manifestly warranted, or a cool judgment dictated. On some occasions the writer himself, through haste or inadvertence, may have fallen into an awkward use of words, faults of grammar, or inaccuracies of style, and when such occur from this source, I have equally felt bound to correct them. It would be an act of unpardonable injustice to any author, after his death, to bring forth compositions, and particularly letters, written with no design to their publication, and commit them to the press without previously subjecting them to a careful revision. This exercise of an editor's duty, however, I have thought it allowable to extend only to verbal and grammatical mistakes or inaccuracies, maintaining a scrupulous caution that the author's meaning and purpose should thereby in no degree be changed or affected.

As this work is intended to be strictly a collection of Washington's writings, it is deemed unadvisable to encumber it with notes and foreign matter, any farther than is requisite to explain and properly illustrate the text. The notes will for the most part be short, historical, and explanatory, touching only on particulars relevant to the subject in hand. There will be an Appendix at the end of each volume for topics, which may demand additional inquiry or investigation, and also for original materials not suited to the body of the work.

Should the notes in this First Part seem to trespass on the rule of brevity, an apology may be found in the fact, that the history of the events upon which they have a bearing is but little known, and that hardly any of the letters to which they are attached have hitherto been published. Some new matter is thrown into the Appendix, claiming a place there, as containing biographical sketches of Washington's early years, elucidating the transactions of his first campaigns, and, above all, vindicating him from a charge, which the French historians have wrongfully perpetuated as a spot on the brightness of his fame.

Facsimiles.

Æt. 13.

March 12th 1744/5

Geo Washington

Æt. 17.

Beginning this Eleventh Day of November 1749 —

Washington

Æt. 25.

I am Sir, Yr Most Obedt Hble Servt

Fort Loudoun
10th Septr 1757 } —

G: Washington

Æt. 44.

Yr Most Affectn Brother,

G: Washington

New York 29th of April 1776.

Four days before his Death. Æt. 67.

Mount Vernon
December 10th
1799

G: Washington

G. H. Boynton & Co. Sc.

LETTERS

OFFICIAL AND PRIVATE,

BEFORE THE AMERICAN REVOLUTION.

TO ROBERT DINWIDDIE, LIEUTENANT-GOVERNOR OF VIRGINIA.

Alexandria, 9 March, 1754.*

SIR,

In my last, by Mr. Stewart, I slightly mentioned the objection, which many had against enlisting, to wit, not knowing who was to be paymaster, or the times for payment. It is now grown a pretty general clamor; and some of those, who were among the first enlisted, being needy, and knowing it to be usual for his Majesty's soldiers to be paid once a week, or at most

---

* The letters written previously to this date have been lost. For earlier papers see APPENDIX, No. I.

Washington arrived in Williamsburg, from his mission over the Alleganies, on the 16th of January, and the Governor and Council resolved to enlist two companies, of one hundred men each, and send them to the Ohio with orders to construct a fort on that river. The command of the two companies was given to Washington. One company was to be raised by himself, and the other by Captain Trent, who was to collect his men among the traders and people in the back settlements, and proceed immediately to the place of destination. Major Washington, in the mean time, was stationed at Alexandria, till the other company should be completed, and the proper military supplies forwarded to that place.

"Having all things in readiness," says the Governor in his instructions, "you are to use all expedition in proceeding to the Fork of the Ohio, with the men under your command; and there you are to finish, in the best manner, and as soon as you possibly can, the fort, which I expect is there

every fortnight, are very importunate to receive their due. I have soothed and quieted them as much as possible, under pretence of receiving your instructions in this particular at the arrival of the colonel.

I have increased my number of men to about twenty-five, and dare venture to say, that I should have had several more, if the excessive bad weather did not prevent their meeting agreeably to their officers' commands.

We daily experience the great necessity for clothing the men, as we find the generality of those, who are to be enlisted, loose, idle persons, quite destitute of house and home, and, I may truly say, many of them of clothes; which last renders them very incapable of the necessary service, as they must unavoidably be exposed to inclement weather in their marches, and can expect no other than to encounter almost every difficulty, that is incident to a soldier's life. There are many of them without shoes, others want stockings, some are without shirts, and not a few that have scarce a coat or waistcoat to their backs. In short, they are as ill provided as can well be conceived; but I really believe every man of them, for his own credit's sake, is willing to be clothed at his own expense. They are perpetually teazing me to have it done, but I am not able to advance the money, provided there was no risk in it, which there certainly is, and too great for me to run; though it would be nothing to the country, as a certain part of their pay might be deducted and appro-

---

already begun by the Ohio Company. You are to act on the defensive; but, in case any attempts are made to obstruct the works, or interrupt our settlements, by any person whatsoever, you are to restrain all such offenders, or, in case of resistance, to make prisoners of, or kill and destroy them. For the rest, you are to conduct yourself as the circumstances of the service shall require, and to act as you shall find best for the furtherance of his Majesty's service, and the good of this dominion."

priated to that use. Mr. Carlyle, or any of the merchants here, would furnish them with proper necessaries, if there was a certainty of any part of their pay being stopped to reimburse the expense.

But I must here in time put a curb to my requests, and remember that I ought not to be too importunate; otherwise I shall be as troublesome to you, as the soldiers are to me. Nothing but the necessity of the thing could urge me to be thus free; but I shall no more press this affair, as I am well assured, that whatever you may think for the benefit of the expedition, you will cause to have done. I am, &c.

TO RICHARD CORBIN.*

March, 1754.

DEAR SIR,

In a conversation with you at Green Spring, you gave me some room to hope for a commission above that of major, and to be ranked among the chief officers of this expedition. The command of the whole forces is what I neither look for, expect, nor desire; for I must be impartial enough to confess, it is a charge too great for my youth and inexperience to be entrusted with. Knowing this, I have too sincere a love for my country, to undertake that which may tend to the prejudice of it. But if I could entertain hopes, that you thought me worthy of the post of lieutenant-colonel, and would favor me so far as to mention it at the appointment of officers, I could not but entertain a true sense of the kindness.

---

* Mr. Corbin was a member of the Governor's Council, and connected by the ties of friendship and affinity with the Washington family. See Marshall's *Life of Washington*, 2d ed. Vol. 1. p. 3.

I flatter myself, that, under a skilful commander, or man of sense, (whom I most sincerely wish to serve under,) with my own application and diligent study of my duty, I shall be able to conduct my steps without censure, and, in time, render myself worthy of the promotion, that I shall be favored with now. I am, &c.

TO GOVERNOR DINWIDDIE.*

Alexandria, 20 March, 1754.

SIR,

I was favored with your letter by Mr. Stewart, enclosing a lieutenant-colonel's commission, and I hope my future behaviour will sufficiently testify the true sense I have of this kindness.†

---

* Dinwiddie was lieutenant-governor of Virginia, yet, as he was the acting governor, all Colonel Washington's letters are addressed to him as bearing that title.

† The Virginia Assembly, at a recent sitting, had voted ten thousand pounds towards supporting the expedition to the Ohio. With this aid the Governor was induced to increase the military establishment to three hundred men, divided into six companies, and Colonel Joshua Fry was appointed to command the whole. Major Washington was in consequence raised to the rank of lieutenant-colonel, and made second in command. Ten cannon, and other military equipments, were sent to Alexandria for the use of the expedition. These had recently arrived from England.

As early as the first of March, also, Governor Dinwiddie received a letter from the Earl of Holdernesse, enclosing an order to the governor of New York to send two Independent companies to Virginia, for the purpose of coöperating with the forces destined to the Ohio; and an order to the governor of South Carolina to furnish another Independent company for the same service. The troops, called *Independent Companies*, were raised in the colonies, under the direction of the governors, but they were paid by the King, and the officers had King's commissions. Hence they were not subject to colonial regulations, but could be marched to any point at the King's command.

By the laws of Virginia, the militia could not be marched more than five miles from the boundary line of the colony. It was doubtful whether the

At present there are about seventy-five men at Alexandria, near fifty of whom I have enlisted. The others have been sent by Messrs. Polson, Mercer, and Waggener to this place. Very few officers have repaired hither yet, which has occasioned a fatiguing time to me, in managing a number of self-willed, ungovernable people. I shall implicitly obey your commands, and march out with all expedition. Major Carlyle is now preparing wagons for the conveyance of provisions, which till now could not move, on account of the heavy roads.

I doubt not but your Honor has been informed before this of Mr. Vanbraam's ill success in Augusta, by the express, who was sent from thence for that purpose.

Major Muse's promotion, and Messrs. Rose and Bently's declining, will occasion a want of officers; in which case I would beg leave to mention Mr. Vanbraam for a command, who is the oldest lieutenant, and an experienced soldier. Unless the officers come in, I shall be obliged to appoint him to that office, till I have your Honor's further directions. It would be con-

---

territory invaded by the French was within the limits of Virginia, as the western bounds of Pennsylvania had not been defined. Hence the governor could not order the militia on this service, but was obliged to rely on volunteer enlistments.

To encourage these enlistments, and give spirit to this enterprise, Governor Dinwiddie issued a proclamation, granting two hundred thousand acres of land on the Ohio River, which were to be divided among the officers and soldiers engaged in the present expedition. The grant was confirmed by the King, but it was not till the war had been long at an end, that the land was surveyed and appropriated. This was effected at last chiefly, if not entirely, through the active and persevering agency of Washington.

Governor Dinwiddie wrote to Governor Delancey of New York, that his orders from the King were, "to prevent the French and their Indians from settling on his lands on the Ohio, and to build two or three forts on that river; and that he had been pleased to send thirty cannon to be mounted on those forts, and eighty barrels of gunpowder." — Dinwiddie's *Manuscript Letter-Books*, 21 March, 1754.

ferring a very great obligation on him, were you to confirm the appointment. I verily believe his behaviour would not render him displeasing to you. I have given Captain Stephen orders to be in readiness to join us at Winchester with his company, as they were already in that neighbourhood, and raised there.

I have nothing further to add at present, but my sincere thanks for the indulgent favors I have met with, and I am your Honor's most obedient, &c.*

TO GOVERNOR DINWIDDIE.

Will's Creek, 25 April, 1754.

SIR,

Captain Trent's ensign, Mr. Ward, has this day arrived from the Fork of the Monongahela, and brings the disagreeable account, that the fort, on the 17th instant, was surrendered at the summons of Monsieur Contrecœur to a body of French, consisting of upwards of one thousand men, who came from Venango with eighteen pieces of cannon, sixty batteaux, and three hundred canoes. They gave him liberty to bring off all his men and working-tools, which he accordingly did the same day.†

---

* Colonel Washington marched from Alexandria on the 2d of April, with two companies of troops, and arrived at Will's Creek on the 20th, having been joined on the route by a detachment under Captain Stephen.

† The position occupied by Captain Trent's men was at the junction of the Monongahela and Allegany Rivers (now Pittsburg), which had been visited by Major Washington on his mission from the governor of Virginia to the French, and which he described in his Journal as well situated for a fort. The Ohio Company had already a small establishment there. When Contrecœur appeared before the fort, very little progress had been made in the work. Captain Trent was absent at Will's Creek, and Lieu-

Immediately upon this information I called a council of war, to advise on proper measures to be taken in this exigency. A copy of their resolves, with the proceedings, I herewith enclose by the bearer, whom I have continued express to your Honor for more minute intelligence.

Mr. Ward has the summons with him, and a speech from the Half-King,* which I also enclose, with the wampum. He is accompanied by one of the Indians mentioned therein, who were sent to see where we were, what was our strength, and to know the time to expect us out. The other young man I have prevailed upon to return to the Half-King with the following speech.

" Sachems, Warriors of the Six United Nations, Shannoahs, and Delawares, our friends and brethren. I

---

tenant Frazier was at his residence ten miles distant. Ensign Ward, therefore, was left in the command. His whole number of men amounted only to forty-one.

Contrecœur approached within a short distance of the fort, halted his troops, and sent in an officer with a summons, allowing Ensign Ward an hour to consider the subject, and directing him then to repair to the French camp with his determination in writing. He immediately counselled with the Indians, and the Half-King advised him to inform the French, that he was not an officer of rank, nor invested with powers to answer their demands, and to request them to wait the arrival of the chief commander. He went accordingly with this reply to the French camp, accompanied by the Half-King; but Contrecœur refused to wait, and demanded an immediate decision, saying that he should otherwise take possession of the fort by force. Hereupon a capitulation was agreed to, and Ensign Ward marched off his men the next day, and ascended the Monongahela to the mouth of Red-stone Creek. Contrecœur invited him to supper the evening of the capitulation, and treated him with much civility.

A full narrative of the particulars was given under oath by Ensign Ward to Governor Dinwiddie, who communicated it to the English government. The original is now in the Plantation Office, where it was examined by the editor. This seizure of a post by a military force was considered, at the time, as the first overt act of hostility in the memorable war which followed, and which raged for seven years both in Europe and America.

* A Chief of the Six Nations, devoted to the interests of the English.

received your speech by the Buck's brother [Mr. Ward], who came to us with the two young men five sleeps after leaving you. We return you thanks from hearts glowing with affection for your steadfast adherence to us, for your kind speech, and for your wise counsels and directions to the Buck's brother.

"The young man will inform you where he met a small part of our army advancing towards you, clearing the road for a great number of our warriors, who are immediately to follow with our great guns, our ammunition, and our provisions.

"I could not delay to let you know our hearts, and have sent back one of the young men with this speech to acquaint you with them. I have sent the other, according to your desire, to the governor of Virginia, with the Buck's brother, to deliver your speech and wampum, and to be an eyewitness of the preparations we are making to come in haste to support you, whose interest is as dear to us as our lives. We resent the usage of the treacherous French, and our conduct will henceforth plainly show you how much we have it at heart.

"I cannot be easy without seeing you before our forces meet at the fork of the roads, and therefore I have the greatest desire that you and Escuniate, or one of you, should meet me on the road as soon as possible to assist us in council.

"To assure you of the good will we bear you, and to confirm the truth of what has been said, I herewith present to you a string of wampum, that you may thereby remember how much I am your brother and friend."

I hope my proceedings in these affairs will be satisfactory to your Honor, as I have, to the utmost of my knowledge, consulted the interest of the expedition and good of my country; whose rights, while they are asserted in so just a cause, I will defend to the last remains of life.

Hitherto the difficulties I have met with in marching have been greater, than I expect to encounter on the Ohio, when possibly I may be surrounded by the enemy, and these difficulties have been occasioned by those, who, had they acted as becomes every good subject, would have exerted their utmost abilities to forward our just designs. Out of seventy-four wagons impressed at Winchester, we got but ten after waiting a week, and some of those so badly provided with teams, that the soldiers were obliged to assist them up the hills, although it was known they had better teams at home. I doubt not that in some points I may have strained the law; but I hope, as my sole motive was to expedite the march, I shall be supported in it, should my authority be questioned, which at present I do not apprehend, unless some busybody intermeddles.*

Your Honor will see by the resolves in council, that I am destined to the Monongahela with all the diligent despatch in my power. We will endeavour to make the road sufficiently good for the heaviest artillery to pass, and, when we arrive at Red-stone Creek, fortify our-

---

* By the militia law of Virginia the commander could impress provisions, boats, wagons, draft-horses, utensils, tools, and the like, necessary to facilitate military movements and operations. But no article could be impressed, till its value had been appraised, and an estimate of the proper allowance for its daily use had been made, by two reputable persons under oath. A receipt for the same was then to be given in writing to the owner, by the commanding officer. — Hening's *Statutes at Large*, Vol. VI. p. 114. Under the difficulties of the service mentioned in the text, it was doubtless not possible to comply literally in every instance with these formalities of the law.

Although the troops now raised were volunteers, and enlisted for a special purpose, yet they were regulated in every respect by the militia laws of the colony. This was the cause of great inconvenience and embarrassment to Washington afterwards, particularly in regard to discipline, as the militia laws were extremely ill suited to an army in active service.

selves as strongly as the short time will allow. I doubt not that we can maintain a possession there, till we are reinforced, unless the rising of the waters shall admit the enemy's cannon to be conveyed up in canoes, and then I flatter myself we shall not be so destitute of intelligence, as not to get timely notice of it, and make a good retreat.

I hope you will see the absolute necessity for our having, as soon as our forces are collected, a number of cannon, some of heavy metal, with mortars and grenadoes to attack the French, and put us on an equal footing with them.

Perhaps it may also be thought advisable to invite the Cherokees, Catawbas, and Chickasaws to march to our assistance, as we are informed that six hundred Chippewas and Ottawas are marching down Scioto Creek to join the French, who are coming up the Ohio. In that case I would beg leave to recommend their being ordered to this place first, that a peace may be concluded between them and the Six Nations; for I am informed by several persons, that, as no good harmony subsists between them, their coming first to the Ohio may create great disorders, and turn out much to our disadvantage.

As I had opportunities I wrote to the governors of Maryland and Pennsylvania, acquainting them with these advices, and enclosed the summons and Indian speech, which I hope you will not think me too forward in doing. I considered that the Assembly of Maryland was to sit in five days, that the Pennsylvania Assembly is now sitting, and that, by giving timely notice, something might be done in favor of this expedition, which now requires all the force we can muster.*

* Governor Dinwiddie had likewise written to the governors of all the provinces, from New York to South Carolina, setting forth the alarming

By the best information I can get, I much doubt whether any of the Indians will be in to treat in May. Are the Indian women and children, if they settle amongst us, to be maintained at our expense? They will expect it. I have the honor to be, &c.

TO JAMES HAMILTON, GOVERNOR OF PENNSYLVANIA.

Will's Creek, 27 April, 1754.

SIR,

It is with the greatest concern I acquaint you, that Mr. Ward, ensign in Captain Trent's company, was compelled to surrender his small fort at the Fork of the Monongahela to the French, on the 17th instant, who fell down from Venango, with a fleet of three hundred and sixty batteaux and canoes, upwards of one thousand men, and eighteen pieces of artillery, which they planted against the fort, drew up their men, and sent the enclosed summons to Mr. Ward, who, having but

---

state of affairs in Virginia, and pressing for assistance. But nothing was done. Several of the governors brought the matter before their Assemblies, with moving appeals to their patriotism and sympathy. The evil was too distant to be felt, and was little heeded. The Assemblies of New York and Pennsylvania, and some persons in that of Virginia, professed to doubt, whether his Majesty's dominions actually extended to the French encroachments. Governor Glen of South Carolina was perplexed with similar misgivings. This idea was shocking to the zeal and loyalty of Dinwiddie and others, who supposed the question of right to have been put at rest by the treaties of Utrecht and Aix-la-Chapelle, and by certain diplomatic arrangements with the Indians of recent date. — *Review of Military Operations in North America*, p. 10. — *Votes of the Assembly of Pennsylvania*, Vol. IV. pp. 287 - 513. — Dinwiddie's *Letter-Books*.

Pennsylvania and Maryland were more immediately concerned, as their frontiers were threatened. In both these colonies the Assemblies passed money bills for general protection, but so clogged with what the governors called attacks upon the prerogative, that they would not sign them. Long feuds had existed between the governors and the Assemblies on this subject of granting money, and the Assemblies were generally adroit enough to connect a full assertion of their claims with those cases, in which the

an inconsiderable number of men, and no cannon, to make a proper defence, was obliged to surrender. They suffered him to draw off his men, arms, and working-tools, and gave leave that he might retreat to the inhabitants.

I have heard of your Honor's great zeal for his Majesty's service, and for all our interests on the present occasion. You will see, by the enclosed speech of the Half-King, that the Indians expect some assistance from you; and I am persuaded you will take proper notice of their moving speech, and their unshaken fidelity.

I thought it more advisable to acquaint your Honor with it immediately, than to wait till you could get intelligence by the way of Williamsburg and the young man, as the Half-King proposes.

I have arrived thus far with a detachment of one hundred and fifty men. Colonel Fry, with the remainder of the regiment and artillery, is daily expected. In the mean time, we advance slowly across the mountains, making the roads, as we march, fit for the carriage of

---

public exigencies were the most urgent, hoping thereby to bring the governors to proper terms, and in this they sometimes succeeded. As the people gave the money, it was said, they ought to be allowed to raise and appropriate it in their own way. To this broad principle the governors objected instructions, prerogative, and precedent.

Governor Dinwiddie's official dignity was severely tried in the affair of the ten thousand pounds, granted by the Virginia legislature. By the bill, making the grant, a committee was appointed to act in concert with the governor in appropriating the money. In writing to the Board of Trade, he says, "I would by no means have given my assent to the bill, if his Majesty's service had not immediately called for a supply." He averred, that the business of appropriating the money, granted for the defence of the colony, was vested wholly in the hands of the governor.

He wrote at the same time to the Earl of Halifax: — "I am sorry to find the House of Burgesses in a republican way of thinking; and, indeed, they do not act in a proper constitutional way, but make encroachments upon the prerogative of the crown, in which some former governors have submitted too much to them; and, I fear, without a very particular instruction, it will be difficult to bring them to order." — Dinwiddie's *Letter-Books*, 12 March, 1754.

our great guns; and are designed to proceed as far as the mouth of Red-stone Creek, which enters the Monongahela about thirty-seven miles above the fort taken by the French, from whence we have a water carriage down the river. And there is a storehouse built by the Ohio Company, which may serve as a receptacle for our ammunition and provisions.

Besides these French, that came from Venango, we have credible accounts, that another party are coming up the Ohio. We also have intelligence, that six hundred of the Chippewas and Ottawas are marching down Scioto Creek to join them. I hope your Honor will excuse the freedom I have assumed in acquainting you with these advices; it was the warm zeal I owe my country, that influenced me to it, and occasioned this express.

I am, with all due respect and regard, your Honor's most obedient and very humble servant.*

---

* This letter was immediately laid before the legislature by the governor. A bill was then pending for a grant of ten thousand pounds for the King's use, but it was obstructed in its progress by the opposition of the Governor to the plan proposed by the Assembly for raising the money, and no relief was obtained for the expedition. — *Votes of the Pennsylvania Assembly*, Vol. IV. p. 313.

Whatever doubts there may have been in the minds of some members of the Assembly, as to the King's title to the Western lands, these doubts were not publicly urged as a reason for withholding a grant of money. But the truth is, that, when the contest between France and England began, neither power had any just title to the lands west of the Ohio River. There could be no pretence, by either party, of conquest, purchase, or occupancy. The French had been accustomed to pass from Canada and the Lakes down the Wabash and through the Illinois country to Louisiana, and a few English traders had recently gone over the mountains and bartered with the Indians. The English government had even granted five hundred thousand acres of land there to the Ohio Company. The claim by the English was founded on the treaties of Utrecht and Aix-la-Chapelle, in which France consented that Great Britain should have jurisdiction over all the regions possessed by the Iroquois, or Six Nations. But there is no proof, that the territory in question belonged to the Iroquois. In fact, there is the strongest evidence to the contrary.

TO GOVERNOR DINWIDDIE.

Little Meadows, 9 May, 1754.

SIR,

I acquainted you by Mr. Ward with the determination, which we prosecuted four days after his departure, as soon as wagons arrived to carry our provisions. The want of proper conveyances has much retarded this expedition, and at this time it unfortunately delays the detachment I have the honor to command. Even when we came to Will's Creek, my disappointments were not less than before; for there I expected to find a sufficient number of packhorses provided by Captain Trent, conformably to his promise, and to Major Carlyle's letters and my own, that I might prosecute my first intention with light, expeditious marches; but instead of that, there was none in readiness, nor any in expectation that I could perceive, which reduced me to the necessity of waiting till wagons could be procured from

---

The only rightful owners were the Indian occupants, and these were not the Iroquois. This point is very clear from the whole tenor of Indian history, and is fully confirmed by Heckewelder, though in some things that venerable missionary was credulous, and too much influenced by the traditions of his favorite Delawares.

Besides the above memorable treaties of the high European powers, Governor Dinwiddie gave great weight to an Indian treaty made at Lancaster, in 1744, between a large number of delegates from the Iroquois tribes, and Commissioners from Pennsylvania, Maryland, and Virginia. This treaty was conducted with much parade and formality, after the Indian manner, and the Iroquois professed to give up their claim to the lands on the west of the Allegany Mountains for *four hundred pounds*, paid to them by Virginia in money and goods; but the extent of these lands is not defined; and the Commissioners themselves seem to doubt the title of the Iroquois, when they tell them, "We are informed that the Southern Indians claim these very lands that you do." During the whole transaction, which lasted several days, the Indian negociators expressed more solicitude about the rum, that was given them from time to time, than the affairs of state in which they were engaged.

There was much good sense, however, in the following remarks of the Sachem Gachradodow, in his speech to the Commissioners from Virginia;

the Branch, forty miles distant. However, in the mean time, I detached a party of sixty men to make and mend the road, which party since the 25th of April, and the main body since the 1st instant, have been laboriously employed, and have got no farther than these Meadows, about twenty miles from the New Store.* We have been two days making a bridge across the river, and have not done yet.†

The great difficulty and labor, that it requires to mend

—"You know very well, when the white people first came here, they were poor; but they have got our lands, and are by them become rich, and we are now poor; what little we have had for the land goes soon away, but the land lasts for ever." And again;—"The great king might send you over to conquer the Indians; but it looks to us, that God did not approve it; if he had, he would not have placed the great sea where it is, as the limits between us and you."—Colden's *History of the Five Nations*, Vol. II. pp. 86, 87.

When Mr. Gist went over the Alleganies, in February, 1751, on a tour of discovery for the Ohio Company, "an Indian, who spoke good English, came to him, and said that their great man, the Beaver, and Captain Oppamyluah, (two Chiefs of the Delawares) desired to know where the Indians' land lay, for the French claimed all the land on one side of the Ohio River, and the English on the other." This question Mr. Gist found it hard to answer, and he evaded it by saying, that the Indians and white men were all subjects of the same king, and all had an equal privilege of taking up and possessing the land, in conformity with the conditions prescribed by the King.—Gist's *Manuscript Journal*.

* A storehouse, or magazine, established by the Ohio Company at Will's Creek.

† A council of war had been called, when the news of Ensign Ward's capitulation reached Will's Creek, in which it was agreed to be impossible to march towards the fort without reinforcements; but it was resolved to advance to the mouth of Red-stone Creek on the Monongahela, and raise a fortification, clearing the roads on the way, so that the artillery and baggage could pass, and there wait for fresh orders.

The reasons for this decision were, that the mouth of the Red-stone was the nearest convenient position on the Monongahela; that the storehouses already built there by the Ohio Company would receive their munitions and provisions; that the heavy artillery might be easily transported by water from that place, whenever it should be expedient to attack the French fort; and that by this movement the soldiers would be kept from the ill consequences of inaction, and the Indians encouraged to remain true to their alliance.

and alter the road, prevent our marching above two, three, or four miles a day; and I fear, though no diligence shall be spared, that we shall be detained some considerable time before it can be made good for the carriage of the artillery with Colonel Fry.

We daily receive intelligence from Ohio by one or another of the traders, who are continually retreating to the inhabitants with their effects. They all concur, that the French are reinforced with eight hundred men; and this day, by one Kalendar, I received an account, which he sets forth as certain, that there are six hundred at the Falls of the Ohio, from whence they intend to move up to the lower Shawnese Town, at the mouth of Scioto Creek, to erect fortresses. He likewise says, that the forces at the Fork are erecting their works with their whole strength; and as he was coming he met at Mr. Gist's new settlement Monsieur La Force with four soldiers, who, under the specious pretence of hunting after deserters, were reconnoitring and discovering the country. He also brings the agreeable news, that the Half-King has received, and is much pleased with, the speech I sent him, and is now upon his march with fifty men to meet us. The French down the river are sending presents and invitations to all the neighbouring Indians.

We have heard nothing from the Catawbas, or any of the Southern Indians, though this is the time we mostly need their assistance. I have not above one hundred and sixty effective men with me, since Captain Trent's have left us, whom I discharged from this detachment, and ordered them to wait your commands at Captain Trent's; for I found them rather injurious to the other men, than serviceable to the expedition, till they could be upon the same establishment with us, and come under the rigor of martial law. I am, &c.

TO GOVERNOR DINWIDDIE.

Youghiogany, 18 May, 1754.

SIR,

I am heartily concerned, that the officers have such real cause to complain of the Committee's resolves; and still more to find my inclinations prone to second their just grievances.

I have endeavoured, as far as I was able, to see in the best light I could the trifling advantages that may accrue; yet nothing prevents their throwing down their commissions, (with gratitude and thanks to your Honor, whose good intentions of serving us we are all well assured of,) but the approaching danger, which has too far engaged their honor to recede till other officers are sent in their room, or an alteration made regarding their pay, during which time they will assist with their best endeavours voluntarily, that is, without receiving the gratuity allowed by the resolves of the Committee.

Giving up my commission is quite contrary to my intention. Nay, I ask it as a greater favor, than any amongst the many I have received from your Honor, to confirm it to me. But let me serve voluntarily; then I will, with the greatest pleasure in life, devote my services to the expedition without any other reward, than the satisfaction of serving my country; but to be slaving dangerously for the shadow of pay, through woods, rocks, mountains, — I would rather prefer the great toil of a daily laborer, and dig for a maintenance, provided I were reduced to the necessity, than serve upon such ignoble terms; for I really do not see why the lives of his Majesty's subjects in Virginia should be of less value, than of those in other parts of his American dominions; especially when it is well known, that we must undergo double their hardship.

I could enumerate a thousand difficulties that we have met with, and must expect to meet with, more than other officers who have almost double our pay; but as I know you reflect on these things, and are sensible of the hardships we must necessarily encounter, it would be needless to enlarge.

Besides, as I have expatiated fully (and, perhaps, too warmly) in a letter to Colonel Fairfax, who, I suppose, will accompany you to Winchester, upon the motives that occasion these my resolves, I shall not trouble you with them; for the subject leads me too far when I engage in it.*

Another thing resolved by the Committee is, that only one sergeant and one corporal be allowed to a company; with whom it is as much impossible to do the necessary duty, as it is to conquer kingdoms with my handful of men.

Upon the whole, I find so many clogs upon the expe-

---

* The Governor was at this time in Winchester, having previously made arrangements for meeting there several Indian chiefs, to brighten the chain of friendship by a new treaty, or rather to give them presents, and exchange belts of wampum. He assigned this as a reason, why Virginia did not send delegates to the Albany Convention, which was recommended by the Board of Trade, and attended by commissioners from the northern and middle colonies, and which acquired notoriety from the celebrated *Plan of Union* drawn up by Franklin, and adopted by the Convention. The attempt to treat at Winchester was a failure, as two or three subordinate Chiefs only appeared, though Washington used his best endeavours to bring down the Half-King and some of his friends. They made excuses, that they were planting corn, and engaged in other affairs at home.

The Albany Plan of Union was disapproved in Virginia, as it was everywhere else, and by the Governor particularly, because he had already matured a project of his own. He communicated the year before to Lord Halifax a scheme for colonial government, which he deemed "more reasonable and more constitutional," than the one proposed by the commissioners at Albany. The prominent feature of his scheme was, that the colonies should be divided into two districts, a northern and southern, in each of which there should be a congress, or some kind of general council. for the regulation of their respective interests.

dition, that I quite despair of success; nevertheless, I humbly beg it, as a particular favor, that your Honor will continue me in the post I now enjoy, the duty whereof I will most cheerfully execute as a volunteer, but by no means upon the present pay.

I hope what I have said will not be taken amiss; for I really believe, were it as much in your power, as it is your inclination, we should be treated as gentlemen and officers, and not have annexed to the most trifling pay, that ever was given to English officers, the glorious allowance of soldier's diet, — a pound of pork, with bread in proportion, per day. Be the consequence what it will, I am determined not to leave the regiment, but to be amongst the last men that quit the Ohio, even if I serve as a private volunteer, which I greatly prefer to the establishment we are now upon. I am, &c.

TO GOVERNOR DINWIDDIE.

Youghiogany, 18 May, 1754.

SIR,

I received your Honor's favor by Mr. Ward, who arrived here last night, just as two Indians came to us from the Ohio.

These Indians contradict the report of the French having received reinforcements, though they agree that eight hundred men are very shortly expected. Those on the spot are busily employed in erecting the fort, which they have removed to the point I recommended for the country's use, whose walls they have now made two fathoms thick, and raised them breast high.

They are daily sending out scouts, some of whom about five days ago were seen within six or seven miles of our camp; but as I did not receive timely notice of it, they may have escaped, unless they have fallen in with a party sent out about eight days ago to Red-stone Creek, to reconnoitre the country thereabouts, and to get intelligence of the motions of the French.

It is imagined that the Half-King will be here in two or three days, but to hurry him I have sent the Indian, that came up with Mr. Ward, with a short speech, acquainting him with my desire of his coming as expeditiously as possible, to receive the speech which your Honor sent by Mr. Ward, and which Colonel Fry wrote me I was to deliver. When he arrives I will endeavour to send him on to meet you at Winchester.

These Indians, and all the traders that I have been able to get any information from, of late, agree that it is almost impracticable to open a road, in which a wagon can pass from this to Red-stone Creek. But most of them assure me, that, except at one place, water carriage may be had down this river, which will be a most advantageous discovery if it proves true, as it will save forty miles' land carriage over almost impassable roads and mountains.

The water is now so high, that we cannot possibly cross over with our men, which likewise secures us from any immediate attacks of the enemy. I have therefore resolved to go down the river to the fall, which is at the Turkey Foot, to inform myself concerning the nature and difficulty attending this fall. I have provided a canoe, and shall, with an officer and five men, set out upon this discovery to-morrow morning.

Captain Trent's men, who by their refractory behaviour obliged me to separate them from the other soldiers, have now left the New Store and dispersed, contrary to my positive orders till they received your commands.

As I shall have frequent communications with the Indians, which are of no effect without wampum, I hope you will order some to be sent. Indeed, we ought to have shirts, and many other things of this sort, which are always expected by every Indian that brings a message, or good report. Also the chiefs, who visit and converse in council, look for the same. If it would not be thought too bold in me, I would recommend some of the treaty goods to be sent for that purpose with Colonel Fry, or after him. This is the method the French pursue, and a trifle judiciously bestowed, and in season, may turn to our advantage. If I find this river navigable, I am convinced it cannot but be agreeable to your Honor, that we should build canoes in order to convey our artillery down. As the road to this place is made as good as it can be, much time and great labor having been spent upon it, I believe a wagon may travel now with fifteen or eighteen hundred weight, by doubling the teams at one or two places only. I am, &c.

TO COLONEL JOSHUA FRY.

23 May, 1754.

SIR,

This day I returned from my discoveries down the Youghiogany, which, I am sorry to say, can never be made navigable. We traced the watercourse near thirty miles, with the full expectation of succeeding in the much desired aim; but, at length, we came to a fall, which continued rough, rocky, and scarcely passable, for two miles, and then fell, within the space of fifty yards, nearly forty feet perpendicular.*

---

* In his Journal, as published by the French government, Colonel Washington gives the following account of this tour of discovery.

"On the 20th of May I embarked in a canoe, with Lieutenant West,

As I apprehended there would be difficulty in these waters, I sent the soldiers forward upon the road, when I left the camp, which was as soon as they could cross; therefore, no time has been lost; but the roads are so exceedingly bad, that we proceed very slow.

By concurring intelligence, which we received from the Indians, the French are not above seven or eight hundred strong, and by a late account we are informed, that one half of them were detached in the night, without even the Indians' knowledge, on some secret expedition; but the truth of this, though it is affirmed by an Indian lately from their fort, I cannot yet vouch for, nor tell where they are bound.

---

three soldiers, and an Indian. Having followed the river for about half a mile we were obliged to go ashore, where we found a trader, who seemed to discourage my attempting to seek a passage by water, which caused me to change my intention of having canoes made. I ordered the troops to wade the river, as the waters had now sufficiently subsided. I continued to descend the river, but, finding our canoe too small for six persons, we stopped to construct a bark, with which and the canoe we reached Turkey Foot just as the night began. Eight or ten miles further onward we encountered several difficulties, which were of little consequence. At this point we stopped some time to examine the position, and found it well suited for a fort, being at the mouth of three branches or small rivers, and having a gravelly foundation.

"We went down about two miles to examine the course of the river, which is straight, with many currents, and full of rocks and rapids. We crossed it, though the water was high, which induced me to believe the canoes would easily pass, but this was not effected without difficulty. Besides these rapids we met with others, but, the water being more shallow and the current smoother, we passed them easily. We then found the water very deep, and mountains rising on both sides. After proceeding about ten miles, we came to a fall in the river, which arrested our progress, and compelled us to go ashore and desist from any further attempt." — *Mémoire contenant le Précis des Faits*, &c. p. 121.

The full title of the book, which is here quoted, is as follows; — "MÉMOIRE *contenant le Précis des Faits, avec leurs Pièces Justificatives, pour servir de Réponse aux* OBSERVATIONS *envoyées, par les Ministres d'Angleterre, dans les Cours de l'Europe. À Paris; de l'Imprimerie Royale*. 1756." Four or five years had been consumed in unavailing attempts at a negotiation between England and France, with the ostensible

I would recommend, in the strongest terms possible, your writing to the Governor for some of the treaty goods, or any others suitable for the Indians. Nothing can be done without them. All the Indians that come expect presents. The French take this method, which proves very acceptable; besides, if you want one or more to conduct a party, to discover the country, to hunt, or for any particular service, they must be bought; their friendship is not so warm, as to prompt them to these services gratis; and that, I believe, every person, who is acquainted with the nature of Indians, knows. The Indian, that accompanied me down the river, would go no further than the Forks, about ten miles, till I promised him a ruffled shirt, which I must take from my own, and a watch-coat. He said the French always had Indians to show them the woods, because they paid well for so doing; and this may be laid down as a standing maxim amongst them. I think were the goods sent out, and delivered occasionally, as you see cause, that four or five hundred pounds' worth would do more good, than as many thousands given at a treaty.

---

design on both sides to effect a reconciliation of difficulties, but neither party in reality was solicitous to avoid a war. At length hostilities were commenced in time of peace, and each nation charged the other with being the aggressor. Two French vessels on their way to Canada were taken by the British Admiral Boscawen, and, to justify this procedure, the "*Observations*" above mentioned were published, in which the position was maintained, that the French had actually begun the war, by their encroachments with a military force on the Ohio frontiers. To repel this charge, the French government circulated among the courts of Europe the *Mémoire*, whose title is here given, the object of which was to prove, that the British had been the first to transgress.

This *Mémoire* is curious, as containing many official and other documents relating to the question at issue, which are nowhere else to be found, and particularly selections from the manuscripts of General Braddock and of Washington, which the French had captured at the disastrous battle of the Monongahela. Among other things are Braddock's instructions, several of his letters to the ministry, and extracts purporting to be from a

I hope I may be excused for offering my opinions so freely, for I can aver we shall get no intelligence, or other services from them, unless we have goods to apply to these uses. I am, &c.

TO GOVERNOR DINWIDDIE.

Great Meadows, 27 May, 1754.

SIR,

On the 25th ultimo, by an express from Colonel Fry, I received the news of your arrival at Winchester, and desire of seeing the Half-King and other chiefs of the Six Nations. I have by sundry speeches and messages invited him, Monacawacha, and others, to meet me, and have reason to expect the Half-King is on his way, as he only designed to settle his people to planting, at a place up the Monongahela chosen for that purpose. But fearing something might have retarded his march, I immediately, upon the arrival of the express, despatched a messenger with a speech. He is not yet returned. About four days ago I received a message from the Half-King to the following purport; —

---

journal kept by Washington during his preceding campaign. With what fidelity these were published cannot now be known, but as it was the object of the *Mémoire* to prove a contested point, it may be presumed, that such parts of the papers only were brought forward, as would make for that end. Coming out as they did, however, under the name and sanction of the government, there can be no room for doubt, that the official papers at least were given with accuracy.

These papers were originally published by the French government in a duodecimo volume. A copy was soon afterwards found in a French prize, that was brought to New York. It was there translated into English, and printed the year after its appearance in Paris. The translation was hastily executed, and is worthy of little credit, being equally uncouth in its style, and faulty in its attempts to convey the sense of the original.

"To the first of his Majesty's officers, whom this may concern.

"It is reported, that the French army is coming to meet Major George Washington. I exhort you, therefore, my brethren, to be on your guard against them, for they intend to strike the first English, whom they shall see. They have been on their march two days. I know not their number. The Half-King and the rest of the Chiefs will be with you in five days to hold a council. No more at present, but my remembrance to my brothers the English."

His account was strengthened in the evening by another, that the French were at the Crossing of Youghiogany about eighteen miles distant. I hereupon hurried to this place as a convenient spot. We have, with nature's assistance, made a good entrenchment, and, by clearing the bushes out of these meadows, prepared a charming field for an encounter. I detached, immediately upon my arrival here, a small light party of horse (wagon horses) to reconnoitre the enemy, and discover their strength and motion. They returned yesterday without having seen any thing of them; nevertheless, we were alarmed in the night, and remained under arms from two o'clock till near sunrise. We conceived them to be our own men, as six of them deserted, but cannot be certain whether it was they or our enemies. Be it as it will, they were fired at by my sentries, but I believe without damage.

This morning Mr. Gist arrived from his place, where a detachment of fifty men was seen yesterday at noon, commanded by M. La Force. He afterwards saw their tracks within five miles of our camp. I immediately detached seventy-five men in pursuit of them, who, I hope, will overtake them before they get to Red-stone, where their canoes lie. As Mr. Gist has been an eyewitness of our proceedings, and is waiting for this without my knowing till just now that he intends to visit you, I refer you to him for particulars. I expect my messenger in to-night from the Half-King, and shall write more fully to-morrow by the express that came from Colonel Fry.

The numbers of the French have been greatly magnified, as your Honor may see by a copy of the enclosed journal of a person, whom I sent out to gain intelligence. I have received letters from the Governors of Pennsylvania and Maryland, copies of which I also enclose. I am, &c.

TO COLONEL JOSHUA FRY.

Great Meadows, 29 May, 1754.

SIR,

This is by an immediate express, whom I send to inform you, that yesterday I engaged a party of French, whereof ten were killed, one wounded, and twenty-one taken, with the loss of only one of mine killed and two or three wounded, among whom was Lieutenant Waggener. By some of their papers we can discover, that large detachments are expected every day, which we may reasonably suppose are to attack us, especially since we have begun.

This is therefore to acquaint you with the necessity of a reinforcement, which I hope you will detach immediately, as you can be in no manner of danger in your march; for the French must pass our camp, which I flatter myself is not practicable without my having intelligence of it, especially as there will be Indians always scouting. If a sufficient reinforcement does not come, we must either quit our ground and retreat to you, or fight very unequal numbers, which I will do, before I will give up one inch of what we have gained. The great haste I am in, to despatch the bearer, prevents me from being particular at this time. I shall conclude, Sir, with assuring you how sincerely concerned I am for your indisposition, which I hope you will soon recover from, and be able to join us, with the artillery, that we may attack the French in their forts. I am, &c.*

TO GOVERNOR DINWIDDIE.

Camp at the Great Meadows, 29 May, 1754.

SIR,

In answering your letter by Mr. Birney, I shall begin with assuring you, that nothing was farther from my intentions than to recede, though I then pressed, and

---

* Colonel Fry died at Will's Creek two days after this letter was written, and the command of the expedition devolved of course on Washington, as second in rank. Reinforcements were forwarded, so that the whole number of troops under his immediate command amounted to somewhat more than three hundred.

The death of Colonel Fry was considered an essential loss to the service. He was born in Somersetshire, England, and educated at Oxford. Excelling in the mathematical sciences, he was at one time Professor of the Mathematics in the college of William and Mary; and, after resigning that station, he was a member of the House of Burgesses, and otherwise employed in public affairs, particularly in running the boundary line at the westward between Virginia and North Carolina. In concert with Peter Jefferson he made a map of Virginia, which had much repute. By these employments he had gained such a knowledge of the interior country, as, with other qualifications, pointed him out for this command. He was one of the commissioners from the government of Virginia for making a treaty with the Indians at Logstown, June, 1752. In a notice of him written at the time, it is said, "he was a man of so clear a head, so mild a temper, and so good a heart, that he never failed to engage the love and esteem of all who knew, or were concerned with him, and he died universally lamented."

still desire, that my services may be voluntary, rather than on the present pay. I am much concerned, that you should seem to charge me with ingratitude for your generous, though undeserved favors; for I assure you, Sir, nothing is more a stranger to my breast, or a sin that my soul more abhors, than that black and detestable one of ingratitude. I retain a true sense of your kindness, and want nothing but opportunity to give my testimony of willingness to oblige you, as far as my life or fortune will extend.

I could not object to the pay before I knew it. I dare say you remember, that the amount allowed by the first estimate to a lieutenant-colonel was fifteen shillings, and to a major twelve shillings and sixpence, of which I then complained very much, till your Honor assured me that we were to be furnished with proper necessaries, and offered that as a reason why the pay was less than that of British officers. After this, when you were so kind as to prefer me to the command I now hold, and at the same time informed me, that I was to have but twelve shillings and sixpence, after this, influenced also by some other reasons, I was induced to acquaint Colonel Fairfax with my intention of resigning, which he must well remember, as it happened at Bellhaven; and it was there that he dissuaded me from it, and promised to represent the trifling pay to you, who would endeavour (as I at the same time told him that the Speaker thought the officers' pay too small) to have it enlarged.

As to the numbers that applied for commissions, and to whom we were preferred, I believe, had those gentlemen been as well acquainted with this country, and as sensible of the difficulties that would attend a campaign here as I then was, that your Honor would not have been so troublesomely solicited as you were. Yet I do not offer this as a reason for quitting the service.

For my own part I can answer, that I have a constitution hardy enough to encounter and undergo the most severe trials, and, I flatter myself, resolution to face what any man dares, as shall be proved when it comes to the test, which I believe we are upon the borders of.

There is nothing, Sir, I believe, more certain, than that the officers in the Canada expedition had British pay allowed, while they were in the service.* Lieutenant Waggener, Captain Trent, and several others, whom I have conversed with on that head, and who were engaged in that expedition, affirm it for truth. Therefore, Sir, as this cannot be allowed, suffer me to serve as a volunteer, which, I assure you, will be the next reward to British pay; for, as my services, so far as I have knowledge, shall equal those of the best officer, I make it a point of honor not to serve for less, or accept a medium.

Nevertheless, I have communicated your sentiments to the other officers, and, as far as I could put on the hypocrite, set forth the advantages that may accrue, and advised them to accept the terms, as a refusal might reflect dishonor upon their character, leaving it to the world to assign what reason it pleases for their quitting the service. I am very sensible of the pernicious con-

* This Canada expedition was the one projected by Governor Shirley, and approved by the British government, in 1746, during the previous war between England and France. The memorable capture of Louisburg the year preceding, effected mainly by colonial troops from Massachusetts, had raised to a high pitch the martial spirit of the people; and large numbers were easily enlisted for this new expedition, in the northern and middle provinces. They were disbanded the next year, without having accomplished any thing, but were all paid at the same rate as the troops on the King's establishment. — Belknap's *History of New Hampshire*, Vol. II. p. 235.

From the tenor of this letter to Governor Dinwiddie, it is evident, that the parsimony of the Virginia government, on this occasion, was as ill-judged as it was unprecedented.

sequences that will attend their resigning, as they have gained some experience of the military art, have a tolerable knowledge of the country, having been most of them sent out at different times with parties, and are now accustomed to the hardships and fatigues of living as we do, which, I think, were it truly stated, would prevent your Honor from many troublesome solicitations from others for commissions. This last motive has induced and will induce me to do what I can to reconcile matters, though I really believe there are some, who will not remain long without an alteration. They have promised to consider it, and give you an answer. I was not ignorant of the allowance, which Colonel Fry has for his table; but, being a dependent there myself, I am deprived of the pleasure of inviting an officer, or friend, which to me would be more agreeable, than any benefits I shall meet with there.

And here I cannot forbear answering one thing more in your letter on this head, which, too, is more fully expressed in a paragraph of Colonel Fairfax's letter to me, as follows; — "If, on the British establishment, officers are allowed more pay, the regimentals they are obliged annually to furnish, and their necessary table and other incidental expenses, being considered, little or no savings will be their portion."

I believe it is well known, that we have been at the expense of regimentals, and it is still better known, that regimentals, and every other necessary, which we were under an indispensable necessity of purchasing for this expedition, were not to be bought for less in Virginia currency, than they would cost British officers in sterling money; which ought to have been the case, to put us upon a parity in this respect. Then Colonel Fairfax observes, that their table and other incidental charges prevent them from saving much. They have the enjoyment of their pay, which we neither have in one sense nor the other. We are debarred the pleasure of good living; and, Sir, I dare say you will acknowledge, that, with one who has always been used to it, it must go somewhat hard to be confined to a little salt provision and water, and to do duty, hard, laborious duty, which is almost inconsistent with that of a soldier, and yet have the same reductions as if he were allowed luxuriously. My pay, according to the British establishment and common exchange, would be near twenty shillings per day; in the room of which, the Committee (for I cannot in the least imagine your Honor had any hand in it) has provided twelve shillings and sixpence, so long as the service continues, whereas one half of the other is confirmed to British officers for life. Now if we should be fortunate enough to drive the French from the Ohio, as far as your Honor would please to have them sent, in any short time, our pay will not be sufficient to discharge our first expenses.

I would not have you imagine from this, that I have said all these things to have the pay increased, but to justify myself, and show you that our complaints are not frivolous, but founded upon strict reason. For my own part, it is a matter almost indifferent whether I serve for full pay, or as a generous volunteer; indeed, did my circumstances correspond with my inclinations, I should not hesitate a moment to prefer the latter; for the motives that have led me here are pure and noble; I had no view of acquisition, but that of honor, by serving faithfully my king and country.

As you have recommended Mr. Willis, you may depend I shall with pleasure do all I can for him. But above all, Sir, you may rely, that I shall take all possible means of procuring intelligence, and guarding against surprises; and be assured nothing but very unequal numbers shall compel me to submit or retreat.

Now, Sir, as I have answered your letter, I shall beg leave to acquaint you with what has happened since I wrote by Mr. Gist. I then informed you, that I had detached a party of seventy-five men to meet fifty of the French, who, we had intelligence, were upon their march towards us. About nine o'clock the same night, I received an express from the Half-King, who was encamped with several of his people about six miles off, that he had seen the tracks of two Frenchmen crossing the road, and that, behind, the whole body were lying not far off, as he had an account of that number passing Mr. Gist's.

I set out with forty men before ten, and it was from that time till near sunrise before we reached the Indians' camp, having marched in small paths, through a heavy rain, and a night as dark as it is possible to conceive. We were frequently tumbling one over another, and often so lost, that fifteen or twenty minutes' search would not find the path again.

When we came to the Half-King, I counselled with him, and got his assent to go hand-in-hand and strike the French. Accordingly, he, Monacawacha, and a few other Indians set out with us; and when we came to the place where the tracks were, the Half-King sent two Indians to follow their tracks, and discover their lodgement, which they did at half a mile from the road, in a very obscure place surrounded with rocks. I thereupon, in conjunction with the Half-King and Monacawacha, formed a disposition to attack them on all sides, which we accordingly did, and, after an engagement of about fifteen minutes, we killed ten, wounded one, and took twenty-one prisoners. Amongst those killed was M. de Jumonville, the commander. The principal officers taken are M. Drouillon and M. La Force, of whom your Honor has often heard me speak, as a bold enterprising man, and a person of great subtlety and cunning. With these are two cadets.

These officers pretend they were coming on an embassy; but the absurdity of this pretext is too glaring, as you will see by the Instructions and Summons enclosed. Their instructions were to reconnoitre the country, roads, creeks, and the like, as far as the Potomac, which they were about to do. These enterprising men were purposely chosen out to procure intelligence, which they were to send back by some brisk despatches, with the mention of the day that they were to serve the summons; which could be with no other view, than to get a sufficient reinforcement to fall upon us immediately after. This, with several other reasons, induced all the officers to believe firmly, that they were sent as spies, rather than any thing else, and has occasioned my detaining them as prisoners, though they expected, or at least had some faint hope, that they should be continued as ambassadors.

They, finding where we were encamped, instead of coming up in a public manner, sought out one of the most secret retirements, fitter for a deserter than an ambassador to encamp in, and stayed there two or three days, sending spies to reconnoitre our camp, as we are told, though they deny it. Their whole body moved back near two miles, and they sent off two runners to acquaint Contrecœur with our strength, and where we were encamped. Now thirty-six men would almost have been a retinue for a princely ambassador, instead of a *petit*. Why did they, if their designs were open, stay so long within five miles of us, without delivering their message, or acquainting me with it? Their waiting could be with no other design, than to get detachments to enforce the summons, as soon as it was given. They had no occasion to send out spies, for the name of an ambassador is sacred among all nations; but it was by the track of those spies, that they were discovered, and that we got intelligence of them. They would not have retired two miles back without delivering the summons, and sought a skulking-place (which, to do them justice, was done with great judgment), but for some special reason. Besides, the summons is so insolent, and savors so much of gasconade, that if two men only had come to deliver it openly, it would have been too great an indulgence to send them back.*

---

* In the part of Washington's Journal published by the French government, among the *Pièces Justificatives* attached to the *Mémoire* heretofore mentioned, the narrative of this affair is related nearly in the same words, as will be seen by the following extract.

"As I marched on with the prisoners (after the action), they informed me, that they had been sent with a summons for me to depart; a specious pretext, that they might discover our camp, and reconnoitre our force and situation. This was so evident, that I was astonished at their assurance in telling me, that they came as an embassy. By their instructions they were to obtain a knowledge of the roads, rivers, and country, as far as the Potomac. Instead of coming as an ambassador, public, and in an open manner, they came secretly, and sought out the most hidden retreats, much better suited for deserters than an ambassador. Here they encamped, here they remained concealed for whole days together within five miles of us. They sent out spies to reconnoitre our camp. The whole body then moved back two miles. Thence they sent messengers, as directed in the instructions, to acquaint M. Contrecœur with the place we were in, and with our disposition, that he might forward his detachments to enforce the summons, as soon as it should be given.

"An ambassador has no need of spies; his character is always sacred. Since they had so good an intention, why should they remain two days within five miles of us, without giving me notice of the summons, or of any thing which related to their embassy? This alone would be sufficient to raise the strongest suspicions; and the justice is certainly due them, that, as they wished to conceal themselves, they could not have chosen better places than they did." See *Mémoire*, &c. p. 127.

"They pretend that they called to us, as soon as we were discovered, which is absolutely false; for I was at the head of the party in approaching them, and I can affirm, that, as soon as they saw us, they ran to their arms without calling, which I should have heard, if they had done so." — p. 129.

The sense of the Half-King on this subject is, that they have bad hearts, and that this is a mere pretence; that they never designed to come to us but in a hostile manner, and if we were so foolish as to let them go again, he never would assist us in taking another of them. Besides, La Force would, if released, I really think, do more to our disservice, than fifty other men, as he is a person whose active spirit leads him into all parties, and has brought him acquainted with all parts of the country. Add to this a perfect use of the Indian tongue, and great influence with the Indians. He ingenuously enough confessed, that, as soon as he saw the commission and instructions, he believed,* and then said he expected some such tendency, though he pretends to say he does not believe the commander had any other than a good design.

In this engagement we had only one man killed and two or three wounded, among whom was Lieutenant Waggener slightly, — a most miraculous escape, as our right wing was much exposed to their fire and received it all.†

The Half-King received your Honor's speech very kindly, but desired me to inform you, that he could not leave his people at this time, thinking them in great danger. He is now gone to the Crossing for their families, to bring them to our camp; and he desired I would furnish some men and horses to assist them up, which I have accordingly done. I have sent thirty men and

---

* That is, he believed there was some hostile intention. La Force appears not to have seen the instructions, which were in possession of M. Jumonville. Whether he knew their import before his capture is doubtful.

The original Summons and Instructions are printed among the *Pièces Justificatives* affixed to the *Mémoire* of the French government.

† Washington and his soldiers were on the right, and the Indians on the left.

upwards of twenty horses. He says, if your Honor has any thing to say, you may communicate it by me, and that, if you have a present for them, it may be kept till another occasion, after sending out some things for their immediate use. He has declared that he will send these Frenchmen's scalps, with a hatchet, to all the nations of Indians in union with them, and did that very day give a hatchet, and a large belt of wampum, to a Delaware man to carry to Shingiss.* He promised me to send down the river for all the Mingoes † and Shawanees to our camp, where I expect him to-morrow with thirty or forty men, and their wives and children, to confirm what he has said here. He has sent your Honor a string of wampum.

As these runners went off to the fort on Sunday last,‡ I shall expect every hour to be attacked, and by unequal numbers, which I must withstand if there are five to one; for I fear the consequence will be, that we shall lose the Indians, if we suffer ourselves to be driven back. I despatched an express immediately to Colonel Fry with this intelligence, desiring him to send me reinforcements with all imaginable speed.

Your Honor may depend I will not be surprised, let them come at what hour they will; and this is as much as I can promise. But my best endeavours shall not be wanting to effect more. I doubt not, if you hear I am beaten, but you will hear at the same time, that we have done our duty, in fighting as long as there was a shadow of hope.

I have sent Lieutenant West, accompanied by Mr.

---

* King, or chief, of the Delaware Indians.

† The confederated Indians of the Six Nations were designated by various names. They were usually called *Iroquois* by the French, *Mingoes* by the English, *Maquas* by the Dutch, and *Mengwe* by the Indians of other tribes.

‡ The two French runners mentioned above, who had been sent to Fort Duquesne by Jumonville before the attack.

Spiltdorph and a guard of twenty men, to conduct the prisoners in, and I believe the officers have told him what answer to return to you. *

Monsieur La Force and Major Drouillon beg to be recommended to your notice, and I have promised that they shall meet with all the favor due to prisoners of war. I have shown all the respect I could to them here, and have given them some necessary clothing, by which I have disfurnished myself; for, having brought no more than two or three shirts from Will's Creek, that we might be light, I was ill provided to supply them. I am, &c.

P. S. I have neither seen nor heard any particular account of the Twigtwees since I came on these waters.† We have already begun a palisadoed fort, and hope to have it up to-morrow. I must beg leave to acquaint you, that Captain Vanbraam and Ensign Peyrouny have behaved extremely well since they came out, and I hope they will meet with your favor. ‡

---

* Respecting the regulations for pay discussed at the beginning of this letter.

† Mr. Gist, who visited the Twigtwees in February, 1751, described them as follows. "The Twigtwees are a very numerous people, consisting of many different tribes under the same form of government. Each tribe has a particular chief, or king, one of whom is chosen indifferently out of any tribe to rule the whole nation, and is vested with greater authority than any of the others. They are accounted the most powerful nation to the westward of the English settlements, and much superior to the Six Nations, with whom they are now in amity. They formerly lived on the farther side of the Wabash, and were in the French interest. They have now revolted from them, and have left their former habitations for the sake of trading with the English." The town visited by Mr. Gist was on the North bank of the Miami river, about a hundred and fifty miles from its mouth. The town consisted of about four hundred families. — Gist's *MS. Journal.* Wynne says that the Twigtwee Indians were the same as the Ottawas. The French wrote the name *Twigtuis.*

‡ Vanbraam and Peyrouny were foreigners then resident in Virginia. Peyrouny was a Frenchman, well esteemed and of a respectable charac-

TO GOVERNOR DINWIDDIE.

Camp at the Great Meadows, 29 May, 1754.

SIR,

The bearer hereof, Monsieur Drouillon, and Monsieur La Force and two cadets, I beg leave to recommend to your particular notice, as prisoners of war, and officers whom I had the honor of taking.

I have assured them, that they will meet with all the respect and favor due to their character and personal merit; and I hope they will do me the justice to inform you, that I have neglected no means in my power to render their confinement easy here.

Lieutenant West will conduct these gentlemen, with sixteen privates, prisoners, to your Honor at Winchester, who will acquaint you with the profound respect with which I am your Honor's most obedient and most humble servant.

TO GOVERNOR DINWIDDIE.

Without date.

SIR,

Since writing my last I have still stronger presumption, indeed almost confirmation, that they were sent as spies, and were ordered to wait near us, till they were truly informed of our intentions, situation, and strength, and were to have acquainted their commander therewith, and to have lain lurking here for reinforcements before they served the summons, if served at all.

I doubt not but they will endeavour to amuse you

---

ter. He was afterwards killed at Braddock's defeat. Vanbraam was a Dutchman, and had the year before been Washington's interpreter, in his mission from the governor of Virginia to visit the French posts on the Ohio.

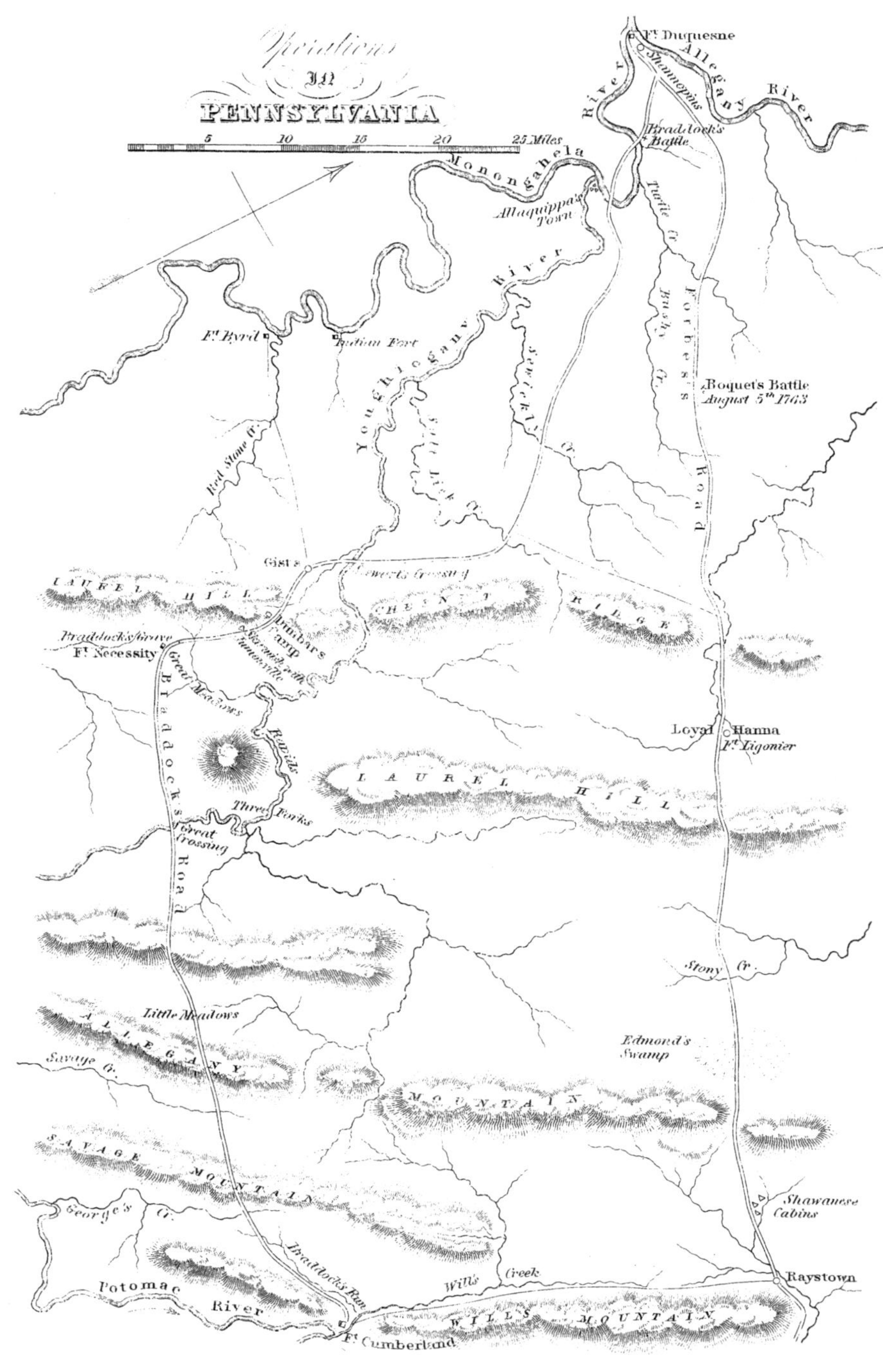
Operations
in
PENNSYLVANIA
5 10 15 20 25 Miles
Ft. Duquesne
Allegany River
Shannopins
River
Monongahela
Braddock's Battle
Allaquippa's Town
Turtle Cr.
Youghiogany River
Bushy Cr.
Forbes's Road
Sewickly Cr.
Ft. Byrd
Indian Fort
Boquet's Battle August 5th 1763
Red Stone Cr.
Salt Lick Cr.
Gists
Stewarts Crossing
LAUREL HILL
CHESNUT RIDGE
Braddock's Grave
Ft. Necessity
Dunbars Camp
Great Meadows
Braddock's Road
Loyal Hanna
Ft. Ligonier
LAUREL HILL
Three Forks
Great Crossing
Stony Cr.
Little Meadows
ALLEGANY
Savage Cr.
Edmond's Swamp
MOUNTAIN
SAVAGE MOUNTAIN
George's Cr.
Shawanese Cabins
Braddock's Run
Will's Creek
Raystown
Potomac River
WILLS MOUNTAIN
Ft. Cumberland

with many smooth stories, as they did me; but they were confuted in them all, and, by circumstances too plain to be denied, almost made ashamed of their assertions. I dare say you will treat them with respect, which is due to all unfortunate persons in their condition. But I hope you will give no ear to what they will have an opportunity for displaying to the best advantage, having none present to contradict their reports.

I have heard, since they went away, that they should say they called to us not to fire; but that I know to be false, for I was the first man that approached them, and the first whom they saw, and immediately upon it they ran to their arms, and fired briskly till they were defeated.

We have heard of another being killed by the Indians, that made his escape from us; so that we are certain of thirty-three killed and taken.* I thought it expedient to acquaint your Honor with the above, as I fancy they will have the assurance of asking the privileges due to an embassy, when in strict justice they ought to be hanged as spies of the worst sort, being authorized by their commander, at the expense of a character, which should be sacred to all nations, and never trifled with or used in an equivocal way.† I am, &c.

---

* It appears by M. de Contrecœur's orders to M. de Jumonville, (See *Mémoire*, &c. p. 104) that his party consisted of thirty-five men, that is, himself and another officer, three cadets, a volunteer, an interpreter, and twenty-eight soldiers. Two of the party had returned the day before, whose tracks had been seen by the Half-King, as he reported to Colonel Washington, thus leaving thirty-three, who were engaged in the skirmish. As two cadets only were taken, one of the men, who returned, must have been a cadet.

† For other particulars respecting this skirmish, see APPENDIX, No. II.

In Horace Walpole's *Memoirs of George the Second* is the following passage.

"In the express, which Major Washington despatched on his preceding little victory, (the skirmish with Jumonville), he concluded with these

TO GOVERNOR DINWIDDIE.

Great Meadows, 10 June, 1754.

SIR,

Yours I received by the post, and return you my hearty thanks for your kind congratulation on our late success, which I hope to improve without risking the imputation of rashness, or hazarding what a prudent conduct would forbid. I rejoice that I am likely to be happy under the command of an experienced officer, and man of sense. It is what I have ardently wished

---

words, — '*I heard the bullets whistle, and, believe me, there is something charming in the sound.*' On hearing of this the king said sensibly, — '*He would not say so, if he had been used to hear many.*' However, this brave braggart learned to blush for his rhodomontade, and, desiring to serve General Braddock as aid-de-camp, acquitted himself nobly." Vol. I. p. 347.

The above letter is the despatch communicated by Major Washington to Governor Dinwiddie, giving an account of the rencounter with Jumonville's party, a copy of which was probably sent by the Governor to England. It contains nothing about the *whistling of bullets*, nor is such a sentiment uttered in any of his letters, that have been preserved. As the writer refers to no authority, it may be presumed, that he had none but rumor, either for the saying of Washington, or the more sensible reply of the King. Yet this anecdote is not wholly without foundation, if we may rely on a statement of Gordon, in which he says; — "A gentleman, who had heard the Reverend Mr. Davies relate, that Colonel Washington had mentioned, he knew of no music so pleasing as the whistling of bullets, being alone in conversation with him at Cambridge, asked him whether it was as he had related. The General answered, 'If I said so, it was when I was young.'" Gordon's *History*, Vol. II. p. 203.

The *Memoirs* of Horace Walpole, Earl of Orford, quoted above, are understood to have been written near the time of the events, but they were not published till after his death. The Editor remarks, in a note on the word *braggart*, — "It is wonderful, that Lord Orford should have allowed this expression to remain, after he had lived to witness and admire the subsequent career of that great man General Washington." It may be added, that it was not by his own *desire*, but at the solicitation of General Braddock, that Washington joined him as aid-de-camp.

There is another passage in these *Memoirs*, purporting to have been written in 1754, which is remarkable for the declaration with which it concludes. The author is censuring the government for the course pur-

for.* I shall here beg leave to return my grateful thanks for your favor in promoting me to the command of the regiment. Believe me, Sir, when I assure you, that my breast is warmed with every generous sentiment, which your goodness can inspire. I want nothing but opportunity to testify my sincere regard for your person, to whom I stand indebted for so many unmerited favors.

Your Honor may depend, I shall myself, and will endeavour to make my officers, show Captain Mackay all the respect due to his rank and merit; but I should have been particularly obliged, if you had declared whether he was under my command, or independent of it.† However, I shall be studious to avoid all disputes that may tend to the public prejudice, but, as far as I am able, will inculcate harmony and unanimity. I hope Captain Mackay will have more sense, than to insist upon any unreasonable distinction because he and his officers have commissions from his Majesty. Let him consider, though we are greatly inferior in respect to advantages of profit, yet we have the same spirit to serve our gracious King as they have, and are as ready

---

sued towards the colonies, and observes; — "The instructions to Sir Danvers Osborn, a new governor of New York, seemed better calculated for the latitude of Mexico, and for a Spanish tribunal, than for a free, rich British settlement, and in such opulence and such haughtiness, *that suspicions had long been conceived of their meditating to throw off their dependence on the mother country.*" Vol. I. p. 343.

* Colonel Innes, from North Carolina, had arrived with about three hundred and fifty troops, raised in that colony. He was now at Winchester. After Colonel Fry's death, he had been appointed, by Governor Dinwiddie, commander-in-chief of all the forces destined for the western expedition. Colonel Washington was promoted to the command of the Virginia regiment. The North Carolina troops never joined him, nor rendered any service. Colonel Innes had been an officer in the former war, and was intimate with Major Lawrence Washington at the siege of Carthagena.

† Captain Mackay commanded an *Independent Company* of one hundred men from South Carolina, who were now on their march from Alexandria to join Colonel Washington.

and willing to sacrifice our lives for our country's good. And here, once more, and for the last time, I must say, that it will be a circumstance, which will act upon some officers of this regiment beyond all measure, to be obliged to serve upon such different terms, when their lives, their fortunes, and their operations are equally, and, I dare say, as effectually exposed, as those of others, who are happy enough to have King's commissions.

I have been solicitous on this head, and have earnestly endeavoured to reconcile the officers to their appointments, and flatter myself that I have succeeded, having heard no mention thereof lately. I considered the pernicious consequences, that would attend a disunion, and was therefore too much attached to my country's interests to suffer it to ripen, after I received your letters.

I am very thankful to you for ordering an assortment of Indian goods, which we daily find still more necessary. I shall take care, while they are under my direction, that they are judiciously applied, and shall be particularly careful in consulting Mr. Croghan and Mr. Montour, by whom I shall be advised in all Indian affairs agreeably to your directions. *

I shall with great pleasure wear the medal, which you were pleased to compliment me with, and shall present the others to Indian chiefs, as I have already done one to the Half-King.

We have been extremely ill used by Major Carlyle's deputies, which I am heartily sorry for, since he is a gentleman so capable of the business himself, and has taken so much pains to give satisfaction. He, I believe, has been deceived, and we have suffered by those

* Croghan was an Indian trader of note, and had been employed on public affairs in the Indian country by the governor of Pennsylvania. Montour was a Canadian, and also an Indian trader and interpreter. He was of Indian extraction, and a man of weight among the Six Nations.

under him, and by those who have contracted for provisions. We have been six days without flour, and there is none upon the road for our relief that we know of, though I have by repeated expresses given him timely notice. We have not provisions of any sort enough in camp to serve us two days. Once before we should have been four days without provisions, if Providence had not sent a trader from the Ohio to our relief, for whose flour I was obliged to give twenty-one shillings and eight pence per hundred.

In a late letter to Major Carlyle, I have complained of the tardiness of his deputies. I likewise desired, that suitable stores of ammunition might be sent up speedily, for till that is done we have it not in our power to attempt any advantageous enterprise; but must wait its arrival at Red-stone, for which I shall set off the moment provisions arrive to sustain us on the march. Major Carlyle mentioned a contract he had made with Mr. Croghan for flour, likewise Mr. Croghan's offer of furnishing more if required. I have therefore desired to have all that Mr. Croghan can furnish.

Major Muse, with Captain Montour, joined us yesterday, and brought the wampum you sent to the Half-King, which I presented, with the medal and speech. He is very thankful for the notice you have taken of him. Major Muse brought nine of the swivels, with some powder and balls; and this day I have engaged fifty or sixty horses to bring up more of the balls and other stores from Will's Creek, if there should be no provisions to load them with. The balls are to be brought in leather bags made for the purpose. I hear that Captain Mackay, who was to have brought the artillery, has marched without it, as wagons could not be procured. I shall write to Mr. Gist to procure wagons, if he is obliged to go to Pennsylvania for them, to bring out the artillery, if not, when Colonel Innes comes up we shall have nothing in readiness, and shall let slip this best season for action.

The Indians are drawing off from the River daily, one of whom last night brought news of Monacawacha. He went from Logstown about five nights ago with the French scalps, and four hatchets, with which he intended to visit the four tribes of Indians between this and Lake Erie, and present to each tribe a scalp and hatchet, and at the same time acquaint them that it was expected, as the English and Six Nations had hand-in-hand struck the French, they would join our forces. This messenger likewise says, that Monacawacha was determined not only to counsel with the chiefs of those tribes, but with their great warriors also, which is customary in these cases, and was to return as soon as possible, which he imagined would be in fifteen days; but in case he should not return in that time, he left orders for the Indians at Logstown to set off for Red-stone Creek, so that they would all meet at Red-stone to join their brothers the English. He also desired there might be no attack made against the French fort, till he should return, by which time he hoped all the forces would be gathered, and then they would make a general attack together, and gain a complete victory at once.

The Half-King has sent messengers to other places for warriors, who are to meet us also at Red-stone Creek. Besides these, he has sent two messengers, by the advice of Mr. Croghan, Mr. Montour, and myself, one to invite the Shawanees to come and receive one of their men, who was imprisoned in Carolina, and to counsel with us, and the other to the Delawares for the same purpose, as we hear both these nations have accepted the hatchet against us. This report was first brought by an Indian sent from Logstown to the Half-

King, and since confirmed by nine French deserters, who arrived at our camp to-day. These men farther say, that the fort at the Fork is completed, and proof against any attempts, but with bombs, on the land side. There were not above five hundred men in it, when they left it, but they suppose by this time two hundred more are arrived. Nine hundred were ordered to follow them, who might be expected in fourteen or fifteen days.

I was as much disappointed when I met these persons to-day, as ever I was in my life. By misunderstanding the scouts that brought me intelligence, that is, mistaking ninety for nine, I marched out at the head of one hundred and thirty men (the major part of the effective men in the regiment), full with the hope of procuring another present of French prisoners for your Honor. Judge then my disappointment at meeting nine only, and those coming for protection. I guarded against all casualties, that might happen to the camp, and ordered Major Muse to repair into the fort, and erect the small swivels for the defence of the place, which he could do in an hour's time.

Agreeably to your desire I shall here mention the names of the gentlemen, who are to be promoted. Lieutenant George Mercer will worthily succeed to a captaincy. Captain Vanbraam has acted as captain ever since we left Alexandria. He is an experienced, good officer, and very worthy of the command he has enjoyed. Mr. James Towers is the oldest ensign, for whom you will please to send a lieutenancy. To Captain Stephen I have already given a major's commission, finding one blank among Colonel Fry's papers. If merit, Sir, will entitle a gentleman to your notice, Mr. Peyrouny may justly claim a share of your favor. His conduct has been governed by the most consummate prudence, and all his actions have sufficiently testified his readiness to serve his country, which I really believe he looks upon Virginia to be. He was sensibly chagrined, when I acquainted him with your pleasure, of giving him an ensigncy. This he had twelve years ago, and long since commanded a company. He was prevailed on by Colonel Fry, when he left Alexandria, to accept the former commission, and assist my detachment, as I had very few officers, till we all met on the Ohio, which commission he would now have resigned, and returned to Virginia, but for my great dissuasion to the contrary. I have promised to solicit your Honor to appoint him adjutant, and continue him ensign, which will induce a very good officer to remain in the regiment. The office of adjutant, Sir, is most necessary to a regiment, in distributing the daily orders, receiving all reports, and seeing orders executed. In short, an adjutant is an indispensable officer. Should you be pleased to indulge me in this request, I shall look upon it in a very particular light, as I think the personal merit of the gentleman, his knowledge of military duty, and his activity will render him highly worthy of the favor. An ensign is still wanting, whom I hope you will send, if you know of any one suitable for the office. A young man in the camp, who came with Captain Lewis, has solicited, but I am yet ignorant of his character and qualities. He is a volunteer, and recommended by Captain Lewis.

In a letter by Mr. Ward, you acquainted me, that you had given orders to Colonel Fry to examine into the proceedings of Captain Trent, and his lieutenant, Frazier, by a court-martial. I shall be glad if you will repeat your orders and instructions to me, or rather to Colonel Innes; for an officer cannot be tried by those of his own regiment only, but has a right to be heard in a general court-martial. Captain Trent's behaviour has been very tardy, and has convinced the world of what they before suspected, his great timidity. Lieutenant Frazier, though not altogether blameless, is much more excusable, for he would not accept of the commission, till he had a promise from his captain, that he should not reside at the fort, nor visit it above once a week, or as he saw necessary. *

Queen Aliquippa desired that her son, who is really a great warrior, might be taken into council, as he was declining and unfit for business, and that he should have an English name given him. I therefore called the Indians together by the advice of the Half-King, presented one of the medals, and desired him to wear it in remembrance of his great father, the King of England, and called him by the name of *Colonel Fairfax*, which he was told signified *the first of the council.* This gave him great pleasure. I was also informed, that an English name would please the Half-King, which made me presume to give him that of your Honor, and call him *Dinwiddie;* interpreted in their language, *the head of all.* † I am, &c.

P. S. These deserters corroborate what the others said and we suspected. La Force's party were sent

---

* Complaint was made against Captain Trent for being absent from his post when the French compelled his ensign to capitulate.

Mr. Frazier had lived for some time in the Ohio country as an Indian trader. He had a house at the mouth of the Creek, ten miles up the Monongahela from the Fork of the Ohio River, and near the spot afterterwards rendered memorable by Braddock's disastrous rencounter. Hence his stipulation, when he accepted the commission to act as lieutenant, not to be obliged to reside at the fort, then about to be constructed at the Fork of the River, nor to visit it except at stated times.

† The Indians were likewise fond of giving names to the whites. Washington they named *Connotaucarius.* The governor of Pennsylvania was called *Onas,* the governor of Maryland *Tocarryhogan,* and the gover-

out as spies, and were to show that summons if discovered, or overpowered, by a superior party of ours. They say the commander was blamed for sending so small a party.

Since writing the foregoing, Captain Mackay, with the Independent Company, has arrived, whom I take to be a very good sort of a gentleman. For want of proper instructions from your Honor, I am much at a loss to know how to act, or proceed in regard to his company. I made it my particular study to receive him (as it was your desire) with all the respect and politeness, that were due to his rank, or that I was capable of showing; and I do not doubt from his appearance and behaviour, that a strict intimacy will ensue, when matters shall be put in a clear light. But at present, I assure you, they will rather impede the service, than forward it; for, as they have commissions from the King, they look upon themselves as a distinct body, and will not incorporate and do duty with our men, but keep separate guards, and encamp separately. I have not offered to control Captain Mackay in any thing, nor showed that I claimed a superior command, except in giving the patrole and countersign, which must be the same in an army consisting of different nations, to distinguish friends from foes. He knows the necessity of this, yet does not think he is to receive it from me. Then who is to give it? Am I to issue these orders to a company? Or is an independent captain to prescribe rules to the Virginia regiment? This is the question. But its absurdity is obvious.

It now behoves you, Sir, to lay your absolute commands on one or the other to obey. This is indispen-

---

nor of Virginia *Assaragoa*. These names pertained to the office, and not to the individual, each successive governor being designated by the same appellation. Giving a name was attended with much ceremony.

sably necessary, for nothing clashes more with reason, than to conceive our small bodies can act distinctly, without having connexion with one another, and yet be serviceable to the public. I do not doubt that Captain Mackay is an officer of sense, and I dare say will do the best for the service; but, Sir, two commanders are so incompatible, that we cannot be as useful to one another, or the public, as we ought; and I am sincerely sorry, that he has arrived before your instructions by Colonel Innes, who I doubt not will be fully authorized how to act. But as we have no news of Colonel Innes, I have, in the mean time, desired Major Carlyle to send this by an immediate express to you, who, I hope, will satisfy these doubts.

Captain Mackay and I have lived in the most perfect harmony since his arrival, and have reasoned on this calmly; and, I believe, if we should have occasion to exert our whole force, we shall do as well as divided authority can do. We have not had the least warmth of dispute. He thinks you have not a power to give commissions, that will command him. If so, I can very confidently say, that his absence would tend to the public advantage. I have been particularly careful in discovering no foolish desire of commanding him, neither have I intermeddled with his company in the least, nor given any directions concerning it, except, in general, the countersign, and place to repair to in case of an alarm, none of which he thinks he should receive. I have testified to him, in the most serious manner, the pleasure I should take in consulting and advising with him upon all occasions, and I am satisfied that we shall never differ after you have decided this point. I am convinced, that your own just discernment and consideration will prove to you, that there can be no medium. The nature of the thing will not allow of it. Before orders will be observed, it must be known who is to command; and I am very confident you will see the absurdity, and consider the effects, of Captain Mackay's having the direction of the regiment; for it would certainly be the hardest thing in life, if we are to do double and treble duty, and neither be entitled to the pay nor rank of soldiers. That the first column of the Virginia regiment has done more for the interest of this expedition, than any company, or corps, that will hereafter arrive, must be obvious to all. This, Sir, Captain Mackay did not hesitate one moment to allow, since he has seen the work we have done upon the roads. We shall part to-morrow. I shall continue my march to Red-stone, while his company remains here. This, Sir, I found absolutely necessary for the public interest. Captain Mackay says, that it is not in his power to oblige his men to work on the road, unless he will engage them a shilling sterling a day, which I would not choose to do. And to suffer them to march at their ease, whilst our faithful soldiers are laboriously employed, carries with it an air of such distinction, that it is not to be wondered at, if the poor fellows were to declare the hardship of it. He also assures me, that this is not peculiar to his company, but that no soldiers subject to martial law can be obliged to work for less. I shall continue to complete the work we have begun with my own men. We shall have the whole credit, as no others have assisted.

I hope, from what has been said, your Honor will see the necessity of giving your speedy order on this head; and I am sensible you will consider the evil tendency, that will accompany Captain Mackay's arrival. The rank of office to me, Sir, is much more important than the pay.

Captain Mackay brought none of the cannon, very little ammunition, about five days' allowance of flour, and sixty beeves. I am much grieved to find our stores so slowly advancing. God knows when we shall be able to do any thing to deserve better of our country.*

I am, Sir, with the most sincere and unfeigned regard, your Honor's most obedient and most humble servant.

TO WILLIAM FAIRFAX.†

Alexandria, 11 August, 1754.

SIR,

Since my last to you, I have received, by Mr. Spiltdorph, the letter therein alluded to, the contents of which are nearly the same as in the one received from

---

* As intimated in this letter, Colonel Washington marched forward with the Virginia regiment, and left Captain Mackay with his company to guard Fort Necessity. Thus the difficulty about command was for the time removed. He advanced slowly as far as Gist's house, thirteen miles from the Great Meadows, employing the soldiers on the way in repairing the road, and sending out scouting parties to watch the motions of the French. In the mean time, he held councils with several Indian chiefs, who came to him for that purpose, delivered speeches, exchanged belts of wampum, and went through the usual ceremonies on such occasions. But all to little purpose, for some of the Indians were treacherous spies from the French, and others had no higher motive than that of obtaining presents of goods and provisions. In this mode of gaining friends, the French were much the most successful, as they were better supplied with all the articles wanted by the Indians. A party of men was likewise despatched to clear the road beyond Gist's house, towards the junction of Red-stone Creek with the Monongahela.

While these operations were going on, reports were constantly brought in by French deserters and Indians, that large reinforcements had arrived at Fort Duquesne, and that a formidable force would soon come out to attack the English. On the 28th of June a council of war was held at Gist's house, in which it was unanimously resolved, that it was necessary to return to the fort, and wait there at all events till they should receive a larger supply of provisions. They retreated accordingly. The enemy appeared before the fort on the 3d of July, and the action of the Great Meadows was fought on that day. See APPENDIX, No. III.

† William Fairfax was the son of Henry Fairfax, of Yorkshire, England, and grandson of Thomas the fourth Lord Fairfax. His father died when

the Governor four days before. The following is an exact copy of it.

"The Council met yesterday, and, considering the present state of our forces, and having reason to think the French will be reinforced next spring, it was resolved, that the forces should immediately march over the Allegany mountains, either to dispossess the French of their fort, or build one in a proper place, that may be fixed upon by a council of war. Colonel Innes has my orders for executing the above affair. I am, therefore, now to order you to get your regiment completed to three hundred men, and I have no doubt, that you will

---

he was young, and he was educated under the care of his uncle, Lord Lonsdale. At the age of twenty-one he entered the army, and served in Spain. He went also to the East Indies, and after his return engaged in the expedition against Providence Island, at that time in possession of the pirates. He was appointed governor of the Island, after its reduction, and married, in the year 1724, the daughter of Thomas Walker, a major in the army, who had accompanied the expedition, and received the appointment of chief justice of the Bahama Islands. The climate not agreeing with the health of Mr. Fairfax, he removed to New England, where he resided, holding an office of considerable trust and emolument, till he was desired by his kinsman, Lord Fairfax, to remove to Virginia, and become the agent for managing his large tract of lands in that colony. His first residence was in Westmoreland county, where he remained several years; but he afterwards established himself at Belvoir, on the Potomac River, a little below Mount Vernon. He died at that place on the 3d of September, 1757. He was a gentleman of great worth and respectability, held the offices of lieutenant of the county of Fairfax, and collector of the customs of South Potomac, and was one of the King's Council in Virginia, which last station he retained many years, and was for a considerable time president of the Council.

From him have descended the various branches of the Fairfax family in Virginia. He was twice married; first, to Sarah Walker, by whom he had four children, George William, Thomas, Anne, and Sarah; secondly, to Deborah Clarke, of Salem, Massachusetts, by whom he had three children, Bryan, William, and Hannah.

George William was educated in England. On his return to Virginia he married the daughter of Colonel Cary, of Hampton, became one of his Majesty's Council, and resided at Belvoir till the year 1773, when, some estates in Yorkshire having devolved to him, he went to England. The political troubles, which followed, induced him to remain. Part of his

be able to enlist what you are deficient of your number very soon, and march directly to Will's Creek to join the other forces; and, that there may be no delay, I order you to march what companies you have complete, and leave orders with the officers remaining to follow you, as soon as they shall have enlisted men sufficient to make up their companies. You know the season of the year calls for despatch. I depend upon your former usual diligence and spirit to encourage your people to be active on this occasion. Consult with Major Carlyle as to the ammunition which may be wanted, that I may send it up immediately. I trust much to your diligence and despatch in getting your regiment to Will's Creek as soon as possible.

---

property in Virginia was sequestered, by which his income was reduced, and he removed to Bath, in England, where he lived in a private manner, and during the war contributed generously to the relief of the American prisoners. He died at Bath, on the 3d of April, 1787, in the sixty-third year of his age. *Thomas*, the second son, was an officer in the navy, and was killed in the East Indies, on board the ship of war, Harwich, in an action with the French squadron, 26 June, 1746. *Anne*, the eldest daughter of William Fairfax, was married to Lawrence Washington; and, after the death of her husband, she was married a second time to George Lee of Virginia. *Sarah*, the second daughter, was married to John Carlyle, a merchant of Alexandria. *Bryan*, the third son, who afterwards became the eighth Lord Fairfax, married a daughter of Wilson Cary, and lived at a place called Towlston, in Fairfax county. He had two sons, Thomas and Ferdinando, and two daughters. As George William Fairfax, who died in England, had no children, he bequeathed his estates in Virginia to Ferdinando, this second son of his youngest and only surviving brother. *William*, the fourth son of William Fairfax, was educated in England He entered the army, and was killed at the famous siege of Quebec. He was a young man of much promise. It is related, that when General Wolfe had landed, he saw young Fairfax sitting near the bank of the river, and, touching him on the shoulder, said, "Young man, when we come to action remember your name." *Hannah*, the youngest child, was married to Warner Washington, cousin-german to General Washington. — Burnaby's *Travels in America*, 3d edition, p. 159.

Mr. William Fairfax was an early, constant, and valuable friend to Washington, and it was doubtless chiefly through the influence of Mr. Fairfax with the Governor and Council, that he received his appointment,

"Colonel Innes will consult you in the appointment of officers for your regiment. Pray consider, if practicable, that, to send a party of Indians to destroy the corn at the fort and Logstown would be of great service to us, and a considerable disappointment to the enemy. I can say no more, but to press the despatch of your regiment to Will's Creek."

Thus, Sir, you will see I am ordered, with the utmost despatch, to repair to Will's Creek with the regiment; to do which, under the present circumstances, is as impracticable, as it is (as far as I can see into the thing) to dispossess the French of their fort; both of which, with our means, are morally impossible.

The Governor observes, that, considering the state of our forces at present, it is thought advisable to move out immediately to dispossess the French. Now that very reason, "the state of our forces," is alone sufficient against the measure, without a large addition to them. Consider, I pray you, Sir, under what unhappy circumstances the men at present are; and their numbers, compared with those of the enemy, are so inconsiderable, that we should be harassed and driven from place to place at their pleasure. To what end the building of a fort would be, unless we could proceed as far as Red-stone, where we should have to take

---

while yet a youth, as adjutant to the northern division of the Virginia militia, and his mission to the French posts on the Ohio, as well as his subsequent commission in the army.

While Washington was encamped at the Great Meadows, Mr. Fairfax wrote to him: "I will not doubt your having public prayers in the camp, especially when the Indian families are your guests, that they, seeing your plain manner of worship, may have their curiosity excited to be informed why we do not use the ceremonies of the French, which being well explained to their understandings will more and more dispose them to receive our baptism, and unite in strict bonds of cordial friendship."

It may be added, that it was Washington's custom to have prayers in the camp, while he was at Fort Necessity.

water, and where the enemy can come with their artillery, I cannot see, unless it be to secure a retreat, which we should have no occasion for, were we to go out in proper force and properly provided, which I aver cannot be done this fall; for, before our force can be collected, with proper stores of provisions, ammunition, and working-tools, the season would approach in which horses cannot travel over the mountains on account of snows, want of forage, slipperiness of the roads, and high waters. Neither can men, unused to that life, live there, without some other defence from the weather than tents. Of this I am certain from my own knowledge, as I was out last winter from the 1st of November till some time in January; and notwithstanding I had a good tent, was as properly prepared, and as well guarded, in every respect, as I could be against the weather, yet the cold was so intense, that it was scarcely supportable. I believe, out of the five or six men that went with me, three of them, though they were as well clad as they could be, were rendered useless by the frost, and were obliged to be left upon the road.

But the impossibility of supporting us with provisions is alone sufficient to discourage the attempt; for, were commissaries with sufficient funds to set about procuring provisions, and getting them out, it is not probable that enough could be conveyed out this fall to support us through the winter; for you are to consider, Sir, as I before observed, that the snows and hard frosts set in very early upon those mountains; and, as they are in many places almost inaccessible at all times, it is then more than horses can do to clamber up them. But, allow that they could, for want of provender they will become weak and die upon the road, as ours did, though we carried corn with us for their use, and purchased from place to place. This reason holds good, also, against driving out live-stock, which, if it could be done, would save some thousands of loads for horses, that might be employed in carrying flour, which alone, not to mention ammunition and tools, we shall find will require more horses, than at this present moment can be procured with our means.

His Honor also asks, whether it is practicable to destroy the corn at the fort and at Logstown. At this question I am a little surprised, when it is known we must pass the French fort and the Ohio to get to Logstown; and how this can be done with inferior numbers, under our disadvantages, I see not; and, as to the ground for hoping, that we may engage a sufficient party of Indians for this undertaking, I have no information, nor have I any conception; for it is well known, that notwithstanding the expresses, whom the Indians sent to one another, and all the pains that Montour and Croghan (who, by vainly boasting of their interest with the Indians, involved the country in great calamity, by causing dependence to be placed where there was none,) could take, they never could induce above thirty fighting men to join us, and not more than one half of those were serviceable upon any occasion.

I could make many other remarks equally true and pertinent; but to you, Sir, who, I am sensible, have acquired a pretty good knowledge of the country, and who see the difficulties that we labor under in getting proper necessaries, even at Winchester, it is needless. Therefore I shall only add some of the difficulties, which we are particularly subjected to in the Virginia regiment. And to begin, Sir, you are sensible of the sufferings our soldiers underwent in the last attempt, in a good season, to take possession of the Fork of the Allegany and Monongahela. You also saw the disorders those sufferings produced among them at Winchester after they returned.

These are yet fresh in their memories, and have an irritating effect. Through the indiscretion of Mr. Spiltdorph, they got some intimation that they were again ordered out, and it immediately occasioned a general clamor, and caused six men to desert last night. This, we expect, will be the consequence every night, unless prevented by close confinement.

In the next place, I have orders to complete my regiment, and not a sixpence is sent for that purpose. Can it be imagined, that subjects fit for this service, who have been so much impressed with, and alarmed at, our want of provisions, which was a main objection to enlisting before, will more readily engage now without money, than they did before with it? We were then from the 1st of February till the 1st of May, and could not complete our three hundred men by forty; and the officers suffered so much by having their recruiting expenses withheld, that they have unanimously refused to engage in that duty again, unless they are repaid for the past, and a sufficient allowance is made to them in future. To show you the state of the regiment, I have sent you a report by which you will perceive what great deficiencies there are of men, arms, tents, kettles, screws (which was a fatal want before), bayonets, cartouch-boxes, and every thing else. Again, were our men ever so willing to go, for want of the proper necessaries of life they are unable to do it. The chief part are almost naked, and scarcely a man has either shoes, stockings, or a hat. These things the merchants will not credit them for. The country has made no provision; they have not money themselves; and it cannot be expected, that the officers will engage for them again, personally, having suffered greatly on this head already; especially, now, when we have all the reason in the world to believe, that they will desert whenever they have an opportunity. There is not a man that has a blanket to secure him from cold or wet. Ammunition is a material article, and that is to come from Williamsburg, or wherever the governor can procure it. An account must be first sent of the quantity which is wanted; this, added to the carriage up, with the necessary tools, that must be had, as well as the time for bringing them round, will, I believe, advance us into that season, when it is usual, in more moderate climates, to retreat into winter-quarters, but here, with us, to begin a campaign! *

The promises of those traders, who offer to contract for large quantities of flour, are not to be depended upon;

* It is hardly necessary to add, after the reasons so ably urged in this letter, that the wild project of a campaign over the Allegany Mountains, without money, men, or provisions, was abandoned. It is sufficiently obvious, that the Governor and Council were not practised in military affairs, and that they needed the advice of this young officer of twenty-two, whose wisdom and foresight so much exceeded his experience and his years. This letter is characterized by the same comprehensive grasp of mind, the same attention to details, and the same cool reflection, which marked his whole career in after life, and particularly his military transactions during the Revolution.

There was a misunderstanding between the governor and the House of Burgesses, which prevented any appropriation of money at this juncture. It had been a custom in former times, that when the governor signed a patent for land, he should receive a fee of a pistole (about $3,60) for every such signature, which was a perquisite of his office. This fee had been revived by Governor Dinwiddie, but the House of Burgesses considered it an onerous exaction, and determined to resist it. As the governor refused to sign patents on any other terms, the Burgesses had the year before passed some spirited resolves, and sent an agent to England with a petition to the King's Council, that this custom might be abolished. The agent was Peyton Randolph, then Attorney-General of Virginia, and afterwards President of the first American Congress. While he was absent, the governor wrote to a correspondent in England; — "I have had a great deal of trouble and uneasiness from the factious disputes and violent heats of a most impudent troublesome party here, in regard to that silly fee of a pistole; they are very full of the success of their agent, which I give small notice to." The Attorney-General returned, without effecting his whole object, but the Board of Trade made new regulations, by which relief was afforded in certain cases, and the fee was prohibited except where the

a most flagrant instance of which we experienced in Croghan, who was under obligation to Major Carlyle for the delivery of this article in a certain time, and who was an eyewitness to our wants; yet he had the assurance, during our sufferings, to tantalize us, and boast of the quantity he could furnish, as he did of the number of horses he could command. Notwithstanding, we were equally disappointed of these also; for out of two hundred he had contracted for, we never had above twenty-five employed in bringing the flour engaged for the camp; and even this, small as the quantity was, did not arrive within a month of the time it was to have been delivered.

Another thing worthy of consideration, is, that if we depend on Indian assistance, we must have a large quantity of proper Indian goods to reward their services, and make them presents. It is owing to this alone, that the French command such an influence among them, and that we have conciliated so few. This, with the scarcity

---

quantity of land patented was more than one hundred acres.—*Journal of the House of Burgesses for November*, 1753.

The agent's expenses were two thousand five hundred pounds. The governor refused to sanction any bill for their payment. Piqued by this obstinacy, the House of Burgesses affixed the amount to a bill for raising twenty thousand pounds for his Majesty's service. Equally indignant at this presumption, the governor sent back the bill without his signature, and prorogued the Assembly for six weeks. Thus no supplies were granted, and the governor was induced to write, that "there appeared to him an infatuation in all the Assemblies in this part of the world." The treasurer of the colony had already paid the agent by order of the Assembly, without any special grant, which was no doubt a high disrespect to the Governor and Council. In giving an account of this affair to Governor Sharpe of Maryland, Governor Dinwiddie says, "I am now persuaded, that no expedition can be conducted here with dependence on American Assemblies; and I have written to that purpose home, and proposed a British act of Parliament to compel the subjects here to obedience to his Majesty's commands, and to protect their property from the insults of the French." The governor seemed not aware, that the people who owned the property, and lived on the spot, were well qualified to judge for themselves how far it needed protection.

of provisions, would induce them to ask, when they were to join us, if we meant to starve them as well as ourselves. But I will have done, and only add assurances of the regard and affection with which I am, &c.

TO GOVERNOR DINWIDDIE.

Alexandria, 20 August, 1754.

SIR,

Mr. Peyrouny, soliciting for leave to attend the Assembly, with the hope of having some allowance made for his loss of clothes and other articles, which he sustained in common with us all, and being not thoroughly cured of his wounds,* which have hitherto rendered him unfit for duty, I thought it proper to indulge him in this request. By him I again take the liberty of reminding your Honor of the great necessity there is of a regulation in the soldiers' pay, and that a deduction be made for the country to furnish them with clothes; otherwise they never will be fit for service; they are now naked, and cannot get credit even for a hat, and are teazing the officers every day to furnish them with these and other necessaries.

Another thing, which should be fixed indisputably, is the law we are to be guided by, whether martial or military. If the former, I must beg the favor of your Honor to give me some written orders and indemnification; otherwise I cannot give my assent (as I am liable for all proceedings) to any judgment of a court-martial, that touches the life of a soldier; though at this time there is an absolute necessity for it, as the soldiers are

* Received in the action of Fort Necessity at the Great Meadows.

deserting constantly. Yesterday, while we were at church, twenty-five of them collected, and were going off in the face of their officers, but were stopped and imprisoned before the plot came to its height.

Colonel Innes did not fill up any commissions for the Virginia regiment, which has given those entitled to promotion some uneasiness. His reasons were, that it would be an unnecessary expense to the country, till there were orders to recruit; but this, I think, should not have been considered, while it is remembered how small encouragement is shown them upon every occasion. Another motive, which, I believe, served to prevent it, was his dislike to the form of the commissions, as it savoured so much of the militia. He told me he would send down another form for your approbation, and Colonel Fairfax has also taken another, both of which are greatly preferable to those by which we act. And here I must beg leave to acquaint you, that the one you sent me is not signed.

The officers are uneasy about their pay, and think it hard to be kept out of it so long. They hope you will order the dates of their commissions to be from the time of the vacancies that happened, of which I have enclosed a list for your information, hoping with them, that you will be kind enough to fill them up yourself, and return such commissions as were sent for precedents.

Mr. West, lieutenant of Vanbraam's company, has resigned his commission, which I herewith send. I also enclose a list of medicines, which the doctor desires may be procured for the use of the regiment. He solicits much for an assistant, and I believe it necessary, as he often has more business than he can well manage, and, were a large detachment sent upon duty, it would be imprudent to go without the surgeon.

If you should think proper to promote Mr. Peyrouny,

we shall be at a loss for a good disciplinarian to do adjutant's duty, which requires a perfect knowledge of all the kinds of duty. I should, therefore, take it extremely kind, if you would be pleased to confer the office upon Mr. Frazier, whom I think I can fully answer for, let his former conduct have been what it may.

We have caught two deserters, whom I shall keep imprisoned till I receive your answer how far the martial law may be extended. It is necessary that an example be made of some, as a warning to others; for there is scarcely a night, or an opportunity, when there are not desertions, and often two, three, or four at a time. We always advertise and pursue them as quickly as possible, but seldom to any purpose. The expenses attending this will fall heavily upon the country while this spirit prevails. I am, &c.

TO GOVERNOR DINWIDDIE.

Without date.

Sir,

As I wrote so lately and fully to you, by Mr. Polson, on the subject of the orders I had received, I have little to add now, only to acquaint your Honor, that as far as it is in my power, I shall endeavour to comply with them. What men we can, we do enlist; but to send officers into different parts for that purpose, would be unavailing, as they neither have money, nor can get any. I have given Major Carlyle memorandums of several questions to ask your Honor, to which I beg your answers, that I may be governed thereby. I have also sent some of the soldiers' accounts, in hope of getting the money for them, as they are uneasy on that head. Others of them are rendered useless by their late wounds; therefore I hope you will recommend it to the consideration of the Assembly, that some provision may be made to keep them from want.

I have also desired Major Carlyle to mention to you the great necessity there is for regulation in the soldiers' pay; and that a certain part may be deducted and appropriated for clothing. Unless this be done, we shall ever be in the distressed condition we are in at present, concerning which Major Carlyle can fully inform you. I refer you to him for many particulars, especially the consequences of going as high as Will's Creek, if we cannot march farther; as, for the reasons which have been alleged, I fear we cannot, if we attempt it; and, at that place, for want of proper conveniences, we could not remain.* I have the honor to be, &c.

---

* After the battle of the Great Meadows, Colonel Innes was ordered to Will's Creek to construct a fort, which should serve as a rallying point to the remaining forces, and a guard to the frontiers. This was afterwards called Fort Cumberland. It was built chiefly by the three Independent Companies, namely, Captain Mackay's from South Carolina, and two others from New York, which were on their march from Alexandria to join Washington at the time of the action at the Great Meadows. A company of recruits from Maryland also repaired to Will's Creek in November. Ten four-pounders, besides swivels, were mounted in the fort. But Colonel Innes was left with a small command; for the North Carolina troops, to the number of three hundred and fifty, all disbanded themselves in a very disorderly manner at Winchester, and went off without ceremony. North Carolina had granted twelve thousand pounds, and enlisted soldiers at the extravagant rate of three shillings a day. The money was of course soon exhausted, and the troops, finding there was no pledge for future payment, very naturally consulted their own interest, and went home.

This unmilitary conduct, and lack of patriotism, put an end to all hopes of further operations against the French for the present season, and added much to the despair of Governor Dinwiddie. He began to think the colonies would be ruined without remedy, and urged anew the measure, which he had before recommended to the British government. It was his favorite scheme, that a poll-tax should be laid on all the colonies by *an act of Parliament*, and that the amount thus raised should be held at the King's disposal for the defence of the country. In a letter to the Board of Trade he expressed himself thus. "I beg leave to give my humble

TO COLONEL WILLIAM FITZHUGH.

15 November, 1754.*

DEAR SIR,

I was favored with your letter from Rousby Hall, of the 4th instant. It demands my best acknowledgments for the particular marks of esteem you have expressed therein, and for the kind assurances of his Excellency Governor Sharpe's good wishes towards me. I also thank you, and sincerely, Sir, for your friendly intention of making my situation easy, if I return to the service; and I do not doubt, could I submit to the terms, that

---

opinion, that the progress of the French will never be effectually opposed, but by means of an act of Parliament to compel the colonies to contribute to the common cause independently of Assemblies, who in these parts are either ignorant, or do not foresee danger at a distance, or at least are so obstinate as to pay little regard to it." And, again, to the Secretary of State; "I know of no method to compel them to their duty to the King, but by an act of Parliament for a general poll-tax of two shillings and sixpence a head from all the colonies on this continent." — Dinwiddie's *Letter-Books*.

Had this counsel of Governor Dinwiddie been followed, it would probably have hastened the Revolution a few years, which, as it was, happened only twenty years afterwards. From the tenor of this correspondence, we may also learn what kind of intelligence and advice the government in England was in the habit of receiving from its governors, and may account in some degree for the extraordinary delusion, that finally prevailed, respecting the character, temper, and feelings of the colonists.

* At this time Colonel Washington had resigned his commission, and retired from the service. When the Assembly met in October, they granted twenty thousand pounds for the public exigencies, and the governor received from England ten thousand pounds sterling in specie, with the promise of ten thousand more, and two thousand firearms. Thereupon he resolved to enlarge the army to ten companies, of one hundred men each, and to reduce them all to Independent Companies, by which there would be no officer in the Virginia regiment above the rank of a captain. This expedient, he supposed, would remedy the difficulties about command. Washington accordingly resigned, as he would not accept a lower commission, than the one he had held, and under which he had exhibited a rare example of bravery and good conduct, that had gained him the applause of the country.

Meantime Governor Sharpe, of Maryland, had received the King's commission as commander-in-chief of all the forces engaged against the

I should be as happy under your command in the absence of the General, as under any gentleman's whatever. But I think the disparity between the present offer of a company and my former rank too great, to expect any real satisfaction or enjoyment in a corps, where I once had, or thought I had, a right to command; even if his Excellency had power to suspend the orders received in the Secretary of War's letter; which, by the by, I am very far from thinking he has, or that he will attempt to do it, without fuller instructions than I believe he has received; especially, too, as there has been a representation of this matter by Governor Dinwiddie, and, I believe, the Assembly of this province.

All that I presume the General can do, is, to prevent the different corps from interfering, which will occasion the duty to be done by corps, instead of detachments; a very inconvenient way, as found by experience. *

You make mention in your letter of my continuing in

French. Colonel Fitzhugh was to have the command of the army, during General Sharpe's absence in visiting the military posts, and in executing his official duties as governor. Knowing the value of Colonel Washington's experience and reputation, the commander-in-chief wished to bring him back to the service; and, to effect this object, Colonel Fitzhugh wrote him a letter, in which he tried the force of argument and persuasion. "I am confident," he observes, "that the General has a very great regard for you, and will by every circumstance in his power make you very happy. For my part, I shall be extremely fond of your continuing in the service, and would advise you by no means to quit it. In regard to the Independent Companies, they will in no shape interfere with you, as you will hold your post during their continuance here, and, when the regiment is reduced, will have a separate duty." The letter, from which this extract is taken, Colonel Washington answered as above.

* That is, the Independent and Colonial companies must always act separately, and not in concert by detachments from each. The inconvenience of this method was proved in the case of Captain Mackay, previously to the battle of the Great Meadows. Colonel Innes, at Will's Creek, contrived to keep up a nominal command, by acting under two commissions, his old one from the King received in the former war, and his new one from Governor Dinwiddie, to each of which he appealed as occasion required.

the service, and retaining my colonel's commission. This idea has filled me with surprise; for, if you think me capable of holding a commission, that has neither rank nor emolument annexed to it, you must entertain a very contemptible opinion of my weakness, and believe me to be more empty than the commission itself.

Besides, Sir, if I had time, I could enumerate many good reasons, that forbid all thoughts of my returning; and which to you, or any other person, would, upon the strictest scrutiny, appear to be well founded. I must be reduced to a very low command, and subjected to that of many, who have acted as my inferior officers. In short, every captain, bearing the King's commission, every half-pay officer, or others appearing with such a commission, would rank before me. For these reasons I choose to submit to the loss of health, which I have, however, already sustained, (not to mention that of effects,) and the fatigue I have undergone in our first efforts, rather than subject myself to the same inconveniences, and run the risk of a second disappointment.

I shall have the consolation of knowing, that I have opened the way, when the smallness of our numbers exposed us to the attacks of a superior enemy; that I have hitherto stood the heat and brunt of the day, and escaped untouched in time of extreme danger; and that I have the thanks of my country, for the services I have rendered it.*

The information I have received shall not sleep in silence, that those peremptory orders from home, which you say could not be dispensed with, for reducing the regiment into Independent Companies, were generated and hatched at Will's Creek. Ingenuous treatment and

* See APPENDIX, No. III.

plain dealing I at least expected.* It is to be hoped the project will answer; it shall meet with my acquiescence in every thing except personal services. I herewith enclose Governor Sharpe's letter, which I beg you will return to him, with my acknowledgments for the favor he intended me. Assure him, Sir, as you truly may, of my reluctance to quit the service, and of the pleasure I should have received in attending his fortunes. Inform him, also, that it was to obey the call of honor, and the advice of my friends, that I declined it, and not to gratify any desire I had to leave the military line. My inclinations are strongly bent to arms.

The length of this letter, and the small room I have left, tell me how necessary it is to conclude; which I will do, with the assurance that you shall always find me

Truly and sincerely your most humble servant.

---

* It would seem, that some unfair purpose was suspected in this matter of reducing the regiment, and thereby throwing out the higher officers. Nor was this a groundless suspicion. Governor Dinwiddie wrote to the Earl of Halifax, on the 25th of October; — "As there have been some disputes between the regulars, and the officers appointed by me, I am now determined to reduce our regiment into Independent Companies, so that from our forces there will be no other distinguished officer above a captain." — It is clear, therefore, that this was done at the governor's own motion, probably in concert with General Sharpe, and not by any orders, which had as yet been received from higher authority. He had written for instructions, but none had then arrived, nor in fact did they arrive, till brought out by General Braddock the winter following. It is no wonder, that a high-minded officer should be displeased at such a manœuvre, cloaked as it was under the pretence of "peremptory orders from home." Doubtless the arrangement was considered essential to the prosperity of the service, but this would hardly be taken as an apology for a concealed design, by a man of spirit and high motives, who felt himself entitled to frankness and confidence.

TO ROBERT ORME.

Mount Vernon, 15 March, 1755.*

SIR,

I was not favored with your polite letter, of the 2d instant, until yesterday; acquainting me with the notice his Excellency, General Braddock, is pleased to honor me with, by kindly inviting me to become one of his family the ensuing campaign. It is true, Sir, I have, ever since I declined my late command, expressed an inclination to serve in this campaign as a volunteer; and this inclination is not a little increased, since it is likely

---

* General Braddock landed in Virginia, as commander-in-chief of all the military forces in North America, on the 20th of February. The transports with the British troops, who were to act under him, came into the Chesapeake soon afterwards. These he ordered up the Potomac to Alexandria, or, as it was then sometimes called, Bellhaven, where the troops debarked. By the plan first proposed, one company was to be stationed at Dumfries, six companies at Fredericksburg and Falmouth, three and a half companies at Winchester, and half a company at Conococheague. In Maryland one company was to be cantoned at Bladensburg, another at Upper Marlborough, and two at Frederic Town. Some of the troops were to be landed below Alexandria, at the nearest point to Fredericksburg. But this plan was finally abandoned, and the troops were all landed at Alexandria.

The following order of the King, dated at St. James's, November 12th, 1754, respecting the rank of colonial officers, was brought out by General Braddock.

"All troops serving by commission signed by us, or by our general commanding in chief in North America, shall take rank before all troops, which may serve by commission from any of the governors, lieutenant or deputy governors, or president for the time being. And it is our further pleasure, that the general and field officers of the provincial troops shall have no rank with the general and field officers, who serve by commission from us; but that all captains and other inferior officers of our forces, who are or may be employed in North America, are, on all detachments, courts-martial, and other duty, wherein they may be joined with officers serving by commission from the governors, lieutenant or deputy governors, or president for the time being of the said provinces, to command and take post of the said provincial officers of the like rank, though the commissions of the said provincial officers of like rank should be of elder date."

Since his resignation in October, Colonel Washington had remained

to be conducted by a gentleman of the General's experience.

But, besides this, and the laudable desire I may have to serve, with my best abilities, my King and country, I must be ingenuous enough to confess, that I am not a little biassed by selfish considerations. To explain, Sir, I wish earnestly to attain some knowledge in the military profession, and, believing a more favorable opportunity cannot offer, than to serve under a gentleman of General Braddock's abilities and experience, it does, you may reasonably suppose, not a little contribute to influence my choice. But, Sir, as I have taken the liberty to express my sentiments so freely, I must beg your indulgence while I add, that the only bar, which can check me in the pursuit of this object, is the inconveniences that must necessarily result from some proceedings, which happened a little before the General's arrival, and which, in some measure, had abated the ardor of my desires, and determined me to lead a life

---

inactive at Mount Vernon, and if he found it derogatory to his honor to hold a commission under Governor Dinwiddie's scheme of Independent Companies, it could not be expected, that he would subject himself to the humiliating terms of this order from the King. His passion for a military life, however, had not abated. General Braddock, knowing his value, and the importance of securing his services to the expedition, directed Mr. Orme, his aid-de-camp, to write to him the following letter, proposing an expedient by which the chief obstacles would be removed.

"Williamsburg, 2 March, 1755.

"SIR,

"The General, having been informed that you expressed some desire to make the campaign, but that you declined it upon some disagreeableness that you thought might arise from the regulations of command, has ordered me to acquaint you, that he will be very glad of your company in his family, by which all inconveniences of that kind will be obviated.

"I shall think myself very happy to form an acquaintance with a person so universally esteemed, and shall use every opportunity of assuring you how much I am, Sir, your most obedient servant.

"ROBERT ORME, *Aid-de-camp.*"

of retirement, into which I was just entering, at no small expense, when your favor was presented to me.

But, as I shall do myself the honor of waiting upon his Excellency, as soon as I hear of his arrival at Alexandria, (I would do it sooner, were I certain where to find him,) I shall decline saying any thing further on this head till then; begging you will be pleased to assure him, that I shall always retain a grateful sense of the favor with which he is pleased to honor me, and that I should have embraced this opportunity of writing to him, had I not recently addressed a congratulatory letter to him on his safe arrival in this country.

I flatter myself you will favor me in making a communication of these sentiments.

You do me a singular favor, in proposing an acquaintance. It cannot but be attended with the most flattering prospects, on my part, as you may already perceive, by the familiarity and freedom with which I now enter upon this correspondence; a freedom, which, even if it is disagreeable, you must excuse, and lay the blame of it at your own door, for encouraging me to throw off that restraint, which otherwise might have been more obvious in my deportment on such an occasion.

The hope of shortly seeing you will be an excuse for my not adding more, than that I shall endeavour to approve myself worthy of your friendship, and that I beg to be esteemed your most obedient servant.

TO ROBERT ORME.

Mount Vernon, 2 April, 1755.

DEAR SIR,

The arrival of a good deal of company (among whom is my mother, alarmed at the report of my intention to attend your fortunes,) deprives me of the pleasure of waiting upon you to-day, as I had designed.* I therefore beg, that you will be kind enough to make my compliments and excuse to the General, who I hope to hear is greatly recovered from his indisposition, and recruited sufficiently to prosecute his journey to Annapolis.†

I find myself much embarrassed with my affairs, having no person in whom I can confide, to entrust the management of them with. Notwithstanding, I am determined to do myself the honor of accompanying you, upon this proviso, that the General will be kind enough to permit my return, as soon as the active part of the campaign is at an end, if it is desired; or, if there should be a space of inaction, long enough to admit a visit to my home, that I may be indulged in coming to it.

I need not add, how much I should be obliged by joining you at Will's Creek, instead of doing it at an earlier period.‡

These things, Sir, in whatever light they may appear

---

* Captain Orme was now with the army at Alexandria, nine miles from Mount Vernon.

† Soon after General Braddock arrived in Virginia, he wrote to the governors of Massachusetts, New York, and Pennsylvania, requesting them to meet him at Annapolis in Maryland, to concert measures for future operations. The General and Governor Dinwiddie proceeded to Annapolis, but the place of meeting was afterwards changed to Alexandria, where they all assembled on the 13th of April, and concerted measures for the united action of the middle and northern colonies. It was thought by some, that New York ought to be the centre of operations, as affording greater facilities for attacking the French at their strongest points; but Braddock's instructions were positive to proceed to the Ohio. He marched from Alexandria on the 20th of April.

‡ In reply Captain Orme wrote;—"The General orders me to give you his compliments, and to assure you his wishes are to make it agreeable to yourself and consistent with your affairs, and, therefore, he desires you will so settle your business at home, as to join him at Will's Creek if more convenient to you; and, whenever you find it necessary to return, he begs you will look upon yourself as entirely master, and judge what is proper to be done."

to you at first sight, will not, I hope, be thought unreasonable, when it is considered how unprepared I am to quit a family, and an estate I was just about to settle, which is in the utmost confusion.

I enclose a letter from Colonel Fairfax to Governor Shirley, which, with his compliments, he desired might be given to that gentleman. He also sends his blessing to you. At present he entertains sanguine hopes of you; this for your comfort.

I herewith send you a small map of the back country, which, though imperfect and roughly drawn, for want of proper instruments, may give you a better knowledge of the designated parts, than you have hitherto had an opportunity of acquiring.

I shall do myself the honor of waiting upon the General, as soon as I hear of his return from Annapolis. My compliments attend him, and Mr. Shirley. I am, &c.

TO JOHN ROBINSON, SPEAKER OF THE HOUSE OF DELEGATES, VIRGINIA.

Mount Vernon, 20 April, 1755.

DEAR SIR,

I little expected, when I wrote you last, that I should so soon engage in another campaign; but, in doing it, I may be allowed to claim some merit, if it is considered that the sole motive, which invites me to the field, is the laudable desire of serving my country, not the gratification of any ambitious or lucrative plans. This, I flatter myself, will manifestly appear by my going as a volunteer, without expectation of reward, or prospect of obtaining a command, as I am confidently assured it is not in General Braddock's power to give me a commission that I would accept. Perhaps by many others the above declaration might be construed into self-applause, which, unwilling to lose, I proclaim myself. But by you, Sir, I expect it will be viewed in a different light, because you have sympathized in my disappointments, and lent your friendly aid to reinstate me in a suitable command; the recollection of which can never be lost upon a mind, that is not insensible of obligations, but always ready to acknowledge them.

This is the reason why I am so much more unreserved in the expression of my sentiments to you, than I should be to the world, whose censures and criticisms often place good designs in a bad light. But, to be ingenuous, I must confess I have other intentions in writing you this letter; for, if there is any merit in my case, I am unwilling to hazard it among my friends, without this exposition of facts, as they might conceive that some advantageous offers had engaged my services, when, in reality, it is otherwise, for I expect to be a considerable loser in my private affairs by going. It is true I have been importuned to make this campaign by General Braddock, as a member of his family, he conceiving, I suppose, that the small knowledge I have had an opportunity of acquiring of the country, Indians, &c., is worthy of his notice, and may be useful to him in the progress of the expedition.

I heartily wish a happy issue to all your resolves, and am, Sir,

Your most obedient servant.

TO WILLIAM FAIRFAX.

Mount Vernon, 23 April, 1755.

DEAR SIR

I cannot think of quitting Fairfax,* without embracing this last opportunity of bidding you farewell. I shall *this day set out for Will's Creek*, where I expect to meet the General, and to stay, I fear, too long, as the march must be regulated by the slow movements of the train; which, I am sorry to say, will be tedious, very tedious indeed, as I have long predicted, though few believed. Alexandria has been honored with five governors in consultation; a favorable presage, I hope, not only of the success of this expedition, but of the future greatness of that town; for surely such a meeting must have been occasioned by the commodious and pleasant situation of the place, which prognosticates population, and increase of a flourishing trade.

I have had the honor to be introduced to several governors, and of being well received by them; especially Mr. Shirley, whose character and appearance have perfectly charmed me. I think his every word and action discover in him the gentleman and politician. I heartily wish the same unanimity may prevail among us, as appeared to exist between him and his Assembly, when they, to expedite the business, and to forward his journey hither, sat till eleven and twelve o'clock every night.

It will be needless, as I know your punctuality requires no stimulus, to remind you of an affair, about which I wrote some time ago; therefore I shall only beg my compliments to Mr. Nicholas and his lady, and to all friends who think me worthy of their inquiries. I am, &c.

---

* Mount Vernon is in Fairfax county.

TO WILLIAM FAIRFAX.

Winchester, 5 May, 1755.

DEAR SIR,

I overtook the General at Frederic Town, in Maryland. Thence we proceeded to this place, where we shall remain till the arrival of the second division of the train, which we hear left Alexandria on Tuesday last. After that, we shall continue our march to Will's Creek; from whence, it is imagined, we shall not stir till the latter end of this month, for want of wagons and other conveniences of transport over the mountains.

You will naturally conclude, that to pass through Maryland, when no object required it, was an uncommon, and an extraordinary route for the General and for Colonel Dunbar's regiment to this place. The reason, however, was obvious. Those who promoted it had rather the communication should be opened that way, than through Virginia; but I believe the eyes of the General are now opened, and the imposition detected; consequently, the like will not happen again. I am, &c.

TO JOHN A. WASHINGTON.*

Fort Cumberland, 14 May, 1755.

DEAR BROTHER,

As wearing boots is quite the mode, and mine are in a declining state, I must beg the favor of you to procure me a pair that are good and neat, and send them to

* John Augustine Washington was a younger and favorite brother. He was the father of Bushrod Washington, who, after having been more than thirty years one of the associate justices of the Supreme Court of the United States, died at Philadelphia, on the 26th of November, 1829.

Major Carlyle, who, I hope, will contrive to forward them, as quickly as my necessity requires.

I see no prospect of moving from this place soon, as we have neither horses nor wagons enough, and no forage, except what is expected from Philadelphia; therefore, I am well convinced, that the trouble and difficulty we must encounter in passing the mountains, for the want of proper conveniences, will equal all the difficulties of the campaign; for I conceive the march of such a train of artillery, in these roads, to be a tremendous undertaking. As to any danger from the enemy, I look upon it as trifling, for I believe the French will be obliged to exert their utmost force to repel the attacks to the northward, where Governor Shirley and others, with a body of eight thousand men, will annoy their settlements, and attempt their forts.

The General has appointed me one of his aids-decamp,* in which character I shall serve this campaign agreeably enough, as I am thereby freed from all commands but his, and give his orders, which must be implicitly obeyed.

I have now a good opportunity, and shall not neglect it, of forming an acquaintance, which may be serviceable hereafter, if I find it worth while to push my fortune in the military line.

I have written to my two female correspondents by this opportunity, one of whose letters I have enclosed to you, and beg your deliverance of it. I shall expect a particular account of all that has happened since my departure.

I am, dear Jack,

Your most affectionate brother.

---

* This appointment was proclaimed to the army in general orders, on the 10th of May.

TO WILLIAM FAIRFAX.

Camp, at Will's Creek, 7 June, 1755.

SIR,

I arrived with my charge safe in camp, on the 30th of last month, after waiting a day and part of another in Winchester, expecting the cavalry to escort me up; in which being disappointed, I was obliged to make use of a small guard of the militia of Frederick county.*

The General, from frequent breaches of contract, has lost all patience; and, for want of that temper and moderation, which should be used by a man of sense upon these occasions, will, I fear, represent us in a light we little deserve; for, instead of blaming the individuals, as he ought, he charges all his disappointments to public supineness, and looks upon the country, I believe, as void of honor and honesty. We have frequent disputes on this head, which are maintained with warmth on both sides, especially on his, as he is incapable of arguing without it, or giving up any point he asserts, be it ever so incompatible with reason or common sense.†

* Colonel Washington had been despatched to Williamsburg, to obtain four thousand pounds in money for the use of the army, and bring it to the camp at Will's Creek. He executed this commission with promptness and effect, and the guard here mentioned was to protect him with this charge on his return between Winchester and the camp.

† General Braddock had good grounds for complaint, if we may judge from his letters published in the French *Mémoire*, as translations from the originals found among his papers taken at his defeat, which bear every mark of being genuine. The contractors deceived and disappointed him in nearly every instance, and paralyzed his most strenuous efforts to proceed with the army. This, to be sure, was not the fault of the country, but it would seem to have been the duty of the adjoining colonies to take care, that supplies were promptly forwarded through some channel or other, and not to leave the expedition at the mercy of faithless and peculating contractors. It is evident, that the sense of the people was but little wakened to the necessity, or importance, of these enterprises against the French, and that they looked upon them rather as the results of political

A line of communication is to be opened from Pennsylvania to the French fort Duquesne, along which, after a little time, we are to receive all our convoys of provisions, and to give all possible encouragement to a people, who ought rather to be chastised for their insensibility to danger, and disregard of their sovereign's expectations. They, it seems, are to be the favored people, because they have furnished what their absolute interest alone induced them to do, that is, one hundred and fifty wagons, and an equivalent number of horses.*

Major Chapman, with a detachment of five hundred men, and the Quartermaster-General, marched two or

objects in Great Britain, than as immediately concerning themselves. The perpetual broils with their governors, also, had created a willingness to thwart any schemes proposed by these staunch and obstinate defenders of the prerogative and of prescriptive abuses.

* These remarks are applied to the Pennsylvanians, who were singularly backward in rendering any aids for the public service. The merit of procuring the wagons and horses, here mentioned, was wholly due to Franklin, and not to any agency or intention of the Assembly. Being at that time postmaster-general in the colonies, he visited General Braddock at Frederic Town, for the purpose of maturing a plan for transmitting despatches between the general and the governors. Becoming acquainted with the obstacles, which opposed the progress of the army, he stipulated with General Braddock to furnish within a given time one hundred and fifty wagons, and a proportionable number of horses, for which a specified sum was to be allowed. He immediately returned to York and Lancaster, sent out an advertisement among the farmers, and in two weeks all the wagons and horses were in readiness at Will's Creek. He gave his personal security, that the compensation agreed on should be duly paid according to contract.

General Braddock was fully aware of the nature and value of this service. On the 5th of June he wrote from Will's Creek to the Secretary of State as follows.

"Before I left Williamsburg, the Quartermaster-General told me, that I might depend upon twenty-five hundred horses, and two hundred wagons from Virginia and Maryland; but I had great reason to doubt it, having experienced the false dealings of all in this country, with whom I had been concerned. Hence, before my departure from Frederic I agreed with Mr. Benjamin Franklin, postmaster in Pennsylvania, who has great credit in that province, to hire one hundred and fifty wagons, and the necessary number of horses. This he accomplished with promptitude and fidelity,

three days before I arrived here, to open the roads, and lay in a deposite of provisions at a small fort, which they are to erect at the Little Meadows.

To-morrow, Sir Peter Halket, with the first brigade, is to begin his march, and on Monday the General, with the second, is to follow. One hospital is filled with sick, and the numbers increase daily, with the bloody flux, which has not yet proved mortal to many.

By a letter received from Governor Morris, of Pennsylvania, we have advice, that a party of three hundred men passed Oswego on their way to Fort Duquesne, and that another and a larger detachment was expected to pass that place every moment. By the public accounts from Pennsylvania, we are farther assured, that nine hundred men have certainly passed Oswego to reinforce the French on the Ohio; so that from these accounts we have reason to believe, that we shall have more to do than to go up the hills and come down.

We are impatient to hear what the powers at home are doing; whether peace, or war, is likely to be the issue of all these preparations.

I am, Sir,

Your most obedient servant.

---

and it is almost the only instance of address and integrity, which I have seen in all these provinces." — *Mémoire*, &c. p. 198.

When Franklin returned to Philadelphia, the House of Assembly was in session, and unanimously passed a vote of thanks "to Benjamin Franklin, a member of this House, for the great services done to the King's forces, and to this province, in his late journey through Maryland and our back counties." It should be added, also, that no profit on his own account was either expected or received. On the contrary, after General Braddock's death, the owners of the wagons and horses came upon Franklin for their pay, amounting in all to nearly twenty thousand pounds; and he was much embarrassed with these claims, till they were finally allowed and settled by General Shirley, who succeeded Braddock in the command. — *Votes of the Pennsylvania Assembly*, Vol. IV. p. 397. — *Franklin's Works*, Vol. I. pp. 142-152.

TO JOHN A. WASHINGTON.

Youghiogany, 28 June, 1755.

DEAR BROTHER,

Immediately upon our leaving the camp at George's Creek, on the 14th instant, from whence I wrote to you, I was seized with a violent fever and pain of the head, which continued without intermission until the 23d, when I was relieved, by the General's absolutely ordering the physician to give me Dr. James's powders, one of the most excellent medicines in the world. It gave me immediate ease, and removed my fever and other complaints in four days' time. My illness was too violent to suffer me to ride; therefore I was indebted to a covered wagon for some part of my transportation; but even in this, I could not continue far. The jolting was so great, that I was left upon the road with a guard, and some necessaries, to wait the arrival of Colonel Dunbar's detachment, which was two days' march behind us, the General giving me his word of honor, that I should be brought up, before he reached the French fort. This promise, and the doctor's declaration, that, if I persevered in my attempts to go on, in the condition I then was, my life would be endangered, determined me to halt for the above mentioned detachment.

As the communication between this and Will's Creek must soon be too dangerous for single persons to pass, it will render the intercourse of letters slow and precarious; therefore I shall attempt (and will go through it if I have strength) to give you an account of our proceedings, our situation, and prospects at present; which I desire you will communicate to Colonel Fairfax, and others, my correspondents, for I am too weak to write more than this letter.

In the letter, which I wrote to you from George's

Creek, I acquainted you, that, unless the number of wagons was retrenched, and the carriage-horses increased, we should never be able to see Fort Duquesne.* This, in two days afterwards (which was about the time they got to the Little Meadows, with some of their foremost wagons, and strongest teams), they themselves were convinced of; for they found, that, besides the extreme difficulty of getting the wagons along at all, they had often a line of three or four miles in length; and the soldiers guarding them were so dispersed, that, if we had been attacked either in front, centre, or rear, the part so attacked must have been cut off, or totally routed, before they could be sustained by any other corps.

At the Little Meadows a second council was called (for there had been one before), wherein the urgency for horses was again represented to the officers of the different corps, and how laudable a farther retrenchment of their baggage would be, that the spare ones might be turned over for the public service. In order to encourage this, I gave up my best horse, which I have never heard of since, and took no more baggage than half my portmanteau would easily contain. It is said, however, that the number reduced by this second attempt was only from two hundred and ten or twelve, to two hundred, which had no perceivable effect.

The General, before they met in council, asked my private opinion concerning the expedition. I urged him, in the warmest terms I was able, to push forward, if he even did it with a small but chosen band, with such

* In the letter here referred to he says;—"The difficulties arising in our march, from having such a number of wagons, will, I fear, prove an insurmountable obstacle, unless some scheme can be fallen upon to retrench the wagons, and increase the number of bat-horses, which is what I recommended at first, and which I believe is now found to be the best means of transporting our provisions and stores to the Ohio."

artillery and light stores as were necessary; leaving the heavy artillery, baggage, and the like with the rear division of the army, to follow by slow and easy marches, which they might do safely, while we were advanced in front. As one reason to support this opinion, I urged, that, if we could credit our intelligence, the French were weak at the Fork at present, but hourly expected reinforcements, which, to my certain knowledge, could not arrive with provisions, or any supplies, during the continuance of the drought, as the Buffalo River (Rivière aux Bœufs), down which was their only communication to Venango, must be as dry as we now found the Great Crossing of the Youghiogany, which may be passed dry-shod.

This advice prevailed, and it was determined, that the General, with one thousand two hundred chosen men, and officers from all the different corps, under the following field officers, viz.; Sir Peter Halket, who acts as brigadier; Lieutenant-Colonel Gage, Lieutenant-Colonel Burton, and Major Sparks, with such a number of wagons as the train would absolutely require, should march as soon as things could be got in readiness. This was completed, and we were on our march, by the 19th, leaving Colonel Dunbar and Major Chapman behind, with the residue of the two regiments, some Independent Companies, most of the women, and, in short, every thing not absolutely essential, carrying our provisions and other necessaries upon horses.

We set out with less than thirty carriages, including those that transported the ammunition for the howitzers, twelve-pounders, and six-pounders, and all of them strongly horsed; which was a prospect that conveyed infinite delight to my mind, though I was excessively ill at the time. But this prospect was soon clouded, and my hopes brought very low indeed, when I found, that, instead of pushing on with vigor, without regarding a little rough road, they were halting to level every mole-hill, and to erect bridges over every brook, by which means we were four days in getting twelve miles.

At this camp I was left by the Doctor's advice, and the General's positive orders, as I have already mentioned, without which I should not have been prevailed upon to remain behind; as I then imagined, and now believe, I shall find it no easy matter to join my own corps again, which is twenty-five miles in advance. Notwithstanding, I had the General's word of honor, pledged in the most solemn manner, that I should be brought up before he arrived at Fort Duquesne.* They have had frequent alarms, and several men have been scalped; but this is done with no other design, than to retard the march, and to harass the men, who, if they are to be turned out every time a small party attacks the guards at night (for I am certain they have not sufficient force to make a serious assault), the enemy's aim will be accomplished by the gaining of time.

I have been now six days with Colonel Dunbar's corps, who are in a miserable condition for want of horses, not having enough for their wagons; so that the only method he has of proceeding, is to march with as many wagons as these will draw, and then halt till the remainder are brought up with the same horses, which requires two days more; and shortly, I believe, he will not be able to stir at all. There has been vile management in regard to horses.

---

* Captain Roger Morris, one of the General's aids-de-camp, wrote to Colonel Washington from the Great Crossing of the Youghiogany in the following language. "I am desired by the General to let you know, that he marches to-morrow and next day, but that he shall halt at the Meadows two or three days It is the desire of every individual in the family, and the General's positive commands to you, not to stir, but by the advice of the person under whose care you are, till you are better, which we all hope will be very soon."

My strength will not admit of my saying more, though I have not said half that I intended concerning our affairs here. Business I shall not think of, but depend solely upon your management of all my affairs, not doubting that they will be well conducted. I am, &c.

July 2d. — A serious inconvenience attended me in my sickness, and that was losing the use of my servant; for poor John Alton was taken about the same time that I was, and with nearly the same disorder, and was confined as long; so that we did not see each other for several days. He is also tolerably well recovered.

We are advanced almost as far as the Great Meadows, and I shall set out to-morrow morning for my own corps, with an escort of one hundred men, who are to guard some provisions up, so that my fears and doubts on that head are now removed.

I had a letter yesterday from Orme, who writes me word, that they have passed the Youghiogany for the last time; that they have sent out parties to scour the country thereabouts, and have reason to believe the French are greatly alarmed at their approach.

TO ROBERT ORME.

Great Crossing, 30 June, 1755.

DEAR ORME,

I came to this camp on Thursday last, with the rear of Colonel Dunbar's detachment, and should have continued on with his front to-day, but was prevented by rain.

My fevers are very moderate, and, I hope, near terminating. Then I shall have nothing to encounter but weakness, which is excessive, and the difficulty of getting to you, arising therefrom; but this I would not miss doing, before you reach Duquesne, for five hundred pounds. However, I have no doubt now of doing it, as I am moving on, and the General has given me his word of honor, in the most solemn manner, that it shall be effected.

As the Doctor thinks it imprudent for me to use much exercise for two or three days, my movements will be retarded. I should be glad, therefore, to be advised of your marches from Gist's, and how you are likely to proceed, for you may rest assured, that Colonel Dunbar cannot remove from this present encampment in less than two or three days; and I believe, really, it will be as much as he possibly can do to reach the Meadows at all, so that you will be greatly in advance of him.

I am too weak to add more, than my compliments to the General and the family, and again to desire, that you will oblige me in the above request, and devise the most effectual means for me to join you. I am, dear Orme, your most obedient servant.*

---

* This letter and the preceding are the last on record, previous to the battle of the Monongahela. The following memorandum, written at a later date, is entered in the Letter-Book.

"On the 8th of July I rejoined (in a covered wagon) the advanced division of the army, under the immediate command of the General. On the 9th I attended him on horseback, though very low and weak. This day he was attacked and defeated by a party of French and Indians. When all hope of rallying the dismayed troops, and recovering the ground, had expired, our provisions and stores being given up, I was ordered to Dunbar's camp."

Colonel Dunbar had advanced seven miles beyond the Great Meadows, which was the position of his camp at the time of the action. Here he remained till he was met by General Braddock, and his flying troops, after the defeat at the Monongahela, when he speedily retreated with the whole army to Fort Cumberland.

TO GOVERNOR INNES, AT FORT CUMBERLAND.*

Little Meadows, 15 July, 1755.

SIR,

Captain Orme, being confined to his litter, and not able to write, has desired me to acknowledge the receipt of yours. He begs the favor of you to have the room the General lodged in prepared for Colonel Burton, himself, and Captain Morris, who are all wounded; also, that some small place may be had convenient for cooking; and, if any fresh provision, and other necessaries for persons in their condition, may be had, that you will engage them.

The horses, which carry the wounded gentlemen in litters, are so much fatigued, that we dread their performance; therefore, it is desired that you will be kind enough to send out eight or ten fresh horses for their relief, which will enable us to reach the fort this evening.

I doubt not but you have had an account of the poor gentlemen's death by some of the affrighted wagoners, who ran off, without taking leave. I am, Sir, your most obedient servant.

TO MRS. MARY WASHINGTON, NEAR FREDERICKSBURG.

Fort Cumberland, 18 July, 1755.

HONORED MADAM,

As I doubt not but you have heard of our defeat, and, perhaps, had it represented in a worse light, if possible, than it deserves, I have taken this earliest opportunity to give you some account of the engagement as it hap-

---

* General Braddock had left Colonel Innes with the command at Will's Creek, under the title of Governor of Fort Cumberland.

pened, within ten miles of the French fort, on Wednesday the 9th instant.

We marched to that place, without any considerable loss, having only now and then a straggler picked up by the French and scouting Indians. When we came there, we were attacked by a party of French and Indians, whose number, I am persuaded, did not exceed three hundred men;* while ours consisted of about one thousand three hundred well-armed troops, chiefly regular soldiers, who were struck with such a panic, that they behaved with more cowardice than it is possible to conceive. The officers behaved gallantly, in order to encourage their men, for which they suffered greatly, there being near sixty killed and wounded; a large proportion of the number we had.

The Virginia troops showed a good deal of bravery, and were nearly all killed; for I believe, out of three companies that were there, scarcely thirty men are left alive. Captain Peyrouny, and all his officers down to a corporal, were killed. Captain Polson had nearly as hard a fate, for only one of his was left.† In short, the dastardly behaviour of those they call regulars exposed all others, that were inclined to do their duty, to almost certain death; and, at last, in despite of all the efforts of the officers to the contrary, they ran, as sheep pursued by dogs, and it was impossible to rally them.‡

---

* This estimate was erroneous, as will be seen hereafter.

† The Virginia Assembly gave a generous proof of their gratitude for the services and bravery of Captain Polson, by granting his widow an annual pension of twenty-six pounds.—*Journal of the House of Burgesses*, August 13th, 1755.

‡ Washington wrote to Governor Dinwiddie;—"The dastardly behaviour of the regular troops (so called) exposed those, who were inclined to do their duty, to almost certain death; and, at length, in spite of every effort to the contrary, they broke and ran as sheep before hounds, leaving the artillery, ammunition, provisions, baggage, and in short every thing a prey to the enemy; and when we endeavoured to rally them, in hopes of

The General was wounded, of which he died three days after. Sir Peter Halket was killed in the field, where died many other brave officers. I luckily escaped without a wound, though I had four bullets through my coat, and two horses shot under me. Captains Orme and Morris, two of the aids-de-camp, were wounded early in the engagement, which rendered the duty harder upon me, as I was the only person then left to distribute the General's orders, which I was scarcely able to do, as I was not half recovered from a violent illness, that had confined me to my bed and a wagon for above ten days. I am still in a weak and feeble condition, which induces me to halt here two or three days in the hope of recovering a little strength, to enable me to proceed homewards; from whence, I fear, I shall not be able to stir till towards September; so that I shall not have the pleasure of seeing you till then, unless it be in Fairfax. Please to give my love to Mr. Lewis and my sister; and compliments to Mr. Jackson, and all other friends that inquire after me. I am, honored Madam, your most dutiful son.

TO JOHN A. WASHINGTON.

Fort Cumberland, 18 July, 1755.

Dear Brother,

As I have heard, since my arrival at this place, a cir-

---

regaining the ground, and what we had left upon it, it was with as little success as if we had attempted to stop the wild bears of the mountains, or the rivulets with our feet.

"It is supposed, that we had three hundred or more killed, and about that number were brought off wounded. It is conjectured (I believe with much truth), that two thirds of both received their shot from our own cowardly regulars, who gathered themselves into a body, contrary to orders, ten or twelve deep, — would then level, fire, and shoot down the men before them."

cumstantial account of my death and dying speech, I take this early opportunity of contradicting the first, and of assuring you, that I have not as yet composed the latter. But, by the all-powerful dispensations of Providence, I have been protected beyond all human probability or expectation; for I had four bullets through my coat, and two horses shot under me, yet escaped unhurt, although death was levelling my companions on every side of me!

We have been most scandalously beaten by a trifling body of men, but fatigue and want of time prevent me from giving you any of the details, until I have the happiness of seeing you at Mount Vernon, which I now most ardently wish for, since we are driven in thus far. A feeble state of health obliges me to halt here for two or three days, to recover a little strength, that I may thereby be enabled to proceed homewards with more ease. You may expect to see me there on Saturday or Sunday fortnight, which is as soon as I can well be down, as I shall take my Bullskin Plantations* in my way. Pray give my compliments to all my friends. I am, dear Jack, your most affectionate brother. †

---

* An estate left to him by his brother Lawrence Washington.

† He arrived at Mount Vernon on the 26th of July. He still retained the office of adjutant of the northern division of militia, and he immediately wrote to the county lieutenants, ordering the militia to be ready and properly equipped in each county on certain days, when he should be present to review and exercise them.

Such was the alarm created by the success of the French at Braddock's defeat, that volunteer companies embodied themselves in different parts of Virginia to march to the frontiers. The Reverend Samuel Davies, at that time a clergyman in Hanover county, preached a sermon to one of these companies, on the 17th of August, which was printed in Philadelphia and London, and entitled "*Religion and Patriotism the Constituents of a Good Soldier.*" After applauding the patriotic spirit and military ardor, which had begun to manifest themselves, the preacher adds, —

"As a remarkable instance of this, I may point out to the public that

TO ROBERT JACKSON.

Mount Vernon, 2 August, 1755.

DEAR SIR,

I must acknowledge you had great reason to be terrified at the first accounts, that were given of our unhappy defeat; and, I must own, I was not a little surprised to find, that Governor Innes was the means of alarming the country with a report so extraordinary, without having better confirmation of the truth, than the story of an affrighted wagoner!

It is true, we have been beaten, shamefully beaten, by a handful of men, who only intended to molest and disturb our march. Victory was their smallest expectation. But see the wondrous works of Providence, and the uncertainty of human things! We, but a few moments before, believed our numbers almost equal to the Canadian force; they only expected to annoy us. Yet, contrary to all expectation and human probability, and even to the common course of things, we were totally defeated, and sustained the loss of every thing. This, as you observe, must be an affecting story to the colony, and will, no doubt, license the tongues of people to censure those, whom they think most blamable; which, by the by, often falls very wrongfully. I join very heartily with you in believing, that when this story comes to be related in future annals, it will meet with unbelief and indignation, for had I not been witness to

---

heroic youth, Colonel Washington, whom I cannct but hope Providence has hitherto preserved in so signal a manner for some important service to his country."

This prophetic passage may at least serve as an evidence of the elevated standing, to which Washington had already raised himself in the esteem of his countrymen, by his bravery and good conduct. Mr. Davies was afterwards President of the College at Princeton, in New Jersey.

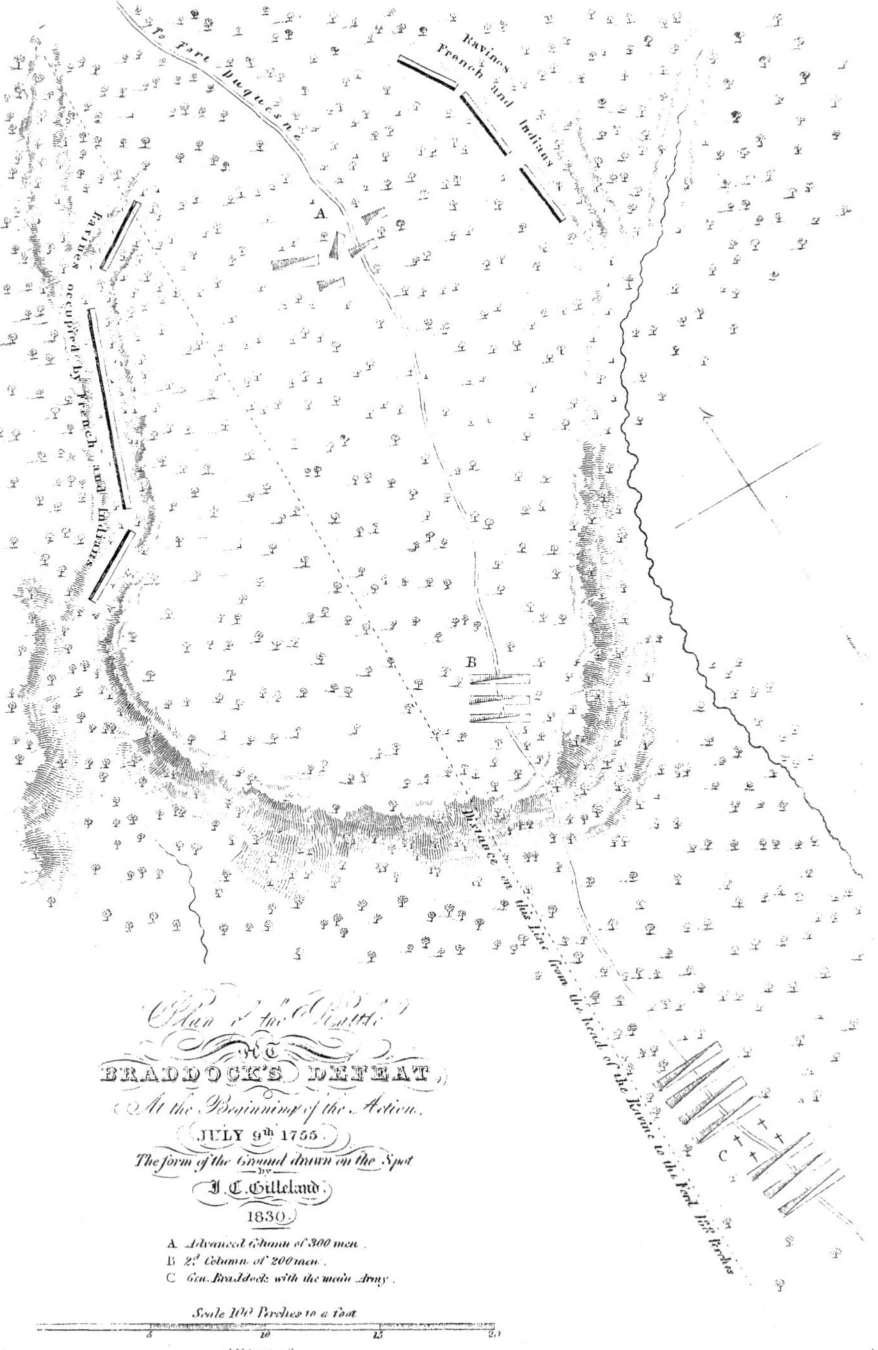

Plan of the Battle
of
BRADDOCK'S DEFEAT,
At the Beginning of the Action,
JULY 9th 1755.
The form of the Ground drawn on the Spot
by
J. C. Gilleland,
1830.

A. Advanced Column of 300 men.
B. 2d Column of 200 men.
C. Gen. Braddock with the main Army.

Scale 100 Perches to a foot

5 10 15 20

G. W. Boynton Sc.

the fact on that fatal day, I should scarcely have given credit to it even now.*

Whenever it suits you to come into Fairfax, I hope you will make your home at Mount Vernon. I assure you, nothing could have added more to the satisfaction of my safe return, than hearing of the friendly concern that has been expressed on my supposed death. I am, &c.

TO AUGUSTINE WASHINGTON.†

Mount Vernon, 2 August, 1755.

DEAR BROTHER,

The pleasure of your company at Mount Vernon always did, and always will, afford me infinite satisfaction; but, at this time, I am too sensible how needful the country is of all the assistance of its members, to have a wish to hear that any are absent from the Assembly.

I most sincerely wish, that unanimity may prevail in all your counsels, and that a happy issue may attend your deliberations at this important crisis.

I am not able, were I ever so willing, to meet you in town, for, I assure you, it is with some difficulty, and much fatigue, that I visit my plantations; so much has a sickness of five weeks' continuance reduced me. But though it is not in my power to meet you there, I can nevertheless assure you, and others "whom it may concern," (to borrow a phrase from Governor Innes,) that, so little am I dispirited at what has happened, I am

---

* For a further account of Braddock's defeat, in the action of the Monongahela, see APPENDIX, No. IV.

† Augustine Washington was an elder brother by the father's first marriage, and was now at Williamsburg as a member of the Assembly.

always ready, and always willing, to render my country any services that I am capable of, but never upon the terms I have done; having suffered much in my private fortune, besides impairing one of the best of constitutions.

I was employed to go a journey in the winter, when, I believe, few or none would have undertaken it, — and what did I get by it? My expenses borne! I then was appointed, with trifling pay, to conduct a handful of men to the Ohio. What did I get by that? Why, after putting myself to a considerable expense, in equipping and providing necessaries for the campaign, I went out, was soundly beaten, and lost them all! — came in, and had my commission taken from me, or, in other words, my command reduced, under pretence of an order from home! I then went out a volunteer with General Braddock, and lost all my horses, and many other things. But this being a voluntary act, I ought not to have mentioned it; nor should I have done it, were it not to show, that I have been upon the losing order ever since I entered the service, which is now nearly two years. So that I think I cannot be blamed, should I, if I leave my family again, endeavour to do it upon such terms, as to prevent my suffering; — to gain by it being the least of my expectations.

I doubt not but you have heard the particulars of our shameful defeat, which really was so scandalous, that I hate to mention it. You desire to know what artillery was taken in the late engagement. It is easily told. We lost all that we carried out, excepting two six-pounders, and a few cohorns, which were left with Colonel Dunbar; and the cohorns have since been destroyed to accelerate his flight. You also ask, whether I think the forces can march out again this fall. I answer, I think it impossible, at least, for them to do the French any damage (unless it be by starving them), for the want of a proper train of artillery; yet they may be very serviceable in erecting small fortresses at convenient places to deposit provisions in, by which means the country will be eased of an immense expense in the carriage, and it will also be a means of securing a retreat, if we should be put to the rout again. The success of this measure, however, will depend greatly upon what Governor Shirley does at Niagara; for, if he succeeds, their communication with Canada will be entirely cut off.

It is impossible for me to guess at the number of recruits, that may be wanted, as that must depend altogether upon the strength of the French on the Ohio, which, to my great astonishment, we were always strangers to.

I thank you, very heartily, for your kind offer of a chair, and for your goodness in sending my things; and, after begging you to excuse the imperfections of this letter, which, in part, are owing to my having much company that hurries me, I shall conclude, dear Sir,

Your most affectionate brother.

TO MRS. MARY WASHINGTON.

Mount Vernon, 14 August, 1755.

HONORED MADAM,

If it is in my power to avoid going to the Ohio again, I shall; but if the command is pressed upon me, by the general voice of the country, and offered upon such terms as cannot be objected against, it would reflect dishonor upon me to refuse it; and that, I am sure, must or ought to give you greater uneasiness, than my going in an honorable command. Upon no other terms will I accept of it. At present I have no proposals made to me, nor have I any advice of such an intention, except from private hands. I am, &c.

TO WARNER LEWIS.

Mount Vernon, 14 August, 1755.

DEAR SIR,

After returning you most sincere and grateful thanks, for your kind condolence on my late indisposition, and for the generous and (give me leave farther to say) partial opinion, you have entertained of my military abilities, I must express my concern for not having it in my power to meet you, and other friends, who have signified their desire of seeing me in Williamsburg.*

Your letter only came to hand at nine last night, and you inform me, that the Assembly will break up the latter end of the week, which allows a time too short in which to perform a journey of a hundred and sixty miles, especially by a person in my feeble condition; for, although I am happily recovered from the disorder, which brought me to so low an ebb, by a sickness of nearly five weeks' continuance, yet my strength

---

* Mr. Ludwell, another of his friends in the Assembly, had written to him on the 8th of August.—"I most heartily congratulate you on your safe return from so many dangers and fatigues, and by this time I hope you are well enough recovered to give us the pleasure of seeing you here, which all your friends are extremely desirous of. The House has voted twelve hundred men, but it is very probable they will determine at last for four thousand. In conversation with the Governor I said, if this should be done I supposed his Honor would give the command of them to Colonel Washington, for I thought he deserved every thing his country could do for him. The Governor made reply much in your favor, though I understand there is another warm solicitation for it. If we could be so happy as to have you here at this time, and it were known that you are willing to take such a command, I believe it would greatly promote the success of our endeavours with the Assembly."

is not returned. Had I received timely notice, I would have attempted the ride, by slow and easy journeys, if it had been only for the satisfaction of seeing my friends, who, I flatter myself, from what you say, are kind enough to sympathize in my good and evil fortunes.

The chief cause, next to indisposition, that prevented me from going down to this Assembly, was a determination not to offer my services; and that determination proceeded from the following reasons. First, a belief that I could not get a command upon such terms as I should incline to accept; for I must confess to you, that I never will quit my family, injure my fortune, and, above all, impair my health, to run the risk of such changes and vicissitudes, as I have met with, but shall expect, if I am employed again, to have something certain. Again, were I to accept the command, I should insist upon some things, which ignorance and inexperience made me overlook before, particularly that of having the officers appointed, in some measure, with my advice and with my concurrence. It appears to me strange, that a commanding officer should not have this liberty, when it is considered how much the conduct and bravery of an officer influence the men, how much a commanding officer is answerable for the behaviour of the inferior officers, and how much his good or ill success, in time of action, depends upon the conduct of each particular one, especially too, in this kind of fighting, where, being dispersed, each and every one of them has a greater liberty to misbehave, than if he were regularly and compactly drawn up under the eyes of his superior.

On the other hand, how little credit is given to a commander, who, after a defeat, in relating the cause of it, justly lays the blame on some individual, whose cowardly behaviour betrayed the whole to ruin. How little does the world consider the circumstances, and how apt are mankind to level their vindictive censures against the unfortunate chief, who perhaps merited least of the blame.

Does it not appear, then, that the appointing of officers is a thing of the utmost consequence; a thing that requires the greatest circumspection? Ought it to be *left to blind chance, or, what is still* worse, to partiality? Should it not be left to a man, whose life, and, what is still dearer, whose honor, depends on their good behaviour?

Officers are yet wanting, for whom no provision has been made. A small military chest is so necessary, that it is impossible to do without it, nor can any man conduct an affair of this kind, who has it not.

These things I should expect, if the appointment should fall upon me.

But, besides all these, I had other reasons, which withheld me from offering my services. I believe our circumstances are brought to such an unhappy dilemma, that no man can gain any honor by conducting our forces at this time, but will rather lose in his reputation if he attempts it. I am confident, that the progress of military movements must be slow, for want of conveniences to transport our provisions, ammunition, and stores, over the mountains; occasioned, in a great measure, by the late ill treatment of the wagoners and horse-drivers, who have received little compensation for their labor, and nothing for their lost horses and wagons; which will be an infallible cause of preventing all from assisting, who are not compelled. Hence I am fully sensible, that whoever undertakes this command will meet with such insurmountable obstacles, that he will soon be viewed in the light of an idle, indolent body, have his conduct criticized, and meet perhaps with abuse, when it may be as much out of his power to avoid delays, as it would be to command the raging seas in a storm.

This view of things has had no small influence upon me, as I am very apprehensive I should lose, what at present constitutes the chief part of my happiness, that is, the esteem and notice, which the country has been pleased to honor me with.

It is possible you may infer from what I have said, that my intentions are to decline, at all events; but this is not my meaning. I am determined not to offer; because to solicit the command, and, at the same time, to make my proposals, would be a little incongruous, and carry with it the face of self-sufficiency. But if the command should be offered to me, the case will then be altered, as I should be at liberty to make such objections, as reason and my small experience have pointed out.*

I am, dear Warner, your most affectionate friend, and obedient servant.

---

* While Colonel Washington was writing this letter, he had already been appointed to the command. The Assembly voted forty thousand pounds for the public service, and the Governor and Council immediately resolved to increase the Virginia regiment to sixteen companies. In the same act, the Assembly also granted to George Washington the sum of three hundred pounds, to the captains seventy-five pounds each, to the lieutenants and surgeon thirty pounds, and to every soldier five pounds, as "a reward and compensation for their gallant behaviour and losses," at the battle of the Monongahela.

The Governor's commission and instructions to Colonel Washington, as commander-in-chief of the Virginia forces, are dated on the 14th of August. He was allowed all that is demanded in the above letter, and also to appoint an aid-de-camp and secretary. The next officers in rank under him were Lieutenant-Colonel Adam Stephen, and Major Andrew Lewis. The following extract from a letter, written by Governor Dinwiddie to Sir Thomas Robinson, Secretary of State, is a proof of the estimation in which Colonel Washington was at this time held, and that he was recommended to the favorable notice of the King.

"I have granted commissions to raise sixteen companies, augmenting our forces to one thousand men, and have incorporated them into a regiment, the command thereof being given to Colonel George Washington, who was one of General Braddock's aids-de-camp, and I think a man of great merit and resolution. Our officers are greatly dispirited for want of his Majesty's commissions, that, when they join the regulars, they may

TO MAJOR ANDREW LEWIS.

Fredericksburg, 6 September, 1755.*

SIR,

The country has come to a resolution to raise sixteen companies, which are to be formed into a regiment, and of which they have honored me with the command. I am allowed the liberty of appointing my field officers; in consequence of which, I have commissioned you as major, and must desire you will, as soon as Captain Hogg arrives, and takes the command of your company, repair to Fredericksburg with all imaginable despatch, to take charge of the recruits, that shall be brought to that place of rendezvous. I know your diligence and punctuality require little or no spur; yet, as this is an affair that calls for the greatest despatch, I must earnestly recommend it to you. Be careful in getting a proper return of your company, that I may order things accordingly.

A return must also be delivered to Captain Hogg, not only of the men, but of the arms, tools, &c., and his receipt taken. I am, &c.

---

have some rank; and I am persuaded it would be of infinite service, if his Majesty would graciously please to honor them with his commissions, the same as in General Shirley's and Sir William Pepperell's regiments; and I am convinced, if General Braddock had survived, he would have recommended Mr. Washington to the royal favor, which I beg your interest in recommending."

* As soon as Colonel Washington was informed of his appointment, he repaired to Williamsburg to consult with the governor respecting future operations. When he wrote this letter he was on his return to Winchester, which place was fixed upon as his head-quarters. The two other points of rendezvous for the recruits were Fredericksburg and Alexandria.

TO JOHN ROBINSON, SPEAKER OF THE HOUSE OF BURGESSES, VIRGINIA.

Alexandria, 11 September, 1755.

SIR,

After a small halt at Fredericksburg, to issue orders to the recruiting officers appointed to that rendezvous, I proceeded to this place, in order to collect a return of the provisions and clothing, that were lodged here; an exact copy of which I herewith send you. I find, after the soldiers have their short allowances, there will arise great inconveniences, if stores of clothing are not laid in to supply their wants; particularly shoes, stockings, and shirts, for these are the least durable and most needed.

The method I would recommend is, for the country to provide these things, and lodge them, or a convenient part of them, in the hands of the quartermaster, who may be appointed to receive and deliver them to the soldiers, by particular orders from their captains, taking care to produce these orders and proper vouchers for the delivery, each pay-day, when the amount must be deducted out of the soldier's pay, who receives them. This, I think, will be a means of keeping them always provided and fit for duty, and of preventing the officers from supplying the men, which is generally attended with misunderstandings. It will also be a means of discouraging followers of the army from demanding such exorbitant prices, as is usually practised on these occasions.

However, I only offer this as the most efficacious method I can at present think of. If any more eligible one can be found, I should be glad to see it executed, as something of the kind must be done, otherwise the soldiers will be barefoot, which is always a plea for exemption from duty; and, indeed, in the approaching season it will be a very just one. You will be a judge, when you see the returns, what had best be done with the provisions. The quantity is too great for the present consumption, and to wagon it up can never answer the expense.

Major Carlyle thinks the West India market best, as the returns will be in rum, which he can soon turn into flour at the camp.

I am afraid I shall not be able to push things with vigor this fall, for want of a commissary who will act with spirit. Mr. Dick seems determined not to enter into any further contracts, unless he is better supported, or until he meets the Committee in October; by which time the best season for engaging beef will be almost over. The Governor, by the advice of Sir John St. Clair, expressed, just as I was coming away, his desire of having him continued; so that I am entirely ignorant how to act. The making of contracts myself is foreign to my duty; neither have I time; and to see the service suffer will give me infinite uneasiness, as I would gladly conduct every thing, as far as I am capable, with life and spirit. This never can be done unless a fund of money is lodged in camp for defraying the contingent charges. As I believed it difficult to get all the clothing in any one part of the country, I engaged it where I could, and have got shoes, stockings, shirts, and hats enough upon tolerably good terms, as you may see by the enclosed.

Major Carlyle is also willing to engage one hundred complete suits, as good as those imported, for three pounds, or less; with which I have acquainted the Governor. I believe them to be as cheap as can be got below, as it is the making chiefly, that occasions the difference between those imported, and those provided here. I am, &c.*

* The following particulars are entered in the book of *Military Orders and Instructions,* which was kept by Colonel Washington. "After giv-

TO GOVERNOR DINWIDDIE.

Fredericksburg, 8 October, 1755.

SIR,

I arrived at this place in less than three hours after I wrote you from Colonel Baylor's. Shortly afterwards arrived also Colonel Stephen, who gives a worse account, than he related in his letter; but as he is the bearer of this, I shall be the less prolix, referring to him for particulars.

I shall set out this evening for Winchester, where I expect to be joined by the recruits from Alexandria and this place, as soon as they can possibly march that distance; also, by one hundred men from Prince William and Frederic. I have written to Fairfax county, desiring that a troop of horse may hold themselves in readiness to march at an hour's warning. So that I doubt not, that, with this assistance, I shall be able to repulse the enemy, if they are still committing their outrages upon the inhabitants. We are at a loss for want of almost every necessary, — tents, kettles, arms, ammunition, and cartridge-paper. I hope, as your Honor did not send to Philadelphia for them, you will, if possible, endeavour to get them below, and send them

ing the necessary orders, and collecting returns of the provisions and clothing at Alexandria, and stores at Rock Creek, I proceeded to Winchester, where I arrived on the 14th of September. Thence I went to Fort Cumberland, and took upon me the command of the troops there, issuing the daily orders, and giving such instructions and directions as appeared necessary. Thence to Fort Dinwiddie on Jackson's River. After examining the state of things there, I set out for Alexandria, and arrived on the 2d of October. On the 5th reached Fredericksburg in my way to Williamsburg. Continued my journey to Colonel Baylor's, where I was overtaken by an express sent from Colonel Stephen (commanding at Fort Cumberland), informing me that a body of Indians had fallen upon the inhabitants, killed many of them, and destroyed and burnt several of their houses. Thereupon I wrote to the Governor, and returned immediately to Fredericksburg."

by the first opportunity to this place, or Alexandria, with orders that they may be forwarded immediately to Winchester.

I must again take the liberty of mentioning to you the necessity of putting the militia, when they are drawn out into actual service, under better regulation than they are at present, as well as of putting us under a military law. Otherwise we shall only be a burthensome charge to the country, and the others will prove its ruin. That this may not appear an unmeaning expression, I refer you to Lieutenant-Colonel Stephen, who can give you some late proofs of their disobedience and inconsistent behaviour.

As these affairs will take some time, I find I cannot possibly be in Williamsburg till the 6th, 7th, or 8th of November, when I should be glad to meet a committee, in order to settle with them and your Honor some points, that are very necessary for the good of the expedition.

Colonel Stephen has orders to receive some money below, that we may be enabled to pay the troops, keep them in spirits, and answer such immediate charges as cannot be dispensed with, until I come down. I should be glad if your Honor would order him to repair therewith (as soon as he has done his business with the committee) to Winchester; and from thence, with a proper guard, to Fort Cumberland. I hope the treasury will have a sufficient sum of money prepared against I come down, that I may meet with no delay.

There are about seventy recruits at this place, and I left twenty-five at Alexandria. I suppose they are augmented before this time by officers, who, I am sorry to say, have paid slight regard to orders, by not being in at the time appointed. I am, &c.

TO GOVERNOR DINWIDDIE.

Winchester, 11 October, 1755.

SIR,

As I think it my indispensable duty to inform you particularly of my proceedings, and to give the most plain and authentic accounts, from time to time, of our situation, I must acquaint you that, immediately after giving the necessary orders at Fredericksburg, and despatching expresses to hurry the recruits from Alexandria, I rode post to this place. I passed by Lord Fairfax's, who was not at home, but was here, where I arrived yesterday about noon, and found every thing in the greatest hurry and confusion, by the back inhabitants flocking in, and those of this town moving out, which I have, as far as was in my power, prevented. I was desirous of proceeding immediately, at the head of some militia, to put a stop to the ravages of the enemy, believing their numbers to be few; but I was told by Colonel Martin, who had attempted to raise the militia for the same purpose, that it was impossible to get above twenty or twenty-five men, they having absolutely refused to stir, choosing, as they say, to die with their wives and families.

Finding this expedient likely to prove abortive, I sent off expresses to hurry on the recruits from below, and the militia from Fairfax and Prince William, who had been ordered out by Lord Fairfax. I also hired spies to go out and discover the numbers of the enemy, and to encourage the rangers, who, we were told, were blocked up by the Indians in small fortresses. But, if I may offer my opinion, I believe they are more encompassed with fear, than by the enemy. I have also impressed wagons and sent them to Conococheague for flour, musket-balls, and flints. Powder, and a trifling quantity of paper, bought at extravagant prices, for cartridges, I expect from below.

Six or eight smiths are now at work, repairing the firearms that are here, which are all that we have to depend upon. A man was hired, on the 24th of last month, to do the whole, but neglected it, and was just moving off to Pennsylvania in wagons. I impressed his wagons, and compelled him by force to assist in this work. In all things I meet with the greatest opposition.

No orders are obeyed, but such as a party of soldiers, or my own drawn sword, enforces. Without this, not a single horse, for the most earnest occasion, can be had, — to such a pitch has the insolence of these people arrived, by having every point hitherto submitted to them. However, I have given up none, where his Majesty's service requires the contrary, and where my proceedings are justified by my instructions; nor will I, unless they execute what they threaten, that is, "blow out our brains."

I have invited the poor distressed people, who were driven from their habitations, to lodge their families in some place of security, and to join our parties in scouring the woods, where the enemy lie; and I believe some will cheerfully assist. I have also taken, and shall continue to take, every previous step to forward the march of the recruits, as soon as they arrive here. Your Honor may depend, that nothing in my power shall be wanting for the good of the service. I would again hint the necessity of putting the militia under a better regulation, had I not mentioned it twice before, and a third time may seem impertinent. But I must once more beg leave to declare, for here I am more immediately concerned, that, unless the Assembly will pass an act to enforce the military law in all its parts, I must, with great regret, decline the honor that has been so generously intended me. I am urged to this, by the foreknowledge I have of failing in every point, that might justly be expected from a person invested with full power to execute his authority. I see the growing insolence of the soldiers, and the indolence and inactivity of the officers, who are all sensible how limited their punishments are, compared with what they ought to be. In fine, I can plainly see, that under the present establishment, we shall become a nuisance, an insupportable charge to our country, and never answer any one expectation of the Assembly. And here I must assume the freedom to express some surprise, that we alone should be so tenacious of our liberty, as not to invest a power, where interest and policy so unanswerably demand it, and whence so much good must consequently ensue. Do we not know, that every nation under the sun finds its account therein, and that, without it, no order or regularity can be observed? Why then should it be expected from us, who are all young and inexperienced, to govern and keep up a proper spirit of discipline without laws, when the best and most experienced can scarcely do it with them? If we consult our interest, I am sure it loudly calls for them. I can confidently assert, that recruiting, clothing, arming, maintaining, and subsisting soldiers, who have since deserted, have cost the country an immense sum, which might have been prevented, were we under restraints, that would terrify the soldiers from such practices.

One thing more on this head I will recommend, and then quit the subject; that is, to have the inhabitants liable to certain heavy fines, or corporal punishments, for entertaining deserters, and a reward offered for taking them up. If this were done, it would be next to an impossibility for a soldier to escape; but, as things now stand, they are not only seduced to run away, but are also harboured and assisted with every necessary means to do it.

Sunday noon.—Last night arrived an express, just spent with fatigue and fear, reporting that a party of Indians were seen about twelve miles off, at the plantation of one Isaac Julian, and that the inhabitants were flying in the most promiscuous manner from their dwellings. I immediately ordered the town guards to be strengthened, Perkins's lieutenant to be in readiness with his companies, some recruits, who had only arrived about half an hour before, to be armed, and sent two men, well acquainted with the roads, to go up that road, and lie in wait, to see if they could discover the number and motion of the Indians, that we might have timely notice of their approach. This morning, before we could parade the men, arrived a second express, ten times more terrified than the former, with information, that the Indians had got within four miles of the town, and were killing and destroying all before them, and that he himself had heard constant firing, and shrieks of the unhappy murdered! Upon this, I immediately collected what force I could, which consisted of twenty-two men, recruited for the rangers, and nineteen of the militia, and marched directly to the place, where these horrid murders were said to be committed. When we came there, whom should we find occasioning all this disturbance, but three drunken soldiers of the light-horse, carousing, firing their pistols, and uttering the most unheard-of imprecations? These we took, and marched them as prisoners to town, where we met the men I sent out last night, and learned that the party of Indians, discovered by Isaac Julian, proved to be a mulatto and negro, seen hunting cattle by his child, who alarmed the father, and the father the neighbourhood.

These circumstances are related only to show what a panic prevails among the people; how much they are alarmed at the most usual and customary cries; and yet how impossible it is to get them to act in any respect for their common safety. As an instance of this, Colonel Fairfax, who arrived in town while we were upon a scout, immediately sent to a noble captain, not far off, to repair with his company forthwith to Winchester. With coolness and moderation this great captain answered, that his wife, family, and corn were all at stake; so were those of his soldiers; therefore it was impossible for him to come. Such is the example of the officers; such the behaviour of the men; and upon such circumstances depends the safety of our country!

Monday morning. — The men I hired to bring intelligence from the Branch returned last night, with letters from Captain Ashby, and the other parties there; by which I learn, that the Indians are gone off; scouts having been dispersed upon those waters for several days, without discovering tracks or other signs of the enemy.

I am also informed, that it is believed their numbers amounted to about one hundred and fifty; that seventy of our men are killed and missing, and several houses and plantations destroyed, but not so great havoc made as was represented at first. The rangers, and a small company of militia, ordered there by Lord Fairfax, I am given to understand, intend to march down on Monday next. They will be immediately followed by all the inhabitants of those parts, that had come together under their protection. I have, therefore, sent peremptory orders to the contrary; but what obedience will be paid to them a little time will reveal. I have ordered those men, that were recruited for the rangers, to join their respective companies. A party of militia, commanded by Captain Harden, also marched with them. Captain Waggener is this instant arrived with thirty recruits, whom he marched from Bellhaven in less than three days, — a great march indeed! Major Lewis and his recruits from Fredericksburg I expect in to-morrow, when, with these and twenty-two of Captain Bell's now here, I shall proceed by quick marches to Fort Cumberland, in order to strengthen that garrison. Besides these, I think it absolutely essential, that there should be two or three companies exclusively of rangers, to guard the Potomac waters, until such time as our regiment is completed. Indeed, the rangers and volunteer companies in Augusta, with some of their militia, should be properly disposed of on those frontiers, for fear of an attack from that quarter. But this is submitted to your Honor's judgment, and waits your orders for its execution, if thought expedient.

Captain Waggener informs me, that it was with difficulty he passed the Ridge for crowds of people, who were flying as if every moment was death. He endeavoured, but in vain, to stop them; they firmly believing that Winchester was in flames. I shall send expresses down the several roads in hopes of bringing back the inhabitants, who are really frightened out of their senses. I despatched an express immediately upon my arrival at this place, with a copy of the enclosed letter to Andrew Montour, who I heard was at a place called Long Island, with three hundred Indians, to see if he could engage him and them to join us. I also wrote to Gist, acquainting him with the favor you intended him, and desired he would repair home, in order to raise his companies of scouts.*

* Mr. Gist had been sent to Philadelphia for some object connected

I shall defer writing to the Speaker and Committee upon any other head, than that of commissary, still hoping to be down by the time mentioned in my last, provided no new disturbances happen, having some points to settle, that I am uneasy and urgent about. I have been obliged to do duty very foreign to my own; but that I shall never hesitate about, when the good of the service requires it.

In a journey from Fort Cumberland to Fort Dinwiddie, which I made purposely to see the situation of our frontiers, how the rangers were posted, and how troops might be disposed of for the defence of the country, I purchased six hundred and fifty beeves, to be delivered at Fort Cumberland by the 1st of November, at ten shillings per hundred weight, except a few for which I was obliged to give eleven shillings. My own bonds are now out for the performance of these covenants. This is the commissary's business, who, I am sorry to say, has hitherto been of no use, but of disservice to me, in neglecting my orders, and leaving this place without flour, and Fredericksburg without any provisions for the recruits, although he had timely notice. I must beg, that, if Mr. Dick will not act, some other person may be appointed; for, if things remain in this uncertain situation, the season will pass without having provision made for the winter, or the summer campaign.

---

with the service, and on the 15th of October he wrote to Colonel Washington; — "Your name is more talked of in Pennsylvania, than that of any other person in the army, and every body seems willing to venture under your command. If you would send some discreet person, I doubt not he would enlist a good number, especially to be irregulars, for all their talk is of fighting the Indian way. The Assembly of Pennsylvania is now sitting. Mr. Franklin and Mr. Peters both told me, that, if you would write a pressing letter to them, informing them of the damages and murders, and desiring their assistance, you would now get it sooner than any one in America."

I have appointed Captain George Mercer (whose seniority entitled him to it) my aid-de-camp; and Mr. Kirkpatrick, of Alexandria, my secretary, a young man bred to business, of good character, well recommended, and a person of whose abilities I had not the least doubt.

I hope your Honor will be kind enough to despatch Colonel Stephen, with orders to repair hither immediately, and excuse the prolixity of this letter. I was willing to give a circumstantial account of our situation, that you may be the better enabled to judge what orders are necessary. I am, &c.

TO GOVERNOR DINWIDDIE.

Winchester, 17 October, 1755.

Sir,

Last night by the return of the express, who went to Captain Montour, I received the enclosed from Mr. Harris at the Susquehanna. I think no means should be neglected to preserve the few Indians, who still remain in our interest. For which reason I shall send Mr. Gist, as soon as he arrives (which I expect will be to-day), to Harris's Ferry, in hopes of engaging and bringing with him the Belt of Wampum and other Indians at that place. I shall further desire him to send an Indian express to Andrew Montour, to try if he cannot be brought with them.

In however trifling a light the attempts of the French to alienate the affections of our southern Indians may at first appear, I must look upon it as a thing of the utmost consequence, requiring our greatest and most immediate

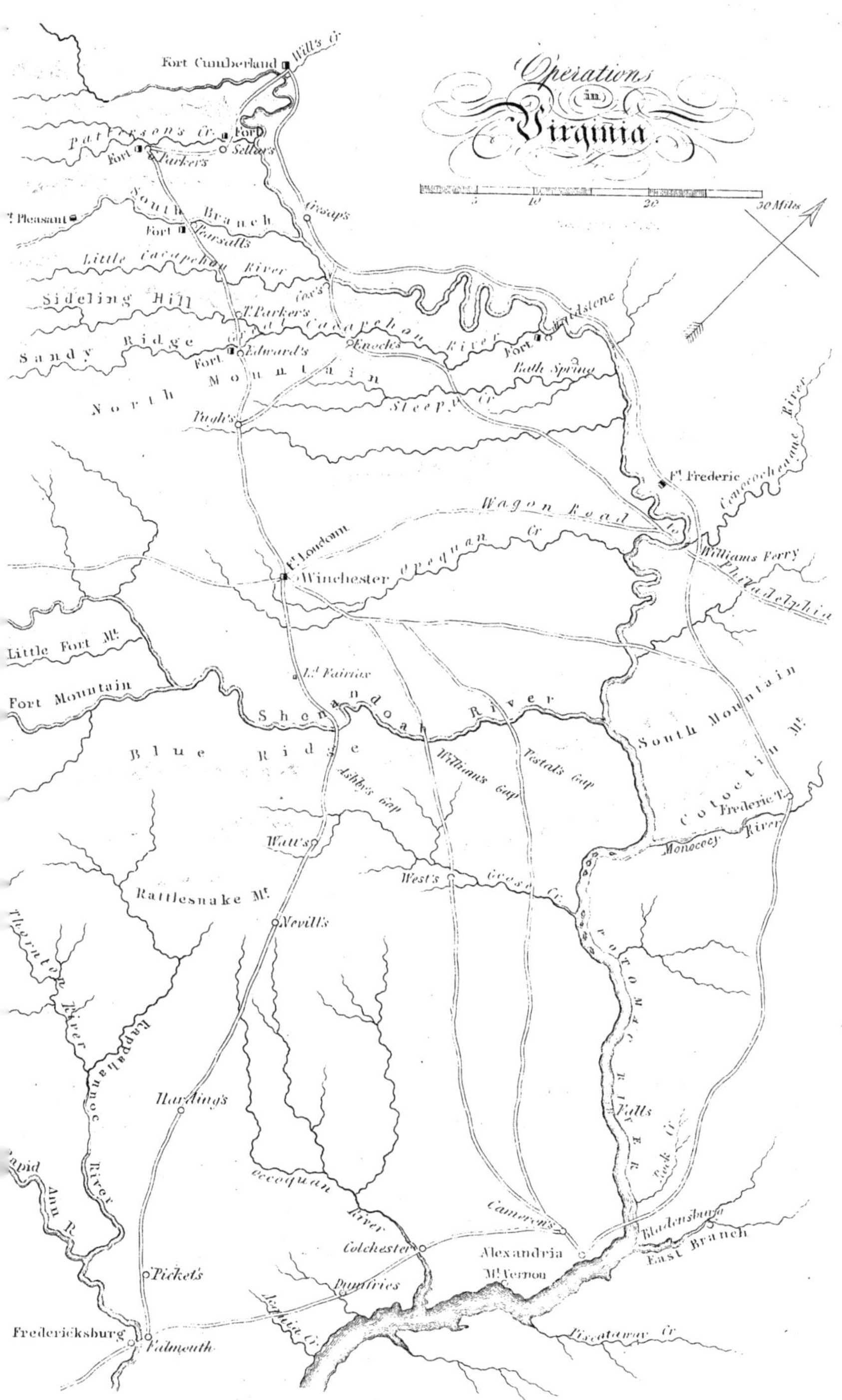
Operations in Virginia
5
10
20
30 Miles
Fort Cumberland
Will's Cr.
Pattersons Cr.
Fort
Fort
Sellars
Parkers
Pleasant
South Branch
Fort
Pearsalls
Cresaps
Little Cacapehon River
Cox's
Sideling Hill
T. Parker's
Sandy Ridge
Cacapehon River
Enock's
Fort
Edward's
Fort
Maidstone
Bath Spring
North Mountain
Sleepy Cr.
Pugh's
Ft. Frederic
Conococheague River
Wagon Road
Williams Ferry
Philadelphia
Ft. Loudoun
Winchester
Opequan Cr.
Little Fort Mt.
Fort Mountain
Ld. Fairfax
Shenandoah River
South Mountain
Blue Ridge
Ashby's Gap
Williams Gap
Vestal's Gap
Cotoctin Mt.
Frederic T.
Monococy River
Watt's
West's
Goose Cr.
Rattlesnake Mt.
Nevill's
Thornton River
Rappahannoc River
Potomac River
Harding's
Falls
Rock Cr.
Occoquan River
Cameron's
Bladensburg
Colchester
Alexandria
East Branch
Mt. Vernon
Dumfries
Rapid Ann R.
Pickets
Fredericksburg
Falmouth
Piscataway Cr.

attention. I have often wondered at not hearing this was attempted before, and had it noted among other memorandums to acquaint your Honor with, when I should come down.

The French policy in treating with the Indians is so prevalent, that I should not be in the least surprised, were they to engage the Cherokees, Catawbas, and others, unless timely and vigorous measures are taken to prevent it.

A pusillanimous behaviour now will ill suit the times; and trusting to traders and common interpreters, who will sell their integrity to the highest bidder, may prove the destruction of these affairs. I therefore think, that if a person of distinction, acquainted with their language, is to be found, his price should be come to at any rate. If no such person can be had, a man of sense and character, who may conduct the Indians to a council, or superintend any other matters, will be found extremely necessary. It is impertinent, I own, in me to offer my opinion in these affairs, when better judges may direct; but my steady and hearty zeal for the cause, and the great impositions I have known practised by the traders upon these occasions, would not suffer me to be quite silent. I have heard, from undoubted authority, that some of the Cherokees, introduced to us as sachems and princes by the interpreter, who shares the profits, have been no other than common hunters, and bloodthirsty villains.

We have no accounts yet of the militia from Fairfax. This day I march with about one hundred men to Fort Cumberland. Yesterday an express informed me of eighty recruits at Fredericksburg, whom I have ordered to proceed to this place; but, for want of that regularity being observed, by which I should know where every officer is, my orders are only conditional, and always confused.* The commissary is much wanted. I hope you will send him up immediately; if not, things will greatly suffer here. I am, &c.

TO LIEUTENANT-COLONEL ADAM STEPHEN.

Fredericksburg, 18 November, 1755.

SIR,

I came to this place on Sunday last, and intended to proceed immediately up; † but your letter and others, contradicting the late reports, determined me to go to Alexandria, where I shall wait a few days, hoping to meet the express from General Shirley, to whom the Governor sent for commissions for the field-officers. ‡

---

* To a captain he wrote;—"Your late disobedience of orders has greatly displeased me. It is impossible to carry on affairs as they ought to be, when you pay so little regard to a military order. You must be conscious, that your crime is sufficient to break the best officer, that ever bore a commission."

† He was now returning from Williamsburg to head-quarters at Winchester, having previously made a journey to Fort Cumberland.

‡ The old difficulty about rank between the provincial officers, and those with King's commissions, had been revived at Fort Cumberland.

Immediately after the affair of the Great Meadows, the Assembly of Maryland granted the small sum of six thousand pounds for the defence of the frontiers, and in the December following they passed an act authorizing the Governor to raise a military force. A few soldiers only were enlisted, and at this time a Maryland company of thirty men was stationed at Fort Cumberland, under the command of Captain Dagworthy, who had been an officer in the Canada expedition during the last war, and had received a King's commission. Governor Innes had gone home to North Carolina on his private affairs. Dagworthy assumed the command, and refused to obey any orders of a provincial officer, however high in rank. This created wranglings and insubordination among the inferior officers, who took sides. The Governor of Maryland was tardy in giving any decisive orders to Dagworthy, because the fort was in that province, and he seemed willing to consider it under his command. Governor Dinwiddie argued, that it was a King's fort, built by an order sent to him from the King, chiefly by forces in the King's pay, and that it could in no sense

I beg that you will be particularly careful in seeing strict order observed among the soldiers, as that is the life of military discipline. We now have it in our power to enforce obedience; and obedience will be expected from us, the men being subject to death, as in military law. The Assembly have also offered a reward to all who will apprehend deserters, and a severe punishment upon those, who shall entertain or suffer them to pass, and upon any constable, who refuses to convey them to the company or troop to which they belong, or shall suffer them to escape, after such deserters are committed to his custody.

---

be regarded as subject to the authority of Maryland. And, moreover, as Captain Dagworthy had commuted his half-pay for a specific sum of money, his commission had thereby become obsolete, and there was no propriety in his pretending to act under it; and it was an absurdity for a captain with thirty men, who in reality had no other commission than that from the Governor of Maryland, to claim precedence of the commander-in-chief of all the Virginia forces.

Colonel Washington refused to interfere, but made a forcible remonstrance to the Governor and Council at Williamsburg, and insisted on a speedy arrangement, that should put an end to the difficulty. To effect this purpose, Governor Dinwiddie sent an express to General Shirley, commander of his Majesty's forces in North America, stating the particulars of the case, and requesting from him brevet commissions for Colonel Washington, and the field-officers under him; proposing, at the same time, that these commissions should only imply rank, without giving any claim to pay from the King. — Dinwiddie's *Letter-Books*. — *Laws of Maryland*, 1754.

The Governor's troubles seemed to thicken at this crisis. On the 15th of November he wrote to the Earl of Halifax; —

"Our Assembly met on the 29th ultimo, but not above one half of them gave their attendance. They fell into cabals, and wanted to emit two hundred thousand pounds in paper money for a loan-office, to be discharged in eight years, which I thought to be contrary to act of Parliament and my instructions. They further proposed a secret committee, which, in course, would have been the beginning of great dissensions. They likewise were very mutinous and unmannerly. For their not meeting in a body when summoned, and for the above conduct, I thought it for his Majesty's service, and for the good of this Dominion, to dissolve them, and take my chance of a new election, which I think cannot be so bad as the last."

These things, with the articles of war and a proper exhortation, I would have you read immediately to the men, and see that it is frequently done hereafter. I must desire, that you will use all possible means to facilitate the salting of our provisions, and give the commissary such assistance as he shall reasonably require. The Governor approves of the Committee's resolve, in not allowing either the Maryland or Carolina companies to be supported out of our provisions. This you are to make them acquainted with, and, in case any of the companies should be discharged, to use your utmost endeavours to enlist as many of the men as you can. Lieutenant McManners has leave to go to Carolina, if he desires it. The Assembly would make no alteration in our militia law; nor would the Governor order the militia to be drafted to complete our regiment, so that the slow method of recruiting is likely to be our only means of raising the men. I think, could a brisk officer, and two or three sergeants, be sent among the militia stationed on the South Branch, they would have a probable chance of engaging many, as some were inclined to enlist at Winchester. Doctor Craik is expected round to Alexandria in a vessel, with medicines and other stores for the regiment. As soon as he arrives, I shall take care to despatch him to you.

The Colonels Byrd and Randolph are appointed commissioners,* and will set out very shortly with a present for the Cherokees, in order to engage them in our interest. I am, &c.

---

* Commissioners appointed by the Governor to visit and conciliate the Cherokees, Catawbas, and other southern Indians, who were inclined to the French interest, and threatened hostilities in that quarter.

TO COLONEL ADAM STEPHEN.

Alexandria, 28 November, 1755.

SIR,

I received your two letters by Jenkins last night, and was greatly surprised to hear that Commissary Walker was not arrived at camp, when he came away. He set out from Williamsburg about the 12th instant, with orders to proceed immediately up; but such disobedience of commands, as I have generally met with, is insufferable, and shall not go unpunished. The account you enclosed of the method of receiving the beef, I suppose, is customary; but for want of knowledge in those affairs, I can neither applaud nor condemn it.

The Governor did not seem inclined to promote the removal of the fort; however, the Committee have lodged a discretionary power in my hands, and have resolved to pay for all extraordinary labor. I would, therefore, have as little labor lost at Fort Cumberland as possible; at least, until I come up, which will be very shortly, my stay here being only for a few days, in order to receive recruits, and hurry up the stores to Winchester.

I believe those, who say Governor Sharpe is to command, can only wish it. I do not know that General Shirley has a power to appoint a chief to our forces,— to regulars he may. As to that affair of turning the store-house into a dwelling-room, I do not know what better answer to give, than saying, that this is one among the many instances, which might be offered, of the inconvenience of having the fort in Maryland. As soon as I hear from Governor Shirley, which is hourly expected, I can then send a more determinate answer.

There has been such total negligence among the recruiting officers in general, such disregard of the service they were employed in, and such idle proceedings, that I am determined to send out none until we all meet, when each officer shall have his own men, and have only this alternative, either to complete his number, or lose his commission. Several officers have been out six weeks, or two months, without getting a man, spending their time in all the gayety of pleasurable mirth, with their relations and friends; not attempting, nor having a possible chance to recruit any but those, who, out of their inclination to the service, will proffer themselves.

I should be glad to have ten or twelve wagons sent to this place. Salt enough may be had here to load that number, and it is obtained upon easier terms than at Fredericksburg, by sixpence or eight pence per bushel. Those stores at Watkins's Ferry should be hurried up as fast as the water affords opportunities, if it were only to prevent disputes.

If the paymaster is at Winchester, and not on his way to Fort Dinwiddie, order him down here immediately. If he should be going with pay to Captain Hogg, he is to proceed with despatch; but if he is at Fort Cumberland, order him down to Winchester, to wait there until I arrive. I am, &c. *

* The following letter from Colonel Gage to Colonel Washington may be thought worthy of preservation, considering the relations that subsisted between these two persons twenty years afterwards, when the former commanded the British forces in Boston, and the latter was at the head of the American army at Cambridge.

"Albany, 23 November, 1755.

"DEAR SIR,

"Your obliging letter of the 17th of October was forwarded from Philadelphia to this place, and came to my hands yesterday. It gave me great pleasure to hear from a person, of whom the world has justly so good an opinion, and for whom I have so great an esteem. I shall be extremely happy to have frequent news of your welfare, and hope soon to hear, that your laudable endeavours, and the noble spirit you have exerted in the service of your country, have at last been crowned with the success they merit.

"We expect the next intelligence from your parts will inform us, that

TO GOVERNOR DINWIDDIE.

Alexandria, 5 December, 1755.

SIR,

I have sent the bearer, Captain John Mercer (who has accounts to settle with the Committee), to the treasurer for the balance of the ten thousand pounds; and to acquaint your Honor, that, meeting with letters at Fredericksburg, as I returned from Williamsburg, informing me that all was peaceable above, and that nothing was so immediately wanting as salt, I got what I could at that place, and hastened on hither to engage more, to receive the recruits expected in, and to wait the arrival of the vessel with arms from James River, in order to forward them up with the greater despatch. The vessel is not yet arrived.

I have impatiently waited to hear the result of your letter to General Shirley, and wish that the delays may not prove ominous. In that case, I shall not know how to act; for I can never submit to the command of Captain Dagworthy, since you have honored me with the command of the Virginia regiment.

The country has sustained inconceivable losses, by delaying the commissaries at Williamsburg. Many of

---

those merciless barbarians, that have ravaged your frontiers, are repulsed and driven back to their woods. The account we have received of their barbarities gave me infinite concern, when I reflected on the many poor families that I had seen in that part of the world, who had been massacred by those murderers. Nothing would give me greater pleasure, than to hear they had met with the fate their villanies deserve, and which I hope they will sooner or later meet with.

"General Johnson has finished his fort at Lake George, which will be garrisoned by the New England forces, as well as Fort Edward. There is an end of this campaign, and nothing remains now but to prepare for the next, which I hope will be more successful than the last. I sincerely wish you all health and happiness, and beg you will believe me, dear Sir, &c.

"THOMAS GAGE."

the Carolina beeves are dead, through absolute poverty, and the chief part of them too poor to slaughter.

We are at a loss how to act, for want of the mutiny *bill*; and I should be *obliged* to your Honor, if you will have fifty or a hundred printed, and sent by the bearer. There is a clause in that bill, which, if you are not kind enough to obviate it, will prevent entirely the good intention of it, that is, delaying the execution of sentences, until your Honor shall be made acquainted with the proceedings of the court. This, at times when there is the greatest occasion for examples, will be morally impossible; I mean, while we are on our march, perhaps near the Ohio, when none but strong parties can pass with safety. At all times it must be attended with great expense, trouble, and inconvenience. I represented this to Colonel Corbin, and some other gentlemen of the Council, when I was down, who said that the objection would be removed, by your giving blank warrants, to be filled up as occasion should require. This would effectually remedy all those evils, and put things in their proper channel.

We suffer greatly for want of kettles; those sent from below, being tin, are of short duration. We shall, also, in a little time, suffer as much for the want of clothing; none can be got in these parts. Shoes and stockings we have, and can get more if wanted, but nothing else. I wish your Honor would direct what is to be done in these cases; and that you would be kind enough to desire the treasurer to send some part of the money in gold and silver. Were this done, we might often get necessaries for the regiment in Maryland, or Pennsylvania, when they cannot be had here. But with our money it is impossible; our paper not passing there.

The recruiting service goes on extremely slow. Yesterday being a day appointed for the rendezvous at this place, there came in ten officers with twenty men only. If I had any other than paper money, and you approved of it, I would send to Pennsylvania and the borders of Carolina. I am confident men might be had there. Your Honor never having given any particular directions about the provisions, I should be glad to know, whether you would have more laid in, than will serve for twelve hundred men, that I may give orders accordingly.

As I cannot now conceive, that any great danger can be apprehended at Fort Cumberland this winter, I am sensible, that my constant attendance there cannot be so serviceable, as riding from place to place, making the proper dispositions, and seeing that all our necessaries are forwarded up with despatch. I therefore think it advisable to inform your Honor of it, hoping it will correspond with your own opinion.

Captain Mercer's pay as aid-de-camp seems yet doubtful. I should be pleased if you would fix it; as also Captain Stewart's. If Captain Stewart's is increased, I suppose all the officers belonging to the light-horse will expect to have theirs augmented also. Colonel Stephen, in a late letter, discovered an inclination to go to the Creek and Cherokee Indians this winter. I told him where to apply, if he had any such thoughts. I believe, on so useful a business, he might be spared until the spring.

If you think proper to order the act of Assembly for apprehending deserters, and against harbouring them, to be published every Sunday in each parish church, until the people are made acquainted with the law, it would have a very good effect. The commonalty in general err more through ignorance than design. Few of them know that such a law exists, and there is no other certain way of bringing it to their knowledge. A great many of the men, that once belonged to our companies, and deserted from the regiments into which they were drafted, would now gladly return, if they could be sure of indemnity. If you would be kind enough to intimate this to General Shirley, or the colonels of those regiments, it would be of service to us. Without leave, we dare not receive them. I am, &c.

TO COLONEL ADAM STEPHEN.

Winchester, 28 December, 1755.

SIR,

Captain John Mercer only returned last night from Williamsburg, and brings no satisfactory answers to any thing I questioned the Governor upon.

The express, that was sent to General Shirley, has returned without seeing him. However, the Governor writes that he expects answers to his letters by Colonel Hunter, who is now at New York, and waits the arrival of the General at that place. The Governor is very strongly of opinion, that Captain Dagworthy has no right to contend for the command; and in his letter he says, after mentioning the return of the express, and his expectation of satisfactory letters, "But I am of opinion you might have obviated the inconsistent dispute with Captain Dagworthy, by asking him if he did not command a provincial company by virtue of Governor Sharpe's commission; as that he had formerly from his Majesty now ceases, as he is not on the half-pay list. If so, the method you are to take is very obvious, as your commission from me is greater than what he has." And in Williamsburg, when I was down there, both he and Colonel Fitzhugh told me, that Dagworthy could have no more pretensions to command me, or either of the field-officers of the Virginia regiment, than we have to command General Shirley; and further gave it as their opinion, that as Dagworthy's was only a botched-up commission at best, and as he commanded a provincial company, and by virtue of a governor's commission, he ought to be arrested for his presumption. They say, allowing his commission from the King to be valid, yet, as he is not there by order of his Majesty, he can have no better pretensions to assume the command, than a visiting half-pay officer, who transiently passes through the camp.

I wish you would sound him on this head, and hear how he will answer these things, and let me know when you come down, which I desire may be immediately, as I want much to consult you upon several accounts. The paymaster, and commissary, if not very much engaged, must accompany you. Desire both to have their accounts settled, and brought with them, as that is necessary before I can give more money.

I have sent you one of the mutiny bills, which I received from below, but I believe it is necessary, as we still want the power, to postpone trials until after your return.

Enclosed is a commission for Captain Waggener, which I have neglected giving before. Desire him, as the command upon your leaving the place will devolve upon him, to be very circumspect in his duty, and to see that the troops are duly drawn out and trained to their exercise, and practised to bush-fighting.

As I expect in a very few days to have the pleasure of seeing you, I shall only add, I am, &c.

TO ROBERT HUNTER MORRIS, GOVERNOR OF PENNSYLVANIA.

Winchester, 5 January, 1756.

SIR,

I am sorry it has not been in my power to acknowledge the receipt of yours until now. At the time your letter came to Winchester, I was at Williamsburg; before I got back, it was conveyed thither; and so from place to place it has been tossing almost until this time.

There is nothing more necessary than good intelligence to frustrate a designing enemy, and nothing that requires greater pains to obtain. I shall, therefore, cheerfully come into any measures you can propose to settle a correspondence for this salutary end; and you may depend upon receiving (when the provinces are threatened) the earliest and best intelligence I can procure.

I sympathized in a general concern to see the inactivity of your province in a time of imminent danger; but am pleased to find, that a feeling sense of wrongs has roused the spirit of your martial Assembly to vote a sum, which, with your judicious application, will turn to a general good.*

---

* The warm contest between the Governor and Assembly of Pennsylvania, respecting the mode of raising money, had hitherto prevented any efficient aid being rendered by that colony for the public service. As the Proprietaries owned large estates in the province, the Assembly insisted that these estates should be taxed for the common defence, in the same proportion as the estates of the inhabitants, and reported all their bills accordingly. Prohibited by his instructions, the Governor had no power to sanction such bills. In a case so manifestly just, and involving a principle of great importance, the Assembly would not yield, and no money was granted.

At last, when the news of Braddock's defeat reached England, the Proprietaries, alarmed at the progress of the enemy, or, as Dr. Franklin has said, "intimidated by the clamor raised against them for their meanness

We took some pretty vigorous measures to collect a force upon our frontiers, upon the first alarm, which has kept us peaceable ever since. How long this may last is uncertain, since that force, which consisted of militia, is disbanded, and the recruiting service almost stagnated.

If you propose to levy troops, and their destination is not a secret, I should be favored were I let into the scheme, that we may act conjunctly, so far as the nature of things will admit.

Pray direct to me at Alexandria, to which place I intend to go in about ten days. I am, &c.

ADDRESS TO THE OFFICERS OF THE VIRGINIA REGIMENT.*

8 January, 1756.

This timely warning of the effects of misbehaviour

---

and injustice in giving their governor such instructions," ordered the receiver-general to add five thousand pounds to such sums, as the Assembly should grant for the security of the province. When this was made known to the House, a new bill was formed, granting *sixty thousand pounds* for the use of the crown, with a clause exempting the proprietary estates from the tax. — *Votes of the Pennsylvania Assembly for November*, 1755.

In the May preceding, the Assembly had given fifteen hundred pounds for the King's use, by an order appropriating funds then within their control. Five thousand pounds of this money were applied to victualling the King's troops in Virginia, and ten thousand pounds to procuring and transporting provisions for the Massachusetts troops engaged in the King's service.

At the same time that the above grant of sixty thousand pounds was made, a bill for establishing and disciplining a voluntary militia was drafted by Franklin, which, as he says, passed through the House with little difficulty, as the Quakers were left at liberty. Several companies were organized, but none ever joined the Virginians in any expedition against the Indians. The money was chiefly expended in building forts on the Pennsylvania frontiers, under the superintendence of Franklin, who was commissioned for that purpose by the Governor. — See *Franklin's Works*, Vol. I. p. 153.

* An officer had been tried by a court-martial, and suspended. In

will, I hope, be instrumental in animating the younger officers to a laudable *emulation* in the service of their country. Not that I apprehend any of them can be guilty of offences of this nature, but there are many other misdemeanors, that will, without due circumspection, gain upon inactive minds, and produce consequences equally disgraceful.

I would, therefore, earnestly recommend, in every point of duty, willingness to undertake, and intrepid resolution to execute. Remember, that actions, and not the commission, make the officer, and that more is expected from him, than the title. Do not forget, that there ought to be a time appropriated to attain knowledge, as well as to indulge in pleasure. And as we now have no opportunities to improve from example, let us read for this desirable end. Bland's and other treatises will give the proper information.

I think it my duty, gentlemen, as I have the honor to preside over you, to give this friendly admonition; especially since I am determined, as far as my small experience, my abilities, and interest in the service may dictate, to observe the strictest discipline. On the other hand, you may as certainly depend upon having rigid justice administered to all, and that I shall make it the most agreeable part of my duty to study merit, and reward the brave and deserving. I assure, you, gentlemen, that partiality shall never bias my conduct, nor shall prejudice injure any; but, throughout the whole tenor of my proceedings, I shall endeavour, as far as I am able, to reward and punish, without the least departure from equity.

---

communicating this sentence, the commander addressed to the officers generally the above remarks and admonition.

TO GOVERNOR DINWIDDIE.

Alexandria, 14 January, 1756.

SIR,

Major Lewis, being at Winchester when your letter came to hand, was immediately despatched to Augusta, to take upon him the command of the troops destined against the Shawanese Town;* with orders to follow such directions as he should receive from you. This scheme I am apprehensive will prove abortive, as we are told that those Indians are removed up the river, into the neighbourhood of Fort Duquesne.

I have given all necessary orders for training the men to a proper use of their arms, and the method of Indian fighting, and hope in a little time to make them expert. I should be glad to have your Honor's express commands, either to prepare for taking the field, or for guarding our frontiers in the spring, because the steps for these two operations are very different. I have already built two forts on Patterson's Creek, which have caused the chief part of the inhabitants to return to their plantations; and have now ordered Captain Waggener with sixty men to build and garrison two others, at places I have pointed out high up the South Branch, which will be a means of securing near a hundred miles of our frontiers, exclusive of the command at Fort Dinwiddie, on Jackson's River. And, indeed, without a much greater number of men than we have a prospect of raising, I do not see how it is possible to think of passing the mountains, or acting more than defensively. This seems to be the full determination of the Pennsylvanians; so that there can be no hope of assistance from that quarter. If we only act defensively, I would most earnestly recommend the building of a strong fort

* Situated at the junction of the Great Kenhawa and Ohio Rivers.

at some convenient place in Virginia, as that in Maryland [Fort Cumberland], not to say any thing of its situation, which is extremely bad, will ever be an eyesore to this colony, and attended with more inconveniences than it is possible to enumerate. One instance of this I have taken notice of, in a letter that accompanies this, and many more I could recite, were it necessary.

If we take the field, there is not time to carry on a work of this kind, but we should immediately set about engaging wagons, horses, forage, pack-saddles, &c. And here I cannot help remarking, that I believe it will be impossible to get wagons or horses sufficient, unless the old score is paid off; as the people are really ruined for want of their money, and complain justly of their grievances.

I represented in my last the inconveniences of the late act of Assembly, which obliges us first to send to your Honor for a commission to hold general courts-martial, and then to delay execution until a warrant can be had from Williamsburg. I hope you will take the thing into consideration. We have several deserters now on hand, whom I have taken by rigorous measures, and who should be made examples to others, as this practice is continued with greater spirit than ever.

Unless clothing is soon provided, the men will be unfit for any kind of service. And I know of no expedient to procure clothes, but by sending to the northward, as cloth cannot be had here. I left, among other returns, an exact account of the clothing at every place, when I was in Williamsburg. I shall not care to lay in provisions for more than a thousand men, unless I have your orders. We have put out such of the beeves as were unfit for slaughtering. If they survive the winter, they may be useful in the summer.

Ensign Polson has received a commission in Colonel Gage's regiment, and has thus left a vacancy, which, with your approbation, will be filled by Mr. Dennis McCarty, whom you once appointed a captain. He has continued a volunteer ever since, and has recruited several men. I hope your Honor will allow me the liberty, as you once promised, of filling up the vacancies, as they happen, with the volunteers, who serve with that expectation. We have several with us, who appear to be very deserving young gentlemen. I shall observe the strictest justice in promoting them according to their merit, and their time of entering the service.

The skipper of the vessels has embezzled some of the stores; but for want of a particular invoice of them, we cannot ascertain the loss. He is kept in confinement until your Honor's pleasure is known. I am, &c.

TO GOVERNOR DINWIDDIE.

Alexandria, 14 January, 1756

SIR,

When I was down, the Committee among other things resolved, that the Maryland and Carolina companies should not be supported with our provisions. This resolve, I think, met with your approbation; upon which I wrote to Colonel Stephen, desiring him to acquaint Captain Dagworthy therewith, who paid slight regard to it, saying they were in the King's garrison, and all the troops had an equal right to draw provisions with us, by his order, as commanding officer, and that we, after the provisions were put there, had no power to remove them without his leave. I would, therefore, request your Honor's peremptory orders what to do in this case, as I do not care to act without instructions, lest it should appear to proceed from pique and resentment at having the command disputed. This is one among the numberless inconveniences of the fort being in Maryland. Captain Dagworthy, I dare venture to affirm, is encouraged to say this by Governor Sharpe, who we know has written him to keep the command. With this Captain Dagworthy himself acquainted Colonel Stephen.

As I have not yet heard how General Shirley has answered your request, I fear for the success of it, especially as it is next to an impossibility (since Governor Sharpe has been there to plead Captain Dagworthy's cause) to make the General acquainted, by writing, with the nature of the dispute. The officers have drawn up a memorial to be presented to the General, and, that it may be properly strengthened, they humbly beg your solicitation to have us put upon the establishment, as we have certain advices that it is in his power. This would at once put an end to contention, which is the root of evil, and destructive to the best operations; and it would turn all our movements into a free and easy channel.

They have urged it to me, in the warmest manner, to appear personally before the General for that end. This I would gladly do, even at this disagreeable season, if I had your permission; which I the more freely ask, since I am determined to resign a commission, which you were generously pleased to offer me, and for which I shall always retain a grateful sense, rather than submit to the command of a person, who has not such superlative merit as to balance the inequality of rank. However, he adheres to what he calls his rights, in which I know he is supported by Governor Sharpe. He says, that he has no commission from the province of Maryland, but acts by virtue of that from the King; that this was the condition of his engaging in the Maryland service; and that, when he was sent up there the 1st of last October, he was ordered by Governor Sharpe and Sir John St. Clair not to give up his right. To my certain knowledge his rank was disputed before General Braddock, who gave it in his favor; and he accordingly took place of every captain upon the expedition, except Captain James Mercer and Captain Rutherford, whose commissions were older than his; so that I should not by any means choose to act, as your Honor hinted in your last, lest I should be called to an account myself.*

I have, during my stay at Winchester from the 20th of December to this time, disposed of all the men and officers, that are not recruiting, and can be spared from the fort, in the best manner I could for the defence of the inhabitants, and they will need no further orders till I could return. And the recruiting officers are allowed till the 1st of March to repair to their rendezvous, which leaves at present nothing to do at the fort, but to train and discipline the men, and prepare and salt the provisions. For the better perfecting both these, I have left full and clear directions.

Besides, in other respects, I think my going to the northward might be of service, as I should thereby become acquainted with the plan of operations, so far as it may be thought proper to be communicated.

Should you comply with my request, I would thank you for such letters, as you think may enforce the petition to the General, or any of the governors in my way. I am, &c.

---

* See above, the letter to Colonel Stephen dated, December 28th.

TO LIEUTENANT-COLONEL STEPHEN.

Alexandria, 1 February, 1756.

SIR,

Looking upon our affairs at this critical juncture to be of such importance, and having a personal acquaintance with General Shirley, which I thought might add some weight to the strength of our memorial, I solicited leave, which is obtained, to visit him in person. I shall accordingly set out in two days for Boston, having procured letters from the Governor. You may depend I shall leave no stone unturned for this salutary end; and, I think, if reason, justice, and every equitable right can claim attention, we deserve to be heard.

As I have taken the fatigue of this tedious journey upon myself, which I had never thought of until I left Winchester, I hope you will conduct every thing in my absence for the interest and honor of the service. And I must exhort you in the most earnest manner to strict discipline and due exercise of arms.

You may tell Mr. Livingston from me, that, if the soldiers are not skilled in arms equal to what may reasonably be expected, he most assuredly shall answer for it at my return. And I must frankly tell you, that I also expect to find them expert at bush-fighting. You are to order a particular account to be taken of the provisions, that are delivered to the Maryland and Carolina companies by the commissary.

The Governor seems determined to make the officers comply with the terms of holding their commissions, or forfeit them. He approves of Dekeyser's suspension, and orders, that he shall not be admitted into the camp. He seems uneasy at what I own gives me much concern, namely, that gaming is introduced into the camp.

I am ordered to discourage it, and must desire that you will intimate the same.

As money may be wanted for paying the troops, and other incidental charges, order the paymaster down to Alexandria, where he may receive of Mr. Kirkpatrick the sum requisite.

I think of nothing else at present; so, with once more exhorting you to strict observation of discipline, I conclude, yours, &c.

TO GOVERNOR DINWIDDIE.

Alexandria, 2 February, 1756.

SIR,

I can but return my very hearty thanks for your kind condescension in suffering me to wait upon General Shirley, as I am very well assured it was done with the intention to favor my suit.

There is as yet an unanswerable argument against our taking the field, which I forgot to mention in my last; that is, the want of a train of artillery, and, what is full as necessary, engineers to conduct the affair, if we hope to approach Fort Duquesne.

By the advices, which we have received hitherto from the northward, the Pennsylvanians are determined to act defensively. For that purpose they have posted their newly raised levies upon their frontiers at different passes, and have received the additional strength and favor of a detachment or two from the regulars.

I have ordered, besides the forts that are built, and now building, that a road which I had reconnoitred, and which proves nearer and better, should be immediately opened for the more easy transportation of stores from Winchester to Fort Cumberland; so there is not the least fear that the soldiers will be corrupted through idleness.

The commission for calling general courts-martial appears to me imperfect, notwithstanding it was drawn by the attorney-general, as it rather, by the words, appoints me, or whomever it is directed to, president of the said court, than invests a power to hold a court-martial without its being first ordered by you; whereas, the commission should empower the officer to appoint a court, of which he is to be president. But as I hope there will be little occasion for any, until I come back, it may be deferred until then, when that and other things, I trust, will be properly settled.

I have always, so far as was in my power, endeavoured to discourage gaming in the camp; and always shall while I have the honor to preside there.

I have delivered the skipper to Mr. Carlyle, who proposes, in order to save expense, to send him round by water, in the vessel that brought up the stores. The evidences in this affair will be Mr. Carlyle, Ensigns Buckner and Deane, and one of the men now in the vessel.

I cannot help observing, that your Honor, if you have not seen the clothes lately sent up, has been imposed upon by the contractors, for they are really unfit for use; or, at least, will soon be so.

I have nothing in particular to add, but to assure you, that I shall use my utmost diligence in the prosecution of my journey and pretensions, and that I am, with very great esteem, your Honor's, &c.*

* Colonel Washington left Alexandria, on his journey to Boston, February 4th, with his aid-de-camp, Captain Mercer. He returned on the 23d of March. In his route he passed through Philadelphia, New York, New London, Newport, and Providence, visited the governors of Pennsylvania and New York, and spent several days in each of the principal cities. He was well received, and much noticed, by General Shirley, with whom

TO GOVERNOR DINWIDDIE.

Winchester, 7 April, 1756.

SIR,

I arrived here yesterday, and think it advisable to despatch an express (notwithstanding I hear two or three are already sent down) to inform you of the unhappy situation of affairs in this quarter. The enemy have returned in greater numbers, committed several murders not far from Winchester, and even are so daring as to attack our forts in open day, as you may see by the enclosed letters and papers. Many of the inhabitants are in a miserable situation by their losses, and

---

he continued ten days, mixing constantly in the society of the town, and attending with interest to the proceedings of the legislature of Massachusetts, then engaged in affairs of great moment respecting the requisite aids for promoting the grand scheme of military operations, recently agreed upon by a council of several governors assembled at New York. He also visited Castle William, and other objects worthy of a stranger's notice.

In the purpose of his mission he was successful, as may be seen by the following order, given under the hand of General Shirley.

"Boston, 5 March, 1756.

"Governor Dinwiddie, at the instance of Colonel Washington, having referred to me concerning the right of command between him and Captain Dagworthy, and desiring that I should determine it, I do therefore give it as my opinion, that Captain Dagworthy, who now acts under a commission from the Governor of Maryland, and where there are no regular troops joined, can only take rank as a provincial captain, and of course is under the command of all provincial field-officers; and, in case it should happen, that Colonel Washington and Captain Dagworthy should join at Fort Cumberland, it is my order that Colonel Washington shall take the command.

"W. SHIRLEY."

As soon as he returned from this tour, he proceeded onward to Williamsburg. He had been there but a short time, when an express arrived with intelligence, that the French and Indians had broken into the frontier settlements, murdered several of the inhabitants, and excited great alarm in all that region. Upon hearing this news, he hastened back to his headquarters at Winchester.

so apprehensive of danger, that, I believe, unless a stop is put to the depredations of the Indians, the Blue Ridge will soon become our frontier.

I find it impossible to continue on to Fort Cumberland, until a body of men can be raised. I have advised with Lord Fairfax, and other officers of the militia, who have ordered each captain to call a private muster, and to read the exhortation enclosed (for orders are no longer regarded in this county), in hopes that this expedient may meet with the desired success. If it should, I shall, with such men as are ordered from Fort Cumberland to join these, scour the woods and suspected places, in all the mountains and valleys, on this part of our frontiers; and doubt not but I shall fall in with the Indians and their more cruel associates. I hope the present emergency of affairs, assisted by such good news as the Assembly may by this time have received from England, and from the Commissioners, will determine them to take vigorous measures for their own and country's safety, and no longer depend on an uncertain way of raising men for their own protection. However absurd it may appear, it is nevertheless certain, that five hundred Indians have it more in their power to annoy the inhabitants, than ten times their number of regulars. Besides the advantageous way they have of fighting in the woods, their cunning and craft, their activity and patient sufferings, are not to be equalled. They prowl about like wolves, and, like them, do their mischief by stealth. They depend upon their dexterity in hunting and upon the cattle of the inhabitants for provisions. For these reasons, I own, I do not think it unworthy of the notice of the legislature to compel the inhabitants (if a general war is likely to ensue, and things are to continue in this unhappy situation for any time,) to live in townships, working at each other's farms by turns, and to drive their cattle into the thickly settled parts of the country. Were this done, they could not be cut off by small parties, and large ones could not subsist without provisions.*

It seemed to be the sentiment of the House of Burgesses when I was down, that a chain of forts should be erected upon our frontiers, for the defence of the people. This expedient, in my opinion, without an inconceivable number of men, will never answer their expectations.

I doubt not but your Honor has had a particular account of Major Lewis's unsuccessful attempt to get to the Shawanese Town. It was an expedition, from which, on account of the length of the march, I always had little hope, and often expressed my uneasy apprehensions on that head. But since they are returned, with the Indians that accompanied them, I think it would be a very happy step to prevail upon the latter to proceed as far as Fort Cumberland. It is in their power to be of infinite use to us; and without Indians, we shall never be able to cope with those cruel foes to our country.†

I would therefore beg leave to recommend in a very

---

* Colonel Washington wrote a similar account to the Speaker of the House of Burgesses, and added; — "I would beg leave to recommend, that more men should be drafted, than are necessary to complete our numbers, and then, out of the whole, our complement may be chosen of active and resolute men. To encourage such men to go with the less reluctance, I think it not amiss, that they should serve only eighteen or twenty months, and then be discharged. Twenty months will embrace two full campaigns, which will, I apprehend, bring matters to a crisis one way or another."

† Major Lewis's party suffered greatly on this expedition. The rivers were so much swoln by the rains and melting snow, that they were unable to reach the Shawanese Town; and after being six weeks in the woods, having lost several canoes with provisions and ammunition, they were reduced nearly to a state of starvation, and obliged to kill their horses for food.

earnest manner, that your Honor would send an express to them immediately for this desirable end. I should have done it myself, but was uncertain whether it might prove agreeable or not. I also hope you will order Major Lewis to secure his guides, as I understand he attributes all his misfortunes to their misconduct. Such offences should meet with adequate punishment, or else we may ever be misled by designing villains. I am your Honor's, &c.

P. S. Since writing the above, Mr. Paris, who commanded a party, is returned. He relates, that, upon the North River, he fell in with a small body of Indians whom he engaged, and, after a contest of half an hour, put them to flight. Monsieur Donville, commander of the party, was killed and scalped, and his instructions found about him, which I enclose. We had one man killed, and two wounded. Mr. Paris sent the scalp by Jenkins; and I hope, although it is not an Indian's, they will meet with an adequate reward. The whole party jointly claim the reward, no person pretending solely to assume the merit. *

---

* At this time there was no law in Virginia fixing the reward for scalps, and it was probably left to the discretion of the governor. Shortly afterwards a reward of ten pounds was established by law, for every hostile Indian taken prisoner or killed. This law was to remain in force during the war. It applied only to Indians, and not to enemies of any other description. In Maryland at one time the bounty for each Indian prisoner, or scalp, taken within the province, was as high as fifty pounds. But this allowance was not made to soldiers in public pay. — Hening's *Statutes at Large*, Vol. VI. p. 551. — *Acts of the Maryland Assembly, September*, 1756.

From early times it had been customary to offer high bounties for service in Indian wars. The Commissioners of the United Colonies of Massachusetts, Plymouth, and Connecticut, in their instructions to Major Church, September 18th, 1689, confirm, that the soldiers should have "the benefit of the captives, and all lawful plunder, and the reward of eight pounds per head for every fighting Indian man slain by them, over and above their stated wages." By the "benefit of the captives" is here

Your Honor may in some measure penetrate into the daring designs of the French by their instructions, in which orders are given to burn, if possible, our magazine at Conococheague, a place that is in the midst of a thickly settled country.

I have ordered the party there to be made as strong as time and our present circumstances will permit, lest they should attempt to execute the instructions of Dumas.* I have also ordered up an officer and twenty recruits to assist Joseph Edwards, and the people on those waters. The inhabitants of this town are under dreadful apprehensions of an attack, and all the roads between this and Fort Cumberland are much infested. As I apprehend you will be obliged to draft men, I hope care will be taken, that none shall be chosen but active, resolute men, who are practised in the use of arms, and are marksmen.

TO GOVERNOR DINWIDDIE.

Winchester, 16 April, 1756.

SIR,

All my ideal hopes of raising a number of men to scour the adjacent mountains have vanished into nothing.

---

meant the privilege of selling them into slavery, a practice which seems gradually to have been abandoned. At a later period Massachusetts and New Hampshire offered by law a bounty of fifty pounds for each scalp, and on some occasions as high as one hundred pounds. — Penhallow's *Indian Wars*, in the *Collections of the New Hampshire Historical Society*, Vol. I. pp. 52, 105, 110.

* Dumas had succeeded Contrecœur in the command of Fort Duquesne. The following is a translation of the orders found on Donville, which, at least, give a favorable indication of the commandant's humanity.

"Fort Duquesne, 23 March, 1756.

"The Sieur Donville, at the head of a detachment of fifty savages, is

Yesterday was the appointed time for a general rendezvous of all, who were willing to accompany me for that desirable end, and only fifteen appeared; so that I find myself reduced to the further necessity of waiting at this place a few days longer, until the arrival of a party ordered from Fort Cumberland to escort me up; the roads being so infested, that none but hunters, who travel the woods by night, can pass in safety.

I have done every thing in my power to quiet the minds of the inhabitants, by detaching all the men, that I have any command over, to the places most exposed. There have also been large detachments from Fort Cumberland in pursuit of the enemy these ten days past; yet nothing, I fear, will prevent the people from abandoning their dwellings, and flying with the utmost precipitation.

No murder has been committed since I came up; but the express, whom I sent to Colonel Stephen, notwithstanding he was an excellent woodsman, and a very active fellow, was fired upon five times at a place called the Flats, within six miles of Fort Cumberland. He had several bullets through his clothes, and his horse shot under him, yet he made his escape.

By a letter from a gentleman in Williamsburg we are informed, that the Assembly have generously given the

---

ordered to go and observe the motions of the enemy in the neighbourhood of Fort Cumberland. He will endeavour to harass their convoys, and burn their magazines at Conococheague; should this be practicable. He must use every effort to take prisoners, who may confirm what we already know of the enemy's designs. The Sieur Donville will employ all his talents, and all his credit, to prevent the savages from committing any cruelties upon those, who may fall into their hands. Honor and humanity ought, in this respect, to serve as our guide.

"DUMAS."

This is doubtless the same officer, who commanded the French and Indians at Braddock's defeat, after the death of M. de Beaujeu.

further sum of twenty thousand pounds, and voted the augmenting of our forces to two thousand men, from whom, under good regulations, we may have some expectations, if they are properly appointed. For this purpose, as I have not heard your Honor offer your opinion, I have been free enough to propose a scheme, which is now enclosed. The plan is to have the whole two thousand formed into one regiment consisting of two battalions, of ten companies each, with five field-officers, each of whom to have a company; and every other company to consist of one captain, two lieutenants, one ensign, four sergeants, four corporals, two drummers, and eighty-seven private men. This will save to the country the annual sum of five thousand and six pounds, sixteen shillings, and eight pence, and we shall be better established, and appointed more after the British manner, than we now can, or should be, if formed into two regiments, or into one regiment with only fifty men in a company. And I humbly conceive, where we can pattern after our mother country upon as easy terms as pursuing plans of our own, that we should at least pay that deference to her judgment and experience.

The country will save the pay of many commissioned, as well as non-commissioned officers, who are the persons that enhance the expenses. For, the whole annual pay of the two thousand men, including all the staff-officers, and other commissioned officers, sergeants, corporals, drummers, and private men, amounts only to thirty-four thousand one hundred and forty-five pounds ten shillings; whereas, were they formed into regiments, or into one regiment of fifty in a company, (but that would be quite incongruous,) the expense would amount to thirty-nine thousand one hundred and fifty-two pounds, six shillings, and eight pence, which makes the aforesaid difference. Then, again, we do not allow companies to our field-officers, which I believe is the only instance that can be given in which they are not, and this makes the difference of three captains' pay.

I have been free enough to offer my opinion very candidly, and in that light I hope it will be received, though it may meet with your Honor's disapprobation. I had no other motive in proposing this scheme, than the pleasing hope of serving my country. If I have mistaken the means, I am sorry for it, and beg pardon for my presumption.

As I am convinced, that no other method can be used to raise two thousand men, but by drafting, I hope to be excused, when I again repeat, that great care should be observed in choosing active marksmen. The manifest inferiority of inactive persons, unused to arms, in this kind of service, (although equal in numbers,) to men who have practised hunting, is inconceivable. The chance against them is more than two to one. Another thing I hope will merit the consideration of the Assembly, and that is, that they will put all such men as are raised for the expedition in actual pay, and under the same discipline as ours at present; otherwise, I am very well convinced their good intentions will prove abortive, and all the drafts will very soon quit the service.

I do not conceive it to be a hardship to put even drafts under martial law, if they are only taken for a certain time, which I could wish to be the case, as I thereby hope for better men.

I have the honor to be, with high consideration, &c.

TO GOVERNOR DINWIDDIE.

Winchester, 18 April, 1756.

SIR,

It gave me infinite concern to find in yours by Governor Innes, that any representations should inflame the Assembly against the Virginia regiment, or give cause to suspect the morality and good behaviour of the officers. How far any of the individuals may have deserved such reflections, I will not take upon me to determine, but this I am certain of, and can call my conscience, and what, I suppose, will be a still more demonstrative proof in the eyes of the world, my orders, to witness how much I have, both by threats and persuasive means, endeavoured to discountenance gaming, drinking, swearing, and irregularities of every other kind; while I have, on the other hand, practised every artifice to inspire a laudable emulation in the officers for the service of their country, and to encourage the soldiers in the unerring exercise of their duty. How far I have failed in this desirable end, I cannot pretend to say. But it is nevertheless a point, which does in my opinion merit some scrutiny, before it meets with a final condemnation. Yet I will not undertake to vouch for the conduct of many of the officers, as I know there are some, who have the seeds of idleness very strongly implanted in their natures; and I also know, that the unhappy difference about the command, which has kept me from Fort Cumberland, has consequently prevented me from enforcing the orders, which I never failed to send.

However, if I continue in the service, I shall take care to act with a little more rigor, than has hitherto been practised, since I find it so necessary.

I wrote your Honor in my last how unsuccessfully we attempted to raise the militia, and that I was reduced to the necessity of waiting here for the arrival of an escort from Fort Cumberland. The garrison there is barely manned. The rest are out on parties; yet the Indians continue to haunt the roads, and pick up straggling persons. This you may see by the enclosed from Captain John Mercer, who, being out with a scouting party of one hundred men, has been ordered to search the Warm-Spring Mountain, where, it is lately reported, the Indians rendezvous. The commission you have sent for holding courts-martial is yet insufficient, as it is copied, I suppose, too literally after Governor Innes, who had no power to hold a general court-martial, or to try commissioned officers. But this may be postponed until I come down, which will be in a short time after I arrive at Fort Cumberland. I am your Honor's, &c.

TO GOVERNOR DINWIDDIE.

Winchester, 19 April, 1756.

SIR,

Since writing my letter of yesterday's date, the enclosed came to hand, by which you will be informed of a very unlucky affair.*

I immediately consulted Governor Innes, and such officers of my regiment as were at this place, on the necessary steps to be taken. They unanimously advised, that I should remain here with the fifty recruits that are in town, for the defence of the place, until the militia be raised, that we may thereby be enabled to compose a formidable body, and march out against the enemy.

---

* A skirmish with the Indians at Edwards's Fort, in which Captain John Mercer and several of his party were killed.

This engagement happened within twenty miles of Winchester, and the sergeant, who brought the letter, assures me there is reason to imagine, that their numbers are greater than the letter informs. He says there were many French among them, and that the chief part of the whole were mounted on horseback; so that there is a great probability of their having a design upon this place.

I have sent an express to Lord Fairfax, with a copy of Stark's letter, and have desired, in the most earnest manner, that he will be expeditious in calling the militia; but, alas! that is an unhappy dependence; yet the only one we have. I am your Honor's, &c.

TO GOVERNOR DINWIDDIE.

Winchester, 22 April, 1756.

SIR,

This encloses several letters, and the minutes of a council of war, which was held upon the receipt of them. Your Honor may see to what unhappy straits the distressed inhabitants and myself are reduced. I am too little acquainted, Sir, with pathetic language to attempt a description of the people's distresses, though I have a generous soul, sensible of wrongs, and swelling for redress. But what can I do? I see their situation, know their danger, and participate their sufferings, without having it in my power to give them further relief, than uncertain promises. In short, I see inevitable destruction in so clear a light, that, unless vigorous measures are taken by the Assembly, and speedy assistance sent from below, the poor inhabitants that are now in forts, must unavoidably fall, while the remainder are flying before the barbarous foe. In fine, the melancholy situation of the people, the little prospect of assistance, the gross and scandalous abuses cast upon the officers in general, which is reflecting upon me in particular, for suffering misconduct of such extraordinary kinds, and the distant prospect, if any, of gaining honor and reputation in the service, — cause me to lament the hour, that gave me a commission, and would induce me, at any other time than this of imminent danger, to resign, without one hesitating moment, a command, from which I never expect to reap either honor or benefit; but, on the contrary, have almost an absolute certainty of incurring displeasure below, while the murder of helpless families may be laid to my account here!

The supplicating tears of the women, and moving petitions of the men, melt me into such deadly sorrow, that I solemnly declare, if I know my own mind, I could offer myself a willing sacrifice to the butchering enemy, provided that would contribute to the people's ease.

Lord Fairfax has ordered men from the adjacent counties, but when they will come, or in what numbers, I cannot pretend to determine. If I may judge from the success we have met with here, I have but little hope, as three days' incessant endeavours have produced but twenty men.

I have too often urged my opinion for vigorous measures, and shall only add, that, besides the accounts you will receive in the letters, we are told from all parts, that the woods appear to be alive with Indians, who feast upon the fat of the land. As we have not more than a barrel or two of powder at this place, the rest being at Fort Cumberland, I could wish that some might be sent up. I have written to Alexandria and Fredericksburg, desiring that two barrels may be sent from each place, but whether there is any at either, I know not. I have sent orders to Captain Harrison to be diligent on the waters where he is posted, and to use his utmost endeavours to protect the people; and, if possible, to surprise the enemy at their sleeping-places. Ashby's letter is a very extraordinary one. The design of the Indians was only, in my opinion, to intimidate him into a surrender. For which reason I have written him word, that if they do attack him, he must defend that place to the last extremity, and when bereft of hope, lay a train to blow up the fort, and retire by night to Fort Cumberland.

A small fort, which we have at the mouth of Patterson's Creek, containing an officer and thirty men guarding stores, was attacked smartly by the French and Indians; they were as warmly received, upon which they retired. Our men at present are dispersed in small bodies, guarding the people and public stores.

I am your Honor's, &c.*

---

* The Governor, on receiving this letter, immediately ordered out one half of the militia in ten of the upper counties. Colonel Fairfax, one of the Council, wrote at the same time to Colonel Washington; —

"The House of Burgesses are pleased with the Governor's orders, and depend on your vigilance and success. Your endeavours in the service and defence of your country must redound to your honor; therefore do not let any unavoidable interruptions sicken your mind in the attempts you may pursue. Your good health and fortune are the toast at every table. Among the Romans, such a general acclamation and public regard, shown to any of their chieftains, were always esteemed a high honor, and gratefully accepted."

Landon Carter also wrote as follows. — "Virginia has been neglected by the mother country. Had there been a more active king on the throne of France, she would have made a conquest of it long ago. If we talk of obliging men to serve their country, we are sure to hear a fellow mumble over the words 'liberty' and 'property' a thousand times. I think as you do. I have endeavoured, though not in the field, yet in the senate, as much as possible to convince the country of danger, and she knows it; but such is her parsimony, that she is willing to wait for the rains to wet the powder, and rats to eat the bow-strings of the enemy, rather than attempt to drive them from her frontiers."

TO GOVERNOR DINWIDDIE.

Winchester, 24 April, 1756.

SIR,

Not an hour, nay scarcely a minute, passes, that does not produce fresh alarms and melancholy accounts. Nor is it possible to give the people the necessary assistance for their defence, on account of the small number of men we have, or that are likely to be here for some time. The inhabitants are removing daily, and in a short time will leave this country as desolate as Hampshire, where scarce a family lives.

Three families were murdered the night before last, at the distance of less than twelve miles from this place; and every day we have accounts of such cruelties and barbarities, as are shocking to human nature. It is not possible to conceive the situation and danger of this miserable country. Such numbers of French and Indians are all around, that no road is safe; and here we know not the hour when we may be attacked.

As it is not in my power to give you a full account of every thing, I have sent Captain Peachey to wait upon you, who can be more ample and satisfactory in every point, that requires your notice. I have written for the militia of Fairfax, Prince William, and Culpeper, and expect them here in a very few days. But how they are to be supplied with ammunition and provisions, I am quite at a loss to know. The distance of Fort Cumberland from us, where these supplies are, renders them useless, in a manner, and puts us to the greatest straits; and as the inhabitants are leaving their farms, it will be impossible for the militia to subsist without a supply of provisions, which are now very scarce, and will be more so. I should therefore be glad if your Honor would send up arms, ammunition, and provisions, and give immediate orders for the Irish beef at Alexandria, which cannot be had without your consent.

You spoke of sending some Indians to our assistance, in which no time should be lost, nor any means omitted to engage all the Catawbas and Cherokees, that can possibly be gathered, and immediately to despatch them hither. Unless we have Indians to oppose Indians, we may expect but small success. And I should think it no bad scheme, while the Indians remain here in such numbers, to have a detachment sent out with some friendly Indians to make an attempt upon the hostile towns, though this should be executed with all imaginable secrecy.

I hear the Assembly is for augmenting the forces in pay to fifteen hundred only, which are far too few to defend the frontiers against so numerous an enemy. But I have often written you my sentiments upon this and other subjects, and shall not now enlarge. I have also written to the Speaker by Captain Peachey, who will, I imagine, communicate to you what demands your immediate regard.

I wish your Honor would inform me, whether the militia expected here must be supplied out of the public stock of provisions laid up for the soldiers, or are to supply themselves. The want of due direction in matters of this nature causes great inconvenience. Give me leave to urge your speedy care in sending men and ammunition to our assistance, else the consequence may prove very fatal in a little time.

I have been just now told, that numbers about the neighbourhood hold councils and cabals for very dishonorable purposes, and unworthy the thoughts of a British subject. Despairing of assistance and protection from below (as they foolishly conjecture), they talk of capitulating and agreeing upon terms with the French and Indians, rather than lose their lives and fortunes through obstinacy. My force, at present, is very weak, and unable to take the necessary measures, as to those suspected persons; but, as soon as the militia arrive, be assured I will do my utmost to detect and secure such pests of society, if my information is not groundless, which I should be pleased to find so.

I enclose a copy of a council of war lately held here, and copies of some letters received since my last to you; one of which, for Colonel Martin, has been just sent to me from Fort Hopewell, on the South Branch. They have had an engagement there, with the French and Indians, the particulars of which you will see by the enclosed. Captain Waggener, with a party of his men, joined them the next day, and went in pursuit of the enemy, but could not come up with them. The waters were so high, that although Captain Waggener heard them engaged, he could send them no assistance. From these and other circumstances, you may form but a faint idea of the wretched situation of this country, nor can it be adequately conceived.

My extreme hurry, confusion, and anxiety must plead an excuse for incorrectness. I am your Honor's, &c.

TO JOHN ROBINSON, SPEAKER OF THE HOUSE OF BURGESSES, VIRGINIA.

Winchester, 24 April, 1756.

Dear Sir,

Yesterday I received yours by Mr. Kirkpatrick, and am sorry to hear of the reflections upon the conduct of the officers. I could wish that their names had been particularized, that justice might be done to the innocent and guilty; for it is extremely hard, that the whole corps should suffer reproaches for the inadvertence and misconduct of a few.*

The deplorable situation of this people is no more to be described, than my anxiety and uneasiness for their relief. You may expect, by the time this comes to hand, that, without a considerable reinforcement, Frederic county will not be mistress of fifteen families. They are now retreating to the securest parts in droves of fifties. In short, every thing has too melancholy an appearance for pen to communicate. I have therefore sent an officer, whose good sense and judicious observations will be a more effectual way of transmitting an account of the people's distresses.

I wish the Assembly had given two thousand, instead of fifteen hundred men, and that I had been acquainted with the dispositions they intended to make. Since I am ignorant of these, I hope it will not be thought presuming in me to offer my sentiments upon the subject.

We are, Sir, first to consider, that, if a chain of forts is to be erected upon our frontiers, it will be done with a design to protect the people; therefore, if these forts

* His orders for preserving discipline must be allowed to have been sufficiently rigid. The following is a specimen.

"Any commissioned officer, who stands by and sees irregularities committed, and does not endeavour to quell them, shall be immediately put under arrest. Any non-commissioned officer present, who does not interpose, shall be immediately reduced, and receive corporal punishment.

"Any soldier, who shall presume to quarrel or fight, shall receive five hundred lashes, without the benefit of a court-martial. The offender, upon complaint made, shall have strict justice done him. Any soldier found drunk shall receive one hundred lashes, without benefit of a court-martial."

To the major of his regiment he wrote on another occasion;—"Your own good sense has sufficiently prompted you to study the nature of your duty; but at the same time permit me, as a duty incumbent on myself, to recommend in the strongest terms to you the necessity of qualifying yourself *by reading* for the discharge of the duty of major, a post which requires a thorough knowledge of the service, and on the due execution of which your own credit, as well as that of the regiment, greatly depends."

are more than fifteen or eighteen miles, or a day's march, asunder, and garrisoned with less than eighty or a hundred men each, the object is not answered, and for these reasons. First, if they are at greater distances, it will be inconvenient for the soldiers to scout, and will allow the enemy to pass between undiscovered. Secondly if they are garrisoned with less than eighty or a hundred men, the number will be too few to afford detachments. Then, again, our frontiers are so extensive, that, were the enemy to attack us on the one side, they might, before the troops on the other could reach the spot, overrun and destroy half the country. And it is more than probable, if they had a design in one direction, they would make a feint in another. We are also to consider what sums the building of twenty forts, and the removing of stores and provisions to each, would cost. In the last place, we are to inquire where and when this expense will end. For, unless we endeavour to remove the cause, we shall be liable to the same incursions seven years hence as now, if the war continues, and the enemy is allowed to remain on the Ohio.

I shall next give the reasons, which I think make for a defensive plan. If the neighbouring colonies refuse us their assistance, we have neither strength nor ability to conduct an expedition; and, if we had, and were the whole to join us, I do not see to what purpose, since we have neither a train of artillery, artillery-men, nor engineers to execute any scheme beyond the mountains against a regular fortress. Again, we have neither stores nor provisions, arms nor ammunition, wagons nor horses, in any degree proportioned to the service; and to undertake an affair, where we are sure to fall through, would be productive of the worst consequences. By another defeat we should entirely lose the interest of every Indian.

If, then, we cannot act offensively with a prospect of success, we must be upon the defensive; and that there is no way to protect the people, or save ourselves, but by a chain of forts, is certain.

I would beg leave, in that case, to propose that a strong fort should be erected at this place, for a general receptacle of all the stores, and a place of residence for the commanding officers, which may be garrisoned by one company for the security of the stores, serving also as escorts for wagons, that are going higher up. It is the most public and convenient post for intelligence of any in the country, and approaches nearest to the parts, that will ever be attacked by numbers.

I have found by experience, that being just within the inhabitants is essential, in giving orders for the defence of the people; and that Fort Cumberland is of no more use towards that defence, than Fort George at Hampton. For the people, as soon as they are alarmed, immediately fly inwards, and at this time there is not an inhabitant living between this place and Fort Cumberland, except a few settlements upon the Manor around a fort we built there, and a few families at Edwards's, on Cacapehon River, with a guard of ours, which makes this very town at present the outermost frontier. Though a place trifling in itself, it is yet of the utmost importance, as it commands the communication from east to west, and from north to south. At this place almost all the roads centre. It secures the great roads from one half our frontiers to the markets of the neighbouring colonies, as well as to those on Rappahannoc and Potomac. At Fort Cumberland I would have one company garrisoned to secure the place, to procure the earliest intelligence, and to cover the detachments that may be sent towards the Ohio, which is all the use it can ever be put to. In the next place, I would propose, that a good fort should be erected between this and Fort Cumberland, in a line with the chain of forts across the country, and garrisoned by two companies. This I would advise, because, as I before observed, if we are ever attacked by a large body, it must be here, since there is no other road to our frontiers, either for transporting men or necessaries.

These three forts will employ four companies, which will be a tolerable body, if the companies are large, as they would be, according to the plan I sent you. And it would be a trifling expense to augment each company to one hundred privates, making two thousand, exclusive of officers, who were included in the scheme last sent.

After this is done, I would post the remaining companies equidistant, or at proper passes, along our frontiers, agreeably to the enclosed sketch, and order communications to be opened between fort and fort, and large detachments to scout and discover the tracks of the enemy.

It needs now only to be inquired, upon what part of our frontiers these forts are to be built. The Great Ridge, or North Mountain, so called in Evans's map, to which I refer, is now become our exterior bound, there not being one inhabitant beyond, on all the Potomac waters, except a few families on the South Branch, and at Joseph Edwards's, on Cacapehon, as already mentioned. So that it requires some consideration to determine whether we are to build near this place, with a view to protect the present inhabitants; or on the South Branch, or at Patterson's Creek, in the hope of drawing back those, who have forsaken their dwellings.

If we do not build there, that country will ever want settlers; and if we do, there is so great a blank, with such a series of mountains between, that it will be next to impossible to guard the people effectually. I could again wish, that the Assembly had given two thousand men, exclusive of officers, to be formed into two battalions of ten companies each. Indeed, fifteen hundred men are a greater number than ever was in a regiment of only one battalion, and they should be divided into two, with four field-officers, who should be so posted as to have the immediate care of a certain number of forts, with orders to draw from one to another, as occasion should require.*

I could add more on this subject, but I am so hurried, that I am obliged to refer you for further particulars to the bearer, who will tell you, that, to carry on all these works, a number of tools, as well as many other necessaries, will be wanting.

I have given my opinion with candor, and submit to correction with the greatest pleasure. Confusion and hurry must be an apology for the incoherence and incorrectness of this letter.

I am, dear Sir, yours, &c.

---

* Governor Dinwiddie had formed a project of a much more extensive chain of forts, embracing the whole line of frontier from Crown Point to the country of the Creek Indians. This project he communicated to the Board of Trade on the 23d of February.

A peculiar feature of his plan was, that the expenses of erecting and supporting these forts should be provided for by a land and poll-tax, to be levied *by an act of Parliament*, which should take effect equally throughout *all the colonies*. He proposed a poll-tax of one shilling sterling for two years, which he thought would be sufficient for building the forts; and a perpetual land-tax of two shillings on every hundred acres of land, as a fund for keeping up the garrisons. "I know," he adds, "that our people will be inflamed, if they hear of my making this proposal, as they are averse to all taxes; but in my duty, and in obedience to your commands, I cannot but think it the most eligible, and it will remain as long as the land; but, if not done by an act of the British Parliament, I may venture to affirm, that no governors on this continent will be able to prevail on the Assemblies to pass laws for this purpose."

By his calculation there were at least a million of taxable polls in the colonies. Hence this tax would produce fifty thousand pounds a year.

TO GOVERNOR DINWIDDIE.

Winchester, 27 April, 1756.

SIR,

I sent an express to Fort Cumberland on Tuesday last, who is just returned with the enclosed letters, which I forward, to prevent the trouble of extracting a part.

In my letter to Colonel Stephen, I informed him, among other things, of the accusations laid to his charge, and that he must expect to have the matter inquired into. You will see what he says upon the subject.

Desolation and murder still increase, and no prospects of relief. The Blue Ridge is now our frontier, no men being left in this county, except a few that keep close with a number of women and children in forts, which they have erected for that purpose. There are now no militia in this county. When there were, they could not be brought to action. If the inhabitants of the adjacent counties pursue the same system of disobedience, the whole must fall an inevitable sacrifice; and there is room to fear, that they have caught the infection, as I have sent, besides divers letters to Lord Fairfax, express after express to hurry them on, and yet I have no tidings of their march. We have the greatest reason to believe, that the number of the enemy is very considerable, as they are spread all over this part of the country; and that their success, and the spoils with which they

---

And the land-tax, estimated by the quitrents paid in Virginia, he believed would yield annually sixty thousand pounds.

The population of Virginia he considered at this time to be 293,472, of whom 173,316 were white, and 120,156 black. The militia were computed at 35,000 men fit to bear arms. The Governor wrote to Mr. Fox, one of the Secretaries of State; — "We dare not venture to part with any of our white men any distance, as we must have a watchful eye over our negro slaves, who are upwards of one hundred thousand." — *Letter Books.*

have enriched themselves, dished up with a good deal of French policy, will encourage the Indians of distant nations to fall upon our inhabitants in greater numbers, and, if possible, with greater rapidity. They enjoy the sweets of a profitable war, and will no doubt improve the success, which must ever attend their arms, unless we have Indians to oppose theirs. I would therefore advise, as I often have done, that there should be neither trouble nor expense omitted to bring the few, who are still inclined, into our service, and that, too, with the greatest care and expedition. A small number, just to point out the wiles and tracks of the enemy, is better than none; for which reason I must earnestly recommend, that those, who accompanied Major Lewis, should be immediately sent up, and such of the Catawbas as can be engaged in our interest. If such another torrent as this has been, (or may be ere it is done,) should press upon our settlements, there will not be a living creature left in Frederic county; and how soon Fairfax and Prince William may share its fate is easily conceived, if we only consider a cruel and bloodthirsty enemy, conquerors already possessed of the finest part of Virginia, plenteously filled with all kinds of provisions, pursuing a people overcome with fear and consternation at the inhuman murders of these barbarous savages.

The inhabitants, who are now in forts, are greatly distressed for the want of ammunition and provision, and are incessantly importuning me for both; neither of which have I at this place to spare. And if I had, I should be much embarrassed to know how to act, as I could not be safe in delivering them without your orders; but to hear the cries of the hungry, who have fled for refuge to these places, with nothing more than they carried on their backs, is exceedingly moving. I hope, therefore, that you will give directions concerning this matter.

I have written to the Assembly, setting forth the great necessity of erecting a large and strong fort at this place, to serve as a receptacle for all our stores, and a place of refuge for the women and children in times of danger. Were this work completed, the men would upon any alarm, as they say themselves, immediately lodge their families here, and turn out against the enemy. But without some such place of defence, they must always fly in the manner they have done, in order to secure their wives and children.

This is the place generally fixed upon, as it has a free and open communication with all the country, from its peculiar situation. It also secures the communication with the neighbouring colonies, and is conveniently situated for procuring intelligence. This is now fully proved by the experience I have had since I came here. From the time the first murders were committed by the Indians, I have never missed of receiving intelligence of their motions, while Colonel Stephen has, in a manner, lived in total ignorance. The reason is obvious. Fort Cumberland is detached so far beyond the inhabitants, that no person thinks of alarming it, but immediately, upon the first fright, they retire within the settlements.

You will observe some parts of Colonel Stephen's letters, about reinforcements from the second division, and the number of men, which were only meant as a finesse, in case they should fall into the enemy's hands. The letters, conveying the true accounts, were put into the pummel of the saddle, as were mine to him.

I have been formerly, and am at present, pretty full in offering my opinion and counsel upon matters, which regard the public safety and interest. These have been solely the object of all my thoughts, words, and actions;

and, in order to avoid censure in every part of my conduct, I make it a rule to obey the dictates of your Honor, the Assembly, and a good conscience.

I shall not hereafter trouble you further on these topics, as I can add nothing to what I have said.

I am your Honor's, &c.

TO GOVERNOR DINWIDDIE.

Winchester, 3 May, 1756.

SIR,

I have sent down an Indian scalp, which was taken at the place where Captain Mercer had his engagement. He was found thrust under some rocks, with stones piled up against them. They believe more were killed, from the quantity of blood found on the ground, and from other discoveries of their attempts to make more graves. But a hard shower of rain prevented their making a farther search.

We have reason to believe, that the Indians have returned to Fort Duquesne, as some scouts from Fort Cumberland saw their tracks that way; and many corroborating accounts affirm, that the roads over the Allegany Mountains are as much beaten, as they were last year by General Braddock's army. From these and other circumstances we may judge their numbers to have been considerable. Whether they are gone for the season, or only to bring in a larger party, I am at a loss to determine.

For this reason, and on account of the scarcity of provisions on this side of Fort Cumberland, I must beg leave humbly to offer it to your Honor's superior judgment, if it would not be advisable to stop all the militia, that are ordered from the ten counties, save about five or six hundred from the adjacent ones. These will serve to cover our frontiers in this quarter, (which is the only part that ever will or can be much exposed,) until the regiment is completed by drafts, and until they can erect fortresses. Drafts, if they are judiciously chosen, will be of infinitely more service, and much less expensive to the country, and they can be immediately sent to their posts.

I am convinced, that, if your Honor has a mind to stop any part of the militia, you will have full time, notwithstanding they are ordered to rendezvous at this place on the 10th instant. I never yet knew any to appear within ten days of the time they were expected; and I am also apprehensive, that having so many of the militia out will be the means of retarding the drafts, which, above all things, I wish to see completed.

Though I have often troubled you on this head, I must again beg leave to desire your particular instructions and information, as, being in a state of uncertainty, without knowing the plan of operations, or what scheme to go upon, I am much embarrassed, and left to guess at every thing. Orders, that are essential one day, appear the next as necessary to be countermanded; so that I really cannot tell how to act for the good of the service, or the satisfaction of any individual. Were the regiment complete, and things put on a proper footing, the whole would go on smoothly and regularly, which is now rendered impossible. So much am I kept in the dark, that I do not know whether to prepare for the offensive or defensive; yet, what might be absolutely necessary in the one, would be quite useless in the other.

Great inconveniences arise from our being so dispersed through the country. The men cannot be regularly paid or supplied. If every company had its proper post assigned, their pay might be sent to them, and necessaries always provided in due season. We could also have the same advantages were we collected into one place. But there are now so many detachments out, that one officer may command men of every company of the regiment, and when necessaries are sent, he may be removed from his command, and those things cannot be stopped out of their pay. By this method the country loses money, the men are badly supplied, and always discontented.

I find the act of Assembly against mutiny and desertion quite insufficient, except in those two particular crimes. No court-martial can be held, by virtue of this act, for trying any officer or soldier charged with cowardice, holding correspondence with the enemy, quitting or sleeping upon his post, nay, many other crimes, which are provided against in the articles of war. I think, at this time, it would be for the good of the service to make an act to enforce the articles of war in general, except two or three particular ones, such as impressing wagons, and the like. They are in force in our mother country, where they are thought best calculated for keeping soldiers under discipline; and none of them would prove burthensome, or inconvenient, either to the public or any individual.

About one hundred and fifty of the Fairfax militia are now in town. Three hundred are expected from Prince William. With the soldiers and militia now here, I intend to go out and scour the woods hereabouts for three or four days until the others arrive.

Clothes for the men are very much wanted. We have none in store, and some men, who have been enlisted these two months, and to whom we could give nothing but a blanket, shoes, and shirt, are justly dissatisfied at having two pence per day stopped from their wages.* Provision here is scarce, and the commissary much wanted to lay in more. I have been, and still am, obliged to do this duty, as well as most others, which I would take upon me, rather than let any thing in my power be wanted for the good of the country.

I enclose your Honor the sentence of a general court-martial, which was held here upon a sergeant for running away with his party. They have, I think, very justly adjudged him to suffer death, which sentence I hope you will approve, as there never was a fitter object to make an example of, this being the second time he has been guilty of the same crime. I am your Honor's, &c.

TO GOVERNOR DINWIDDIE.

Winchester, 23 May, 1756.

SIR,

The method I shall use to inform you of the proceedings of the militia, is to enclose a transcript of my journal relating to that affair, and to send a copy of a council of war held here by the field-officers of those counties, whose militia you were pleased to order to our assistance.†

---

* The soldiers were paid eight pence a day. Out of this amount two pence a day were reserved for supplying them with clothes.

† The militia, who had assembled at Winchester upon the recent alarm, had given the commander infinite trouble and anxiety. On this subject Colonel William Fairfax wrote to him;—

"I am sensible, that such a medley of undisciplined militia must create you various troubles, but, having Cæsar's Commentaries, and perhaps Quintus Curtius, you have therein read of greater fatigues, murmurings, mutinies, and defections, than will probably come to your share; though, if any of those casualties should interrupt your quiet, I doubt not you would bear them with a magnanimity equal to that of any of the heroes of those times.

"The Council and Burgesses are mostly your friends; so that if you

I have found it impossible to go to Fort Cumberland, without letting matters of greater importance here suffer in my absence; such a multiplicity of different kinds of business am I at present engaged in. Governor Innes is gone up, who, I hope, will assist with his advice in setting things in order, if any irregularities have been practised contrary to the rules of the army.

I have ordered a sufficient number of officers to be left at Fort Cumberland, and the rest to repair to this place, that they may proceed to Fredericksburg, agreeably to your Honor's commands. As soon as the gentlemen Associators arrive here, I shall take that place in my way to Williamsburg, to settle my accounts, and receive more money, which is already scarce with me. I am heartily glad, that you have fixed upon those gentlemen to point out the places for erecting forts, but regret to find their motions so slow.* The summer will be so

---

have not always particular instructions from the Governor, which you think necessary and desire, the omission, or neglect, may proceed from the confidence entertained in your ability and discretion to do what is fit and praiseworthy."

* These gentlemen Associators were a company of mounted volunteers, at the head of whom was Peyton Randolph, the attorney-general. They marched towards Winchester, but the alarm subsided before they had an opportunity of putting their martial spirit to the test.

Mr. Robinson, the speaker, after giving notice to Colonel Washington of the organization of this company of gentlemen volunteers, added;—"The Council and House of Burgesses have agreed on a representation to his Majesty, in which you and the other officers are recommended to his Majesty's favor. Our hopes, dear George, are all fixed on you for bringing our affairs to a happy issue."

It was probably in accordance with the above sentiment of the Council and Assembly, that the Governor wrote as follows to Major-General Abercromby, May 28th.

"As we are told the Earl of Loudoun is to raise three regiments [one regiment of four battalions] on this continent, on the British establishment, I do not venture to trouble him immediately on his arrival with any recommendations; but, good Sir, give me leave to pray your interest with his Lordship in favor of Colonel George Washington, who, I will venture to say, is a very deserving gentleman, and has from the beginning com-

far advanced, that, if we meet with opposition in conducting the work, the difficulties and delays attending the execution cannot be described.

It gave me infinite concern to be informed, that the Assembly had levied their troops until December only. By the time they will have entered into the service, they will claim a discharge. They cannot get the least smattering of their duty, and we find by experience, that our poor and ragged soldiers would kill the most active militia in five days' marching, so little are the latter acquainted with fatigue. Men would almost as soon have entered the service for seventeen months, as for seven, and in that time I am convinced we could have enlisted them upon our own terms. As it is, some perhaps may be obtained.

In a recent letter your Honor approved the scheme I sent down for forming the regiment into two battalions of twenty companies, assigning one to each of the field-officers, but never gave any directions concerning the appointments. Nor do I think there can be any plan judiciously concerted, until we know what number of forts is to be built upon our frontiers, as the number of our companies must in a great measure depend upon the divisions of the regiment. There are now several vacancies in the regiment, and I have but one blank commission. Indeed, if I had more, I should not think it prudent to fill them up, until matters are a little better regulated.

At this place I have begun the fort according to your

manded the forces of this dominion. General Braddock had so high an esteem for his merit, that he made him one of his aids-de-camp, and, if he had survived, I believe he would have provided handsomely for him in the regulars. He is a person much beloved here, and he has gone through many hardships in the service, and I really think he has great merit, and believe he can raise more men here, than any one present that I know. If his Lordship will be so good as to promote him in the British establishment, I think he will answer my recommendation." — Dinwiddie's *Letter Books*.

orders, and have found that the work could not be conducted, if I were away, which was one among many reasons, that detained me here.* I have also ordered Captain Stewart, who commands at Conococheague, to fortify that place as well as he can, with such tools as he can procure.

Mr. Dick, who is just returned from the northward, says, orders have been given for drawing out all the ammunition and other stores belonging to the train at Fort Cumberland, and to send them immediately round to New York. I have thought it expedient to give your Honor the earliest advice; for should this be done, it will leave that place entirely defenceless, and stop the source of our supplies. I have given Colonel Stephen previous notice of it, and have desired that he will induce the conductor of the train, in whose care it is left, to have Ashby's, Cox's, and the other forts plentifully furnished, before such an order arrives. I am, &c.

TO GOVERNOR DINWIDDIE.

Winchester, 25 June, 1756.

SIR,

I doubt not but your Honor will be as much surprised, as I have been concerned and vexed, at my stay here.

When I left Williamsburg, I did it with a design to proceed with the utmost expedition to Fort Cumberland. I arrived at Fredericksburg to dinner, the day after I left your Honor, at one o'clock, and gave the officer, posted at that place, a list of such tools as were wanted to build the chain of forts, and ordered them to be sent by a wagon, pressed for that purpose, immedi-

---

* This fort, built at Winchester, was called Fort Loudoun.

ately to Winchester, to which place I repaired to get every thing in readiness, and wait their coming to escort them to Fort Cumberland. I thought it needless to proceed without them, as nothing can be done for want of tools. I have sent two or three expresses to hurry them on, and shall make no delay when they arrive. I intend to take the advice of a council of war, when I arrive at Fort Cumberland, as to the line on which these forts are to be erected, and shall visit all the grounds that I conveniently can, and direct the building.

It is a work, that must be conducted tediously for these reasons, namely, the scarcity of tools, the smallness of our numbers, and the want of conductors.

The strength of our forces will not admit of many divisions, because, in that case, each party may probably be diminished. We can, therefore, only attempt, with such men as can be drawn out of the garrisons already established, to build fort after fort, and not, by attempting too many at a time, thereby run the risk of having the whole demolished. To go on in the manner above mentioned must be extremely tedious, unless you will be pleased to put the militia upon our southern frontiers under the command of Captain Hogg, and order them to begin on the Mayo River, and proceed in their building until they meet our parties, who will advance southward. I can point out no other method at present to expedite this necessary work.

If you approve this scheme, and will let me know it by an express, I shall despatch another with the information to Captain Hogg, and enclose to him such a plan, as the whole will be directed by. Your orders to the militia, and indeed to the inhabitants of these parts, to assist with their advice in fixing upon the places, and with their labor in forwarding the work, are absolutely necessary.

Your Honor never gave me a decisive answer to a question I asked, about assigning companies to the field-officers. For this reason I have presumed to repeat it again, because there are two companies now vacant, by the death of Captain John Mercer, and the resignation of Captain Savage, and they should either be given to field-officers, or to the oldest lieutenants. No advantage can possibly arise to the field-officers from having companies, since they are allowed, I suppose, the same pay now, as they would receive in such a case.

Two hundred and forty-six drafts are the total number brought in. Of these several have deserted. Three were discharged, being quite unfit for service, (and indeed several more ought to be discharged, if men were not so scarce,) and there remain now in confinement six Quakers, who will neither bear arms, work, receive provisions or pay, nor do any thing that tends, in any respect, to self-defence. I should be glad of your directions how to proceed with them. I cannot yet return to you the names of the volunteers, that will be appointed to the vacancies, but as soon as I arrive at Fort Cumberland I shall acquaint you according to request.

Governor Sharpe is building a fort on Potomac River, about fifteen miles above Conococheague, which may be of great service towards the protection of our people on that side. It is thought the fort will cost the province of Maryland near thirty thousand pounds, before it is finished. I am, &c.*

---

* The Governor and Assembly of Maryland had come at last to a temporary reconciliation of their differences, so far as to agree in a bill for raising forty thousand pounds for his Majesty's service. Of this sum eleven thousand pounds were to be appropriated to building a fort on the frontiers, near but not beyond the North Mountain; and twenty-five thousand for carrying on any expedition for the public service, in which the other colonies might join. By the same act the Governor was authorized to raise two hundred men, to be employed in constructing the fort. — *Acts*

TO GOVERNOR DINWIDDIE.

Winchester, 4 August, 1756.

SIR,

Giving the necessary orders and directions, about the chain of forts to be built on the frontiers, has kept me so closely employed, that I could not write fully to you until this time. But I have got that trouble now pretty well off my hands, as I have despatched orders, plans, and tools to all the officers appointed to that duty.

By the enclosed proceedings of a council held at Fort Cumberland, you will see our determination, and where it is necessary to erect the forts. Although we have not kept strictly to the act of Assembly, I hope it will be overlooked, as I am sensible that this will be the best chain that can possibly be erected for the defence of the people, and that the Assembly aimed at that, but, being unacquainted with the situation of the country, had fallen into an error.*

---

of Assembly passed in May, 1756. — McMahon's *History of Maryland*, Vol. I. p. 305. — The fort was called FORT FREDERIC. It was a work of considerable magnitude, situated on an eminence about five hundred yards from the Potomac River, of a quadrangular form, and constructed of durable materials. Parts of it still remain, in a state of good preservation, surrounded by cultivated fields, and the triumphs of industry, which three quarters of a century have effected in one of the most beautiful and fertile regions of the western world.

* Soon after writing the letter of June 25th, Colonel Washington went to Fort Cumberland, where he remained several days, making arrangements and giving orders for constructing the chain of forts, which was to extend southward along the South Branch of the Potomac, till it reached the head waters of Jackson's River, and thence down that river. The gentlemen Associators were to have had some voice in this matter, as intimated heretofore, but their military ardor seems to have subsided, and their resolution to have abated, before they reached Colonel Washington's camp. The direction of the chain, and the position of the principal forts, were determined by a council of officers at Fort Cumberland. The act of Assembly specified certain localities, which the Council decided to be in-

I make no doubt, that you have ere this heard of the defeat of Lieutenant Rutherford of the Rangers, escorting an express to me at Fort Cumberland, and of the dastardly behaviour of the militia, who ran off without one half of them having discharged their pieces, although they were apprised of the ambuscade by one of the flanking parties, before the Indians fired upon them; and ran back to Ashby's Fort, contrary to orders, persuasions, and threats. They are all ordered in, as soon as the people have secured their harvest. Those of King George and Caroline counties are already here. The rest I expect shortly. Through the passive behaviour of their officers they are very refractory.

---

expedient or impracticable.—Hening's *Laws of Virginia*, Vol. VII. p. 18. — The chain was built according to the decisions of the Council.

The following extract from the *Orderly Book*, issued in general orders by the Commander two days after he reached Fort Cumberland, will show that he enforced rigid rules of discipline.

"Colonel Washington has observed, that the men of his regiment are very profane and reprobate. He takes this opportunity to inform them of his great displeasure at such practices, and assures them, that, if they do not leave them off, they shall be severely punished. The officers are desired, if they hear any man swear, or make use of an oath or execration, to order the offender twenty-five lashes immediately, without a court-martial. For the second offence, he will be more severely punished."

To a captain he also wrote, about the same time;—"Your suffering such clamors among the men argues very great remissness in you. I imagined your being put there over them was partly with an intent to keep them quiet and passive, but this express, sent purely to humor them, would indicate that you are afraid to do your duty. Let me tell you, in your own words, that 'I was very much surprised' at the contents of your letter, written in such a commanding style. And your demands were so express and peremptory, that the direction was the only thing, which gave me the least room to suspect it could be written to any but John Roe, or some other of your menial servants.

"I am sorry to find your conduct so disagreeable to all the officers, as to occasion two, who were appointed to your company, to resign. I must therefore desire you will act circumspectly, as I assure you, if I have any just complaints made against you, you may expect to answer them."

This captain was much older in years, than the Commander-in-chief, and had probably taken some liberties on that ground.

Again, to another captain he wrote;—"You are to acquaint Mr. L. that

There is an act of Parliament to allow all servants to enlist, and the owners to be paid a reasonable allowance for them. If we had this privilege, we could soon complete the regiment; and I doubt not but his Majesty would order them to be paid for, if we enlisted them, as soon as for the regulars; nay, should he not, the ten pounds' fine through the country would go a considerable way towards it. And this we may depend upon, if we have not this liberty granted us, the servants will all run off to the regular officers, who are recruiting around us; and that would be to weaken our colony much, when it could receive no immediate benefit from it. For my part, I see no other expedient.*

---

he is to remain at his fort, and act as lieutenant of the Rangers, until further orders. Tell him, also, not to stir from his post at his peril, until he has leave; if he does, I will arrest him for his disobedience of orders, and try him as soon as he arrives here."

* The servants mentioned in this paragraph were emigrants from Europe, or persons imported, whose services were purchased for a term of years, either from the masters of vessels, who brought them over, or from the individuals themselves. By a law of Virginia, all servants, except convicts, imported without indenture, if they were Christians or of Christian parentage, and above nineteen years of age, could be required to serve only five years; if under nineteen, their term of service was limited to the age of twenty-four. No such person could ever be sold as a slave. — Hening, Vol. VI. p. 356. These servants were exempt from military duty.

When Lord Loudoun succeeded Governor Shirley, as commander of the forces in America, he was empowered to raise a regiment in the colonies, consisting of four battalions, to be commanded by officers bearing the King's commission, and called the *Royal American Regiment.* He was authorized, also, to enlist servants of the above description, paying to their masters a proper compensation for the time they had yet to serve. Recruiting officers were now employed in Virginia, enlisting men for the *Royal Regiment*, and interfered essentially with the enlistments for the service of the colony. The Governor endeavoured to prevail on the Assembly to draft militia for this regiment, but without success. They voted eight thousand pounds to be paid for enlisting men, and transporting them to New York. — Dinwiddie's *Letter-Books.*

The Maryland Assembly appropriated five thousand pounds to aid enlistments in that colony for the *Royal Regiment*, and resolved to raise three hundred men. A bounty was given not exceeding five pounds for each man enlisted. A letter was received by the Governor from Henry Fox

You perceive plainly what effect the act of Assembly, in regard to the drafts, has had, and how little our strength has been augmented by that scheme, and in three or four months we shall not be the better for them. They are then to be discharged.

I could wish we were clear of Fort Cumberland. It takes a great part of our small force to garrison it, and I see no service that it renders to our colony; for since the Indians have driven the inhabitants so low down, they do not hesitate to follow them as far as Conococheague and this place. There have been several families murdered within two miles of the mouth of Conococheague, on the Maryland side, this week; and Fort Cumberland is now so much out of the way, that the forces there seldom hear of those things within a month after they are done.

Our men want many necessaries, until the arrival of their regimentals, which cannot be had without sending to Philadelphia; and the great loss, which we shall suffer by sending our paper money for them, has prevented my purchasing them, until the men are almost naked.

I could by no means bring the Quakers to any terms. They chose rather to be whipped to death than to bear arms, or lend us any assistance whatever upon the fort, or any thing for self-defence. Some of their friends

---

one of his Majesty's principal Secretaries of State, directing that the compensation to masters for enlisted servants should be paid by the colony; but the Assembly refused to comply with this order by a majority of more than two to one.— See *Votes and Proceedings for September*, 1756.

The "*ten pounds' fine*," spoken of in the text, was the penalty imposed on such of the drafted militia as refused to march. This fine was so low, that many of the drafts preferred to pay it, and stay at home.

Governor Dinwiddie said in reply;—"If you can enlist servants agreeably to the act of Parliament, the masters of such servants shall be paid for the time they have to serve in proportion to the first purchase, but I think you should be careful not to enlist any convicts, who probably may be factious and bad examples to the others."

have been security for their appearance, when they shall be called for; and I have released them from the guard-house until I receive further orders from you, which they have agreed to apply for.

I have supplied the Nottoway Indians with some necessaries, and allowed them to take their arms with them; but they have received no pay, and they say they were promised a bit* per day. Captain Tom has promised to go to the Tuscaroras with a speech and wampum, which I have given him. He says they have a hundred fighting-men to spare. They would be a great assistance to us, if they could be engaged to come.

I observe your proposal to Lord Loudoun of carrying on an expedition against the Ohio. I have always thought it the best and only method to put a stop to the incursions of the enemy, as they would then be obliged to stay at home to defend their own possessions. But we are quite unprepared for such an undertaking. If it is fixed upon, now is the time for buying up provisions, and laying them in at the most convenient places. The Pennsylvania butchers are buying quantities of beef here, which should be put a stop to, if we are to march towards the Ohio. If we are still to remain on the defensive, and garrison the chain of forts, provisions must be laid in at each of them; and I much fear, if we march from the frontiers, all the inhabitants will quit their plantations. Your sentiments and orders on this head will be very agreeable to me, and shall be punctually complied with. I am, &c.

---

* A small piece of silver, probably the Spanish eighth of a dollar, or twelve cents and a half.

TO JOHN ROBINSON, SPEAKER AND TREASURER.

Winchester, 5 August, 1756.

SIR,

Fort Cumberland at present contains all our provisions and valuable stores, and is not capable of an hour's defence, if the enemy were only to bring a single half-pounder against it; which they might do with great ease on horseback. Besides, it lies so remote from this place, as well as from the neighbouring inhabitants, that it requires as much force to keep the communication open to it, as a fort at the Meadows would do, and employs one hundred and fifty men, who are a dead charge to the country, as they can be of no other use than just to protect and guard the stores, which might as well be lodged at Cox's Fort;* indeed better, for they would then be more contiguous to this place, to the inhabitants, and to the enemy, and more serviceable, if we should ever carry an expedition over the mountains, by opening a road where the Indians have blazed.† A strong garrison there would not only protect the stores, but also the few remaining inhabitants on the Branch,‡ and at the same time waylay and annoy the enemy, as they pass and repass the mountains. Whereas, the forces at Fort Cumberland, lying in a corner quite remote from the inhabited parts, to which the Indians always repair to commit their murders, can have no intelligence of any thing that is doing, but remain in total ignorance of all transactions. When I was down, I applied to the Governor for his particular and positive directions in this

* This fort was on Patterson's Creek, twenty-five miles from Fort Cumberland.

† The Indians and first settlers mark a path through the woods by cutting the bark from the trees. This is called *blazing*.

‡ The South Branch of the Potomac.

affair. The following is an exact copy of his answer.—"Fort Cumberland is a King's fort, and built chiefly at the charge of the colony, therefore properly under our direction, until a governor is appointed." Now whether I am to understand this ay or no, to the plain, simple question asked,—"Is the fort to be continued or removed?"—I know not. But in all important matters, I am directed in this ambiguous and uncertain way.*

Great and inconceivable difficulties arise in the execution of my commands, as well as infinite loss and disrepute to the service, by my not having power to pay for deserters. I would, therefore, humbly recommend it to the consideration of the Committee, whether it would not be more for the interest of the country, were I allowed to pay these demands, rather than have them levied in the public claims. Many of our deserters are apprehended in Maryland, and some in Pennsylvania, and, for the sake of the reward, are brought hither. But since they, who apprehend them, are to receive certificates only, that they are entitled to two hundred pounds of tobacco, and those certificates are to be presented to a court of claims, there to lie perhaps till they are quite forgotten, so much dissatisfaction is created, that many, I believe, rather than apprehend one, would aid fifty to escape, and this, too, among our own people.

Another thing, which I should be glad to know, is, whether the act of Assembly prohibits the whole forces, or only the drafts, from marching out of Virginia, and whether it is contrary to law, even to take the drafts out, provided it is done with their own consent. If we can-

* On this head Mr. Speaker Robinson replied;—"The Committee were all in opinion with you, that the keeping of Fort Cumberland was an unnecessary expense; but upon my mentioning their opinion to the Governor, he appeared very warm, and said Lord Loudoun might do what he pleased, but for his part he would not remove the garrison, nor order the fort to be demolished."

not take any of the forces out of the colony, the disadvantages, which the country may labor under, are not to be described; for the enemy, in that case, may commit the most unheard-of cruelties, and, by stepping across the Potomac, evade pursuit, and mock our best endeavours to scourge them.

The inconveniences that arise from paying the soldiers in large bills, are not to be conceived. We are obliged to give the pay of two or three soldiers to one man. He, ten to one, drinks, games, or pays it away; by which means the parties are all dissatisfied, and perpetually complaining for want of their pay. It also prevents them from laying out their pay for absolute necessaries, and obliges them many times to drink it out; for they put it into the tavern-keeper's hands, who will give no change, unless they will consent to receive the greatest part in liquor. In short, for five shillings cash you may at any time purchase a month's pay from the soldiers; in such contempt do they hold the currency. Besides small bills, if the thing is practicable, I should be extremely glad to receive some part of the money in Spanish and Portugal gold and silver. Many things are wanted for the use of the regiment, which cannot be had here, and may be obtained at Philadelphia; but the depreciation of our money, out of the colony, has prevented my sending thither.

At the repeated instances of the soldiers, I must pay so much regard to their representations, as to transmit their complaints. They think it extremely hard, as it is indeed, Sir, that they, who perhaps do more duty, and undergo more fatigue and hardship, from the nature of the service and situation of the country, than any other troops on the continent, should be allowed the least pay, and smallest encouragements in other respects. The Carolinians receive British pay; the Marylanders, I believe, the same; Pennsylvania is exorbitant in rewarding her soldiers; as to the Jerseys and New York, I am not informed; but the New England governments give more than a shilling per day, our money, besides an allowance of rum, pease, tobacco, vinegar, ginger, and the like.

Our soldiers complain, that their pay is insufficient, even to furnish shoes, shirts, and stockings, which their officers, in order to keep them fit for duty, oblige them to provide. This, they say, deprives them of the means of purchasing any of the conveniences or necessaries of life, and compels them to drag through a disagreeable service, in the most disagreeable manner. That their pay will not afford more than enough to keep them in clothes, I should be convinced for these reasons, if experience had not taught me. The British soldiers are allowed eight pence sterling per day, with many necessaries that ours are not, and can buy what is requisite upon the cheapest terms; and they lie one half the year in camp, or garrison, when they cannot consume the fifth part of what ours do in continual marches over mountains, rocks, and rivers. Then, Sir, is it possible that our men, who receive a fourth less, have two pence per day stopped for their regimental clothing, and all other stoppages made that British soldiers have, and are obliged, by being in continual action, to lay in triple the quantity of ammunition and clothes, and at double the price, should be able to clear themselves? It is not to be done, and this is the reason why the men have always been so bare of clothes.

And I dare say you will be candid enough to allow, that few men would choose to have their lives exposed to the incessant insults of a merciless enemy, without some view or hope of a reward. Another thing gives them great uneasiness, and that is, seeing no regular provision made for the maimed and wounded. They acknowledge the generosity of the Assembly, and have the highest veneration for that respectable House; they look with gratitude on the care, which has been taken of their brother soldiers; but they say, this is only an act of will, and another Assembly may be much less liberal. They have no certainty, that this generosity will continue, and consequently can have nothing in view but the most gloomy prospects, and no encouragement to be bold and active; for as soon as they become unfit for service by their wounds, they may be discharged, and turned upon an uncharitable world to beg, steal, or starve. In short, they have a true sense of all that can happen, and do not think slightly of the fatigues they encounter, in scouring these mountains with their provisions on their backs, lying out and watching for the enemy, with no other covering to shelter them from the inclemency of the weather, than the trees and rocks. The old soldiers are affected, and complain of their hardships and little encouragement in piteous terms; and they give these as reasons for so much desertion. The money expended in paying for deserters, expresses, horse-hire, losses and abuse of horses, would go a great length towards advancing their pay, which I hope would contribute not a little to remove the cause of this expense.

I would not have it understood, however, that I mean to recommend any thing extraordinary; no, I would give them British pay, and allow them the same privileges during their stay in the service, and this as a reward or compliment for their toil, rather than a matter of right. Were the country to give them one suit of regimental clothes a year, without receiving the two pence stoppage, it would be a full allowance, and cause great content and satisfaction. All they want is to be entitled to the privileges and immunities of soldiers, of which they are well informed, by some who have been a number of years in the army. They would then think it no hardship to be subject to the punishments and fatigues. Were this done, and an order given by the Committee empowering me to provide for them, according to the rules and customs of the army, I then should know what I am about. I could do it without hesitation or fear, and, I am convinced, to the satisfaction and interest of the country. As the case now stands, we are upon such an odd establishment, under such uncertain regulations, and subject to so much inconvenience, that I am wandering in a wilderness of difficulties, and am ignorant of the ways to extricate myself, and to act for the satisfaction of the country, the soldiers, or myself. Having no certain rules for the direction of my conduct, I am afraid to turn to this hand or to that, lest it should be censured. If such an order, as I before spoke of, were to issue from your Board, I would then immediately provide upon the best terms a quantity of all kinds of ammunition and clothes for the use of the regiment, and deliver them out to each company, as their wants required, taking care to deduct the value of all such things from their pay. By these means the soldiers would be always provided and fit for duty, and would do it cheerfully, and the country sustain no other loss, than advancing the money for a few months to lay in those stores, as this money would always be restored by the soldiers again.*

I have hitherto been afraid to advance any sums of money for this salutary purpose, and have always bought the articles at extravagant prices, and been obliged to send to different parts, ere they could be had, which

* These requests, in regard to the soldiers, were so far complied with, that they afterwards received full pay without any stoppage for their clothing.

has also contributed to cause the nakedness of the soldiers. The officers are almost as uneasy and dispirited as the men, doing every part of duty with languor and indifference. When ordered to provide themselves with suitable necessaries, they complain of an uncertain establishment, and the probability of being disbanded, and the things rendered useless. So that I really and most heartily wish for a change. The surgeon has entreated me to mention his case, which I shall do by enclosing his letters. He has behaved extremely well, and discharged his duty, in every capacity, since he came to the regiment. He has long discovered an inclination to quit the service, the encouragement being so small; and I believe he would have done it, had not the officers, to show their regard and willingness to detain him, subscribed each one day's pay in every month. This, as they are likely to be so much dispersed, and can receive no benefit from him, they intend to withdraw, and therefore he begs me to solicit the gentlemen of the Committee in his behalf; otherwise he will be obliged to seek some other method of getting his livelihood.

I beg, Sir, with very great earnestness, that the gentlemen of the Committee will communicate their sentiments fully upon all these several matters, and approve or disapprove every thing therein. I only wait to know their intention, and then to act in strict conformity with it.

If the Committee find my account satisfactory and distinct, as I have no doubt they will, it would be conferring a great obligation, if they would make a final settlement to that date, and begin a new account, as it would be the means of keeping matters more clear and intelligible hereafter. Long accounts, and references to doubtful points, instead of gaining any light, are but darkened and confused by procrastination. The late regulation of our companies will occasion more regularity in the paymaster's account, and be more satisfactory in every shape, for the future. Besides, the gentlemen of the Committee will find little trouble, or difficulty, in looking over a short account, kept in a regular method, plain and perspicuous, which is the very life of business.

I would again entreat your regard to my request, for these and many other reasons.

I am, dear Sir, yours, &c.

TO GOVERNOR DINWIDDIE.

Winchester, 14 August, 1756.

Sir,

The return of the express, that came with the account of La Force's escape, (for which accident I am extremely concerned, and fear its consequences if he is not retaken,) affords me an opportunity to inform you of some occurrences, which have happened since my last.*

Repeated complaints and applications from all quarters for men, but more especially from the garrisons, which secure the communication with Fort Cumberland, obliged me to order a company from Captain Wag-

* La Force, it will be remembered, was one of the prisoners taken in the skirmish with Jumonville's party. He was capable, enterprising, active, and had been instrumental, before his capture, in exciting the Indians to commit depredations on the frontiers. This was deemed a sufficient reason, by the Governor of Virginia, for retaining him in custody, contrary to the articles of capitulation at the Great Meadows. He was thrown into the jail at Williamsburg. From this abode, after more than two years' confinement, he had the address to escape, but was seized before he had advanced far into the country, remanded to prison, and loaded with irons.

gener's detachment (for none else could spare a man) to reinforce and enable those garrisons to send escorts with wagons and expresses, going to and returning from that fort. Captain Waggener's command was thus reduced to a number insufficient to disperse parties among the settlers, and retain a strength to conduct the building of the forts. The grand point then turned on this; whether he was to neglect the inhabitants and build the forts, or neglect the forts and protect the inhabitants.

His council were of the latter opinion unanimously, and sent to know my sentiments, which I own corresponded with theirs, and for these reasons. First, I look upon it, that the protection of the inhabitants was the motive for ordering these forts; and to lose them, while we are at work, would be perverting the intention. Secondly, we have built some forts and altered others, as far south on the Potomac waters as any settlers have been molested; and there only remains one body of inhabitants, at a place called the Upper Tract, who need a guard. Thither I have ordered a party. Beyond this, if I am not misinformed, there is nothing but a continued series of mountains uninhabited, until we get over to the waters of James River, not far from the fort, which takes its name from your Honor; and thence to Mayo River. Captain Hogg, by your orders, is to have the direction. If I have done amiss, in not adhering to the letter of the law, I hope you will intimate the same, and give directions how I am to proceed.

Two or three men have been killed and scalped at different places, since my last, though every precaution has been taken to prevent it. The fatiguing service, low pay, and great hardships in which our men have been engaged, cause, notwithstanding the greatest care and vigilance to the contrary, great and scandalous desertions. Yesterday I received an account, from Captain Stewart, of sixteen men deserting in a party. Frequently two or three went off before, as they have done from this place. We never fail to pursue, and use all possible means to apprehend them; but seldom with success, as they are generally aided and assisted by the inhabitants. Two parties are now in pursuit of these fellows, who have made towards the northward to enlist with the recruiting officers in Pennsylvania. Unless a stop can be put to it, I fear we shall lose numbers of our men.

A report prevailed in town yesterday, said to come from a man, who had it from a person that was at Governor Morris's treaty with the Indians, and heard them say, that a large body composed of different nations, and headed by some French, intended to attack Fort Cumberland this fall. Reports of this kind often take rise without good foundation; yet, as this is an affair of great importance, the slightest intelligence ought not to be discountenanced, especially when we consider that our provision, and, what is still more valuable, all our ammunition and stores, are lodged in that defenceless place. The consequence of a successful enterprise of this sort, and the absolute impossibility (considering the weakness of the place, badness of situation, and division of our force) of preventing its falling, are, without previous notice, motives sufficient for apprehending the worst. Therefore, notwithstanding I enlarged upon this subject in a former letter, I think it my duty to hint it again, and to ask directions how I am to proceed.

It is true, I give no credit to this intelligence, because I flatter myself such important information as this would be communicated, in the most distinct and expeditious manner, by Governor Morris; yet, it being an expedition they cannot fail of succeeding in, what should deter them from attempting it? We have certain advice, that two of our deserters have reached Fort Duquesne, who were heard to speak in high terms, before they escaped, of the reward that would be got for communicating the weakness of the works and garrison at Fort Cumberland.

As a general meeting of all the persons concerned in the estate of my deceased brother* is appointed to be held at Alexandria, about the middle of September next, for making a final settlement of all his affairs, and as I am very deeply interested, not only as an executor, and heir of part of his estate, but also in a very important dispute, subsisting between Colonel Lee, who married the widow, and my brothers and self, concerning a devise in the will, which brings the whole personal estate in question, — I say, as this is a matter of very great moment to me, I hope your Honor will readily consent to my attending this meeting, provided no disadvantage is likely to arise during my absence; in which case, I shall not offer to quit my command.

If war is to be declared at this place, I should be glad if your Honor would direct the manner. I know there is ceremony required, but the order I am ignorant of.†

I am, &c.

---

* Lawrence Washington.

† This alludes to the formal declaration of war against France, the intelligence of which had but recently arrived in America. Governor Dinwiddie answered; — "The method, by which you are to declare war, is at the head of your companies, with three volleys of small arms for his Majesty's health and a successful war."

TO LORD FAIRFAX.*

Winchester, 29 August, 1756.

My Lord,

It is with infinite concern, that I see the distresses of the people, and hear their complaints, without being able to afford them relief. I have so often troubled you for aid from the militia, that I am almost ashamed to repeat my demands; nor should I do it again, did I not think it absolutely necessary at this time to save the

---

* Thomas, the sixth Lord Fairfax, possessed by inheritance a large tract of land in what was called the Northern Neck of Virginia, between the Potomac and Rappahannoc Rivers, estimated to contain five millions seven hundred thousand acres. For a time he employed his relative, William Fairfax, as agent to manage these lands, and, about the year 1739, he came himself over to Virginia. He stayed a year, and went back to England. Four years afterwards, that is, in 1745, he returned to Virginia, where he passed the remainder of his days. He resided several years in the family of Mr. William Fairfax, at Belvoir. At length he determined to establish himself on the western side of the Blue Ridge, where he built a house, called Greenway Court, a few miles from Winchester, laid out a beautiful farm, and put it under high cultivation. Here he lived in the exercise of a plain but generous and elegant hospitality till his death, which happened in January or February, 1782, in his ninety-second year.

In this retreat Lord Fairfax devoted himself to the management of the large tracts of land, of which he was the proprietor, and also to the discharge of such public offices, as rendered him useful to his neighbourhood. He was lieutenant of the county of Frederic, presided in the county courts at Winchester, and was overseer of the public roads. He was remarked for some peculiar traits of character, and was fond of the chase and other active amusements; but his mind was highly cultivated, and his literary taste and accomplishments were considerable. As a proof of this, it is enough to refer to Dr. Burnaby's statement, who says, that in his youthful days he was a contributor to the SPECTATOR. He was greatly esteemed by his intimate friends, and died much lamented.

His barony descended to his only surviving brother, Robert Fairfax, who was the seventh Lord Fairfax, and who died at Leeds Castle, in England, 1791. The title next fell upon Bryan Fairfax, of Towlston Hall, in Virginia, who was the eighth and last Lord Fairfax, and who died August 7th, 1802, at the age of seventy-five. During the latter years of his life, he was a clergyman of the Episcopal Church. — Burnaby's *Travels in America*, 3d edition, p. 159.

most valuable and flourishing part of this county from immediate desertion. And how soon the remaining part, as well as the adjacent counties, may share the same fate, is but too obvious to reason, and to your Lordship's good sense. The whole settlement of Conococheague in Maryland is fled, and there now remain only two families from thence to Fredericktown, which is several miles below the Blue Ridge. We are thus quite exposed, and have no better security on that side, than the Potomac River, for many miles below the Shenandoah; and how great a security that is to us, may easily be discerned, when we consider, with what facility the enemy have passed and repassed it already. That the Maryland settlements are all abandoned is certainly a fact, as I have had the accounts transmitted to me by several hands, and confirmed yesterday by Henry Brinker, who left Monocosy the day before, and who also affirms, that three hundred and fifty wagons had passed that place to avoid the enemy, within the space of three days.

I thought it expedient to communicate this intelligence, that your Lordship may know the reasons for asking succours for these unhappy people, and how absolutely necessary it is to use, without delay, such vigorous measures as will save that settlement from total desolation.

We see, my Lord, the absurdity of the people's arguments, and the consequences of leaving one county, nay, one part of a county, or, to go still farther, a single company, that is more exposed than another, to defend itself and the parts in danger. When Hampshire was invaded, and called on Frederic for assistance, the people of the latter refused their aid, answering, "Let them defend themselves, as we shall do if they come to us." Now that the enemy have forced through that county, and begin to infest this, those a little removed from danger are equally infatuated; and it will thus be, I fear, until all in turn fall a sacrifice to an insulting and merciless enemy.

These observations may be improperly offered to your Lordship, but they occur in so strong a light to me, that I could not resist the impulse to make them. I am so weak-handed here, that I cannot, without stopping the public works, spare a man to these people's assistance. Yet I look upon the retaining of them to be so essential to the well-being of the county in general, that I have ordered all the men, that can possibly be spared, to march thitherwards; and they will accordingly set out to-morrow morning, to remain there until your Lordship can relieve them, that they may return to these works, which in my opinion are of no little importance to the safety of the county, if we should be attacked by numbers, as we have reason to apprehend. I hope your Lordship will exert your authority in raising men for this salutary end, and that you will think it advisable to make every company furnish its quota. This will remove the complaints of the people below, who say they cannot leave their families to the mercy of the enemy, while they are scouring the woods.

This is the reason given by some why Caton's party consists of but ten men, while others say it proceeds from dislike to the man. I acquainted the Governor with your Lordship's order for raising fifty men for this service, who approved it, and has been pleased to direct me to continue them as long as I see cause.

I cannot conclude without again mentioning how agreeable it would be, if your Lordship would order a party immediately to those parts, that I may withdraw my men to their duty at this place.

I am, my Lord, &c.

TO GOVERNOR DINWIDDIE.

Mount Vernon, 23 September, 1756.

SIR,

Under your kind indulgence I came to this place a few days ago, expecting to meet the executors of my deceased brother, in order to make a final settlement of his affairs. I was disappointed in this design, by the Assembly having called away the principal persons concerned.

I shall remark, in obedience to your request, such things relating to the Virginia regiment as occur to me now, and require the Assembly's attention; and if any thing further presents itself, I shall communicate it from Winchester, for which place I shall set out this afternoon. I have often urged, for one thing, the necessity of enforcing the articles of war in all their parts, where it is not incompatible with the nature of this service. I have been surprised, as often as I have reflected upon this subject, and really cannot devise any reason, why the Assembly should be so much averse to fixed rules for the regulation of their forces, of which long experience in established armies fully evinces the necessity. My surprise is yet increased, when I consider how cautiously worded the act of Parliament is, to preserve the rights and liberties of the people against the arbitrary proceedings of the military officers.

We are under a kind of regulation at present, that renders command extremely difficult and precarious, as no crimes, I believe, are particularly noticed in the act of Assembly, except mutiny and desertion, notwithstanding there are many others equally punishable by act of Parliament.

One thing more, which particularly requires attention, is the billeting, quartering, and dieting of soldiers upon the inhabitants, which in many cases cannot be avoided.

I have, in several letters to your Honor, expressed my opinion with candor and freedom, about the situation, works, and garrison at Fort Cumberland. I shall, nevertheless, as you command me to lay before you such things as require the Assembly's notice, repeat on this occasion my fears once more for that place, that I may avoid, if any accident should happen to it, the malicious reflections, which inseparably attend misfortunes of this kind. I have upon all occasions said, that Fort Cumberland is a place of no strength, and never can be tenable from the badness of the ground. It is far remote from any of our inhabitants, exposed to the insults of the enemy, contains all our valuable stores (save what I have removed to Winchester), and a garrison of one hundred and seventy men, which is too large a number to be spared from other places, merely to defend the stores at this, and too small to afford detachments to waylay and surprise the enemy. I shall, therefore, beg leave to observe, in regard to Fort Cumberland, that if it is continued, we must be confined to act defensively, and keep our forces dispersed as they now are. The place must be fortified with strong works, or else it will inevitably fall, garrison and stores, into the enemy's hands. I enclose Colonel Stephen's letter on this head, in answer to one I wrote to him.

I did, from the beginning, express my sentiments against having small garrisons in a chain of forts along our frontiers. We have a frontier of such immense extent, that to build forts at convenient distances would employ such numbers of men, and divide our troops into such trifling parties, that no one part could defend itself, much less the inhabitants, were the country invaded.

The most effectual way that I can see, though none

can answer while we act defensively, is to have no more than three or four large, strong forts, built at convenient distances, upon our frontiers; in which strong garrisons must be maintained, that parties able to cope with the enemy may be sent out, and these parties kept in constant succession ranging and scouring the country. Here a difficulty will arise, as others will in every defensive plan, that can be offered. How are these ranging parties, sent out in this manner, and probably remaining on the scout from ten to fourteen days, to be supplied with provisions, the inhabitants being so thinly settled, and the forts so far extended? The difficulty is great, yet not sufficient to render this plan inferior to the former. For in the other case, when the enemy is heard of, the garrison can only send out parties, more fit to reconnoitre than oppose. These parties, if they prove too small (which in all probability they may), are certain of falling a prey to the enemy, whose numbers cannot be known until thus proved. I could urge many things more on this head, but believe it useless. What I have already said, I hope, is sufficient to give your Honor a hint of the matter, and that is all I aim at. We may form many schemes to defend ourselves, but experience will show, that none but removing the cause of the difficulties will prove effectual. Unless the Assembly concerts some measures to augment their force, the country, I fear, must inevitably fall. The frontiers, within twelve months, have been totally deserted for fifty miles and upwards from north to south, and all below that distance greatly thinned by the removal of numbers; occasioned in some measure by Maryland and Pennsylvania giving ground so much faster than we do, which exposes a very fine country of ours on that side, as low as Monocosy in Maryland, several miles on this side of the Blue Ridge.

I believe I might also add, that no person, who regards his character, will undertake a command without the means of preserving it; since his conduct is culpable for all misfortunes, and never right but when successful.

I cannot think any number under two thousand men sufficient to cover our extensive frontiers, and with that number it would be impossible to prevent misfortunes, however easy the world may think it. What means can be used to raise these men, I know not, unless the enlisting of servants is thought expedient; and that alone will prove ineffectual. Some determination should be had about the ranging companies. Under what regulations those are in Augusta, and what service they have done the country, I know not. Those in this quarter have done little, and both companies amount to about thirty men only at this time. I apprehend it will be thought advisable to keep a garrison always at Fort Loudoun; for which reason I would beg leave to represent the number of tippling-houses in Winchester as a great nuisance to the soldiers, who, by this means, in despite of the utmost care and vigilance, are, so long as their pay holds out, incessantly drunk, and unfit for service.

The rates of their liquor are immoderately high, and the publicans throughout the country charge one shilling a meal, currency, for soldier's diet; and the country only allows the recruiting officer eight pence a day for the maintenance of a soldier, by which means he loses in proportion as he obtains men, which is much complained of, and is in reality a discouraging circumstance demanding redress. The want of a chaplain, I humbly conceive, reflects dishonor on the regiment, as all other officers are allowed. The gentlemen of the corps are sensible of this, and proposed to support one at their private expense. But I think it would have a more graceful appearance were he appointed as others are. I could wish some method were practised to bring the commonalty acquainted with the laws against entertaining deserters, and to enforce those laws.

An officer of the *American Regiment* is recruiting at Alexandria, and purposes to go through the country, and pass into Carolina. He has enlisted some servants, and intends to take all he can meet with. This, I believe, may evince the necessity of our following his example, otherwise we shall suffer our colony to be weakened without receiving any immediate advantage; though I imagine the expense will be nearly the same to the country, whether they are in the King's or country's service.

I am, with all due respect, your Honor's, &c.

TO GOVERNOR DINWIDDIE.

Halifax, 10 October, 1756.

SIR,

This day within five miles of the Carolina line, as I was proceeding to the southernmost fort in Halifax, I met Major Lewis on his return from the Cherokees, with seven men and three women only of that nation. The causes of this unhappy disappointment I have desired him to communicate, that you may take measures accordingly.* This account is sent by express, to give the earliest notice while the Assembly is sitting.

I shall defer going into a particular detail of my observations on the situation of our frontiers, until I return to Winchester, as I expect by that time to be more inti-

* There had been sanguine expectations, that four hundred Cherokee Indians would join the Virginia forces; and it was supposed, that Major Lewis would return with that number.

mately acquainted with the unhappy circumstances of the people. Yet I shall not omit mentioning some occurrences, which have happened in my tour to this place. I wrote to you from Winchester, that I should set out the next day for Augusta. I accordingly did so, September 29th, with Captain McNeil; and hearing at the Court-House, that the Indians still continued their depredations, although not so openly as at first, I applied to Colonel Stewart, then present, to raise a party of the militia, and proposed to head them myself, march to Jackson's River, scour the woods, and, if possible, fall in with the enemy. He gave me very little encouragement to expect any men, yet desired I would wait four days, till Monday, and he would use his endeavours to collect a body. Until Tuesday I waited, and only five men appeared. This being too inconsiderable a number to expose to a triumphant enemy, I was advised to apply to Colonel Buchanan for men, between whom and Colonel Stewart there was contention about command.

Colonel Buchanan resided at Luney's Ferry, on James River, sixty miles along the road to Vass's, on the Roanoke, where Captain Hogg was building a fort, and to which place I intended to proceed, if I could get men to range along the frontiers with me. I set out immediately for his house, attended by Captain Preston, who was kind enough to be my conductor; and I acquainted the Colonel with the motives that brought me thither. He told me with very great concern, that it was not in his power to raise men; for that, three days before, some of the militia in a fort, about fifteen miles above his house, at the head of Catawba Creek, commanded by one Colonel Nash, were attacked by the Indians, which occasioned all that settlement to break up totally, even as far as the ferry at Luney's; that he had ordered three companies to repair thither, and march against the enemy, and not one man came, except a captain, lieutenant, and seven or eight men from Bedford.

Finding that it was impossible to get a party to range and scour the frontiers, it remained only to proceed without men to see the situation of the forts, or to return back. The latter I was loath to do, since I had come thus far, and was anxious to see what posture of defence they were in. I therefore determined to come forward, at least to Vass's, and accordingly set out in company with Colonel Buchanan, who, being desirous that I might see and relate their unhappy condition, undertook to accompany me. We arrived safely at Vass's, where Captain Hogg, with only eighteen of his company, was building a fort, which must employ him till Christmas, without more assistance. One Captain Hunt from Lunenburg, was there with thirty men; but none of them would strike a stroke, unless I would engage to see them paid forty pounds of tobacco a day, which is provided by act of Assembly for militia carpenters. This I certainly could not do, as your Honor, who I thought had ordered them purposely out for this duty, had given no directions in the affair. Whatever expectations your Honor may have had from the militia's assistance, I am told they never lent a hand, save a few, that first came out with Captain Hogg, whom he has paid after the same rates with our men, at sixpence a day. Vass's place is a pass of very great importance, affording a road for the enemy, but secure, if strongly garrisoned.

From Vass's I came off with a servant and a guide, to visit the range of forts in this county. In less than two hours after, two men were killed along the same road, as will appear by Captain McNeil's letter, which I have just received, and herewith send, to let you see, by the account of Captain Hunt's behaviour, what dependence may be put on the militia. The inhabitants are so sensible of their danger, if left to the protection of these people, that not a man will stay at his place. This I have from their own mouths, and the principal persons of Augusta county. The militia are under such bad order and discipline, that they will go and come when and where they please, without regarding time, their officers, or the safety of the inhabitants, consulting solely their own inclinations. There should be, according to your orders, one third of the militia of these parts now on duty at once; instead of that, I believe scarce one thirtieth is out. They are to be relieved every month. More than that time is taken up in marching to and from their stations, and they will not wait one day longer than the limited time, whether they are relieved or not, let the necessity for it be ever so urgent. An instance of this kind happened in my presence about four days ago, in the case of Captain Daniel from Albemarle, who was intreated by Colonel Buchanan to stay at the time he was gathering or attempting to gather men, upon the alarm at the Catawba settlement before mentioned. The Captain's month was out, and go he must and did. Nay, I believe I may venture to say, that, whether his month had been out or not, this circumstance would have induced him to go; for the same gentleman went away from Vass's, because he thought it a dangerous post, giving that for his reason, and left Captain Hogg with eighteen men, exposed to the insults of the enemy.

Perhaps it may be thought I am partial in my relation, and reflect unjustly. I really do not, Sir. I scorn to make unjust remarks on the behaviour of the militia, as much as I despise and contemn the persons, who detract from mine and the character of the regiment. Were it not, that I consult the good of the public, and think these garrisons merit attention, I should not deem it worth mentioning. I only wish to make the country sensible, how ardently I have studied to promote its cause, and desire very sincerely, that my successor may fill my place more to its satisfaction in every respect, than I have been able to do. I mentioned in my last, that I did not think a less number than two thousand men would be sufficient to defend our extensive and much exposed frontiers from the ravages of the enemy. I have not had one reason to alter my opinion, but many to strengthen and confirm it. And I flatter myself, that the country will, when my determinations are known, be convinced that I have no sinister views, no vain motives of commanding a number of men, which urge me to recommend this number, but that it proceeds from the knowledge I have acquired of the country and people to be defended.

Your Honor, I hope, will give directions about laying in provisions on our southern frontiers. It is not in my power to do it, as I know not what troops can or will be put there. The regiment is at present too weak to allow any men to march from the quarter in which they are now stationed. I shall set out this day on my return to the fort, at the head of Catawba Creek, where Colonel Buchanan promised to meet me with a party to conduct me along our frontiers, up Jackson's River to Fort Dinwiddie, and higher if needful. If he does not meet me, I shall immediately proceed to Winchester, as it will be impossible to do any thing without men.

If you think proper to advance the pay of the militia, in order to engage them to work, please to acquaint Captain Hogg therewith, and send him money for that purpose. Were more men ordered to cover his party, and assist in the work, it would be highly advantageous, for he is greatly exposed. Major Lewis is extremely unwell. I am hurried a good deal, but have given a plain account of all the several matters mentioned in the foregoing sheet. I am, &c.

TO GOVERNOR DINWIDDIE.

Winchester, 9 November, 1756.

SIR,

In mine from Halifax I promised a particular detail of my observations upon the situation of our frontiers, when I arrived at this place. Although I was pretty explicit in that letter, I cannot avoid recapitulating part of the subject now.

From Fort Trial on Smith's River, I returned to Fort William on the Catawba, where I met Colonel Buchanan with about thirty men, chiefly officers, to conduct me up Jackson's River, along the range of forts. With this small company of irregulars, with whom order, regularity, circumspection, and vigilance were matters of derision and contempt, we set out, and, by the protection of Providence, reached Augusta Court-House in seven days, without meeting the enemy; otherwise we must have fallen a sacrifice, through the indiscretion of these whooping, hallooing *gentlemen* soldiers!

This jaunt afforded me an opportunity of seeing the bad regulation of the militia, the disorderly proceedings of the garrisons, and the unhappy circumstances of the inhabitants.

First, of the militia. The difficulty of collecting them on any emergency, I have often spoken of; and I appeal to sad experience, how great a disadvantage it is, that the enemy should have every opportunity to plunder, kill, and escape, before the militia can afford any assistance. And not to mention the expensiveness of their service in general, I can instance several cases, where a captain, lieutenant, and, I may add, an ensign, with two or three sergeants, and six or eight men, will go upon duty at a time. The proportion of expense in this case is so unjust and obvious, that your Honor wants it not to be proved.

Then these men, when raised, are to be continued only one month on duty, half of which time is lost in their marching out and home, especially those from the adjacent counties, who must be on duty some time before they reach their stations, by which means double sets of men are in pay at the same time, and for the same service. Again, the waste of provision they make is unaccountable; no method or order in being served or purchasing at the best rates, but quite the reverse. Allowance for each man, as in the case of other soldiers, they look upon as the highest indignity, and would sooner starve, than carry a few days' provision on their backs for conveniency. But upon their march, when breakfast is wanted, they knock down the first beef they meet with, and, after regaling themselves, march on till dinner, when they take the same method, and so for supper, to the great oppression of the people. Or, if they chance to impress cattle for provision, the valuation is left to ignorant and interested neighbours, who have suffered by those practices, and, despairing of their pay, exact high prices, and thus the public is imposed upon at all events. I might add, I believe, that, for the want of proper laws to govern the militia (I cannot ascribe it to any other cause), they are obstinate, self-willed, perverse, of little or no service to the people, and very burthensome to the country. Every individual has his own crude notions of things, and must undertake to direct. If his advice is neglected, he thinks himself slighted, abused, and injured; and, to redress his wrongs, will depart for his home. These, Sir, are literally matters of fact, partly from persons of undoubted veracity, but chiefly from my own observations.

Secondly, concerning the garrisons. I found them very weak for want of men; but more so from indolence and irregularity. I saw none in a posture of defence, and few that might not be surprised with the greatest ease. An instance of this appeared at Dickinson's Fort, where the Indians ran down, caught several children playing under the walls, and had got to the gate before they were discovered. Was not Vass's Fort surprised, and a good many souls lost, in the same manner? They keep no guard, but just when the enemy is about, and they are under fearful apprehensions; nor ever stir out of the forts, from the time they reach them, till relieved on their month being expired; at which time they march off, be the event what it will. Of the ammunition they are as careless as of the provisions, firing it away frequently at targets for wagers. On our journey, as we approached one of their forts, we heard a quick fire for several minutes, and concluded for certain that they were attacked; so we marched in the best manner to their relief; but when we came up, we found they were diverting themselves at marks. These men afford no assistance to the unhappy settlers, who are driven from their plantations, either in securing their harvests, or gathering their corn. Lieutenant Bullitt, commanding at Fort Cumberland, sent to Major Lewis of Albemarle, who commanded a party of sixty militia at Miller's, about fifteen miles above him, where were also thirty men of Augusta, for some men to join his small parties to gather the corn. Major Lewis refused assistance, and would not divide his men. I wrote to him, but got no answer. Mr. Bullitt has done what he could with his few men, not quite thirty. Of the many forts, which

I passed by, I saw but one or two that had their captains present, they being absent chiefly on their own business, and had given leave to several of the men to do the same. Yet these persons, I will venture to say, will charge the country their full month's pay.

Thirdly, the wretched and unhappy situation of the inhabitants needs few words, after a slight reflection on the preceding circumstances. They are fully sensible of their misery; they feel their insecurity in relying on militia, who are slow in coming to their assistance, indifferent about their preservation, unwilling to continue, and regardless of every thing but their own ease. In short, they are so affected with approaching ruin, that the whole back country is in a general motion towards the southern colonies; and I expect that scarce a family will inhabit Frederic, Hampshire, or Augusta, in a little time. They petitioned me in the most earnest manner for companies of the regiment. But alas! it is not in my power to assist them with any, unless I leave this dangerous quarter more exposed than they are. I promised, at their particular request, to address your Honor and the Assembly in their behalf, that a regular force may be established in lieu of the militia and ranging companies, which are of much less service, and of infinitely more cost to the country. Were this done, the whole would be under one direction, and any misbehaviour could never pass with impunity. Whereas the others are soldiers at will. And, indeed, the manner in which some of the ranging captains have obtained their commissions, if I am rightly informed, is by imposture and artifice. They produce a list, I am told, to your Honor, of sundry persons, who are willing to serve under them. One part, it is said, consists of fictitious names; another, the names of persons who never saw the list; and the remainder are persons drawn into it by fallacious promises, that cannot be performed without detriment to the service. But were it otherwise, surely any person, who considers the pay of the soldiers and that of the militia, will find a considerable difference, though both under the best regulations.

As defensive measures are evidently insufficient for the security and safety of the country, I hope no arguments are requisite to prove the necessity of altering them to a vigorous offensive war, in order to remove the evil. But, should the Assembly still indulge that favorite scheme of protecting the inhabitants by forts along the frontiers, in which too many of them put their dependence, and as the building of these forts has been encouraged and confirmed by an act of Assembly, I take the liberty to present your Honor with a plan of the number of forts, and strength necessary to each, reaching entirely across our frontiers from north to south. This plan is calculated upon the most moderate and easy terms for sparing expense to the country, and, I believe, with tolerable propriety to answer the wished-for design of protecting the settlers. Besides, most of the forts are already built by the country-people or soldiers, and require but little improvement, save one or two, as Dickinson's and Cox's. Your Honor will see Fort Cumberland excluded in this list.*

The advantage of having the militia in Augusta under one command, I have already hinted at; and I think Major Lewis should have your Honor's orders to take that duty in hand, with directions to secure

* This scheme embraced a line of twenty-three forts, extending along the whole frontier of Virginia, from the Potomac River to the borders of North Carolina. The number of men required to garrison the whole was estimated at two thousand. The project of a chain of forts, as has been seen, was not a favorite one with Colonel Washington; but he had formed this plan in compliance with the views of the Assembly.

those important passes of Dickinson's and Vass's, by building a fort in the neighbourhood of Dickinson's, or by some other means. Were it practicable to get the people to assemble in little towns contiguous to these forts, it would contribute much to their mutual peace and safety, during the continuance of the Indian war. The Augusta people complain greatly for want of money.

The other day eleven Indians of the Catawba tribe came here, and we undoubtedly might have had more of them, had the proper means been used to send trusty guides to invite and conduct them to us; but this is neglected. One Matthew Tool makes his boast of stopping them until he shall be handsomely rewarded for bringing them; and Major Lewis can inform you of one Bemer, who uses every method to hinder the Cherokees from coming to our assistance. Complaint should be made to Governor Littleton of these persons. Indian goods are much wanted to reward the Catawbas, and encourage them to engage in our service.

Your Honor and the Assembly should determine several essential points; namely, a proper method of paying rewards for taking up deserters, the present one being very discouraging, as it delays payment until Courts of Claims have decided; means to replace the drafts, that must be discharged in December; ascertaining the pay of workmen employed on all public works, or empowering the commanding officer to agree on the cheapest terms he can with them; how the masters of servants enlisted for the Virginia regiment are to be paid. We have already recruited more than fifty, and are daily dunned for payment by the masters. A report prevails, to my great surprise, though disbelief, that your Honor had told some persons, who applied to you for satisfaction for their servants, that I had no orders to enlist any. This false rumor occasions strange reflections, and must make me appear in a very unjust light to the world. I have, therefore, desisted from recruiting until you direct me in what manner those already obtained are to be paid for; and I beg you will give me immediate advice on the affair, as the people are impatient, and threaten us with prosecutions from all quarters.

Your Honor has herewith a copy of the council of war, held in behalf of Fort Cumberland, in which the arguments are justly and fully laid down, both with regard to Virginia in particular, and to the three colonies in general.* On the back of the copy are my sentiments candidly offered, and to your Honor I leave the determination of this important affair.†

As to a chaplain, if the government will grant a subsistence, we can readily get a person of merit to accept the place, without giving the commissary any trouble on that point.‡

* That is, Pennsylvania, Maryland, and Virginia.

† In a former letter Governor Dinwiddie had proposed to Colonel Washington, that the affair of Fort Cumberland should be referred to a council of officers, to be held at that place. This had been done, and the council had reported at large, assigning the reasons, which might be urged both for retaining and for abandoning the fort, but forbore to express a decided opinion. Colonel Washington approved their report, and, after adding his remarks, he forwarded the whole to the Governor. The council agreed, that the fort itself was wholly defenceless, imperfectly constructed, and commanded by several hills within gun-shot; but they thought it important that a post should be maintained in that quarter, since the only road to the west for wheel-carriages passed in that direction.

With this view of the subject Colonel Washington concurred, but was still of opinion, that a better position ought to be chosen, and suggested that it should be in advance of Fort Cumberland, and somewhere in the vicinity of the Little Meadows. This he thought a proper enterprise for the combined efforts of Virginia, Maryland, and Pennsylvania, as the main object was to facilitate an expedition to the Ohio, or prevent an irruption of the enemy into either of those colonies.

‡ In reply to a request for the appointment of a chaplain to the regiment, Governor Dinwiddie had written to him;—"I have recommended

Your Honor has had advice of two spies, that were taken at Fort Cumberland; one of whom they quickly hung up as his just reward, being a deserter; the other was sent to Governor Sharpe, to give information of the infernal practices followed by some of the priests of that province, in holding correspondence with our enemy.

I am, &c.

N. B. I am just setting out for Fort Cumberland.

TO GOVERNOR DINWIDDIE.

Alexandria, 24 November, 1756.

SIR,

At this place, on my way to Williamsburg, I received your Honor's letter of the 16th instant.* I shall take

---

to the commissary to get a chaplain, but he cannot prevail with any person to accept of it. I shall again press it to him."

* For some reason, which does not appear, Governor Dinwiddie received the preceding letter in no very good humor. This will be manifest by the following extracts from his reply, which are requisite also to explain some parts of Colonel Washington's rejoinder.

"The abuses mentioned in yours I have been made acquainted with from several hands; but I expected you would have been more particular in regard to the officers neglecting their duty, and the different forts not being properly garrisoned with men, — nay, without their officers. This vague report makes it impossible for me to call on the delinquents."

"I am of opinion the string of forts proposed is only weakening our strength, and will be a poor defence to our frontiers. I hope you will keep the Indians properly employed. Major Lewis has orders to send up the Cherokees. You seem to attribute neglect to me, in not having proper conductors. The charge is unmannerly, as I did what I thought proper, though disappointed by the villanous traders."

"If you had sent down the amount of money due for the servants enlisted, I would have given a warrant for the money. It is probable I might have refused payment to the masters of some of the servants enlisted, for want of certificates, but never said you did not act properly in enlisting them."

"In regard to a chaplain, you should know, that his qualification and the bishop's letter of license should be produced to the commissary and myself; but this person is also nameless.

"I received the opinion of the council of war in regard to Fort Cumbre-

care to pay the strictest obedience to your orders, and the opinion, so far as I can. The detachment ordered from Winchester exceeds, I believe, the number of enlisted men we have there; and the drafts, that made our strength at that place to consist of about one hundred and sixty men, will leave us in seven days. I have no hope of enlisting any, nor of prolonging their stay, as we have heretofore engaged those, who were willing to serve.

I am very sorry any expression in my letter should be deemed *unmannerly*. I never intended insults to any; on the contrary, I have endeavoured to demean myself with the proper respect due to superiors. In the instance mentioned, I can truly say, so far from intending a charge or affront of any kind, it was distant from my thoughts; and I meant no more than to show what strange, what unaccountable infatuation prevailed among the magistrates of the back parts of Carolina; who were so regardless of the common cause, as to allow fifty Catawbas to return, when they had proceeded near seventy miles on their march, for want of provisions and a conductor to entice them along. This was a fact with which I did not suppose your Honor unacquainted, knowing Colonel Cobb had written to

---

land; as it was an affair of great consequence, I called the council for their advice. In consequence thereof, I hereby order you immediately to march one hundred men to Fort Cumberland from the forces you have at Winchester, which, Captain Mercer says, are one hundred and sixty enlisted men. You are to remain at Fort Cumberland, and make the place as strong as you can in case of an attack. You are to send out parties from the fort to observe the motions of the enemy, if they should march over the Allegany mountains. Any stores at the fort, not absolutely necessary for its defence, you are to send to Winchester.

"You are to order one of your subaltern officers, in whom you can confide, to command at Winchester, and to oversee the finishing of the fort building at that place. These orders I expect you will give due obedience to, and I am with respect," &c.

you on the subject. I therefore thought I might be less explicit, and not incur this censure by that means.

I seem also to be reprimanded for giving a vague account of my tour to the southward. I was rather fearful of blame for prolixity and impertinence, in meddling with matters with which I had no immediate concern; and I related them rather as hints, to set you upon inquiring, than as a circumstantial account of the facts. This I chose more especially to do, as Colonels Lewis and Buchanan were there, from whom, being heads of the militia, these representations, fully authenticated, would more properly come. When I went to Augusta, it was with the good design to relieve, if possible, a much distressed settlement; but, finding this impracticable without men, and hearing some complaints of Captain Hogg, and at the same time being desirous of seeing in what manner he proceeded, I continued onward in no small danger; yet pleased with executing this extraordinary duty, and bringing myself more intimately acquainted with the situation of our frontiers, which, Sir, I related as well as I was capable, with a design, from which I have never intentionally swerved, to serve my country. And I am sorry to find, that this, and my best endeavours of late, meet with unfavorable constructions. What it proceeds from, I know not. If my open and disinterested way of writing and speaking has the air of pertness and freedom, I shall correct my error by acting reservedly, and shall take care to obey my orders without offering any thing more.

When I spoke of a chaplain, it was in answer to yours. I had no person in view, though many have offered; and I only said, if the country would provide subsistence, we could procure a chaplain, without thinking there was offence in the expression.

So soon as I march from Winchester, which will be

immediately, I shall write you a more distinct account of the situation of that place, which will be left entirely destitute of all protection, notwithstanding it now contains all the public stores of any importance, as they were removed from Fort Cumberland, and in the most dangerous part of our frontiers, at least in a part that has suffered this summer more than any (which has been so well secured) by the ravages of the enemy. The works, which have been constructed and carried on with infinite pains and labor, will be unfinished and exposed; and the materials for completing the building, *which have been collected with* unspeakable difficulty and expense, left to be pillaged and destroyed by the inhabitants of the town; because, as I before observed, one hundred men will exceed the number, I am pretty confident, which we shall have there, when the drafts go off. So, if I comply with my orders, which I shall literally do, if I can, not a man will be left there to secure the works, or defend the King's stores, which are almost wholly removed to that place.

I am your Honor's, &c.

TO GOVERNOR DINWIDDIE.

Fort Loudoun, 2 December, 1756.

SIR,

When I wrote to you from Alexandria, I expected to have been at or near Fort Cumberland by this time; but, upon coming here, and expecting wagons and provisions in readiness to go up with this escort, I received the enclosed from the commissary, which I send to evince that no delays or protracting of orders proceed from me. The return of our strength, which I called in as soon as I arrived, is herewith sent, signed by the adjutant, amounting, exclusive of the drafts, to eighty-one effectives, including the sick, and young drummers, who were sent here to learn.

When Captain Mercer went down, our strength consisted of about twenty-five more, including drafts, who have been sent over, since the middle of October, to Conococheague and Swearingham's Ferry, to encourage the inhabitants there to stay at their places, who otherwise were determined to forsake them. Your late and unexpected order has caused the utmost terror and consternation in the people, and will, I fear, be productive of numberless evils, not only to this place, and the public works erecting here, but to the people in general, who seem to be in the greatest dread of the consequences. The stores of every kind have all been brought from Fort Cumberland, save those indispensably necessary there, at a very great expense, and lie in the court-house and other public buildings, to the no small inconvenience and detriment of the county. I have frequently been importuned by the members of the court, and other public officers, to remove them, and have as often by gentle persuasives protracted the time; which was the more cheerfully granted, as it was evident there were no other places to receive them, and that I strove with the utmost diligence to prepare the proper receptacles. What course to take now, I know not, and hope you will direct.

I am convinced, were you informed how much this place (which is in every respect our extreme and most exposed frontier, there being no inhabitants between this and the South Branch, and none there but such as are forted in,) — I say, I am convinced, if you were truly informed of the situation of this place, of its importance and danger, you would not think it prudent to leave such a quantity of valuable stores exposed to the insults of a few; for a very few indeed might reduce them and the town to ashes. In the next place, as I observed in my last letter, the works, which have been begun and continued with labor and hardship, lie open, untenable, and exposed to the weather, to say no more; the materials, which have been collected with cost and infinite difficulty, will be at the mercy of every pillager; our timber and scantling, used and burnt by the town's people; our plank, which has been brought from afar, stolen and destroyed; and the lime, if not stolen, left to be wasted. And this is not the worst. A building, which in time might and would have been very strong and defensible, and an asylum in the greatest danger, must be in a manner totally abandoned. As the case now stands, we have no place tenable, no place of safety; all is exposed and open to attacks; and by not having a garrison kept at this place, no convoys can get up to us at Fort Cumberland, and the communication with the inhabitants is entirely cut off, so that soldiers and inhabitants cannot assist each other.

In regard to my residing at Fort Cumberland, I shall lay before you such inconveniences as must unavoidably arise, while we pursue these defensive measures; in doing which, I think I only do my duty. First, as Fort Cumberland lies more advanced, and wide of all other forts, I shall be prevented from having the immediate direction of any but that. Secondly, the stores being at this place, and I at that, it will be impossible to deliver them regularly. I must either trust to a subaltern officer to order them discretionally, or else an express must be first sent to me, and then I must send to the storekeeper to deliver the necessaries wanted for each garrison. Moreover, there is no travelling to Fort Cumberland without endangering life, except with a pretty strong escort. Thirdly, by being at Fort Cumberland a total stagnation of business must ensue, because money is lodged with me for discharging all contingent expenses arising in the service, and no persons will, or can, come to me there. Consequently they will be slack in furnishing us with wagons and necessaries of every kind, which now by due payment may be had at call. Lastly, Winchester is in the centre, as it were, of all the forts, and is convenient for receiving intelligence and distributing orders. It also lies in a vale of land, that has suffered more than any other from the incursions of the enemy.

I hope, after receiving a peremptory order, the mentioning of these things will not appear presuming or odd. I do not hesitate a moment to obey. On the contrary, I shall comply as soon as I can. I mean nothing more than to point out the consequences, that must necessarily attend this step, as I apprehend you were not thoroughly apprised of our situation. Some, Sir, who are inclined to put an unfavorable construction on this ingenuous recital, may say, that I am loath to leave Winchester. I declare, upon my honor, I am not, but had rather a thousand times be at Fort Cumberland, if I could do the duty there. I am tired of this place, the inhabitants, and the life I lead here; and if, after what I have said, you should think it necessary for me to reside at that fort, I shall acquiesce with pleasure and cheerfulness, and be freed from much anxiety, plague, and business. To be at Fort Cumberland sometimes, I think highly expedient, and have hitherto done it. Three weeks ago I came from that place.

I have used every endeavour to detain drafts, but all in vain. They are home-sick and tired of work. They all declare, that, if an expedition is conducted in the spring, they will serve two, three, or four months; but these are words of course. The Catawbas are out on the scout with an officer and some men of ours. They proposed, when I was at Fort Cumberland, to stay only one moon, and then to set out for their nation, with a report of the country and its convenience to the enemy, (but rather with a report of our usage, I believe.) It therefore behoves us to reward them well, and keep them in temper. They applied to me for several necessaries, such as a suit of clothes for each, wampum, pipes, tomahawks, and silver trinkets for the wrists and arms. The wampum and tomahawks I have purchased. The want of the other articles may occasion some murmuring, and there are very few things suitable at Fort Cumberland. They seemed desirous, that an officer should return with them, and gave strong assurances of his bringing in a number. If you approve it, I shall endeavour to fix upon some officer, that falls most within their customs, and send him upon this duty. The Indians expect to be sent back upon horses. Do you approve that they should? I will not take upon me to buy horses without your orders. The Cherokees are not yet arrived, nor the arms from Augusta.

I am your Honor's, &c.

TO CAPTAIN WILLIAM BRONAUGH, ON THE SOUTH BRANCH.

Fort Loudoun, 17 December, 1756.

SIR,

You are strictly required, immediately upon receipt of this, to transmit your provisions and stores to Captain Waggener's Fort, and there leave them. Then march your company to Pearsall's, in order to escort a quantity of flour to Fort Cumberland, where you and your whole company are to remain.

I expect you will pay due regard to this order, and put it in execution with the utmost alacrity, as it is in consequence of express directions from the Governor and Council. I heartily commiserate the poor, unhappy inhabitants, left by this means exposed to every incursion of a merciless enemy, and I wish it were in my power to offer them better support, than good wishes will afford. You may assure the settlement, that this unexpected, and, if I may be allowed to say it, unavoidable step was taken without my concurrence or knowledge; that it is an express order from the Governor, and can neither be evaded nor delayed. Therefore, any representations to me of their danger, and the necessity of continuing troops among them, will be fruitless; for, as I before observed, I have inclination, but no power left, to serve them. It is also the Governor's order, that the forts be left standing for the inhabitants to possess if they think proper. *

I am, Sir, yours, &c.

TO GOVERNOR DINWIDDIE.

Fort Loudoun, 19 December, 1756.

SIR,

Your letter of the 10th came to hand the 15th; in consequence of which I despatched orders immediately to all the garrisons on the Branch to evacuate their forts, repair to Pearsall's, where they would meet the flour from this place, and escort it to Fort Cumberland. I

* An order in the same terms was likewise sent to the commanders of several other forts.

fear the provisions purchased for the support of these forts, and now lying in bulk, will be wasted and destroyed, notwithstanding I have given directions to the assistant commissary on the Branch, and to Waggener's company, to use their utmost diligence in collecting the whole, and securing them where his company is posted. An escort, with all the flour we have been able to procure (amounting to an insufficient quantity for want of water), will set out from this place on Tuesday next. I expect to depart sooner myself, leaving directions with Captain Mercer, whom I have appointed to command here, and I shall repair as expeditiously as possible to Fort Cumberland.

I am a little at a loss to understand the meaning of your orders, and the opinion of the Council, when I am directed to evacuate all the stockade forts, and at the same time to march only one hundred men to Fort Cumberland, and to continue the like number here to garrison Fort Loudoun. If the stockade forts are all abandoned, there will be more men than are required for these two purposes, and the communication between them, of near eighty miles, will be left without a settler, unguarded and exposed. But I mean nothing more by this intimation, than to ascertain your intentions, to which I would willingly pay strict obedience.*

* It is no wonder, that Colonel Washington should complain, as he often did, of the confusion and inconsistency of his orders. In the present case, the Governor first ordered him to march from Fort Loudoun to Fort Cumberland more men than he had under his command at the former post, and still to leave a number sufficient to keep up the garrison, and continue the works. When this order was countermanded as absurd and impracticable, another was issued for calling in all the men at the stockade forts, sending one hundred to Fort Cumberland, and retaining the same number at Fort Loudoun, by which means the smaller forts, essential for the defence of the people, would be evacuated, and a large number of men left unemployed. A third order was necessary to remedy the blunders of the other two, by entrusting the matter to the discretion of the Commander-in-chief.

A return of the stores at this place is enclosed. I should have sent it before, but waited to add a return of those at Fort Cumberland. None has yet come down.

If Captain McNeil goes to the Cherokee nation, it would be well for him to conduct the Catawbas home. But when I recommended an officer's going with them, it was with a view of engaging a body of their men to come to our assistance in the spring, and to march with their warriors, not choosing to trust altogether to their unmeaning promises and capricious humors. But you will be pleased to direct as you see proper in this affair. I have hitherto advanced very little money to the masters of servants, because I waited your directions. I received forty-one last night from Captain McNeil, who desires leave to continue recruiting. I do not consent to it, until I know whether it is agreeable to you, and whether I may send out as many other officers as can be spared for the same service.

I should have been exceedingly glad, if your Honor and the Council had directed in what manner Fort Cumberland is to be strengthened; that is, whether it is to be made cannon-proof or not; and that you would fix the sum beyond which we shall not go, for I must look to you for the expense. I have read that paragraph in Lord Loudoun's letter, which you were pleased to send me, over and over again, but am unable to comprehend its meaning.* What scheme it was, that I was

The Governor's settled determination to sustain Fort Cumberland, contrary to the opinion of Colonel Washington, betrayed him and his Council into a series of hasty resolutions and wild mistakes.

* In this paragraph Lord Loudoun writes to the Governor;—"As to the affair of Fort Cumberland, I own it gives me great uneasiness, and I am of the same opinion with you, that it was very material to have supported that fort this winter, and after that we could easily have made it a better post than ever it has been, from what I hear of it. I cannot agree with Colonel Washington in not drawing in the posts from the stockade forts in order to defend that advanced one; and I should imagine much

carrying into execution without waiting advice, I am at a loss to know, unless it was building the chain of forts along our frontiers, which I not only undertook conformably to an act of Assembly, and by your own orders, but, with respect to the places, in pursuance of a council of war. If, under these circumstances, my conduct is responsible for the fate of Fort Cumberland, it must be confessed, that I stand upon a tottering foundation indeed. I cannot charge my memory with either proposing, or intending, to draw the forts nearer Winchester. The garrison of Fort Cumberland, it is true, I did wish to have removed to Cox's, which is nearer Winchester by twenty-five miles; but not farther from the enemy, if a road were opened from thence to the Little Meadows, which place is about twenty miles distant, and the same from Fort Cumberland, and more in the warriors' path. However, I see with much regret, that Lord Loudoun seems to have prejudged my pro-

more of the frontier will be exposed by retiring your advanced posts near Winchester, where I understand he is retired, for, from your letter, I take it for granted he has before this executed his plan, without waiting for any advice. If he leaves any of the great quantity of stores behind, it will be very unfortunate, and he ought to consider that it must lie at his own door. This proceeding, I am afraid, will have a bad effect, as to the Dominion [Virginia], and will not have a good appearance at home."

From this extract it is manifest, that Lord Loudoun (who was then in New York, and had never visited Virginia,) had no accurate knowledge of the transactions in question, and that he had been misled by the Governor's letters. His remarks, as applied to the acts and designs of Colonel Washington, are literally without meaning. It is extraordinary, that the Governor should send them to him, knowing as he did their inaccuracy, and foreseeing as he must, that Colonel Washington would discover on the face of them an unfair attempt, in some quarter, to prejudice him in the mind of Lord Loudoun. The Governor afterwards thought to add a palliative, by assuring him, that the "paragraph of Lord Loudoun's letter was entirely confined to Fort Cumberland; he was afraid you would have evacuated and dismantled that fort before his letter reached me; nor can you think, that he either prejudges or has any bad opinion of your conduct." This is an evasive reply, unsatisfactory, and suspicious.

ceedings, without being thoroughly informed of the springs and motives, that actuated my conduct. How far I have mistaken the means to recommend my services, I know not, but I am certain of this, that no man ever intended better, or studied the interest of his country with more zeal, than I have done; and nothing gives me greater uneasiness and concern, than that his Lordship should have imbibed prejudices so unfavorable to my character, as to excite his belief that I was capable of doing any thing, "that will have a bad effect as to the Dominion, and no good appearance at home."

As I had your permission to go down when his Lordship shall favor us with a visit, I desired Colonel Carlyle to inform me when he should pass through Alexandria, and I will set out accordingly. I hope nothing has intervened to alter this indulgence. It is a favor I should not have thought of asking, had I believed the service would suffer in my absence, but I am convinced it will not. And I cannot help saying, I believe we are the only troops on this continent, that are kept summer and winter to the severest duty, without the least respite or indulgence.

The delay of the soldiers' clothes occasions unaccountable murmurs and complaints, and I am very much afraid we shall have few men left, if they arrive not in a week or two. You would be astonished to see the naked condition of the poor wretches. How they possibly can subsist, much less work, in such severe weather, is not easy to conceive. Had we but blankets to give them, or any thing to defend them from the cold, they might perhaps be easy.

I have formerly hinted to you our necessity for a speedy supply of cash, and have advised with the Speaker likewise, that he may not be unprepared. I purpose to send down by the 10th of next month.

I cannot furnish a return of our strength as yet, because our scattered disposition hinders a regular discharge of the adjutant's duty. I am, &c.

TO JOHN ROBINSON, SPEAKER OF THE HOUSE OF BURGESSES.

Winchester, 19 December, 1756.

SIR,

You are no stranger, I presume, to the late resolutions of the Governor and Council, the consequence of which I meditate with great concern. We are ordered to reinforce Fort Cumberland with one hundred men, and, to enable me to carry that number thither, all the stockade forts on the Branch are to be evacuated, and in course all the settlements abandoned, except what lie under the immediate protection of Captain Waggener's fort, the only place exempted in their resolve. Surely his Honor and the Council are not fully acquainted with the situation and circumstances of the unhappy frontiers, thus to expose so valuable a tract as the Branch, in order to support a fortification, in itself of very little importance to the inhabitants or the colony. The former order of Council would have endangered not only the loss of Fort Loudoun, the stores, and Winchester, but a general removal of the settlers of this vale, even to the Blue Ridge. This last has the same object in view, namely, Fort Cumberland, and, to maintain it, the best lands in Virginia are laid open to the mercy of a cruel and inhuman enemy.

These people have long struggled with the dangers of savage incursions, daily soliciting defence, and willing to keep their ground. To encourage them, all my little help has been administered, and they seemed satisfied with my intentions, resolving to continue while any probability of support remained. The disposition I had made of our small regiment gave general satisfaction to the settlements, and content began to appear everywhere. The necessary measures for provisions and stores were satisfactorily concerted, and every regulation established for the season. But the late order reverses, confuses, and incommodes every thing; to say nothing of the extraordinary expense of carriage, disappointments, losses, and alterations, which must fall heavy on the country. Whence it arises, or why, I am truly ignorant; but my strongest representations of matters relative to the peace of the frontiers are disregarded, as idle and frivolous; my propositions and measures, as partial and selfish; and all my sincerest endeavours for the service of my country are perverted to the worst purposes. My orders are dark, doubtful, and uncertain; to-day approved, to-morrow condemned. Left to act and proceed at hazard, accountable for the consequences, and blamed without the benefit of defence, if you can think my situation capable of exciting the smallest degree of envy, or affording the least satisfaction, the truth is yet hidden from you, and you entertain notions very different from the reality of the case. However, I am determined to bear up under all these embarrassments some time longer, in hope of a better regulation on the arrival of Lord Loudoun, to whom I look for the future fate of Virginia.

His Lordship, I think, has received impressions tending to my prejudice, by false representations of facts, if I may judge from a paragraph of one of his letters to the Governor, on which is founded the resolve to support Fort Cumberland at all events. The severity of the season, and nakedness of the soldiers, are matters of much compassion, and give rise to infinite complaints. Nor is it possible to obviate them, unless the clothing come in immediately. You would be surprised how the poor creatures live, much more how they can do duty. Had we but blankets, they might be appeased for a little time. As we have not, I fear many will desert.

I advised you formerly of our necessity for cash, and I now earnestly request it soon. I think of sending down by the 10th of next month, or sooner if agreeable. Please to inform me upon what I may depend, as our men are impatient, and with some reason, when without both money and clothes. I need not urge the advantage of small bills. We shall have occasion for at least six thousand pounds to clear us to the 1st of January. The commissary wants above half that sum to furnish his stock of provisions. The remainder will be exhausted in paying the troops. We ought always to have money in hand, as we are often reduced to many inconveniences by waiting for it, not to mention the expense and trouble. *

I am, dear Sir, your most obliged and affectionate humble servant.

---

* In reply to this letter Mr. Speaker Robinson wrote ;—

"I am truly concerned at the uneasiness you are under in your present situation, and the more so, as I am sensible you have too much reason for it. The resolution of defending Fort Cumberland, and evacuating the other forts, was taken before I knew or mistrusted any thing of the matter. I must confess I was not a little surprised at it, and took the liberty to expostulate with many of the Council upon it, who gave me in answer, that Lord Loudoun had insisted that Fort Cumberland should be preserved, and, as we had so few troops, it could not be done without breaking up the small forts, and taking the men from them.

"It was to no purpose to tell them, that our frontiers would thereby be entirely exposed to our cruel and savage enemy, and that they could receive no protection from Fort Cumberland, as it was in another province, and so remote from any of our inhabitants ;— and further, that the act of Assembly, which gave the money solely for the defence and protection of our frontiers, would be violated, and the money applied otherwise than the Assembly intended. Yet, notwithstanding all I could say they persisted

TO THE EARL OF LOUDOUN.

Fort Loudoun, February, 1757.

MY LORD,

The posture of affairs in this quarter is really melancholy, and the prospect was rendered more gloomy while there appeared no hopes of amendment; but, from the presence of your Lordship at this time in the Dominion, we conceive hopes of seeing these threatening clouds dispelled.

The sums of money, which have been granted by this colony to carry on the war, have been very considerable; and to reflect to what little purpose is matter of great concern, and will seem surprising to those, who are not acquainted with the causes, and the confusion with which all our affairs have hitherto been conducted, owing to our having no fixed object, nor pursuing any regular system, or plan of operation.

As I have studied with attention and care the nature of the service, have been myself engaged in it from the beginning of the present broils, and an eyewitness to all the movements and various proceedings, I beg leave to offer a concise and candid account of our circumstances

---

in their resolution, without alleging any other reason, than that it was in pursuance of Lord Loudoun's desire.

"It cannot be a difficult matter to guess, who was the author and promoter of this advice and resolution, or by whom Lord Loudoun has been persuaded, that the place is of such importance. But supposing it were really so, it ought to be defended by the people in whose province it is [Maryland], or at least at the expense of the three colonies jointly, and our own frontiers not left exposed for the defence of a place, from which we cannot receive the least advantage or protection. The present unhappy state of our country must fill the mind of every well-wisher to it with dismal and gloomy apprehensions; and without some speedy alterations in our counsels, which may God send, the fate of it must soon be determined."

to your Lordship; from which many errors may be discovered, that merit redress in a very high degree.

It was not ascertained until too late, that the French were on the Ohio; or rather, that we could be persuaded they came there with a design to invade his Majesty's dominions. Nay, after I was sent out in December, 1753, and brought undoubted testimony even from themselves of their avowed design, it was yet thought a fiction, and a scheme to promote the interest of a private company, even by some who had a share in the government. These unfavorable surmises caused great delays in raising the first men and money, and gave the active enemy time to take possession of the Fork of the Ohio (which they now call Duquesne), before we were in sufficient strength to advance thither, which has been the chief source of all our past and present misfortunes. For by this means, as the French got between us and our Indian allies, they fixed those in their interests, who were wavering, and obliged the others to neutrality, till the unhappy defeat of General Braddock.

The troops under Colonel Dunbar going into quarters in July, the inactivity of the neighbouring colonies, and the incapacity of this, conspired to give the French great room to exult, and the Indians little reason to expect a vigorous offensive war on our side, and induced the defensive plan, which promised the greatest show of protection. This is an undeniable fact, as well as that all the Indians did not forsake the English interests, till three months after the battle of Monongahela, but actually waited to see what measures would be concerted to regain our losses, and afford them the protection we had but too liberally promised.

Virginia, it is true, was not inactive all this time. On the contrary, she voted a handsome supply for raising men to carry on the war, or, more properly, to defend herself; matters being reduced to this extremity for want of assistance. But even in this she signally failed, and, as I apprehend, from the following causes.

The men first levied to repel the enemy marched for the Ohio in the beginning of April, 1754, without tents, without clothes, in short, without any conveniences to shelter them, in that remarkably cold and wet season, from the inclemency of the weather, or to make the service tolerably agreeable. In this state did they continue, notwithstanding, till the battle of the Meadows, in July following, never receiving in all that space any subsistence; and they were very often under the greatest straits and difficulties for want of provisions.

These things were productive of great murmurings and discontent, and rendered the service so distasteful to the men, that, not being paid immediately upon coming in, they thought themselves bubbled, and that no reward for their services was ever intended. This caused desertion; and the deserters, spreading over the country, recounting their sufferings and want of pay, which rags and poverty sufficiently testified, fixed in the mind of the populace such horrid impressions of the hardships they had encountered, that no arguments could remove these prejudices, or facilitate the recruiting service.

This put the Assembly upon enacting a law to impress vagrants, which added to our difficulties, for, as these abandoned miscreants were compelled into the service, they embraced every opportunity to effect their escape, gave a loose to their vicious principles, and invented the most unheard-of stories to palliate desertion and gain compassion; in which they not only succeeded, but obtained protection likewise. So that it was next to impossible, after this, to apprehend deserters, while the civil officers rather connived at their escape, than aided in securing them.

Thus were affairs situated, when we were ordered, in September, 1755, to recruit our force to twelve hundred men. It is easy to conceive, under these circumstances, why we did not fulfil the order, especially when the officers had not a sufficient allowance for this arduous task. We continued, however, using our endeavours until March following, without much success.

The Assembly, meeting about that time, came to a resolution of augmenting our numbers to fifteen hundred men, by drafting the militia, who were to continue in the service until December only. By reason of a clause in the act exempting all those, who should pay ten pounds, our numbers were very little increased, one part of the people paying that sum, and many of the poorer sort absconding. This was not the only pernicious clause, for the funds arising from these forfeitures were thrown into the treasury; whereas, had they been deposited in proper hands for recruiting, the money might have turned to good account. But a greater grievance still was the restraining of the forces from marching out of the colony, or acting offensively, and ordering them to build forts, and garrison them, along a frontier of more than three hundred miles in extent. How far they, or any like number, are equal to such a task, and how repugnant a defensive plan is to the true interest and welfare of the colony, I submit to any one to determine who will consider the following particulars.

First, that erecting forts at greater distances than fifteen or eighteen miles, or a day's march asunder, and garrisoning them with less than eighty or a hundred men each, is not answering the intention; because, if they are at a greater distance from each other, it is inconvenient for the soldiers to scout between them, and it gives the enemy full scope to make incursions without being discovered, until they have fallen on the inhabitants and committed ravages. And, after they are discovered, the time required, in assembling troops from forts more distant, prevents a pursuit being made in time, and allows the enemy to escape without danger into a country so mountainous and full of swamps and hollow ways covered with woods. Then, if garrisoned with less than eighty or a hundred men, the number is too small to afford detachments, that are not very liable to be cut off by the enemy, whose numbers in this close country can scarcely be known till they are proved. Indian parties are generally intermixed with some French, and are so dexterous at skulking, that their spies, lying about these small forts for some days and taking a prisoner, make certain discoveries of the strength of the garrison; and then, upon observing a scouting party coming out, they will first cut it off, and afterwards attempt the fort. Instances of this have lately happened.

Secondly, our frontiers are of such extent, that if the enemy were to make a formidable attack on one side, before the troops on the other could give assistance, they might overrun the country; and it is not improbable, if they had a design on one part, that they would make a feint on the other.

Thirdly, the cost to the country in building these forts, and removing stores and provisions into them.

Fourthly, where and when will this expense end? We may be assured, if we do not endeavour to remove the cause, we shall be as liable to the same incursions seven years hence as now; indeed more so. Because, if the French are allowed to possess those lands in peace, they will have the entire command of the Indians, and grow stronger in their alliance; while we, by our defensive schemes and pusillanimous behaviour, shall exhaust our treasury, reduce our strength, and become the contempt of these savage nations, who are every day enriching themselves with the plunder and spoils of our people.

It will evidently appear from the whole tenor of my conduct, but more especially from reiterated representations, how strongly I have urged the Governor and Assembly to pursue different measures, and tried to convince them, by all the reasonings I could offer, of the impossibility of covering so extensive a frontier from Indian incursions, without more force than Virginia can maintain. I have endeavoured to demonstrate, that it would require fewer men to remove the cause, than to prevent the effects, while the cause subsists. This, notwithstanding, as I before observed, was the measure adopted, and the plan under which we have acted for eight months past, with the disagreeable reflection of doing no essential service to our country, nor gaining honor to ourselves, or reputation to our regiment. However, under these disadvantageous restraints I must beg leave to say, that the regiment has not been inactive; on the contrary, it has performed a vast deal of work, and has been very alert in defending the people. This will appear from the fact, that, notwithstanding we are more contiguous to the French and their Indian allies, and more exposed to their frequent incursions, than any of the neighbouring colonies, yet we have not lost half the number of inhabitants, that others have done, but considerably more soldiers in their defence. In the course of this campaign (since March, I mean, as we have had but one constant campaign, and one continued scene of action, from the time we first entered the service), our troops have been engaged in upwards of twenty skirmishes, and we have had near a hundred men killed and wounded. From a small regiment dispersed over the country, and acting upon the defensive, as ours does by order, this, I conceive, will not appear inconsiderable to those, who are in the least degree acquainted with the nature of this service, and the posture of our affairs; however it may seem to chimney-corner politicians, thirsting for news, and expecting by every express to hear in what manner Fort Duquesne is taken, and the garrison led away captive by our small numbers; although we are restrained from making the attempt, were our hopes of success ever so rational.

The next points, which I shall beg leave to mention, are our military laws and regulations.

The first men raised, if I rightly remember, were under no law; if any, the militia law, which was next of kin to none. Under this we remained a short time, and, by instilling the idea into the soldiers, who knew no better, that they were governed by the articles of war, we felt little inconvenience. The next campaign we were joined by the regulars, and made subject to their laws. After the regulars left us, the Assembly, as I before mentioned, passed an act in September following to raise twelve hundred men, and, in order I suppose to improve upon the act of Parliament, prepared a military code of their own, but such a one as could preserve no military discipline while it existed. This being represented by the most pressing and repeated remonstrances, the Assembly were induced to pass a bill in October following, for one year only, fixing the penalty of death for mutiny and desertion. But they took no cognizance of many other crimes, equally punishable by act of Parliament. So that no officer, or soldier, accused of cowardice, holding correspondence with the enemy, quitting a post, or sleeping upon it, and many other crimes of a capital dye, or pernicious tendency, could be legally tried. Neither was there any provision made for quartering or billeting soldiers, impressing wagons, and the like.

But that which contributed the most towards rendering this law inconvenient and absurd, and at the same time to demonstrate that the Assembly fully intended to prevent any enterprise of their troops out of the colony, was a clause forbidding any courts-martial to sit out of it; by which means all proceedings held at Fort Cumberland (in Maryland) were illegal, and we were obliged to remove to Virginia for the trial of offenders, or act contrary to law, and be open to prosecution.* How then were we to behave upon a march of perhaps fifty, eighty, or a hundred miles beyond? These circumstances concurring to render the law ineffectual, induced me again to recommend an amendment, which I did with all the force and energy of argument I was master of. But no regard has hitherto been paid to my remonstrances. To what cause it is owing, I know not, unless to short sittings and hurry of business; for I can conceive of no reason, why the Assembly should be

* On the 12th of January Colonel Washington wrote to the Governor respecting the trial of several subaltern officers and soldiers for a mutiny. "I thought it needless," said he, "to send you the proceedings of the court-martial, or to ask warrants for execution, as we have no law to inflict punishment, even of the smallest kind. I shall keep those criminals in irons, and, if possible, under apprehensions of death, until some favorable opportunity may countenance a reprieve." The Governor replied, that, as the men were enlisted and paid with money raised for the King's service, he conceived they were subject to the articles of war, in the same manner as the King's regular forces. But so tenacious was Colonel Washington in upholding the rights of the Assembly and the laws of the colony, that he did not accede to this opinion. He considered the Assembly as the only proper authority to prescribe rules of discipline for an army, raised and maintained at their expense; and he believed himself amenable to the civil laws for any acts of severity not countenanced by that code. This was conformable to the scrupulous exactness with which, during all his future military career, and frequently when the interest of the public service offered the strongest temptations to the contrary, he yielded implicit obedience to the civil power.

against instituting rules for the regulation of their forces, of which long experience in established armies has fully evinced the necessity. But, to cut short the account, we are under no government at all, properly speaking. Indeed, there is a jumble of laws that have little meaning or design in them, but to make the command intricate, and to prevent offence to the civil powers, who are tenacious of liberty, and prone to censure and condemn all proceedings not strictly according to the law, not considering what cases may arise to render them necessary.

Another grievance, to which this act subjects us, is the method prescribed to pay for deserters. Many of our deserters are apprehended in Maryland and Pennsylvania, and, for the sake of the reward, are brought to the regiment. But, instead of the reward, the persons thus bringing them in receive a certificate only, that they are entitled to two hundred pounds of tobacco. This certificate is to be presented to a Court of Claims, and they refer it to the Assembly. There it may perhaps remain two or three years before it is paid. This causes great dissatisfaction, and induces the ill-disposed to aid, rather than prevent, the escape of soldiers.

No regular provision is established for the maimed and wounded, which is discouraging, and grievously complained of. The soldiers justly observe, that the result of bravery is often a broken leg, arm, or incurable wound; and when they are disabled, and no longer fit for service, they are discharged, and reduced to the necessity of begging from door to door, or of perishing through indigence. It is true, no instance of this kind has yet appeared. On the contrary, the Assembly have dealt generously by those unfortunate soldiers, who have met with this fate. But then, this provision is not yet established, nor in any manner compulsory, and a man may suffer in the interval of their sitting.

After giving this short and true account of our military laws, and observing that even these laws are now expired, I conceive there need but few arguments to prove the difficulty of keeping soldiers under proper discipline, who know they are not punishable by law for the most atrocious crimes. How then is it to be wondered at, if mutiny, desertion, and all other irregularities should creep into a camp, or garrison, more especially if we consider that hard duty, and want of clothes and of almost every necessary that renders a soldier's life comfortable and easy, are strong incentives,—and, to go further, when these intolerable grievances are set to view in the most glaring point of light by a person, who, lost to all sense of honor and virtue, and building, I am sorry to say, upon a proclamation inviting the deserters from the *Virginia Regiment* to enlist into the *Royal American Regiment*, has made use of every artifice to represent the fatigues and hardships of our service, and the ease and conveniences of the other, to seduce them from their duty?

Want of clothing may be esteemed another principal grievance, which our soldiers have labored under. In the first twelve months of their service they received no clothing; but in March, 1754, they were presented each with a suit made of thin, sleazy cloth without lining, and flannel waistcoats of an inferior sort. After that no others were sent for (although two pence stoppage was drawn from every man's pay, recruits not excepted,) until repeated complaints and remonstrances from me, enforced in June last by a representation of many gentlemen of the Assembly, who had formed an association, and saw the disagreeable situation of the soldiers, induced the Committee, to whom those addresses were presented, to send for clothing. The clothes were to have been here by the middle of October, but no advice is received of them yet, which gives the soldiers some pretence to suspect they are deceived. It is to this irregular pay, and the causes aforementioned, that their late disobedience ought to be ascribed. For I can truly say, and confidently assert, that no soldiers ever were under better command than these were before.

Perhaps it may be asked, by gentlemen not thoroughly acquainted with the nature of our service, why the officers do not see that their men's pay is more properly applied? In answer I must beg leave to observe, that, after the soldiers have appropriated a part for purchasing reasonable and fit necessaries, the remainder is barely sufficient to keep them in shoes, owing, in the first place, to the very great consumption the service occasions, and, in the next, to the exorbitant price, which this article bears. I have known a soldier go upon command with a new pair of shoes, which perhaps have cost him from seven shillings and sixpence to ten shillings, and return without any; so much do they wear in wading creeks, fording rivers, and clambering mountains covered with rocks.

As great a grievance as any I have mentioned is yet unnoticed, and that is the present regulation of the militia; but a representation of this matter will come better and more properly from others.

To point out all the causes, which combine to make our service infinitely hard and disagreeable, would swell these observations into a volume, and require time, and a more able pen than mine. But there are yet some things, that should be mentioned.

An ill-judged economy is shown in raising men. We are either insensible of danger, till it breaks upon our heads, or else, through mistaken notions of economy, evade the expense, till the blow is struck, and then run into an extreme of raising militia. These, after an age, as it were, is spent in assembling them, come up, make a noise for a time, oppress the inhabitants, and then return, leaving the frontiers unguarded as before. And this plan is pursued, notwithstanding former experience convinces us, if reason did not, that the French and Indians are watching their opportunity, when we are lulled into fatal security, unprepared for resisting an attack, to muster their forces to invade the country. By ravaging one part they terrify another, and retreat when our militia assemble, but repeat the stroke as soon as they are dispersed, sending down parties in the interim to discover our motions, procure intelligence, and sometimes to divert our troops. Such an invasion we may expect in March, if measures to prevent it are neglected, as they hitherto have been.

The want of tools occasions insurmountable difficulties in carrying on our works, either offensive or defensive. Cartridge-paper is an article not to be met with in Virginia.

And now, before I conclude, I must beg leave to add, that my unwearied endeavours are inadequately rewarded. The orders I receive are full of ambiguity. I am left, like a wanderer in the wilderness, to proceed at hazard. I am answerable for consequences, and blamed, without the privilege of defence. This, my Lord, I beg leave to declare, is at present my situation. Therefore, it is not to be wondered at, if, under such peculiar circumstances, I should be sick of a service, which promises so little of a soldier's reward. I have long been satisfied of the impossibility of continuing in this service, without loss of honor. Indeed, I was fully convinced of it before I accepted the command the second time, seeing the cloudy prospect before me; and

I did for this reason reject the offer, until I was ashamed any longer to refuse, not caring to expose my character to public censure. The solicitations of the country overcame my objections, and induced me to accept it.

Another reason has of late operated to continue me in the service until now, and that is, the dawn of hope that arose, when I heard your Lordship was destined by his Majesty for the important command of his armies in America, and appointed to the government of his dominion of Virginia. Hence it was, that I drew my hopes, and fondly pronounced your Lordship our patron. Although I had not the honor to be known to your Lordship, yet your name was familiar to my ear, on account of the important services rendered to his Majesty in other parts of the world.

Ever since our defeat at the Meadows, and behaviour under General Braddock, we have been tantalized, nay, bid to expect most sanguinely a better establishment, and have waited in tedious expectation of seeing this accomplished. The Assembly, it is true, have, I believe, done every thing in their power to bring this about; first, by soliciting his Honor, the Lieutenant-Governor, to address his Majesty; and next, by addressing his Majesty themselves in favor of their regiment. What success these addresses have met with, I am yet ignorant. With regard to myself, I cannot forbear adding, that, had General Braddock survived his unfortunate defeat, I should have met with preferment agreeable to my wishes. I had his promise to that purpose, and I believe that gentleman was too sincere and generous to make unmeaning offers, where no favors were asked. General Shirley was not unkind in his promises, but he has gone to England.

I do not know, my Lord, in what light this short and disinterested relation may be received; but it is offered with the utmost candor and submission. It contains no misrepresentations, nor aggravated statement of facts, nor unjust reflections.

Virginia is a country young in war, and, till the breaking out of these disturbances, has remained in the most profound and tranquil peace, never studying war nor warfare. It is not, therefore, to be imagined, that she can fall into proper measures at once. All that can be expected at her hands she cheerfully offers, — the sinews of war, — and these only want your Lordship's ability and experience to be properly applied and directed.

Finally, my Lord, how to apologize for assuming a freedom, which must at any rate give you trouble, I know not, unless an ardent zeal to serve my country, and a steady attachment to her interests, and to the honor of arms, shall plead an excuse, till I am so happy as to have an opportunity of testifying in person how much I admire your Lordship's character, and with what profound respect I have the honor to be, &c. *

* The Earl of Loudoun was expected in Virginia, and Colonel Washington had permission from the Governor to proceed at the same time to Williamsburg. The plan was afterwards changed, and his Lordship requested the governors of the southern colonies to meet him at Philadelphia, where they assembled about the first of March. This letter was written previously, and forwarded to New York. Mr. Cuningham, aid-de-camp to Lord Loudoun, acknowledged the receipt of it on the 27th of February, and added, "His Lordship seems very much pleased with the accounts you have given him of the situation of affairs to the southward."

Colonel Washington had stationed himself, according to orders, at Fort Cumberland. He went likewise to Philadelphia, by consent of the Governor, which was granted, it must be allowed, in no very gracious terms.

"His Lordship has desired all the southern governors," his Honor writes, "to meet him at Philadelphia, and consult what is proper to be done in these parts. As this appears to be the design of this meeting, I cannot conceive what service you can be of in going there, as the plan concerted will in course be communicated to you and the other officers. However, as you seem so earnest to go, I now give you leave."

From the tone of this letter, as well as from many other indications, he

TO RICHARD WASHINGTON, MERCHANT, LONDON.

Fort Loudoun, 15 April, 1757.

DEAR SIR,

After so long silence it may be expected, that I should introduce this letter with an apology for my seeming neglect. I own, Sir, it is necessary to urge something in my defence, and what can be so proper as the truth?

I have been posted, then, for twenty months past upon our cold and barren frontiers, to perform, I think I may say, impossibilities; that is, to protect from the cruel incursions of a crafty, savage enemy a line of inhabitants, of more than three hundred and fifty miles in extent, with a force inadequate to the task. By this means I am become in a manner an exile, and seldom informed of those opportunities, which I might otherwise embrace, of corresponding with my friends.

Experience has convinced every thinking man in this colony, that we must bid adieu to peace and safety whilst the French are allowed to possess the Ohio, and to practise their arts among the numerous tribes of Indian nations that inhabit those regions, and that it must be attended with an expense infinitely greater to defend our possessions, as they ought to be defended against the skulking enemy, than to remove the cause of our groundless fears, by the reduction of Fort Duquesne.

---

had no reason to expect a warm friend in the Governor of Virginia at the councils in Philadelphia. He did not fail, therefore, to embrace the opportunity, reluctantly as it had been granted, of being present and attending personally to the interests of his regiment, and to affairs in which he was so deeply concerned. He was consulted by Lord Loudoun, in regard to the future disposition of the forces on the frontiers of the southern colonies. But after all, he was not successful in his wish to have the Virginia regiment put upon the same footing as the regular army, and to obtain King's commissions for himself and his officers.

Yet, from what strange causes I know not, no attempt this season will be made, I fear, to destroy this hold of the barbarians, for they deserve no better name, who have become a terror to three populous colonies. Virginia may justly say, that she was always willing to furnish her full proportion of men and money for this desirable end; and, I think I may venture to affirm, that there never was, and I verily believe never will be, a more favorable time than the present for an enterprise of this kind, while the enemy's troops are doubtless drawn off to the northward, to defend themselves at home against the more formidable attack of Lord Loudoun.

I have now to add, that I am so little acquainted with the business relative to my private affairs, that I can scarce give you any information concerning it. I know that I ought to have some tobacco, and that it ought to be stripped. I have begged the favor of two persons to do this for me, and I desired them to write you in my behalf, and draw for sundry things, of which I am in want; but whether any part or all of this has been done, I know not. I shall, therefore, desire these two things of you; first, that you will put yourself to no real inconvenience in forwarding goods to a greater amount than my remittance, because I by no means intended to be troublesome, when I solicited your correspondence; and, secondly, that whatever goods you may send me, where the prices are not absolutely limited, you will let them be fashionable, neat, and good in their several kinds. Enclosed is a list of sundries, which I should be glad to receive agreeably to these directions.

I am, dear Sir,

Your affectionate friend, and obedient servant.

TO GOVERNOR DINWIDDIE.

Fort Cumberland, 16 April, 1757.

SIR,

Your letter by express, of the 5th instant, I fear has fallen into the hands of the common enemy, for I never have seen it. The other of the 7th I this day received; and being exceedingly embarrassed to come at your intentions, and really at a loss to know in what manner to act, in such perplexed and difficult circumstances, I called a council of officers to my aid. The result of their advice you will find in the enclosed.*

* According to the plan concerted at Philadelphia for future operations, Fort Cumberland was henceforward to be garrisoned by Maryland forces, and the Virginia troops, provisions, and stores were to be removed to Fort Loudoun. Hence, Colonel Washington's views, as far as Virginia was concerned, were at a late hour adopted, after a tedious winter had been spent, and much money had been wasted, in carrying on the works at that fort.

In a letter, dated on the 5th of April, which had miscarried, Governor Dinwiddie had ordered the immediate evacuation of the place by the Virginia troops; and also, that two companies should be forthwith despatched to Fredericksburg, under Colonel Stephen, destined by direction of Lord Loudoun for South Carolina, where an attack from the enemy was apprehended, both by sea and on the frontiers. In another letter dated on the 7th, the Governor had reiterated his orders. In this dilemma a council of war was called, who decided that the fort ought not to be evacuated, till the Maryland forces under Captain Dagworthy should arrive.

Fort Cumberland seemed destined to be a perpetual source of uneasiness in some quarter. When the Maryland Assembly met, Governor Sharpe requested means to supply provisions for that garrison. The Assembly retorted with a warmth of disapprobation amounting to a reprimand. "That garrison," say they, "was stationed contrary to the plain destination of all the forces raised and to be supported by law; and, if any evil consequences have heretofore or may hereafter follow a want of supplies, let those answer for them, who have, contrary to law, been the means of stationing troops where they had no authority to place them."—*Votes and Proceedings for October*, 1757.

The Maryland Assembly denied the power of Lord Loudoun over the forces raised and paid by that colony, and his right to command them under any exigency without their consent. Whereupon his Lordship wrote a letter to Governor Sharpe, protesting against this doctrine, as

It will not be in my power to be in Williamsburg by the 22d, as your Honor desires; but as soon after as I can, I certainly will. I shall leave orders with Colonel Stephen to march this garrison to Fort Loudoun, as soon as it is relieved, which cannot be before this express may return, and then your further orders may be received. We have no advice of Dagworthy's marching, though orders were sent to him.

I shall order all the country's stores to be carried to Fort Loudoun, and the two companies on Patterson's Creek to be posted on the Branch, to complete the number that was designed for that place. I have ordered a particular return of the provisions to be made out, and Colonel Stephen to take Captain Dagworthy's receipt for the quantity left.

We have been at a good deal of unavoidable expense and trouble to furnish the Indians with such things as they wanted. Some hostile Indians killed two Catawbas on Thursday last, at about one hundred and fifty yards from the fort, and seventy from a sentry, and made their escape, though pursued by other Catawbas and near two hundred men. And the day before yesterday, two soldiers were killed and a third taken prisoner, as they were coming to this place from the fort below. The rest of the party, being ten in number, with Captain Waggener among them, made their escape.

The enclosed remonstrance I have just received, and think it expedient to send it to your Honor, that you may know the temper and disposition of the troops. As I expect to be with you in two or three days after the express, I think it needless to add any thing but an

without precedent, and peculiar to Maryland alone.— *Ibid. for February*, 1758. Governor Dinwiddie, in his usual way, declared it "inconsistent and unmannerly in the Maryland Assembly to make any hesitation, or to dispute his Lordship's power." — *Letter to Governor Sharpe.*

apology for the incoherence of this letter. The Indians are all around teazing and perplexing me for one thing or another, so that I scarce know what I write.

I have the honor to be, &c.

TO JOHN ROBINSON, SPEAKER OF THE HOUSE OF BURGESSES.

Fort Loudoun, 30 May, 1757.*

DEAR SIR,

We receive fresh proofs every day of the bad direction of our Indian affairs. It is not easy to tell what expenses have arisen on account of these Indians, how dissatisfied they are, and how gloomy the prospect of pleasing them appears, while we pursue our present system of management.

I therefore beg leave to propose a plan, which I know is exactly conformable to the French policy, and which may, if properly executed, be a means of retrieving our lost credit with these people, and prove of infinite service to the country. The French have a proper person appointed to the direction of these affairs, who makes it his sole business to study the dispositions of the Indians, and the art of pleasing them. This person is invested with power to treat with and reward them for every

---

* Colonel Washington was now returned from Williamsburg, where he had been for several days concerting with the Governor some new arrangements for the troops. The regiment was remodelled, and reduced to ten companies, of one hundred men each. Head-quarters were fixed at Fort Loudoun.

It had been decided by the Convention at Philadelphia, that four hundred men should be sent from the Virginia regiment to the aid of South Carolina. Colonel Stephen sailed from Hampton with two companies, but no others followed. South Carolina was not attacked, and a timely reinforcement from England quieted the alarms in that quarter.

piece of service, and thus, by timely presents on suitable occasions, to obtain very great advantages. There is always a store of goods committed to his care to answer these purposes, and no other person is suffered to meddle with it; by which means the whole business is thrown into one channel, and it thereby becomes easy and regular. Whereas, with us it is every body's business, and no one's, to afford supplies. Every person attempts to please, and few succeed in it, because one promises this, and another that, and few can perform any thing, but are obliged to shuffle and put the Indians off, to get rid of their importunities.

Hence they accuse us of perfidy and deceit. I could recapitulate a great number of their reproachful complaints, if I judged it necessary to confirm what I have already advanced. But I believe, Sir, you are convinced from what you have seen, that there can be no deception in my story. Therefore, I shall remark with candor, freedom, and submission, that, unless some person is appointed to manage the Indian affairs of this colony, under the direction of the Governor, or the southern agent,* a vast expense and but a little advantage will accrue from the coming of the Indians among us. And I know of no person so well qualified for an undertaking of this sort as the bearer, Captain Gist. He has had extensive dealings with the Indians, is in great esteem among them, well acquainted with their manners and customs, indefatigable, and patient, — most excellent qualities where Indians are concerned. As to his capacity, honesty, and zeal, I dare venture to engage. If he should be appointed to this duty, or, if this plan should take effect, I dare say you will judge it advisable

* Mr. Atkin, recently appointed the King's agent to take charge of all affairs relating to the Indians, who inhabited the country between Pennsylvania and Georgia.

to send for a large assortment of that species of goods best suited for carrying on the abovementioned business.

Bullen, a Catawba warrior, has been proposing a plan to Captain Gist for bringing in the Creek and Chickasaw Indians. If such a scheme could be effected, by the time we shall march for Fort Duquesne, it would be a glorious undertaking, and worthy of the man.

I am, &c.

TO JOHN ROBINSON.

Fort Loudoun, 10 June, 1757.

DEAR SIR,

A person of a readier pen, and having more time, than myself, might amuse you with the vicissitudes, which have happened in the Indian affairs since Mr. Atkin came up. I acknowledge my incompetency, and therefore shall only observe, that the Indians have been pleased and displeased oftener than they ought to have been; and that they are gone off (that party under Warhatalie, I mean,) in different ways, and with far different views; one company southwardly to their nation; and another northwardly to treat with the Pennsylvanians, contrary to the sentiments of Mr. Atkin, who has, I believe, sent to forbid any conference to be held with them.

Major Lewis is returned with part of the Indians, that went out with him, in consequence of their having taken only eight days' provisions with them. He was unable to prevail with those savages to take more. One party of twenty, with ten soldiers, is gone towards Fort Duquesne, under Captain Spotswood; and another party of fifteen, with five soldiers, under Lieutenant

Baker, who are to proceed towards Logstown. God send them success and a safe return.

Unless you will interest yourself in sending money to discharge the public debts, I must inevitably suffer very considerably, as the country people all think me pledged to them, let what will happen. They are grown very clamorous, and will be more than ever incensed, if there should come an inadequate sum, and that sum be appropriated to the payment of the soldiers.

I am convinced it would give pleasure to the Governor to hear that I was involved in trouble, however undeservedly, such are his dispositions towards me.

I am, &c.

TO COLONEL STANWIX.*

Fort Loudoun, 15 June, 1757.

SIR,

A scouting party, consisting of five soldiers and fifteen Cherokee Indians, who were sent out the 20th ultimo towards the Ohio, under Lieutenant Baker, returned the 8th instant to Fort Cumberland with five scalps, and a French officer, prisoner, having killed two other officers of the same party. Mr. Baker met with this party (ten French, three officers) on the head of Turtle Creek, twenty miles from Fort Duquesne, the day after they had parted with fifty Shawanese Indians returning from war, and would have killed and made prisoners of them all, had not the death of the Indian

---

* Colonel Stanwix was stationed by the Earl of Loudoun on the frontiers of Pennsylvania, with the command of five companies of the Royal American Regiment. He was now at Lancaster, but his head-quarters were afterwards at Carlisle. A correspondence, as well friendly as official, was kept up between him and Colonel Washington.

chief, who was killed in that skirmish, prevented their pursuing them. The name of the officer taken, according to his own account, is Velistre; and of those killed, Lasosais and St. Oure; all ensigns.

The commandant at Duquesne and its dependencies is Delignery, a knight of the military order of St. Louis, and captain of a company of detached troops from the marine. This officer likewise says, that the garrison at Fort Duquesne consists of six hundred French and two hundred Indians. We sustained on our side the loss of the brave Swallow warrior, and one other Indian wounded, whom the party brought in on a bier, with no other sustenance for the last four days, than such as they derived from wild onions.

Captain Spotswood, with ten soldiers and twenty Indians, who went out at the same time, but to a different place, is not yet come in, nor any news of him; which makes me uneasy.

Our Assembly have granted a further sum of eighty thousand pounds for the service of the ensuing year, and have agreed, I believe, to complete the regiment of this colony to twelve hundred men, besides three companies of rangers, of one hundred men each. Our strength, since the detachment embarked for Carolina, amounts only to four hundred and twenty rank and file; and these much weakened, by the number of posts we hold. Governor Dinwiddie is apprehensive, that he shall not be able to provide arms for all these men, and he desired me to advise with you thereupon.

Duty and inclination equally induce me to communicate all remarkable occurrences to you, and I shall be punctual in doing so. At present, however, I have only to add, that I am, with very great respect, your most obedient humble servant.

TO GOVERNOR DINWIDDIE.

Fort Loudoun, 16 June, 1757.

SIR,

This instant the enclosed letters came to my hands. I have not lost a moment's time in transmitting them to you, as I look upon the intelligence to be of the utmost importance. If the enemy are coming down in such numbers, and with such a train of artillery, as we are bid to expect, Fort Cumberland must inevitably fall into their hands, as no timely efforts can be made to relieve the garrison. I send you a copy of a council of war held upon this occasion. The advice I intend to pursue, until I receive orders. It is morally certain, that the next object, which the French have in view, is Fort Loudoun, and that is yet in a very untenable posture. They have no roads for carriages into any other province, except through this; and there lies a quantity of stores here, belonging to his Majesty and to this colony, very much exposed and unguarded.

I shall not take up your time, with a tedious detail. You will be a sufficient judge of the present situation of affairs, from the circumstances already related. I have written to the commanding officers of Fairfax, Prince William, and Culpeper counties, (a copy of the letters I enclose,) requesting them to march part of their militia to this place immediately, that no time may be lost. You may be assured, Sir, I shall make the best defence I can, if attacked. I am, &c.

P. S. I have written to Colonel Stanwix an account of this affair, and enclosed him copies of the letters and council of war.*

---

* Six Cherokee Indians came to Fort Cumberland, and told Captain Dagworthy, that they saw the French near Fort Duquesne coming in that

TO COLONEL STANWIX.

Fort Loudoun, 20 June, 1757.

SIR,

Yours of the 18th from the camp at Carlisle I received about noon this day, when, in company with his Majesty's agent for Indian affairs, I was examining the French prisoner brought to this place by Lieutenant Baker and the Cherokee Indian. A copy of this examination I herewith enclose. You will find, Sir, from the tenor of his answers, that a large body of Indians was hourly expected at Fort Duquesne, and that, although there was not (if his intelligence is to be literally credited, and surely it is not) a train of artillery fit for such an expedition; yet this might have been brought by those three hundred men, who arrived there after he left the place.

It is altogether evident, if the Indian accounts may be relied on, that the French are bringing howitzers with them for the easier reduction of the place, if they should attack us. For, say they, your guns are but muskets, compared with those the French have with them. Theirs will admit a fawn in the muzzle, while yours will not take in a man's fist. To any person, in the least degree acquainted with the mountainous country about our settlements, it is clear, that the French can bring artillery along no other road, than that from Fort Duquesne to Fort Cumberland, without spending immense time in mending one. I conceive that the garrison at Fort Augusta has been very negligent and inactive, not

---

direction with wagons and great guns. An attack was apprehended, the country alarmed, the militia called out, and Colonel Stanwix's regulars were put in motion; but it proved to be a false report. Dagworthy was either deceived by the Indians, or, what is more likely, he misunderstood their meaning.

to discover the enemy sooner. On the other hand, a blazed path in the eyes of an Indian is a large road; for he does not distinguish, without a close inspection, between a track which will admit of carriages, and a road sufficient for Indians to march in.

These, Sir, are only my own sentiments, and I submit them to your better judgment. We very well know, that from Fort Duquesne to Fort Cumberland there is a plain road already made, and bridges also. I shall, however, continue to pursue every means in my power to gain the earliest and best intelligence of the approaches of the enemy, and shall transmit it forthwith to you. I have sent Major Lewis fifty miles in advance of this place, with orders to keep out constant spies for intelligence, and to lose no time in forwarding it to me.

We have received nothing new from Fort Cumberland since the 16th. The Indians, who brought the first news, imagine, that some of Spotswood's party are yet watching the motions of the enemy. On the contrary, I apprehend they are all cut off; for a man, who left Fort Cumberland the 16th, says, that the woods appear to be quite alive with hostile Indians, who show themselves openly in the day. This is unusual with them, unless they are strong.

We work on this Fort, both night and day, intending to make it tenable against the worst event. Mr. Croghan and others write you by this express, and will no doubt be more explicit on Indian affairs, than I can pretend to be, and to them I refer. I am, &c.

TO COLONEL STANWIX.

Fort Loudoun, 28 June, 1757.

DEAR SIR,

I have had the pleasure of receiving your two favors both of the 22d instant. We were reinforced, upon the late alarm, by one hundred and seventy militia from the adjacent counties, one half of them unarmed, and the whole without ammunition or provisions.

Had you, Sir, in consequence of Captain Beall's * suggestions, ordered me to reinforce Fort Cumberland, with part of my regiment, I should have given you proof of my willingness to obey your commands, by a speedy compliance with them; but since you are so kind as to leave it discretionary with me, I freely confess, that I cannot entertain any thoughts of parting with the few soldiers I have, to strengthen a place that now seems to be in no actual danger. Nor can I help observing, that I think it a little odd in Captain Beall, after having received subsequent notice of the fallacy of his first intelligence, to intimate that it was reasonable to reinforce Fort Cumberland, at the expense of Virginia, which has a frontier to defend thirty times the extent of that of Maryland, and this frontier left solely to the protection of her few regular troops. †

* Commandant of the garrison at Fort Frederic in Maryland.

† Colonel Washington was in some sort under the command of Colonel Stanwix, but to what extent he did not know, as he had received no instructions on that head, and the Governor continued to issue his orders as formerly. At length the Governor wrote as follows; — "Colonel Stanwix being appointed commander-in-chief [of the middle and southern provinces], you must submit to his orders, without regard to any you may receive from me; he, being near the place, can direct affairs better than I can." This was peculiarly agreeable to the Commander of the Virginia regiment, for Colonel Stanwix was a military man, and a gentleman of an elevated and liberal spirit. His letters bear a high testimony to his good

I flatter myself, that the account of an expected attack upon Fort Augusta [in Pennsylvania], will prove more favorable, than Colonel Weiser imagines; for I have no conception, that a road fit for carriages can be cut within ten miles of a fort, without its being discovered by the garrison.

The friendship and assistance of the Cherokees are well worth cultivating. For my own part, I think them indispensably necessary in our present circumstances, and am sorry to find such unseasonable delays in bringing them amongst us. Since Captain Croghan left this place, Antasity, an Indian warrior of that nation, with twenty-seven followers, has arrived here. He brings an account of many more that are coming; but whether they will wait for Mr. Atkin's passport, or come on with their own, I know not.

I have just received a letter from Governor Dinwiddie, in which he desires me to present his compliments to you. I am, &c.

---

sense, as well as to the delicacy of his feelings, the amenity of his temper, and the generosity of his character.

Notwithstanding the above direction, the Governor did not cease to write, give commands, require returns, and utter complaints as usual, thereby increasing the endless perplexities and bewildering doubts, with which Colonel Washington was harassed in all his plans and operations.

It has heretofore been seen, that he had requested leave of absence for a few days to attend to certain private affairs of a very pressing nature, at Mount Vernon. He afterwards repeated this request, and, as he seemed to be under two commanders, he thought it expedient to consult them both. The Governor answered; — "As to the settlement of your brother's estate, your absence on that account from Fort Loudoun must be suspended, till our affairs give a better prospect." Colonel Stanwix replied to the same request; — "More than two weeks ago I answered your letter, in which you mentioned its being convenient to your private affairs to attend to them for a fortnight. In that answer I expressed my concern, that you should think such a thing necessary to mention to me, as I am sure you would not choose to be out of call, should the service require your immediate attendance; and I hope you will always take that liberty upon yourself, which I hope you will now do."

TO COLONEL STANWIX.

Fort Loudoun, 30 July, 1757.

DEAR SIR,

My former letters would inform you how little share I had in confining the Indians in the public jail at this place.*

Mr. Atkin, in his Majesty's name, applied to me as commanding officer for aid to secure these people, which I thereupon rendered, but not without first representing the consequences, that might and in some measure really did happen. This step was no sooner taken, than the Cherokees in town, about twenty-two in number, despatched a runner to inform their people, that the English had fallen upon their brethren, and desired that they (the Cherokees) would stand upon their defence. Another runner, you know, went to Carlisle to inform the warriors there, who returned fully resolved to rescue the prisoners, or die in the attempt. The former they effected, and were so enraged with Mr. Atkin, that they would hold no conference with him the next day, when he sent to desire it, till they had first been with me for information. I took great pains to convince them, that it was a mistake, and happily succeeded. They agreed to send an Indian to their nation with an express, whom I might procure, to prevent a massacre of all the traders and white people there, which they looked upon as inevitable, unless timely measures were taken to prevent it.

Out of the great number of drafts that have deserted from us, we have been able to apprehend twenty-two; of whom two were hanged on Thursday last. The

* Mr. Atkin had hastily imprisoned ten Indians, upon suspicion of their being spies, or in the French interest.

eight companies now remaining in Virginia are completed to about eighty men each, rank and file, four commanding officers, four sergeants, and two drummers, and are all marched to the several posts assigned them.

The commission, which I have received from Governor Dinwiddie, to hold general courts-martial, is very long, and rather a repetition of the act. I should be obliged, if you would let me know whether this be right or not. I am, &c.

TO GOVERNOR DINWIDDIE.

Fort Loudoun, 27 August, 1757.

SIR,

The drafts from Lunenburg are arrived, to the number of sixteen, which does not replace the soldiers, that have deserted since my last. The drafts, when they were divided among the eight companies in July, completed them to eighty-six rank and file; and there remained over and above forty workmen, whom I detained at this place, as mentioned in a former letter.

What the strength of the companies is just at this time, I am no more able to say, not knowing what casualties may have happened since, than I am to send your Honor a return of the regiment, which is impossible till I get my returns from the several out-posts; and that, I believe your Honor must be sensible, is difficult and precarious, dispersed as the regiment is. I have given express orders, however, that those returns shall be made to me as regularly as the nature of things will admit, and I shall not be wanting in my duty to forward them, nor shall I delay to send the companies' size-rolls, when they come to my hands.

The enclosed is a copy of a report made to me by

two officers, who were instructed to inspect the provisions at Fort Cumberland. Mr. Kennedy, who was entrusted with the care of these provisions, is now there repacking and pickling them; and when he has finished, I shall endeavour to do the best I can with them, but despair of turning them to the least advantage.

A letter, which I received a few days ago from Captain Waggener advises, that the enemy appeared upon the Branch, not far from his neighbourhood, their numbers uncertain, killed several men, and captured others, without his being able to meet with them. On Sunday last, a small party of five Cherokees, who came here a few days ago, set out to war.

Your Honor having asked my opinion concerning recruiting, I shall give it candidly as follows. I believe, unless we are permitted to enlist servants, we should spend much time to little purpose in this service; such a spirit of opposition prevails in one sort of people, and so little spirit of any kind in another. I never thought, in the most distant degree, of recruiting for the additional companies, till the others were complete; nor should I have mentioned that subject, had I not supposed it was required by the act of Assembly.

As you were pleased to leave it to my discretion to punish or pardon the criminals, I have resolved on the latter, since I find example of so little weight, and since those poor unhappy criminals have undergone no small pain of body and mind, in a dark prison, closely ironed.

I have filled up a commission for Sergeant Flint, and will send it to him by the first safe conveyance. Colonel Stanwix, I am told (the truth of which I doubt), has marched to the northward. I have had no account from him these four weeks.

Mr. Boyd, to whom I have spoken on the matter, conceives, that there will be no money left for contingent expenses, when he has paid the troops. I shall do as your Honor directs, with regard to escorting Mr. Boyd to Augusta, and ordering officers to wait upon him at this place, however inconvenient it may prove to the service.

Nothing remarkable has happened, for which reason I have nothing in particular to add. I must beg leave, however, before I conclude, to observe, in justification of my own conduct, that it is with pleasure I receive reproof, when reproof is due, because no person can be readier to accuse me, than I am to acknowledge an error, when I am guilty of one; nor more desirous of atoning for a crime, when I am sensible of having committed it. But, on the other hand, it is with concern I remark, that my best endeavours lose their reward, and that my conduct, although I have uniformly studied to make it as unexceptionable as I could, does not appear to you in a favorable point of light.* Otherwise your Honor would not accuse me of loose behaviour and remissness of duty, in matters where, I believe, I have rather exceeded than fallen short of it. This, I think, is evidently the case in speaking of Indian Affairs at all, after being instructed in very express terms, "*not to have any concern with or management of Indian affairs.*" This has caused me to forbear mentioning the Indians in any of my letters to you of late, and to leave the misunderstanding, which you speak of, between Mr. Atkin and the Indians, to be related by him, knowing that he maintained a correspondence with you on matters rela-

* In the letter to which this was an answer, the Governor had used much freedom of complaint and censure.

"You have sent a detachment from the regiment to Augusta," he observes, "but you do not mention the number; nor do you mention the receipt of the small arms sent from this; nor any account of the misunderstanding with the Indians at Winchester. You must allow this is a loose way of writing, and it is your duty to be more particular to me."

tive to his office. But, with regard to the accounts, when he would have nothing to do with them, and when I was hourly importuned for the payment, and knew I had not the means, what could I do less than promise the people, that I would recommend their cases to your Honor, in hopes that you would appoint a person, in whom you could confide, to take in and pay off their accounts, as I always looked upon it to be a duty distinct from mine, and therefore was unwilling to intermeddle in the affair?

I really thought it unnecessary to say more, than that "the detachment destined for Augusta had marched," because your Honor gave me a copy of the result of the council held at Philadelphia, which directed one hundred and fifty men to be posted at Dickinson's, and one hundred at Vass's, which direction I observed, and I thought it would be sufficiently understood when I wrote as above.

I should have acknowledged the receipt of the arms, had they come to hand, but they were not arrived when my last was written; which obliged me to disarm the men remaining here, in order to supply those who marched, rather than detain them, as I had sent wagons to Falmouth to bring the arms from thence. However, if I have erred in these points, I am sorry for it, and shall endeavour for the future to be as particular and satisfactory, in my accounts of these things, as possible.

I am, with due respect,

Your Honor's most obedient, humble servant.

TO GOVERNOR DINWIDDIE.

Fort Loudoun, 17 September, 1757.

SIR,

Your favor of the 2d instant came safe to hand, and Jenkins's* sickness has prevented my answering it sooner.

I apprehend, that thirteen of the twenty-nine drafts from Lunenburg have deserted, as sixteen only have arrived here, and I have no accounts of any more being on their march. Your Honor may observe by the enclosed list of deserters, all of whom have left the regiment since the last return, and after having received their clothes, arms, and bounty money, how prevalent still is that infamous practice among the dastardly drafts, especially at this garrison, where I indulge them in every thing but idleness, and in that I cannot, the nature of the work requiring the contrary. Lenity, so far from producing its desired effects, rather emboldens them in these villanous acts. One of those condemned to be hanged, deserted immediately upon receiving his pardon. In short, they tire my patience, and almost weary me to death. The expense of pursuing them is very considerable, and to suffer them to escape, without pursuit, is giving up the point, although we have had but little success of late.

The uncertain and difficult communication with the out-posts must apologize for my not sending you a return of our strength for August. The second month will always be far advanced, before I can get in the returns of the preceding, as the month must be first expired, before the returns can be made out, and then

* A person employed to ride express between Williamsburg and the army.

some of them are to come two hundred and fifty miles, and great part of that distance through an uninhabited country.

If special messengers are always sent with these returns, it will be a considerable expense. I should therefore be glad if your Honor would be pleased to direct, whether they are to be sent to me by express, or by the best casual conveyance. In the one case, as I before said, there must be a constant expense, and in the other, great uncertainty. By the enclosed return for July, you will see that our total strength amounted to six hundred and ninety-nine; but, as many changes and casualties happened in that month, by reason of the drafts joining, deserting, and the companies not being properly formed, this return will, I apprehend, appear confused and irregular. Our present strength, I think, is about seven hundred. Major Lewis did, as he wrote you, march from this place with about one hundred and forty men only; but then Captain Woodward, who also marched at the same time, with his company from the South Branch, joined him at Dickinson's; and these troops, with the men under Captain Hogg, formed a body of something more than two hundred and fifty men, agreeably to the number appointed at Philadelphia for the forts at Dickinson's and Vass's.

I never expected, nor ever desired, that there should be an addition made to the number of those persons appointed to transact public business, much less that there should be one to settle every little affair. I only humbly proposed, that, as Captain Gist was empowered with your Honor's approbation to manage the Indian affairs here, and as he is to be paid for that duty by this colony, he should, as a more proper person than myself, take in and adjust the accounts against the Indians, so often mentioned, since it cannot reasonably be supposed that I, who am stripped of the help I once was allowed, and told that I should be freed from these things in consequence, can turn my hands and thoughts to such a multiplicity of business, as naturally arises out of the variety of occurrences, occasioned by our scattered and detached situation and the many extraneous concerns of the Indians. Every person, who sees how I am employed, will readily testify, that very little recreation falls to my lot. Nevertheless, if it is your order, that I shall collect these accounts, I will do it in the best manner I am able, and that with cheerfulness; but it will be some time before it can be accomplished, as I have turned them off once.

The Indian chiefs, before they departed for their nation, warmly solicited me for some drums; and, as I had none but those belonging to the regiment, which could not be spared, I was obliged to promise them, that I would acquaint your Honor with their request, that you might, if you thought proper, provide them against their return.

Since my last, the enemy came to the Branch, where they killed four men, wounded one, captured a man and a woman, and burned some grain, notwithstanding the utmost efforts of the troops, who are constantly scouting. The people in that quarter are terribly frightened by this last irruption, and I fear can hardly be prevented from deserting that valuable settlement.

When your Honor shall be pleased to order the vacancy, occasioned by the death of Captain Spotswood,* to be filled up with the name of Captain McNeil, there will be room for a lieutenant; and should you bestow the commission on Mr. Fairfax, I shall take it infinitely kind, if you will oblige me so far as to send it immediately

* Captain Spotswood, with a party under him, had been cut off by the Indians.

from yourself to that gentleman.* Although I esteem him greatly on account of his father, for whose memory and friendship I shall ever retain a most grateful regard, yet, making him lieutenant over so many ensigns of long standing, will occasion great confusion in the corps, and bring censure on me; for the officers will readily conceive, that my friendship and partiality for the family were the causes of it. If Mr. Fairfax would accept of an ensigncy, the matter might pretty easily be accommodated. The letter under cover to Colonel Fairfax is not yet come to hand.

I have heard nothing yet from Colonel Stanwix; but soon shall, as I wrote to him a few days ago, and expect his answer.

As we have not at this time either commissary or assistant here, it is not in my power to send a return of the provisions with any tolerable exactness. But I do not doubt, that Mr. Rutherford, our acting commissary, who is now below, has satisfied your Honor fully in this particular; if he has not, I will take care to do it in my next.

I doubt not your Honor will see the necessity of making an agreement with the contractors, for furnishing the Indians with provisions; otherwise they will take no concern in this matter. I conceive they are allowed a certain amount for each soldier, that shall be returned, and that Indians are included. If not, no persons will supply them on the same terms, that they do soldiers, for Indians eat and waste triple as much as soldiers.

I am your Honor's, &c.

---

* The commission had not been solicited by Colonel Washington, nor was the application of Mr. Fairfax's friends made through him, but directly to the Governor.

TO GOVERNOR DINWIDDIE.

Fort Loudoun, 17 September, 1757.

SIR,

A letter of the 22d ultimo, from Captain Peachey, came to my hands the other day, the contents of which are herewith forwarded.* I should take it infinitely kind, if your Honor would please to inform me, whether a report of this nature was ever made to you; and, in that case, who was the author of it?

It is evident, from a variety of circumstances, and especially from the change in your Honor's conduct towards me, that some person, as well inclined to detract, but better skilled in the art of detraction, than the author of the above stupid scandal, has made free with my character. For I cannot suppose, that malice so absurd, so barefaced, so diametrically opposite to truth, to common policy, and, in short, to every thing but villany,

* The letter begins by detailing a conversation, which the writer had lately held with Mr. Charles Carter, of Shirley, respecting a transaction in which Captain Peachey had been concerned some months before, on a mission to Williamsburg, when the frontiers were in great alarm from the incursions of the enemy; and then proceeds; —

"Mr. Carter says, that Mr. Christopher Robinson told him he heard Colonel R. C. say, that I affirmed, that my whole business at that time was to execute a scheme of yours to cause the Assembly to levy largely both in men and money, and that there was not an Indian in the neighbourhood; that the frontiers, and even Winchester and the adjacent country, did not appear to be in any more danger at that time than any other. Mr. Robinson also informed Mr. Carter, it was said, that that piece of deceit, or imposition of yours (as they term it), had lessened the Governor's and some of the leading men's esteem for you; or, at least, they make use of it as a reason for their ill treatment, and the worse opinion they say they have of you than formerly.

"I hope you know me better than even to suppose I could be guilty of a thing of this kind; therefore, I shall only add, that you may depend I shall use my endeavour to trace the matter, till I find the person, that dares make himself the author of such a scandalous report. If you think fit to make use of the above, you are at full liberty to do so."

as the above is, could impress you with so ill an opinion of my honor and honesty.

If it be possible, that Colonel C., — for my belief is staggered, not being conscious of having given the least cause to any one, much less to that gentlemen, to reflect so grossly, — I say, if it be possible, that Colonel C. could descend so low as to be the propagator of this story, he must either be vastly ignorant of the state of affairs in this county at that time, or else he must suppose, that the whole body of inhabitants had combined with me, in executing the fraud. Or why did they, almost to a man, forsake their dwellings in the greatest terror and confusion; so that, while one half of them sought shelter in paltry forts, of their own building, the other fled to the adjacent counties for refuge, numbers of them even to Carolina, from whence they have never returned?

These are facts well known; but not better known, than that these wretched people, while they lay pent up in forts, destitute of the common support of life (having in their precipitate flight forgotten, or rather been unable to secure, any kind of necessaries), did despatch messengers of their own (thinking I had not represented their miseries in the piteous manner they deserved), with addresses to your Honor and the Assembly, praying relief. And did I ever send any alarming account, without also sending the original papers, or the copies, which gave rise to it?

That I have foibles, and perhaps many of them, I shall not deny. I should esteem myself, as the world also would, vain and empty, were I to arrogate perfection.

Knowledge in military matters is to be acquired by practice and experience only; and, if I have erred, great allowance should be made for the want of them; unless my errors should appear to be wilful; and then, I conceive, it would be more generous to charge me with my faults, and let me stand or fall according to evidence, than to stigmatize me behind my back.

It is uncertain in what light my services may have appeared to your Honor; but this I know, and it is the highest consolation I am capable of feeling, that no man, that ever was employed in a public capacity, has endeavoured to discharge the trust reposed in him with greater honesty, and more zeal for the country's interest, than I have done; and if there is any person living, who can say with justice, that I have offered any intentional wrong to the public, I will cheerfully submit to the most ignominious punishment, that an injured people ought to inflict. On the other hand, it is hard to have my character arraigned, and my actions condemned, without a hearing.

I must therefore again beg in more plain, and in very earnest terms, to know, if Colonel C. has taken the liberty of representing my character to your Honor with such ungentlemanly freedom as the letter implies? Your condescension herein will be acknowledged, as a singular favor done your Honor's most obedient, humble servant. *

---

* To this request, Governor Dinwiddie replied, in a letter dated September 24th; —

"Your letter of the 17th I perused, and would gladly hope there is no truth in it. I never heard of it before, nor did I ever conceive you would have sent down any alarm without proper foundation. However, I shall show it to Colonel C. when he comes to town; but I would advise you not to give notice to every idle story you hear; for if I was to regard reports of different kinds, I should be constantly perplexed.

"My conduct to you from the beginning was always friendly; but you know I had great reason to suspect you of ingratitude, which I am convinced your own conscience and reflection must allow. I had reason to be angry, but this I endeavour to forget; but I cannot think Colonel C. guilty of what is reported. However, as I have his Majesty's leave to go home, I propose leaving this in November, and I wish my successor may show you as much friendship as I have done."

TO CAPTAIN WILLIAM PEACHEY.

Fort Loudoun, 18 September, 1757.

DEAR SIR,

Your favor of the 22d ultimo came to hand about four days ago. In answer to that part, which relates to Colonel C.'s gross and infamous reflections on my conduct last spring, it will be needless, I dare say, to observe further at this time, than that the liberty, which he has been pleased to allow himself in sporting with my character, is little else than a comic entertainment, discovering at one view his passionate fondness for your friend, his inviolable love of truth, his unfathomable knowledge, and the masterly strokes of his wisdom in displaying it. These several talents he has, I think, exhibited in a most conspicuous manner to every person, who was in the least degree acquainted with the situation of affairs in this county at that juncture. The report of your false musters is equally absurd.

You are heartily welcome to make use of any letter, or letters, which I may at any time have written to you; for, although I keep no copies of epistles to my friends, nor can remember the contents of all of them, yet, I am sensible, that the narrations are just, and that truth and honesty will appear in my writings; of which, therefore, I shall not be ashamed, though criticism may censure my style. I am, &c.

TO GOVERNOR DINWIDDIE.

Fort Loudoun, 24 September, 1757.

SIR,

Enclosed is a copy of a letter, which I received from Captain McKenzie. Since my last, the different parties

I detached in quest of the enemy, who committed the late depredations in this neighbourhood, are returned, after having prosecuted the most feasible measures, and exerted their utmost efforts in vain, in endeavouring to come up with the enemy and prevent their escape. Nor is this in any degree surprising. When the vast extent of country, the scattered condition of the inhabitants, the nature of the ground, and the disposition of the enemy, are collectively considered, it is next to impossible, that any of our parties should ever see the enemy, except when they possess such advantages as render their victory certain.

The inhabitants of this valuable and very fertile valley are terrified beyond expression. Some have abandoned their plantations, and many are packing up their most valuable effects to follow them. Another irruption into the heart of this settlement will, I am afraid, be of fatal consequence. I was always persuaded, and almost every day affords new matter for confirming me in the opinion, that the enemy can, with the utmost facility, render abortive every plan, which can be concerted upon our present system of defence; and that the only method of effectually defending such a vast extent of mountains covered with thick woods, like our frontiers, against such an enemy, is by carrying the war into their country. And I think I may, without assuming uncommon penetration, venture to affirm, that, unless an expedition is carried on against the Ohio next spring, this country will not be another year in our possession.

Sickness, and the different parties, which the distressed situation of affairs here obliged me to detach from this garrison, so greatly retard the works, that the finishing of even the principal parts of them, before the winter sets in, will, I am afraid, prove impracticable.

I understand there is a mortar and a number of shells

at Williamsburg, which would be of great service here. We have a quantity of round and grape-shot for six-pounders, but no cannon for using them. A few pieces of that size would be an essential addition to our strength; and, as this is the only place we have, at which, were it finished, a stand could be made, in case of any formidable attack, I conceive nothing in our power should be omitted to make it as defensible as we can.

Mr. Rutherford is not yet returned. Enclosed is a list of the persons killed and captured by the enemy, when last down. I am, &c.

TO GOVERNOR DINWIDDIE.

Fort Loudoun, 5 October, 1757.

SIR,

Both your Honor's letters of the 24th ultimo I received by Jenkins. As I cannot now send a proper monthly return of the regiment, for want of the remarks of the officers at the out-posts, I enclose an exact return of our effective strength, and how it is disposed of, which will at present answer the end proposed. I likewise send you the return of provisions, specifying the time they will serve.

The assistant commissaries must still be continued, or some persons in their room, who, under the direction of a principal, would have purchased the provisions upon as good terms as any contractor. Besides, the commissary used to act as wagon-master, supply the different garrisons with candles, made from the tallow of the country's beeves, and do many things for the good of the service, not to be expected from a contractor.

I shall take the earliest opportunity of communicating

your intentions, respecting the ranging company, to Captain Hogg, who, I am informed, is lying ill, in consequence of the bite of a snake at Dickinson's Fort, and will, I fear, be unable to raise the men. I apprehend the recruiting of one hundred men will be found a very difficult task. I am quite at a loss how to act, as you did not inform me upon what terms they are to be levied and supported, what bounty-money to allow, what pay to promise the officers and men, how they are to be clothed and supported, and what kind of commissions the officers are to have. If they should have the same bounty, that is allowed by the Assembly for recruits, I shall want money for that purpose. Enclosed is a copy of the last letter I received from Colonel Stanwix. The enemy continue their horrid devastations in this settlement. The day before Captain Lewis was attacked, twenty Cherokees, headed by one of the principal warriors of that nation, marched hence to the South Branch, who, with the troops under Captains Waggener and McKenzie, will, I hope, secure that quarter.

When Mr. Atkin went away, he took with him Mr. Gist and the Indian interpreter. Since that time several parties of Cherokees have been here, by which I and my officers were involved in inconceivable trouble, as we had neither an interpreter, nor any right to hold conferences with them; no articles to satisfy their demands, nor liberty to procure them. These warlike, formidable people, although they seem to have a natural and strong attachment to our interest, will, I am afraid, be induced by such treatment to hearken to the pressing solicitations of the French, who, by the latest and best accounts, are making them vastly advantageous offers. The Chief of the Cherokee party, who went last to the Branch, and who is said to be a man of great weight in that nation, was so incensed on account of what he imagined neglect and contempt, that, had we not supplied him with a few necessaries, without which he could not go to war, he threatened to return, fired with resentment, to his nation. In short, I dread that, by the present management of Indian affairs, we are losing the interest of those people, the preservation of whose friendship is of the last importance to the colonies in general, and to this in particular.

I am sorry to acquaint you, that the quartermaster has misbehaved egregiously, embezzling and disposing of some of the regimental stores, and afterwards running away, and taking a man of the regiment with him. He had leave to go to Alexandria, to order up some of the stores left there, and managed his affairs with such cunning, that he was gone too long to be pursued, before he was suspected.

I do not know, that I ever gave your Honor cause to suspect me of ingratitude, a crime I detest, and would most carefully avoid. If an open, disinterested behaviour causes offence, I may have offended; because I have all along laid it down as a maxim, to represent facts freely and impartially, but not more so to others, Sir, than to you. If instances of my ungrateful behaviour had been particularized, I would have answered them. But I have long been convinced, that my actions and their motives have been maliciously misrepresented.*

* In pursuing the thread of intercourse between Governor Dinwiddie and Colonel Washington, from the beginning of their acquaintance, it will not be easy to detect many acts of the former towards the latter, which deserved expressions of gratitude. His first appointments were solicited by friends, whom it was the Governor's interest to oblige, and the duties of them were executed in such a manner, as not only to extort approbation, but to command the notice and applause of the whole country. By the discretion and good sense, which Colonel Washington displayed in all his early enterprises, by his unexampled toils, courage, energy, and patience in his first campaign among the Alleganies, and by his brilliant conduct on the terrible battle-field of the Monongahela, he had acquired a reputa-

As your Honor proposes to leave the colony in November, I should be glad of liberty to go down to Williamsburg towards the last of this month, or first of the next, if nothing should intervene, to settle some accounts with you and the Committee, which may not be done in so satisfactory a manner after you are gone.*

---

tion, and secured a confidence among powerful friends, that were not to be overlooked or disregarded.

Even after all these proofs of ability and character, it was by no good will of the Governor that he was made commander-in-chief of the Virginia forces. Colonel Innes was the favorite destined for that post. But, aside from the incompetency of this officer, he was an inhabitant of North Carolina, and, as such, unacceptable to the Virginia troops, who naturally preferred a commander from their own colony. Nor did the Governor escape censure for his preference, on the ground of partiality to his countryman, he and Colonel Innes being natives of Scotland. Thus, constrained by the public voice, and contrary to his inclination, he gave the appointment to Colonel Washington. His conduct was ever afterwards ungracious, uncompromising, and indicative of any thing but cordiality and confidence. When he was solicited by the friends of Washington to write to the Earl of Loudoun in his behalf, what did he do? He sent a despatch to General Abercromby, containing a short and cold paragraph, desiring the General to use his interest with his Lordship in favor of Colonel Washington, "who, he ventured to say, was a very deserving gentleman," and "he really thought had great merit." Again, when he asked permission to visit Lord Loudoun at Philadelphia, it was granted reluctantly and with an ill grace, though his presence there was important, not more on his own account, than that of the public.

These facts exhibit but a small claim to gratitude. The defeat of Colonel Washington's warmest wish, that of obtaining a commission in the British army, may be justly ascribed to Governor Dinwiddie. Whether such an event would have been fortunate to himself, to his country, or to the world, is another question. Men are often instruments in the hand of Providence to effect ends beyond their foresight, and contrary to their design.

* This request met with the following peremptory refusal from the Governor; — "I cannot agrée to allow you leave to come down at this time. You have been frequently indulged with leave of absence. You know the fort is to be finished, and I fear when you are away little will be done; and surely the commanding officer should not be absent when daily alarmed with the enemy's intentions to invade our frontiers, and I think you were wrong in asking it. You have no accounts that I know of to settle with me; and what accounts you have to settle with the country may be done at a more proper time."

The last alarm occasioned a great many of the inhabitants of this county to go off, and vast numbers are still moving. I fear that, in a short time, this very valuable valley will be in a great measure depopulated. What further steps to take, and how to obviate so serious a misfortune, I am quite at a loss. As I have hitherto neglected nothing within the compass of my power, it is very evident, that nothing but vigorous offensive measures, next campaign, can save the country, at least all west of the Blue Ridge, from inevitable desolation.

Since writing the above, the express, whom I sent to Major Lewis, is come in, and brings returns of those companies; so that you will now receive proper monthly returns for July and August. By these you will see, that our total strength amounts to thirty-two commissioned officers, forty-eight non-commissioned, and seven hundred and three rank and file; whereof twenty officers, thirty non-commissioned, and four hundred and sixty-four rank and file, are employed in this county and Hampshire. But six women are always allowed to a company, who draw provisions; and the officers receive more or less according to their respective rank, as you will see by the estimate received from Colonel Stanwix, and forwarded to you some time ago; which must be considered in the calculation. I am, &c.

TO COLONEL STANWIX.

Fort Loudoun, 8 October, 1757.

DEAR SIR,

I am favored with an opportunity by Mr. Livingston, to acknowledge the receipt of your agreeable favor of the 19th ultimo; and to inform you of a very extraordinary affair, which has happened at this place, namely, the desertion of our quartermaster. This infamous fellow, as he has proved himself, after having disposed, in a clandestine manner, of many of our regimental stores, being called upon to settle his accounts (not that I, or any officer in the regiment, had the least suspicion of the roguery he was carrying on), pretended, that he could not come to an exact settlement without going to Alexandria, where some of the stores yet lay. Several of our soldiers deserting at the same time, he was sent in pursuit of them, which afforded him the desired opportunity of making his escape. His villany was not laid open, before his departure, and was at last accidentally discovered. This person had been several years a sergeant in one of his Majesty's regiments, and in this character he served three years under me. During that time he gave such signal proofs of his bravery and good behaviour, as bound me, in honor and gratitude, to do something for him. And I therefore got him promoted to be quartermaster, as he was acquainted with the duty, and capable, I thought, of discharging it.

We have had several visitations from the enemy, and much mischief done, since my last to you. About the 17th ultimo upwards of twenty persons were killed only twelve miles from this garrison, and, notwithstanding I sent a strong detachment hence to pursue them, and ordered the passes of the mountains to be waylaid by forces from other places, yet we were not able to meet with these savages.

On Friday sevennight, a body of near or quite a hundred fell upon the inhabitants along the great road between this place and Pennsylvania, and killed or took fifteen more. The mischief would have been much greater, had not an officer and twenty men of the regiment, who were then out, fallen in with and engaged the enemy. Finding, however, that his party was overpowered, and likely to be surrounded, he retreated to a stockade, not far distant, in which they were besieged for three hours; but the firing communicated an alarm from one habitation to another, by which means most of the families were timely apprised of their danger, and happily escaped. Our party killed one Indian, whose scalp they obtained, and wounded several others.

I exert every means in my power to protect a much distressed country, but it is a task too arduous. To think of defending a frontier of more than three hundred and fifty miles' extent, with only seven hundred men, is vain and idle, especially when that frontier lies more contiguous to the enemy than any other. I am, and have for a long time been, fully convinced, that, if we continue to pursue a defensive plan, the country must be inevitably lost.*

You will be kind enough, Sir, to excuse the freedom with which I deliver my sentiments, and believe me to be, as I really am, with unfeigned truth and regard,

Your most obedient, humble servant.

---

* From the time that the Virginia regiment was organized, it had been Colonel Washington's opinion, that an offensive war should be kept up against the enemy. In this sentiment Governor Dinwiddie agreed with him, and he urged upon Lord Loudoun the advantage of an expedition against Fort Duquesne. But the great operations at the north absorbed his Lordship's attention, and he placed the whole southern frontier upon the defensive. Hence the enemy made perpetual inroads, committing murders and ravages. Considering the weak state of the garrison at Fort Duquesne, a large portion of which had been withdrawn to defend the Canada borders, it was deemed an object of easy attainment, as no doubt it was, for Colonel Stanwix, with his five hundred *Royal Americans*, in conjunction with the Virginia and Maryland troops, to seize that Fort. This would have effectually put a stop to all the savage depredations. But such were not his orders, and nothing was done. The Indians were emboldened by this inactivity, and the frontier inhabitants were molested in every quarter.

TO JOHN ROBINSON, SPEAKER OF THE HOUSE OF BURGESSES.

Fort Loudoun, 25 October, 1757.

SIR,

I applied to the Governor for permission to go down and settle my accounts before he leaves the country, and to represent the melancholy situation of our distressed frontiers, which no written narrative can so well describe, as a verbal account to a judicious person inclined to hear. In conversation, the questions resulting from one relation beget others, till matters are perfectly understood; whereas the most explicit writing will be found deficient. But his Honor was pleased to deny his leave, thinking my request unreasonable, and that I had some party of pleasure in view.*

I have, in a letter to the Governor by this conveyance, endeavoured to set in as clear a light as I am able, the situation of our frontiers, and the disposition of the inhabitants; and I shall aim also, in as succinct a manner as possible, to make you acquainted with the same.

The inhabitants of this fertile, and once populous valley, are now become our most western settlers, save the few families that are *forted* on the Branch. The enemy have, in a great measure, ceased committing hostilities on the Branch, and fallen upon the people of this valley, and a considerable part of them have already removed. This, by persons unacquainted with the country, and the enemy we have to deal with, may be attributed to the cowardice of the inhabitants, or inactivity of the soldiers, but by others it will be imputed to neither. No

* In writing to the Governor, he also observed, —"It was not to enjoy a party of pleasure, that I wanted leave of absence. I have been indulged with few of those winter or summer."

troops in the universe can guard against the cunning and wiles of Indians. No one can tell where they will fall, till the mischief is done, and then it is in vain to pursue. The inhabitants see, and are convinced of this, which makes each family afraid of standing in the gap of danger; and by retreating, one behind another, they depopulate the country, and leave it to the enemy, who subsist upon the plunder.

If we pursue a defensive plan next campaign, there will not, by the autumn, be one soul living on this side of the Blue Ridge, except the soldiers in garrison, and such of the inhabitants as may seek shelter therein. This, Sir, I know to be the immovable determination of the people; and, believe me, I have been at great pains, before I could prevail on them to wait the consultations of this winter, and the events of the spring.

I do not know on whom these miserable, undone people are to rely for protection. If the Assembly are to give it to them, it is time that measures were at least concerting, and not when they ought to be going into execution, as has always been the case. If they are to seek it from the Commander-in-chief, it is time their condition was made known to him; for I cannot forbear repeating again, that while we pursue defensive measures we pursue inevitable ruin, the loss of the country being the inevitable and fatal consequence. There will be no end to our troubles, while we follow this plan, and every year will increase our expense. This, my dear Sir, I urge not only as an officer, but as a friend, who has property in the country and is unwilling to lose it. This it is, also, that makes me anxious for doing more than barely to represent these matters, which is all that is expected of an officer commanding.

It is not possible for me to convey a just sense of the posture of our affairs. It would be vain to attempt it.

I, therefore, content myself with entreating you to use your influence to prevent such delays, as we have hitherto met with, if you think this affair depends on the Assembly. If you think the Assembly have done all in their power, and that recourse must be had elsewhere, I am determined, as I will spare neither cost nor pains, to apply to Colonel Stanwix (who commands in this quarter, with whom I am acquainted, and from whom I have received several kind and affectionate letters,) for leave to wait on him with an account of our circumstances. Through these means, perhaps, we may be able to draw a little of Lord Loudoun's attention to the preservation of these colonies.

Pray let me have your sentiments.* I have not time to put my thoughts in a proper dress. The bearer is waiting, and I am in other respects hurried. But the truth of what I have asserted, believe me, is unquestionable; as well as that I am, with the most affectionate regards, your most obedient servant and friend.

TO GOVERNOR DINWIDDIE.

Fort Loudoun, 5 November, 1757.

SIR,

Duty to my country, and his Majesty's interest, indispensably require, that I again trouble your Honor on the

---

* The Speaker, at the conclusion of his answer to this letter, after mentioning the Governor's intended departure, writes, —

"We have not yet heard who is to succeed him. God grant it may be somebody better acquainted with the unhappy business we have in hand, and who, by his conduct and counsel, may dispel the cloud now hanging over this distressed country. Till that event, I beg, my dear friend, that you will bear, so far as a man of honor ought, the discouragements and slights you have too often met with, and continue to serve your country, as I am convinced you have always hitherto done, in the best manner you can with the small assistance afforded you."

subject of Indian affairs here, which have been impeded and embarrassed by such a train of mismanagement, as, if continued, must produce melancholy consequences.

The sincere disposition of the Cherokees heartily to espouse our cause has been demonstrated beyond every doubt; and, if they were rewarded in a proper manner, it would, in all probability, be the means of effecting a favorable change in the present unhappy situation of this part of his Majesty's dominions.

But, instead of meeting with the encouragement, which their services and bravery have merited, several of them, after having undergone the toils and fatigues of long marches, destitute of the conveniences and almost of the necessaries of life, have, in that situation, gone to war, and behaved nobly, from which we have reaped a signal advantage. When returned here, with their trophies of honor, they must have gone home without any kind of reward or thanks, or even provisions to support them on their march, justly fired with resentment, had not I and my officers procured them some things, of which they were in absolute want, and made it the object of our care, in various respects, to please them.*

Another party of those Indians since arrived opportunely to our assistance, at the very juncture the enemy made an irruption into this settlement, pursued their tracks, came up with three of them, scalped two, and wounded the third. They are now returned from the pursuit, and are nearly in the same situation with those abovementioned. I applied to Captain Gist in their behalf, and told him I must represent the matter to your Honor. But he assures me, that he has neither goods, money to procure them, nor even an interpreter, being

* It will be remembered, that Colonel Washington was not now charged with Indian affairs, nor furnished with any instructions on that head. An agent had been appointed for the purpose.

thereby incapable of doing any kind of service. It is surprising, that any man should be entrusted with transacting such important affairs, and not be possessed of the means. Thus he, and several others, who receive high pay from Virginia, are not only rendered useless, but our interest with those Indians is at the brink of destruction. Whenever any of them arrive here, they immediately apply to me; but I have neither any thing to give them, nor any right to do it. Nor is there a person, who can inform them to what these and their other disappointments are owing; which reduces me to a dilemma, from which I would most gladly be extricated.

I must likewise beg leave to mention once more the vast hardships, which many of the people groan under here, from having been so long kept out of the money, that the country owes them on account of the Indians.

When I proposed going down to Williamsburg, several of them brought their accounts to me, which I intended, had you given me liberty, to lay before your Honor. I mention this circumstance, not with any view of being employed in examining and paying off those accounts, which for many reasons I can by no means undertake, but in hope that your Honor will be pleased to give directions, and appoint some person to that duty, by the neglect of which so many poor people greatly suffer.* I am, &c.

---

* This was his last letter to Governor Dinwiddie. It was duly answered, and further provisions were made for the Indians.

Colonel Washington was now laboring under an indisposition, which shortly increased to an alarming illness. He left the army at the pressing request of the surgeon (Dr. Craik, his physician and intimate friend through life), and retired to Mount Vernon, where he was reduced so low by dysentery and fever, that it was more than four months before he was able to resume his command.

The Governor sailed for Europe in January. His departure was viewed with little regret by the inhabitants of Virginia, and perhaps with as little by himself. During his five years' administration, he had shown no de-

TO JOHN BLAIR, PRESIDENT OF THE COUNCIL.*

Fredericksburg, 30 January, 1758.

SIR,

Hearing of the Governor's departure for England, I think it a duty incumbent on me to inform your Honor, that I lingered a long time under an illness, which obliged me to retire from my command, by the surgeon's advice, and with the Governor's approbation, and that I am yet but imperfectly recovered, which is the cause that detains me from my duty.

I have many accounts to settle with the Committee, and should be glad to obtain leave to go down for that purpose, this being the proper season, as our frontiers are quiet. I also wish to receive money for contingent expenses, before I return to Winchester, as there are

---

ficiency of zeal or activity in discharging the duties of his office; but his ignorance of military affairs, his high notions of the royal prerogative and of his own importance, his eagerness to control the money concerns of the public service, and his haughty bearing towards persons in subordinate stations, had neither wrought favorable impressions on the minds of the people, nor gained from them flattering tokens of confidence and esteem. Bold insinuations were thrown out, that his disinterestedness was not of the purest kind. The pistole fee was an irritating topic; and, as it was a perquisite of the Governor, and revived by him contrary to the long usage of his predecessors, it was regarded as a suspicious symptom. When the Assembly appointed a committee to manage their appropriations, he was offended, and declared that his right was infringed. This was also regarded to his disadvantage, as most persons holding a civil office are willing to be as little embarrassed as possible with the responsibility of money affairs.

* Mr. Blair was President of the Council, on whom, according to established usage, the government devolved when the governor left the colony.

George Mason, the neighbour and friend of Colonel Washington, wrote to him on the 4th of January, urging him not to think of joining the army in the present state of his health, and adding, — "You will in all probability bring on a relapse, and render yourself incapable of serving the public at a time, when there may be the utmost occasion. There is nothing more certain, than that a gentleman in your station owes the care of his health and his life not only to himself and his friends, but to his country."

several demands, on the public account, that I should be glad to be provided against. And further, I shall at that time have an opportunity of laying before you a state of the frontier settlements, a matter worthy of great attention, as the well-being of the people depends on seasonable and well concerted measures for their defence.

If you have any orders for the troops under my command, please to favor me with them, and they shall be forwarded, before I go down myself for the purposes aforesaid.

I am, with great esteem,
Your Honor's most obedient, humble servant.

TO THE PRESIDENT OF THE COUNCIL.

Mount Vernon, 20 February, 1758.

SIR,

I set out for Williamsburg the day after the date of my letter, but found I was unable to proceed, my fever and pain increasing upon me to a high degree; and the physicians assured me, that I might endanger my life by prosecuting the journey.

In consequence of that advice I returned to this place again, and informed your Honor of the reason of my detention by the post, whom I met on the road, and who, I have since understood, never lodged my letter in the postoffice at Fredericksburg, which is the cause of my now writing to the same purport. When I shall be sufficiently able to attempt the journey again, I cannot say; but I shall make no delay after I am in a condition to perform it. I am, &c.

TO COLONEL STANWIX.

Mount Vernon, 4 March, 1758.

MY DEAR COLONEL,

Your two favors, with the extract of a letter from Lord Loudoun, were this day delivered to me. In the latter you condescend to ask my opinion of Major Smith. Pray, does not his plan sufficiently indicate the man? Can there be a better index to his abilities, than his scheme for reducing the enemy on the Ohio, and his expeditious march of a thousand men to Detroit? Surely, he intended to provide them with wings to facilitate their passage over so mountainous and extensive a country, or in what way else could he accomplish it?

I am unacquainted with the navigation of the rivers he proposes to traverse, and, consequently, cannot be a competent judge of his scheme in this respect; but the distance is so great, and that through an enemy's country, that, I candidly confess, it appears to me a romantic plan, not to be executed. For, if we are strong enough to attempt the reduction of the Ohio, what necessity is there for our making such a circuitous march, and leaving Fort Duquesne behind us, which is the source of all our ills? If we are too weak to attempt that place, what have we not to dread from leaving it in our rear?

These, Sir, are my sentiments upon Major Smith's project. With regard to the person, if I have been rightly informed, he actually had a commission to command a ranging company, and obtained it by making promises, which he never could comply with. He was adjudged, by persons better acquainted with him than I am, to be quite unfit to command even a company. He lost the Block-House, in which he commanded, by suffering his men to straggle from it at pleasure, which the Indians observing, took advantage of his weakness, and attacked him at a time when he had no men in his works. It is, nevertheless, agreed on all hands, that he made a gallant defence, but I never before heard of any capitulation that was granted to him.

I have not had the pleasure of seeing Major Smith, though I have been favored with a letter from him, in which he politely professes some concern at hearing of my indisposition, as it prevented him from seeing me at Winchester; but he desires, at the same time, that I will *attend him at his house* in Augusta, about two hundred miles off, or in Williamsburg by the 20th instant, when, I suppose, he intends to honor me with *his orders.**

I have never been able to return to my command, since I wrote to you last, my disorder at times returning obstinately upon me, in spite of the efforts of all the sons of Æsculapius, whom I have hitherto consulted. At certain periods I have been reduced to great extremity, and have now too much reason to apprehend an approaching decay, being visited with several symptoms of such a disease.

I am at this time under a strict regimen, and shall set out to-morrow for Williamsburg to receive the advice of the best physicians there. My constitution is much impaired, and nothing can retrieve it, but the greatest care and the most circumspect course of life. This being the case, as I have now no prospect left of preferment in the military way, and despair of rendering that immediate service, which my country may require from the person commanding its troops, I have thoughts of quitting my command, and retiring from all public business, leaving my post to be filled by some other person more

---

* Colonel Stanwix replied,—"I have been favored with your obliging letter, and find your judgment tallies with Lord Loudoun's and mine, in regard to Major Smith's wild scheme."

capable of the task, and who may, perhaps, have his endeavours crowned with better success than mine have been. But, wherever I go, or whatever becomes of me, I shall always retain the sincerest and most affectionate regards for you; being, dear Sir, your most obedient and obliged humble servant.*

TO BRIGADIER-GENERAL STANWIX.

Fort Loudoun, 10 April, 1758.

DEAR SIR,

Permit me,—at the same time that I congratulate you, which I most sincerely do, on your promotion, so justly merited,—to express my concern at the prospect of parting with you. I can truly say, that it is a matter of no small regret to me, and that I should have thought myself happy in serving this campaign under your immediate command. But every thing, I hope, is ordered for the best, and it is our duty to submit. I must, nevertheless, beg, that you will add one more kindness to the many I have experienced, and that is, to mention me in favorable terms to General Forbes, if you are acquainted with that gentleman, not as a person, who would depend upon him for further recommendation to

---

* Soon after writing this letter, he went to Williamsburg. Having attended to the necessary affairs, which called him there, he returned to his command at Fort Loudoun about the 1st of April.

While he was in Williamsburg the Assembly was in session, and an act passed to augment the forces of the colony to two thousand men, besides the three companies of rangers. A bounty of ten pounds was to be paid to every new recruit. A second regiment was organized, and officers appointed. By the same act, all the Virginia forces were to be united, by direction of the president, or commander-in-chief, to such troops as should be furnished by his Majesty, or by the other colonies, for a general expedition against the enemy, and were to be subject to the orders of the commanding officer of his Majesty's forces in America.

military preferment (for I have long conquered all such inclinations, and shall serve this campaign merely for the purpose of affording my best endeavours to bring matters to a conclusion), but as a person, who would gladly be distinguished in some measure from the *common run* of provincial officers, as I understand there will be a motley herd of us.*

Nothing can contribute more to his Majesty's interest in this quarter, than an early campaign, or a speedy junction of the troops to be employed in this service. Without this, I fear the Indians will with difficulty be restrained from returning to their nation before we assemble, and, in that event, no words can tell how much they will be missed. It is an affair of great importance, and ought to claim the closest attention of the commanding officer. On the assistance of these people the security of our march very much depends.

Great care should be taken, also, to lay in a supply of proper goods for them. The Indians are mercenary; every service of theirs must be purchased; and they are easily offended, being thoroughly sensible of their own importance. Upwards of five hundred are already come to this place, the greater part of whom are gone to war. Many others are daily expected, and we have neither arms nor clothes suitable to give them. Nor, indeed, is it reasonable to expect, that the whole expense accruing on account of these people should fall upon this government, which has already in this particular, as well as in many others, exerted its utmost abilities for his Majesty's interest, and, in the present case,

* An expedition against Fort Duquesne had at last been decided on, which was to be conducted by Brigadier-General Forbes. The Virginia troops, and those of the adjoining colonies, were to be under his command. General Stanwix was removed to a station between the Mohawk River and Lake Ontario, where he built a fort, that was honored with his name.

shares only an equal proportion of the advantages arising from Indian services.

These crude thoughts are hastily thrown together. If you find any thing in them, which may be useful, be pleased to turn them to his Majesty's interest. The indulgence, which you have hitherto allowed me, joined to my zeal for the service, has encouraged me to use this freedom with you, Sir, which I should not choose to take unasked with another.

If it is not improper, I should be glad to be informed what regular troops are to be employed under Brigadier-General Forbes, and when they may be expected? Also, where they are to rendezvous.

Fort Frederic, I hear, is mentioned for this purpose, and, in my humble opinion, a little unadvisedly. In the first place, because the country people all around are fled, and the troops will, consequently, lack those refreshments so needful to soldiers. In the next place, I am fully convinced there never can be a road made between Fort Frederic and Fort Cumberland, that will admit the transportation of carriages. I have passed it in company with many others, who were of the same opinion. Lastly, because this is the place [Fort Loudoun] to which all Indian parties, either going to, or returning from war, will inevitably repair.

I am with most sincere esteem, dear Sir, your most obedient and obliged humble servant.

TO MAJOR FRANCIS HALKET.

Fort Loudoun, 12 April, 1758.

MY DEAR HALKET,

Are we to have you once more among us? And shall we revisit together a hapless spot, that proved so fatal to many of our former brave companions? Yes; and I rejoice at it, hoping it will now be in our power to testify a just abhorrence of the cruel butcheries exercised on our friends, in the unfortunate day of General Braddock's defeat; and, moreover, to show our enemies, that we can practise all that lenity of which they only boast, without affording any adequate proofs.

To cut short, I really feel a satisfaction at the prospect of meeting you again, although I have scarcely time to tell you so, as the express is waiting.

I am with most sincere regard, dear Sir, yours, &c.

TO THE PRESIDENT OF THE COUNCIL.

Fort Loudoun, 17 April, 1758.

SIR,

I think it incumbent on me to be informed by your Honor, how the regiment under my command is to be furnished with tents, ammunition, cartridge-paper, and many other requisites, that may be wanted in the course of the campaign. We expect here to be furnished with all those articles from his Majesty's stores, but it is necessary for me to learn this from you.

The last Assembly, in their Supply Bill, provided for a chaplain to our regiment. On this subject I had often without any success applied to Governor Dinwiddie. I now flatter myself, that your Honor will be pleased to appoint a sober, serious man for this duty. Common decency, Sir, in a camp calls for the services of a divine, which ought not to be dispensed with, although the world should be so uncharitable as to think us void of religion, and incapable of good instructions.

I now enclose a monthly return for March, and am, honorable Sir, your most obedient, humble servant.

TO BRIGADIER-GENERAL FORBES.

Fort Loudoun, 23 April, 1758.

SIR,

Permit me to return you my sincere thanks for the honor you were pleased to do me, in a letter to Mr. President Blair, and to assure you, that to merit a continuance of the good opinion you have expressed of me, shall be among my principal endeavours. I have no higher ambition, than to act my part well during the campaign; and if I should thereby merit your approbation, it will be a most pleasing reward for the toils I shall undergo.

It gives me no small pleasure, that an officer of your experience, abilities, and good character should be appointed to command the expedition, and it is with equal satisfaction I congratulate you upon the promising prospect of a glorious campaign.

The Indians seem to anticipate our success, by joining us, thus early, with seven hundred of their warriors. Captain Bosomworth, who held a conference with their chiefs, can fully inform you of their good inclinations to assist his Majesty's troops, and to him I refer you. Two things, however, I must beg leave to indicate, as likely to contribute greatly to their ease and contentment; namely, an early campaign, and plenty of goods. These are matters, which they often remind us of, both in their public councils and private conferences.

I have received no orders yet to assemble the dispersed companies of the Virginia regiment, some of whom are two hundred miles distant from this place; so that, I fear, we shall make a sorry appearance at the general rendezvous. We are very much in want of tents, and have none with which to encamp the regiment when it assembles. This fort cannot yet furnish barracks, nor can the town supply quarters sufficient.*

I am, Sir, with very great respect, your most obedient and most obliged humble servant.

TO THE PRESIDENT OF THE COUNCIL.

Fort Loudoun, 24 April, 1758.

SIR,

Your letter of the 19th instant, intended to come by Colonel Stephen, was received to-day about noon by express. As it contains several matters of an interesting nature, I chose to be aided in my determinations by the advice of my officers, and I now enclose their and my opinions on the several heads.

I could by no means think of executing, willingly, that discretionary power, with which you were pleased to invest me, of ordering out the militia.† It is an affair, Sir, of too important and delicate a nature for me to manage. Much discontent will be the inevitable consequence of this draft.

That was a most extraordinary request of Colonel Mercer's, concerning the exchange of officers, and

* Colonel Stephen had just arrived at Fredericksburg with the two companies returned from South Carolina. These troops were daily expected at Fort Loudoun.

† This power of drafting the militia, with which the forts were to be garrisoned while the regular troops were employed in the expedition, was conferred equally on the President, and the Commander-in-chief; a substantial proof of the confidence reposed in the latter by the Assembly, although in this case, as in all others, he could not be prevailed upon to exercise a delegated power to any greater extent, than was absolutely necessary for a full discharge of the duties of his station. This control of that strong passion, the love of power, was one of the marked traits of his character, and a main cause of his popularity through the whole of his brilliant career.

calculated, it should seem, rather to breed confusion, than to benefit the other regiment.* There is not an ensign there, that would not rather quit the service, than accept of a company in the other regiment, so much do they disapprove Colonel Mercer's proposal; and I have neither inclination nor power to force their compliance. Captain Rutherford's company was raised and posted in this quarter by Governor Dinwiddie's express orders, and can be more useful here, than any other men whatever, being all sons of the neighbouring farmers, men of property, young, active, and acquainted with the woods on these frontiers. Whereas, if they go to the southward, they will be utter strangers to the enemy's haunts, and of no more use there, than the militia of an adjacent county; while their places here must be supplied by militia equally ignorant of these woods; besides giving them a useless march of two hundred miles, and exposing the frontiers in the mean time. Another reason, which may be urged, is, that their property all lies in this county. Interested motives induced them to enlist, and to be vigilant in defending it, and, I believe, they would desert, rather than go to the southward.

Your Honor will please to remember, that one of the last questions, which I had an opportunity of asking, was, whether I should send out recruiting parties. You replied, "that, since the Assembly was so near meeting, you would defer giving any directions on that head." As I had no money for the purpose, I hope it will not seem surprising, that we have recruited but few men since. I have been waiting for orders to complete the regiment. I shall now use my best endeavours, with the very few officers, who can be spared from the garrisons, dispersed as we are. I am, &c.

* Mercer was lieutenant-colonel of the second, or new regiment. The commanding officer of this regiment was Colonel Byrd.

TO SIR JOHN ST. CLAIR.*

Fort Loudoun, 27 April, 1758.

DEAR SIR JOHN,

The post, calling suddenly upon me, only allows me time to acknowledge the receipt of your obliging letter, and to inform you, that I have received Mr. President's orders to obey any command you shall be pleased to honor me with; also to tell you, that the two companies from Carolina were at Fredericksburg, and may be expected here daily.

I have made known the contents of your letter to Mr. Gist, who thinks himself extremely obliged by the care you have taken of Indian affairs. We do all we can to keep the Indians in temper, but I have still apprehensions, that many of them will return home, if the troops are long in assembling.

It gave me real pleasure to learn from you, that my company was desired by the General, Sir John, and Major Halket. I shall think myself quite happy, if I should be able to retain the good opinion, which they seem to entertain of me; for I have long despaired of any other reward for my services, than the satisfaction arising from the esteem of my friends.

I am, with great regard, yours, &c.

TO MAJOR FRANCIS HALKET.

Fort Loudoun, 11 May, 1758.

DEAR SIR,

I am this day favored with yours of the 4th instant, and should have thought myself extremely culpable and

* Sir John St. Clair was quartermaster-general to the forces under General Forbes.

deficient in my duty, had I delayed one moment in transmitting to the General any intelligence I could procure; much more in a matter so material as that upon which he has been informed. I must, therefore, beg that you will, from me, assure the General, that the Catawbas have not this year brought in one prisoner or scalp to this place, nor indeed to any other that I have heard of. No prisoner has been taken by any of our friendly Indians this season, and no scalps, except the two taken near Fort Duquesne by Ucahula,* of which, and all the intelligence of the enemy in that quarter, which that young warrior was able to give, I, by the last post, sent to the General a full and circumstantial account. Nor would I have failed to keep him duly informed of every interesting occurrence, even had it not been recommended to me.

It gave me no small uneasiness to be informed of the resolution of some of the Cherokees, to wander towards the Indian settlements in Maryland and Pennsylvania, clearly foreseeing the bad consequences such a peregrination would produce. I therefore represented the matter to Captain Gist in the strongest manner, and must do him the justice to say, that nothing in his power was omitted to prevent it. But our efforts proved ineffectual, as those two provinces last year, very impoliticly I humbly conceive, made presents to these Indians, and

---

* This Indian went out with a party of six soldiers and thirty Indians, under the command of Lieutenant Gist. After great fatigues and sufferings, occasioned by the snows on the Allegany mountains, they reached the Monongahela river, where Lieutenant Gist, by a fall from a precipice, was rendered unable to proceed, and the party separated. Ucahula, with two other Indians, descended the Monongahela in a bark canoe, till they came near Fort Duquesne. Here they left their canoe, and concealed themselves on the margin of the river, till they had an opportunity of attacking two Frenchmen, who were fishing in a canoe, and whom they killed and scalped. These scalps were brought to Fort Loudoun by Ucahula.

encouraged their returning thither this spring. Such is the nature of Indians, that nothing will prevent their going where they have any reason to expect presents, and their cravings are insatiable.

I and my officers have constantly paid, and always will pay, the strictest regard to every circumstance, that may contribute to keep the Indians in good humor. But, as Governor Dinwiddie ordered me not to meddle with Indian affairs on any pretence whatever, the sole management of them being left to Mr. Atkin and his deputy Mr. Gist, and those orders having never been countermanded, neither I, nor my officers, have adventured to do any thing relative to them, but in a secondary manner through Mr. Gist.

The Raven warrior was on a scout, in which he was unsuccessful. On his return hither, he produced two white men's scalps, which he brought from his own nation, and wanted to pass them for the enemy's, taken in his unsuccessful scout. In this villany he was detected by the other warriors, who were highly offended at so base a deceit, and threatened to kill him. A consciousness of his guilt, and a dread of being called to a severe account by his own countrymen, were the reasons, which many of them assigned for his going away in so abrupt, but by no means unsatisfactory, manner to the English. As Captain Bosomworth was here transacting Indian affairs, under the immediate orders of the Commander-in-chief, when the Raven warrior returned and was detected, I only wrote in mine to General Forbes incidentally on the subject, referring him to Captain Bosomworth for particulars.

Enclosed is my return for April, but you will please to observe, that Captain Woodward's is made out from his last, as his great distance from hence puts it out of his power to send it in due time.

I beg you will inform the General, that I shall, with great alacrity, obey all the orders, with which he may honor me. In the mean time, I am, with unfeigned regard, dear Halket, yours, &c.

TO THE PRESIDENT OF THE COUNCIL.

Williamsburg, 28 May, 1758.

SIR,

I came here at this critical juncture, by the express order of Sir John St. Clair, to represent in the fullest manner the posture of our affairs at Winchester, and to obviate any doubts, that might arise from the best written narrative. I shall make use of the following method, as the most effectual I can at present suggest, to lay sundry matters before you, for your information, approbation, and direction. And I hope, that, when your Honor considers how we are situated, and the importance of despatch, you will please to give me explicit and speedy answers, on the several points here submitted.

First, Sir John St. Clair's letter will, I apprehend, inform you of our principal wants, namely, arms, tents, and other sorts of field-equipage,—articles so absolutely and obviously necessary, as to need no argument to prove, that the men will be useless without them, and that the vast sums of money, expended in levying and marching them to the place of rendezvous, will be entirely lost, besides impeding if not defeating the expedition.

Secondly, the officers will be unprovided with the means of taking the field, till they have an allowance made them of baggage, forage, and bat-money. Governor Dinwiddie, from what cause I could never yet learn, thought proper to discontinue this allowance to the companies that remained in Virginia, at the same time that he allowed it to those who went to Carolina, although I produced evidence under General Stanwix's hand, that all officers were entitled to it, and that it was essential to enable them to take the field. General Forbes has obtained this allowance for the Pennsylvania troops, and desired Sir John St. Clair to urge it strongly on this government also.

Thirdly, the unequal pay of the two Virginia regiments will, I conceive, if a stop is not put to it, be productive of great discontent, and many evils. For the soldiers of the first regiment think their claim upon the country equally as good, if not better than that of the second, because their services are not limited.* They have lacked the great bounty, which the others have received, and have had no clothes for almost two years, although they have an annual call for clothes, and in strictness the same right to expect them.

Fourthly, as our regimental clothing cannot possibly last through the campaign, will it not be advisable to obtain a supply for next winter? I have sent to Philadelphia for one thousand pair of Indian stockings, or *leggins*, the better to equip my men for the woods; and I now inquire whether I am to pay for them in behalf of the country, or deduct the cost out of their pay. As they have not received the clothing, to which they are entitled, they may think this latter a hardship.

Fifthly, should not the pay of the surgeon's mates in the first regiment be equal to that of those in the second? The latter have four shillings and the former

---

* The second regiment was raised only for the campaign, and, by the terms of the act of Assembly, it was to be disbanded, and the men discharged on the first of December; whereas the soldiers of the first regiment were enlisted to serve during the war.

only three per day. Should there not, likewise, be the same number of surgeon's mates allowed to the old as to the new regiment?

Sixthly, it will cause great dissatisfaction in the regiment, if Lieutenant Baker is put over the heads of older officers. It is granted, that Mr. Baker is a very deserving officer, but there are others equally deserving, and who have adventured equally to seek glory, and to merit applause.

Seventhly, Sir John St. Clair directs, in consequence of orders from the General, that the first Virginia regiment shall immediately be completed, and leaves the mode of doing it to your Honor. I should be glad of direction in this affair. The season, I fear, is too far advanced to attempt it now by recruiting.

Eighthly, are the works at Fort Loudoun still to go on? If so, in what manner are they to be forwarded, and under whose direction? Nothing surely will contribute more to the public weal, than this fort when completed; because it will be a valuable repository for our stores, if the event of our enterprise prove successful, and an asylum for the inhabitants, and a place of retreat for our troops, in case of a defeat.

Ninthly, great advantages must arise, by appointing Lieutenant Smith to that direction, and to the command of Fort Loudoun. First, because he has had the charge of the works for nearly two years, and has, by that means, become perfectly well acquainted with every thing intended to be done. Secondly, because there must necessarily be many sick and lame soldiers left at that garrison, who may require the eye of a diligent officer to keep them together. Thirdly, because all the regimental stores and baggage must remain at that place, and ought to be under the care of an officer, who can be made accountable for his conduct; and not left to the mercy of an ungovernable and refractory militia. Fourthly, this is important, if for no other reason than to preserve the materials lying there for finishing the works.

Tenthly, I conceive we shall be ordered to take with us the greatest part of the ammunition now at Fort Loudoun. It will be necessary, therefore, to have a supply laid in at that place for the use of the frontier garrisons.

Eleventhly, in a late letter I endeavoured to point out, in what manner the service would be benefited, by continuing Rutherford's rangers in the parts they at present occupy, and sending the militia of Prince William to the Branch. I again recommend it, for the reasons then given, and for many others, which might be given.

I must now conclude, with once more begging, that your Honor will hasten some speedy determination on these several matters. From what Sir John St. Clair has written, from my orders, and from the statement here made, I conceive it must sufficiently appear, that the greatest despatch is necessary. The success of our expedition will, in a manner, depend on its early commencement. Every delay, therefore, may be attended with pernicious consequences.

The Indians, glad of any pretence for returning home, will make use of delays for a handle; and a spirit of discontent and desertion may spring up among the new levies for want of employment.

These are matters obvious to me, and my duty requires, that I represent them in this free and candid manner.* I am your Honor's most obedient and most humble servant.

* As the government in England had determined to prosecute offensive operations on the southern frontiers, great preparations had been contem-

TO FRANCIS FAUQUIER, LIEUTENANT-GOVERNOR OF VIRGINIA.

Fort Loudoun, 17 June, 1758.

SIR,

Although but little skilled in compliments, permit me nevertheless to offer your Honor my congratulations on your appointment, and your safe arrival at a government, which his Majesty has been pleased to entrust to your administration.

---

plated for a vigorous campaign under General Forbes against Fort Duquesne. Mr. Pitt had lately come into power, and his zeal for the interest of the colonies had produced a change in the counsels of his Majesty's ministers respecting America. On the 30th of December he wrote a circular to the governors of Pennsylvania and the several colonies at the south, requesting a hearty coöperation from the Assemblies in aid of General Forbes's expedition. He stipulated, that the colonial troops raised for this purpose, should be supplied with arms, ammunition, tents, and provisions, in the same manner as the regular troops, and at the King's expense; so that the only charge to the colonies would be that of levying, clothing, and paying the men. The governors were, also, authorized to issue commissions to provincial officers, from Colonels downwards, and these officers were to hold rank in the united army according to their commissions. Had this liberal and just system been adopted at the outset, it would have put a very different face upon the military affairs of the colonies.

Major-General Abercromby, who had succeeded Lord Loudoun to the command in America, assigned six thousand troops to Pennsylvania, Virginia, and Maryland, as their quota for the expedition to the Ohio. Of this number the Pennsylvania Assembly resolved to raise two thousand seven hundred. — *Votes*, &c. *of the Assembly*, Vol. IV. p. 799. — The Maryland Assembly voted one thousand, but their bill was defeated by the usual quarrel with the Governor, who refused his assent to their proposed mode of levying the tax to defray the expense. — *Votes and Proceedings for March*, 1758.

The troops actually employed under General Forbes were twelve hundred Highlanders, three hundred and fifty *Royal Americans*, about twenty-seven hundred provincials from Pennsylvania, sixteen hundred from Virginia, two or three hundred from Maryland, who had been stationed in garrison at Fort Frederic under Colonel Dagworthy; and also two companies from North Carolina; making in all, including the wagoners, between six and seven thousand men. This army was more than five months penetrating to the Ohio, where it was found, at last, that they had to oppose only five hundred of the enemy.

I flattered myself with the hope of seeing your Honor at Williamsburg when I was down, but the business, which carried me there, was of too urgent a nature to admit delay on my part, after it was accomplished. Mr. President Blair has no doubt informed you of the nature of that business, and the state of the troops here, and, generally, of the situation of affairs in this quarter. I will not, therefore, trouble you with a repetition of these particulars, but enclose to you a copy of the last orders, which I have received, and which I am preparing to execute with the greatest exactness.

Sir John St. Clair set out for Conococheague on the 12th instant, to which place I accompanied him, in consequence of a summons from Colonel Bouquet.* He proceeded on to Carlisle, and I returned to this post, where at present I have the honor to command.

When I was last in Williamsburg, I endeavoured to make Mr. President Blair and the Council sensible of the great want of clothing for the first regiment, and how necessary it was to send to England for a supply. They declined doing any thing in the matter at that time, because the funds granted by the late Assembly were almost exhausted. But I hope it will not escape your Honor's notice, if another Assembly should soon be called. Field-equipage of all kinds will also be wanted, and will be better and come much cheaper from England, than it can be had in this country.

I have the honor to be, &c.†

---

* Colonel Bouquet was to have command of the advanced division of the army, and this interview was desired by him, that he might procure information respecting the frontiers from Colonel Washington, and concert arrangements for marching the Virginia troops.

† This letter, and another written on the 19th, were answered by Governor Fauquier. The following are extracts.

"Your congratulations and kind wishes do me the greater honor, as you profess yourself a gentleman not addicted to compliments. I have re-

TO COLONEL HENRY BOUQUET, COMMANDING AT RAYSTOWN.

Camp, near Fort Cumberland, 3 July, 1758.

SIR,

According to orders I marched from Winchester on the 24th ultimo, and arrived at this place yesterday, with five companies of the first Virginia regiment, and a company of artificers from the second, as you may observe by the enclosed returns.* My march, in consequence of bad teams and bad roads, notwithstanding I had sent forward the artificers and a covering party three days before, was much delayed. As I cannot

---

ceived from Mr. President Blair, and all the gentlemen of the Council, all the information I could wish for; but still, as I cannot be master of the state of affairs, I must desire gentlemen will be indulgent where I am wrong. I have enclosed to you the blank commission as you desire, and do not doubt but you will fill it with justice and advantage to his Majesty's service.

"I am extremely sensible of all you say in yours of the 19th relative to the bad condition of the militia, and wish I knew how to redress it. However, I will use my endeavours personally, and will recommend the same to the approaching Assembly at their opening. In some counties they have been mutinous (for so I must term it), and refused to go when drafted out, unless they might pick and choose their own officers. Whether this proceeds from any influence of the officers over the men, or from the caprice and licentiousness of the men themselves, I know not; but this I know, if complied with, there is an end of all discipline. I have ordered the names of all such refusers to be sent up, that they may be prosecuted according to law; for to send fresh orders not to be obeyed is still weakening the hands and loosening the reins of government.

"I have received the returns of the two Virginia regiments. I grieve to see so many sick men, and wish they were complete to a man, to secure the conquest of Fort Duquesne, in which I wish you all possible success, and to obtain which you will oblige me by assuring the General and Commander-in-chief, and all under him, that nothing shall be wanting on my part."

* Colonel Stephen had already marched with a small detachment by way of Shippensburg, in Pennsylvania, and was now at Raystown.

suppose you intended to send any part of my men upon the roads, till joined at this place by Colonel Byrd, I shall decline sending any on that service till he arrives, which I presume will be to-morrow.

There came twenty-eight wagons with me to this place, and I believe, if they were wanted, ten more might be had upon the South Branch, strong and good; but carrying-horses are certainly more eligible for the service to which we are destined. I have received a very scanty allowance of tents for the five companies, namely, sixty-nine only. Out of these most of the officers must either be supplied, or lie uncovered. They will readily pay for what they receive, if required. No bell-tents were sent to us.

My men are very bare of regimental clothing, and I have no prospect of a supply. So far from regretting this want during the present campaign, if I were left to pursue my own inclinations, I would not only order the men to adopt the Indian dress, but cause the officers to do it also, and be the first to set the example myself. Nothing but the uncertainty of obtaining the general approbation causes me to hesitate a moment to leave my regimentals at this place, and proceed as light as any Indian in the woods. It is an unbecoming dress, I own, for an officer; but convenience, rather than show, I think, should be consulted. The reduction of bat-horses alone would be sufficient to recommend it; for nothing is more certain than that less baggage would be required, and the public benefited in proportion. I am, &c.

TO COLONEL BOUQUET.

Camp, near Fort Cumberland, 9 July, 1758.

SIR,

Colonel Byrd, with eight companies of his regiment, arrived here yesterday. He left many sick men behind, and, as he posted a company at Edwards's and Pearsall's, our strength is considerably reduced.

Captain Dagworthy informed me, that Governor Sharpe is to open the road to Town Creek, within fifteen miles of this place, and, as Maryland has nearly two hundred men here fit for duty, I hope you will be of opinion, that they are sufficiently strong to proceed on the Fort Frederic road, without needing a reinforcement from us; especially if you will consider, that they are in a manner covered by the troops here, and by those to be employed on the road to Raystown, to which service I shall send a detachment to-morrow. We have no *hay* at this place; it was *corn*, which I called forage. We shall have tools enough to open the road to Raystown, among the artificers of Colonel Byrd's regiment.

I am sorry to hear that the Catawbas have so egregiously misbehaved. When I write to Governor Fauquier, I shall touch on this subject.*

It gives me great pleasure to find, that you approve the dress I have put my men into.† It is evident, that

* Colonel Bouquet had written;—"The Catawbas, under the command of Captain Johnny, are gone to Winchester. They have behaved in the most shameful manner, and run away like a parcel of thieves, rather than warriors. They have never killed even a deer, and there is the strongest reason to suspect, that the scalp, which they pretend to have taken, was an old one. I think it very necessary to send a message to their nation to complain of their conduct, and know at once if they are friends or enemies. If you approve it, I shall be obliged to you to propose the thing to the Governor of Virginia."

† Alluding to a passage in Colonel Bouquet's letter, in which he says;

soldiers in that trim are better able to carry their provisions, are fitter for the active service we must engage in, less liable to sink under the fatigues of a march, and we thus get rid of much baggage, which would lengthen our line of march. These, and not whim or caprice, were my reasons for ordering this dress. I am, &c.

TO COLONEL BOUQUET.

Camp, at Fort Cumberland, 16 July, 1758.

SIR,

I was favored with your letter of the 14th instant, at eleven o'clock last night. The express, who brought it, informs me, that he was twice fired upon by Indians, and was obliged to abandon his horse to save himself.

Three parties have gone hence towards the enemy within these few days past. The largest of them, consisting of an officer and eighteen Cherokees, marched three days ago. I always send some white men with the Indians, and will, to-day or to-morrow, send an officer and a greater number of white men with another party of Cherokees, because you desire it; although, I must confess, it is my opinion, that small parties of Indians will more effectually harass the enemy, by keeping them under continual alarms, than any parties of white men can do. For small parties of the latter are not equal to the task, not being so dexterous at skulking as Indians; and large parties will be discovered by their spies early enough to have a superior force opposed to

"Major Lewis with two hundred men arrived here last night. I am extremely obliged to you for this extraordinary despatch. Their dress should be our pattern in this expedition." And again, afterwards,— "The dress takes very well here, and, thank God, we see nothing but shirts and blankets."

them. Hence, in either case, there would be a great probability of losing many of our best men, and wearing down the rest, before the more essential services of the campaign would be entered upon, and this, I am afraid, without answering the proposed end.

You are pleased to ask my opinion of the propriety of making an irruption into the enemy's country with a strong party. Such an enterprise, Sir, at this juncture, when we may suppose the enemy have collected, or are collecting, their whole force at Fort Duquesne, would require a formidable detachment, the supplying of which with provisions would be too difficult and cumbersome to be effected undiscovered, as the enemy's parties are continually watching our motions. It is more than likely, therefore, that the enterprise would terminate in a miscarriage, if not in the destruction of the party. I should think it more eligible to defer such an attempt, until the army approaches more nearly to the enemy.

I shall direct the officer, that marches out, to take particular pains in reconnoitring General Braddock's road, though I have had repeated information, that it only wants such small repairs, as could with ease be made as fast as the army would march. It is impossible for me to send out any men to repair it, as I have no tools for that purpose. If we had tools, and should go upon this road, the second company of artificers would no doubt be wanted here; but, as it is, I imagine they will be better employed with you.

The misbehaviour of the Indians at your camp gives me great concern. If they were hearty in our interest, their services would be infinitely valuable. The best white men are not equal to them in the woods. But I fear they are too sensible of their own importance to render us much service.

As the par of exchange between Virginia and Pennsylvania is, by the laws of the two provinces, fixed at twenty-five per cent in favor of the former, I apprehend we can have no right to settle it on any other footing; especially as any material deviation might be productive of very bad consequences.

Since writing the above, the warriors of the party of Cherokees insisted upon marching instantly, and that but one white man should go. They are gone, and I have given the white man the necessary orders relative to the road.

I am, with great sincerity, Sir, your most obedient servant.

TO COLONEL BOUQUET.

Camp, near Fort Cumberland, 19 July, 1758.

SIR,

Your obliging favor of this date I just now had the pleasure of receiving. You flatter me much by coinciding with me in opinion, relative to the proposed expedition.

Captain Dagworthy returned hither yesterday in consequence of orders from Sir John St. Clair, forwarded by the commanding officer at Fort Frederic. I will send out a party on Braddock's road, which I shall be able to reinforce when Colonel Mercer returns.*

I am exceedingly obliged by the handsome and polite manner, in which you are pleased to give me leave to attend the election at Winchester. Although my being there, under any other circumstances, would be

---

* Colonel Mercer had been employed, with a detachment of soldiers, in opening a road from Fort Cumberland to the camp at Raystown, a distance of thirty miles.

very agreeable to me, yet I can hardly persuade myself to think of being absent from my more immediate duty, even for a few days. I will not, however, come to any absolute determination, till I receive answers to some letters on that subject, which I expect this night or to-morrow.* I am, &c.

TO COLONEL BOUQUET.

Camp near Fort Cumberland, 21 July, 1758.

SIR,

I had, before Colonel Stephen came to this place, abandoned all thoughts of attending personally the election at Winchester, choosing rather to leave the

* Having resolved to quit the army, at the close of the present campaign, Colonel Washington had proposed himself to the electors of Frederic county, as a candidate for the House of Burgesses. The election was now approaching, and some of his friends had urged him to be at Winchester on that occasion, fearing the successful activity of three rival candidates.

Regarding his duties in the army, however, as outweighing the considerations of personal interest, he remained at his post, and the election was carried through without his presence. He was chosen by a large majority over all his competitors. "Your friends," said one of his correspondents in a letter, "have been very sincere, so that you have received more votes than any other candidate. Colonel Wood sat on the bench and represented you, and he was carried round the town in the midst of a general applause, and huzzaing for Colonel Washington." Another friend wrote; — "From the bottom of a heart overflowing with gratitude, I beg leave to offer my congratulation on your happy election, — doubly so in its manner, which, considering the vast majority of votes, and your having so long commanded the whole of that country in the worst of times, greatly redounds to your honor."

As an indication of the mode of conducting a Virginia election in those days, it may be stated, that this poll cost the new Burgess thirty-nine pounds and six shillings. Among the items of charge, which have been preserved, are a hogshead and a barrel of punch, thirty-five gallons of wine, forty-three gallons of strong beer, cider, and dinner for his friends.

management of that affair to my friends, than be absent from my regiment, when there is a probability of its being called to duty. I am much pleased now, that I did so. Colonel Byrd has given me your letter of yesterday, in consequence of which I send you a return of the forage. He writes to Mr. Gist, requesting him to send vermilion for the Indians.

We participate in the joy felt for the success of his Majesty's arms at Louisburg, but sincerely lament the loss of the brave, active, and noble Lord Howe.

The bridge is finished at this place, and to-morrow Major Peachey, with three hundred men, will proceed to open General Braddock's road. I shall direct them to go to George's Creek, ten miles in advance. By that time I may possibly hear from you. If they go farther, it may be requisite to reinforce the party. But this matter, I suppose, will be ordered according to the route determined on by the General, for it will be needless to open a road, of which no use will be made afterwards.

Colonel Stephen gives me some room to apprehend, that a body of light troops may soon move on. I pray your interest, most sincerely, with the General, to get my regiment and myself included in the number. If any argument is needed to obtain this favor, I hope without vanity I may be allowed to say, that, from long intimacy with these woods, and frequent scouting in them, my men are at least as well acquainted with all the passes and difficulties, as any troops that will be employed.

The General directs, that the troops shall be provided with covers to their locks. Where to get them I know not. There is but one possible way, and that is, by taking the hides of the cattle, and they will fall short. The commissaries ask eighteen shillings apiece for hides. I should be glad of your advice on this subject. What is to be done with the wagons expected up in our next convoy? I cannot exactly predict their number, but I suppose the provisions, forage, and stores, cannot employ less than fifty.

I am, with very great regard, your most obedient and obliged humble servant.

TO COLONEL BOUQUET.

Camp, near Fort Cumberland, 25 July, 1758.

DEAR SIR,

I do not incline to propose any thing, that may seem officious, but would it not facilitate the operation of the campaign, if the Virginia troops were ordered to proceed as far as the Great Crossing, and construct forts at the most advantageous situations as they advance, opening the road at the same time? In such a case, I should be glad to be joined by that part of my regiment at Raystown. Major Peachey, who commands the working party on Braddock's road, writes to me, that he finds few repairs wanting. To-night I shall order him to proceed as far as Savage River, and then return, as his party is too weak to adventure further.

We have received advice that our second convoy, of more than seventy wagons, will be at the South Branch to-day, where I expect they will be joined by other wagons with forage. They will all proceed to this place immediately.

I shall most cheerfully work on any road, pursue any route, or enter upon any service, that the General or yourself may think me usefully employed in, or qualified for, and shall never have a will of my own, when a duty is required of me. But since you desire me to speak my sentiments freely, permit me to observe, that after having conversed with all the guides, and having been informed by others, who have a knowledge of the country, I am convinced that a road, to be compared with General Braddock's, or, indeed, that will be fit for transportation even by packhorses, cannot be made. I have no predilection for the route you have in contemplation for me, not because difficulties appear therein, but because I doubt whether satisfaction can be given in the execution of the plan. I know not what reports you may have received from your reconnoitring parties; but I have been uniformly told, that, if you expect a tolerable road by Raystown, you will be disappointed, for no movement can be made that way without destroying our horses.

I should be extremely glad of one hour's conference with you, when the General arrives. I could then explain myself more fully, and, I think, demonstrate the advantages of pushing out a body of light troops in this quarter. I would make a trip to Raystown with great pleasure, if my presence here could be dispensed with for a day or two, of which you can best judge.*

I am, my dear Sir, with most sincere regard, your very obedient and affectionate servant.

---

* In reply Colonel Bouquet wrote;—"Nothing can exceed your generous dispositions for the service. I see with the utmost satisfaction, that you are above the influences of prejudice, and ready to go heartily where reason and judgment shall direct. I wish, sincerely, that we may all entertain one and the same opinion; therefore I desire to have an interview with you at the houses built half way between our camps. I will communicate all the intelligence, which it has been in my power to collect; and, by weighing impartially the advantages and disadvantages of each route, I hope we shall be able between us to determine what is most eligible, and save the General trouble and loss of time."

An interview accordingly took place, at which the subject was fully discussed.

TO MAJOR FRANCIS HALKET, BRIGADE MAJOR.

Camp, at Fort Cumberland, 2 August, 1758.

MY DEAR HALKET,

I am just returned from a conference with Colonel Bouquet. I find him fixed, I think I may say unalterably fixed, to lead you a new way to the Ohio, through a road, every inch of which is to be cut at this advanced season, when we have scarce time left to tread the beaten track, universally confessed to be the best passage through the mountains.

If Colonel Bouquet succeeds in this point with the General, all is lost, — all is lost indeed, — our enterprise will be ruined, and we shall be stopped at the Laurel Hill this winter; but not to gather *laurels*, except of the kind that covers the mountains. The southern Indians will turn against us, and these colonies will be desolated by such an accession to the enemy's strength. These must be the consequences of a miscarriage; and a miscarriage is the almost necessary consequence of an attempt to march the army by this new route. I have given my reasons at large to Colonel Bouquet. He desired that I would do so, that he might forward them to the General. Should this happen, you will be able to judge of their weight.

I am uninfluenced by prejudice, having no hopes or fears but for the general good. Of this you may be assured, and that my sincere sentiments are spoken on this occasion.

I am, dear Halket, most affectionately yours.

TO COLONEL BOUQUET.

Camp, at Fort Cumberland, 2 August, 1758.

SIR,

The matters, of which we spoke relative to the roads, have, since our parting, been the subject of my closest reflection; and, so far am I from altering my opinion, that, the more time and attention I bestow, the more I am confirmed in it; and the reasons for taking Braddock's road appear in a stronger point of view. To enumerate the whole of these reasons would be tedious, and to you, who are become so much master of the subject, unnecessary. I shall, therefore, briefly mention a few only, which I think so obvious in themselves, that they must effectually remove objections.

Several years ago the Virginians and Pennsylvanians commenced a trade with the Indians settled on the Ohio, and, to obviate the many inconveniences of a bad road, they, after reiterated and ineffectual efforts to discover where a good one might be made, employed for the purpose several of the most intelligent Indians, who, in the course of many years' hunting, had acquired a perfect knowledge of these mountains. The Indians, having taken the greatest pains to gain the rewards offered for this discovery, declared, that the path leading from Will's Creek was infinitely preferable to any, that could be made at any other place. Time and experience so clearly demonstrated this truth, that the Pennsylvania traders commonly carried out their goods by Will's Creek. Therefore, the Ohio Company, in 1753, at a considerable expense, opened the road. In 1754 the troops, whom I had the honor to command, greatly repaired it, as far as Gist's plantation; and, in 1755, it was widened and completed by General Braddock to within six miles of

Fort Duquesne. A road, that has so long been opened, and so well and so often repaired, must be much firmer and better than a new one, allowing the ground to be equally good.

But, supposing it were practicable to make a road from Raystown quite as good as General Braddock's, — I ask, have we time to do it? Certainly not. To surmount the difficulties to be encountered in making it over such mountains, covered with woods and rocks, would require so much time, as to blast our otherwise well-grounded hopes of striking the important stroke this season.

The favorable accounts, that some give of the forage on the Raystown road, as being so much better than that on the other, are certainly exaggerated. It is well known, that, on both routes, the rich valleys between the mountains abound with good forage, and that those, which are stony and bushy, are destitute of it. Colonel Byrd and the engineer, who accompanied him, confirm this fact. Surely the meadows on Braddock's road would greatly overbalance the advantage of having grass to the foot of the ridge, on the Raystown road; and all agree, that a more barren road is nowhere to be found, than that from Raystown to the inhabitants, which is likewise to be considered.

Another principal objection made to General Braddock's road is in regard to the waters. But these seldom swell so much, as to obstruct the passage. The Youghiogany River, which is the most rapid and soonest filled, I have crossed with a body of troops, after more than thirty days' almost continued rain. In fine, any difficulties on this score are so trivial, that they really are not worth mentioning. The Monongahela, the largest of all these rivers, may, if necessary, easily be avoided, as Mr. Frazer the principal guide informs me.

by passing a defile, and even that, he says, may be shunned.

Again, it is said, there are many defiles on this road. I grant that there are some, but I know of none that may not be traversed; and I should be glad to be informed where a road can be had, over these mountains, not subject to the same inconvenience. The shortness of the distance between Raystown and Loyal Hanna is used as an argument against this road, which bears in it something unaccountable to me; for I must beg leave to ask, whether it requires more time, or is more difficult and expensive, to go one hundred and forty-five miles in a good road already made to our hands, than to cut one hundred miles anew, and a great part of the way over impassable mountains.

That the old road is many miles nearer Winchester in Virginia, and Fort Frederic in Maryland, than the contemplated one, is incontestable; and I will here show the distances from Carlisle by the two routes, fixing the different stages, some of which I have from information only, but others I believe to be exact.* From this com-

* *From Carlisle to Fort Duquesne, by way of Raystown.*

	Miles.
From Carlisle to Shippensburg	21
" Shippensburg to Fort Loudoun	24
" Fort Loudoun to Fort Littleton	20
" Fort Littleton to Juniatta Crossing	14
" Juniatta Crossing to Raystown	14
	93
" Raystown to Fort Duquesne	100
	193

From Carlisle to Fort Duquesne, by way of Forts Frederic and Cumberland.

	Miles.
From Carlisle to Shippensburg	21
" Shippensburg to Chambers's	12
" Chambers's to Pacelin's	12
" Pacelin's to Fort Frederic	12
" Fort Frederic to Fort Cumberland	40
	97
" Fort Cumberland to Fort Duquesne	115
	212

putation there appears to be a difference of nineteen miles only. Were all the supplies necessarily to come from Carlisle, it is well known, that the goodness of the old road is a sufficient compensation for the shortness of the other, as the wrecked and broken wagons there clearly demonstrate.

I shall next give you my reasons against dividing the army, in the manner you propose.

First, then, by dividing our army, we shall divide our strength, and, by pursuing quite distinct routes, put it entirely out of the power of each division to succour the other, as the proposed new road has no communication with the old one.

Secondly, to march in this manner will be attended with many inconveniences. If we depart from our advanced posts at the same time, and make no deposits by the way, those troops that go from Raystown, as they will be light, with carrying-horses only, will arrive at Fort Duquesne long before the others, and must, if the enemy are strong there, be exposed to many insults in their advance, and in their intrenchments, from the cannon of the enemy, which they may draw out upon them at pleasure. If they are not strong enough to do this, we have but little to apprehend from them, in whatever way we may go.

Thirdly, if that division, which escorts the convoy, is permitted to march first, we risk our all, in a manner, and shall be ruined if any accident happens to the artillery and the stores.

Lastly, if we advance on both roads, by deposits, we must double our number of troops over the mountains, and distress ourselves by victualling them at these deposits, besides losing the proposed advantage, that of stealing a march. For, we cannot suppose that the French, who have their scouts constantly out, can be so deficient in point of intelligence, as to be unacquainted with our motions, while we are advancing by slow degrees towards them.

From what has been said relative to the two roads, it appears to me very clear, that the old one is infinitely better, than the other can be made, and that there is no room to hesitate in deciding which to take, when we consider the advanced season, and the little time left to execute our plan.

I shall, therefore, in the last place offer, as desired, my sentiments on advancing by deposits. The first deposit I should have proposed to be at the Little Meadows, had time permitted; but, as the case now stands, I think it should be at the Great Crossing, or the Great Meadows. The Great Crossing I esteem the most advantageous post, on several accounts, especially on those of water and security of passage; but then it does not abound with forage, as the Meadows do, nor with so much level land fit for culture. To this latter place a body of fifteen hundred men may march with three hundred wagons (or with carrying-horses, which would be much better), allowing each wagon to carry eight hundred weight of flour and four hundred of salt meat.

Our next deposit will probably be at Salt Lick, about thirty-five miles from the Meadows. To this place I think it necessary to send two thousand five hundred men, to construct some post, taking six days' provisions only, which is sufficient to serve them till the convoy comes up, by which time an entrenched camp, or some other defensive work, may be effected. From hence I conceive it highly expedient to detach three or four thousand of the best troops to invest the fort, and to prevent, if possible, an engagement in the woods, which of all things ought to be avoided. The artillery and stores may be brought up in four days from Salt Lick.

From that time I will allow eighteen days more, for the carrying-horses to make a trip to Raystown for provisions, passing along the old path by Loyal Hanna. They may do it in this time, as the horses will go down light.

From this statement, and by my calculations, in which large allowance is made for the quantity of provisions, as well as for the time of transporting them, it appears that, from the day on which the front division begins its march, till the whole army arrives before Fort Duquesne, will be thirty-four days. There will be, also, eighty-seven days' provision on hand, allowing for the consumption on the march. Eighteen days added to the above will make fifty-two in all, the number required for our operations. These ought to be finished, if possible, by the middle of October. I am, &c.

TO COLONEL BOUQUET.

Camp, at Fort Cumberland, 18 August, 1758.

DEAR SIR,

I am favored with yours of yesterday, intimating a probability of my proceeding with a body of troops, on General Braddock's road, and desiring me to retain for that purpose a month's provisions at this place, a thing I should be extremely fond of; but, as I cannot possibly know what quantity of provisions may be necessary for that time, without knowing the number of men I may probably march with, and when it is likely I may leave this place, I hope you will be pleased to give me the necessary information on that head; and, also, how this post is to be garrisoned, and what provision and stores should be left here.*

* The General had determined to proceed by the new road, and sixteen hundred men were already in advance of Raystown, making their way

I have talked a good deal with Kelly upon the nature of the intervening ground between the new road and Braddock's, and, from what he says, I apprehend it impracticable to effect a junction with the troops on the new road, till we advance near the Salt Lick, which is at no great distance from Fort Duquesne. How far it may be advisable to send a small body of troops so near the enemy, and at so great a distance from the army, without any tools for repairing the roads, or throwing up any kind of defences in case of need, I shall not presume to say. But I cannot help observing, that all the guides and Indians are to be drawn from hence, and that the

---

across the mountains to Loyal Hanna. It seems there was still a plan for sending out a division by Braddock's road, with the view of forming a junction with the main body on its march. This was discouraged by Colonel Washington, and, indeed, he had been opposed from the beginning to any scheme of dividing the army. It was at length abandoned.

General Forbes had been detained by illness at Carlisle. He was now at Shippensburg, and was expected daily in camp at Raystown. The Virginians and Marylanders believed he had been too much under a Pennsylvania influence, in resolving to make this new road across the mountains, through the heart of that colony, in preference to marching his army over an old one, which required but small repairs. Colonel Washington wrote to Governor Fauquier, — "The Pennsylvanians, whose present as well as future interest it was to have the expedition conducted through their government, and along that way, because it secures their frontiers at present, and their trade hereafter, a chain of forts being erected, had prejudiced the General absolutely against the old road, and made him believe that *we* were the partial people, and determined him at all events to pursue that route."

The Virginia Assembly, when they met on the 14th of September, were so much dissatisfied with the manner in which the expedition had been conducted, and with the partiality, which they imagined was shown to Pennsylvania, that they, thinking no attempt on Fort Duquesne would be made so late in the season, passed an act to withdraw the first regiment from the regulars on the 1st of December, and station it on the frontiers of their own colony. But about a fortnight after the Assembly broke up, the Governor received letters informing him that the expedition would at all events be prosecuted. He immediately called the Assembly together again, and another act was passed, extending the time to the first of January. These particulars were communicated to Colonel Washington by Mr. Speaker Robinson. See the acts in Hening's *Statutes at Large*, Vol. VII. pp. 163, 251.

greater part of my regiment is on the other road,* so that I have but few of the first regiment remaining with me, and eight companies of the second only, whose officers and men cannot be supposed to know much of the service, or of the country, and nearly, if not quite, a fifth of them sick. I thought it incumbent on me to mention these things, that you may know our condition. At the same time I beg leave to assure you, that nothing will give me greater pleasure than to proceed with any number of men, that the General or yourself shall think proper to order.

With regard to keeping out a succession of strong parties on this road, from the troops here, I must beg leave to remark, that we have not so much as one pack-horse upon which to take provisions, having been under the necessity the other day of pressing five horses from some countrymen, who came to camp upon business, before I could equip Captain McKenzie's party for a fourteen days' march. We have not an ounce of salt provision of any kind here, and it is impossible to preserve the fresh, especially as we have no salt, by any other means than *barbacuing* it in the Indian manner. In doing this, nearly half is lost, so that a party receiving ten days' provisions will be obliged to live upon little better than five days' allowance of meat, a thing impracticable.

A great many of Colonel Byrd's men are very sickly; the rest are become dejected. This sickness and depression of spirits cannot arise from the situation of our camp, which is undoubtedly the most healthy of any ground in this vicinity, but is occasioned, I apprehend, by the change in their mode of living, and by the limestone water. The soldiers of the first regiment, like

* The companies of the first regiment were chiefly with Colonel Stephen at Raystown, or on the way to Loyal Hanna.

those of the second, would be sickly, were it not owing to some such causes.

We have reason to believe, that parties of the enemy are about us, a wagoner having been shot yesterday afternoon, and his horse killed under him, not more than three miles from this place.

We have no Indian goods of any kind here. It gives me great pleasure to learn, that the General is getting better, and is expected soon at Raystown. I am, &c.

TO COLONEL BOUQUET.

Camp, at Fort Cumberland, 21 August, 1758.

DEAR SIR,

Twenty-five Catawbas came here this evening, and the convoy may be expected the day after to-morrow, as it was at Pearsall's last night.

Governor Sharpe may be expected here in a day or two. I am at a loss to know how he ranks, and whether he is entitled to the command. In the British army his rank is that of lieutenant-colonel only, but what it may be as a governor, in his own province, I really do not know, nor whether he has any out of the troops of his province. I should, therefore, be glad of your advice, being unwilling to dispute the point with him wrongfully, or to give up the command, if I have a right to it.*

I am, &c.

---

* Colonel Bouquet replied;—"The governors in America have no command of the troops, even in their own provinces, when they are joined with any other of his Majesty's forces, unless they have a commission from the commander-in-chief for that purpose. Governor Sharpe will not expect to have the command as governor, and as lieutenant-colonel he cannot, nor do I suppose he would choose to serve in that rank."

As the Maryland Assembly, in their contests with the Governor and Upper House, had made no provision for supporting the small body of

TO JOHN ROBINSON, SPEAKER OF THE HOUSE OF BURGESSES.

Camp, at Fort Cumberland, 1 September, 1758.

MY DEAR SIR,

We are still encamped here, very sickly, and quite dispirited at the prospect before us.

That appearance of glory, which we had once in view, that hope, that laudable ambition of serving our country, and meriting its applause, are now no more; all is dwindled into ease, sloth, and fatal inactivity. In a word, all is lost, if the ways of men in power, like certain ways of Providence, are not inscrutable. But we, who view the actions of great men at a distance, can only form conjectures agreeably to a limited perception; and, being ignorant of the comprehensive schemes, which may be in contemplation, might mistake egregiously in judging of things from appearances, or by the lump. Yet every fool will have his notions, — will prattle and talk away; and why may not I? We seem then, in my opinion, to act under the guidance of an evil genius. The conduct of our leaders, if not actuated by superior orders, is tempered with something, I do not care to give a name to. Nothing now but a miracle can bring this campaign to a happy issue.

In my last, if I remember rightly, I told you, that I had employed my small abilities in opposing the measures then concerting. To do this, I not only represented the advanced season, the difficulty of cutting a new road over these mountains, the short time left for

---

troops under Colonel Dagworthy, which had now joined the army, General Forbes advanced money for this purpose out of the King's funds, relying on the honor of the Assembly for a future reimbursement. The amount thus advanced was recognised and paid by the succeeding Assembly.

that service, the moral certainty of its obstructing our march, and the consequent miscarriage of the expedition; I endeavoured to represent, also, the hard struggle Virginia had made this year in raising a second regiment *upon so short* a notice, the great expense of doing it, and her inability for future exertion. I spoke my fears concerning the southern Indians, in the event of a miscarriage. But I spoke all unavailingly, for the road was immediately begun, and from one to two thousand men have since constantly wrought upon it. By the last accounts I have received, they had cut it to the foot of Laurel Hill, about thirty-five miles; and I suppose by this time fifteen hundred men have taken post at a place called Loyal Hanna, about ten miles further, where our next fort is intended to be constructed.

We have certain intelligence, that the French strength at Fort Duquesne, on the 13th ultimo, did not exceed eight hundred men, Indians included, of whom there appeared to be about three or four hundred. This account is corroborated on all hands. Two officers of the first Virginia regiment, Chew and Allen, have since come from thence, both in different parties, and at different times, after lying a day or two concealed in full view of the fort, and observing the motions and strength of the enemy. See, therefore, how our time has been misspent. Behold how the golden opportunity has been lost, perhaps never more to be regained! How is it to be accounted for? Can General Forbes have orders for this? Impossible. Will, then, our injured country pass by such abuses? I hope not. Rather let a full representation of the matter go to his Majesty. Let him know how grossly his glory and interest, and the public money, have been prostituted. I wish I were sent immediately home [to England], as an aid to some other on this errand. I think, without vanity, I could set the conduct of this expedition in its true colors, having taken some pains, perhaps more than any other man, to dive to the bottom of it. But no more.

Colonel Byrd, who is unwell, joins me in compliments to you, the Attorney-General, and the rest of our friends.*

I am, &c.

TO GENERAL FORBES, COMMANDING HIS MAJESTY'S FORCES EMPLOYED ON THE OHIO EXPEDITION.

Camp, at Raystown, 8 October, 1758.

SIR,

In consequence of your request of the Colonels assembled at your lodgings, the 15th ultimo, I offer these plans to your consideration. They express my thoughts respecting a line of march through a country covered with woods, and how that line of march may be formed

* A few days after this letter was written, General Forbes arrived at Raystown, and Colonel Washington was called to that place. Fort Cumberland was garrisoned by Maryland militia, under the command of Governor Sharpe. Meantime occurred the strange and unfortunate adventure of Major Grant, who had advanced with eight hundred men to Fort Duquesne. A part of the Virginia troops was in this detachment, and was signalized by its bravery.

"From all the accounts I can collect," says Colonel Washington, in writing to Governor Fauquier, "it appears very clear, that this was a very ill concerted, or a very ill executed plan, perhaps both; but it seems to be generally acknowledged, that Major Grant exceeded his orders, and that no disposition was made for engaging. The troops were divided, which caused the front to give way, and put the whole into confusion, except the Virginians commanded by Captain Bullitt, who were, in the hands of Providence, a means of preventing all our people from sharing one common fate. Our officers and men have gained very great applause for their gallant behaviour during the action. I had the honor to be publicly complimented yesterday by the General on the occasion. Bullitt's behaviour is matter of great admiration."

Major Grant, as also Major Lewis, of the first Virginia regiment, were taken prisoners and sent to Montreal.

quickly into an order of battle. The plan of the order of march and order of battle, on the other side, is calculated for a forced march with field-pieces only, unincumbered with wagons. It represents, first, a line of march; and, secondly, how that line of march may in an instant be thrown into an order of battle in the woods. This plan supposes four thousand privates, one thousand of whom, picked men, are to march in the front in three divisions, each division having a field-officer to command it, besides the commander of the whole; and always to be in readiness to oppose the enemy, whose attack, if the necessary precautions are observed, must always be in front.

The first division must, as the second and third likewise ought to be, subdivided for the captains; these subdivisions to be again divided for the subalterns; and the subalterns again for the sergeants and corporals. By which means every non-commissioned officer will have a party to command, under the eye of a subaltern, as the subalterns will have, under the direction of a captain.

I shall, though I believe it unnecessary, remark here, that the captains, when their subdivisions are again divided, are to take command of no particular part of it, but to attend to the whole subdivision, as the subalterns are to do with theirs, each captain and subaltern acting as commandant of the division he is appointed to, under the field-officer, visiting and encouraging all parts alike, and keeping the soldiers to their duty. This being done, the first division, so soon as the van-guard is attacked (if that gives the first notice of the enemy's approach), is to file off to the right and left, and take to trees, gaining the enemy's flanks, and surrounding them, as described in the second plan.* The flank-guards on

* This plan has not been preserved.

	Captns	Subaltns	Sergts	Corpls	Privts	Captns	Subaltns	Sergts	Corpls	Privts
A. Van Guards consisting of 1st				1	4					
2d			1	1	12					
3d		1	1	1	24					
4th	1	2	2	2	50	1	3	4	5	90
B. Flank Guards each consisting of	1	3	4	5	90	2	6	8	10	180
C. 1st 2d and 3d Division, each					243					730
D. 1st and 2d Brigades, each					950					1900
E. Eight Captain's Guards, each	1	1	1	2	25	8	8	8	16	200
F. Sixteen Subaltern's Guards, each		1	1	1	15		16	16	16	240
G. Sixteen Sergeant's Guards, each			1	1	10			16	16	160
H. Rear and Baggage Guard										500
										1000

PLAN
of
a Line of March
for the Army
under
GENERAL FORBES,
Octr 1758
Drawn by G. Washington.

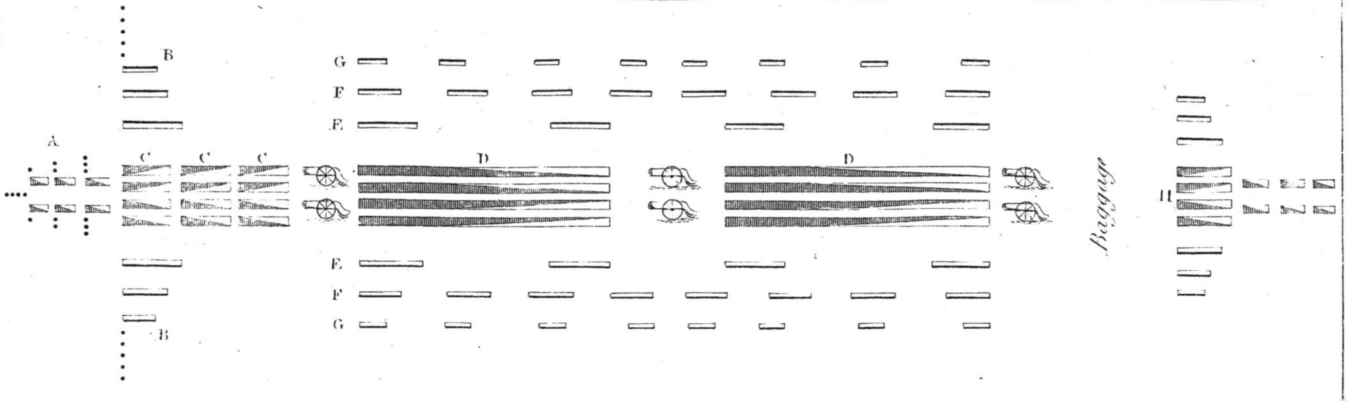

Baggage

the right, which belong to the second division, are immediately to extend to the right, followed by that division, and to form, as described in the aforesaid plan. The rear-guard division is to follow the left flankers in the same manner, in order, if possible, to encompass the enemy, which being a practice different from any thing they have ever yet experienced from us, I think may be accomplished. Such Indians as we have, should be ordered to get round, unperceived, and fall at the same time upon the enemy's rear. The front and rear being thus secured, a body of two thousand five hundred men remains to form two brigades, on the flanks of which six hundred men must march for their safety, and in such order as to form a rank entire, by only marching the captains' and subalterns' guards into the intervals between the sergeants' parties. The main body will now be reduced to nineteen hundred men, who should be kept as a *corps de reserve* to support any part, that shall be found weak or forced.

The whole is submitted with the utmost candor, by Sir, &c.

TO GOVERNOR FAUQUIER.

Camp, at Loyal Hanna, 30 October, 1758. *

SIR,

I am sorry to inform you, that, upon reviewing the six companies of my regiment at this place, which had been separated from me since my last, I found them deficient in the necessaries contained in the enclosed return. I am, therefore, under the duty of providing for them, or more properly of endeavouring to do it, as I

---

* Colonel Washington had now been sent forward, in advance of the main army, to take command of a division employed in opening the road.

doubt very much the possibility of succeeding. You will not, I hope, be surprised, should I draw on you for the amount.

Governor Sharpe in person commanded a garrison of militia, from his province, at Fort Cumberland, when the magazine was blown up.

My march to this post gave me an opportunity of forming a judgment of the road, and I can truly say, that it is indescribably bad. Had it not been for an accidental discovery of a new passage over the Laurel Hill, the carriages must inevitably have stopped on the other side. This fact nobody here takes upon him to deny. The General and great part of the troops being yet behind, and the weather growing very inclement, I apprehend our expedition must terminate for this year at this place. But as our affairs are now drawing to a crisis, and a good or bad conclusion of them will shortly ensue, I choose to suspend my judgment, as well as a further account of the matter, to a future day.*

November 5th. — The General being arrived, with most of the artillery and troops, we expect to move forward in a very few days, encountering every hardship, that an advanced season, want of clothes, and a small stock of provisions will expose us to. But it is no longer a time for pointing out difficulties, and I hope my next will run in a more agreeable strain. In the mean time, I beg leave to assure your Honor, that, with very great respect, I am, &c.

---

* When the General reached Loyal Hanna, a council of war was called, and it was determined not to be advisable to proceed further that season. But the report of three prisoners, who were shortly afterwards brought in, and who communicated the weak state of the garrison at Fort Duquesne, induced a change of opinion, and the enterprise was prosecuted.

TO GENERAL FORBES.

Camp, on Chestnut Ridge, 11 o'clock at night,
15 November, 1758.

SIR,

An express from Colonel Armstrong affords me an opportunity of informing you, that we arrived here about four o'clock this afternoon. I immediately ordered working parties on the road, that no time might be lost in working it; but I fear I shall not proceed so fast as you could wish, since, after all my delays, and waiting for tools, Captain Fields was able to get but forty-two axes. These, and the others that are here, shall be employed to-morrow at daylight to the best advantage. The road intended is but very slightly *blazed*. It may be necessary to send Captain Shelby forward to prevent mistakes.

This camp is about six miles from Loyal Hanna, where the new road strikes out.* I am, &c.

TO GENERAL FORBES.

Camp, near Bushy Run, 17 November, 1758.

SIR,

After the most constant labor from daybreak till night, we were able to open the road only as far as this place, about six miles from our last camp. Captain Shelby here overtook us, and presented me with your and Colonel Bouquet's letters. A junction with Colonel Armstrong this morning would have prevented the good effects of a fortified camp to-night, and retarded our operations a day at least; for which reason I desired

* On leaving Loyal Hanna the command of a division, or brigade, devolved on Colonel Washington. From that date the returns were made to him as *Brigadier*.

him to march forward this morning at two o'clock, and secure himself, as you desired. If he accomplishes that work before night, he is to begin opening the road towards me.

If Indians can ever be of any use to us, it must be now, in the front, for intelligence. I beg you will, therefore, order their conductors to bring them at all events.

Camp, at night. — Colonel Bouquet's letter came to my hands, just as the bearer was passing by, from Colonel Armstrong. I shall punctually observe all its directions, although I at the same time confess, that I think it would have been much safer and more eligible to march briskly forward to our second post, leaving the road for Colonel Montgomery to open. We should by that means have been a covering party to him, while we are fortifying a camp, which may be of great importance to the army. Less time would be lost in this way, and a straggling front, which will ever happen in expeditious cutting, would be avoided; besides the probable advantage of getting into a secure camp before we should be discovered.

I have opened the road between seven and eight miles to day, and am yet three miles short of Colonel Armstrong, who marched at eight o'clock. I understand by Captain Shelby, who is just come from him, that he has not yet begun entrenching his camp, which must again retard us to-morrow. Forwarding provisions is highly necessary; hard labor consumes them fast; but all the men are in high spirits, and are anxious to go on.

I shall be much pleased to see the Indians up, and am very glad to hear that Mr. Croghan is so near at hand. The number with him is not mentioned. I wish they also were in our front.

I was extremely sorry to hear of your indisposition to day, being, Sir, yours, &c.

TO GENERAL FORBES.

Armstrong's Camp, 18 November, 1758.

SIR,

I came to this camp about eleven o'clock to-day, having opened the road before me. I should immediately have proceeded on, but, as the bullocks were to be slaughtered, and provisions dressed, I thought it expedient to halt here till three in the morning, when I shall begin to march with one thousand men, leaving Colonel Armstrong and five hundred more in this camp, until Colonel Montgomery joins him. I took care that the road should not be delayed by this halt, for I ordered out a working party, properly covered, before I came here, to cut it forward till night, and then return.

I fear that we have been greatly deceived, with regard to the distance from this place to Fort Duquesne. Most of the woods-men, that I have conversed with, seem to think that we are still thirty miles from it. I have sent out a party in that direction to ascertain the distance, and the kind of ground to be passed over, and two others to scout on the right and left, for the discovery of tracks.

I found three redoubts erecting for the defence of this camp. Mr. Gordon thinks, that it will be sufficiently secured by these means; but, for my own part, I do not look upon redoubts alone, in this close country, to be half as good as the slightest breastwork; indeed, I do not believe they are any security at all without other works.

I enclose you a return of the total strength of this place, and the time for which we are served with provisions, by which you will see how much a supply is needed. I must beg, that commissaries and steelyards may be sent forward, otherwise a continual dissatisfaction will prevail, as well on the part of the contractors, as on that of the soldiers, who think they have injustice done them in their allowance, notwithstanding that the fifteen bullocks, which were received as provisions for four days, were issued for three only, by the judgment of an officer from each corps, as well as my own, for I took pains to examine into it myself.

I had written thus far, when your favor of this morning came to hand. I shall set out at three o'clock, as above, leaving the Highlanders to finish the redoubts, according to Mr. Gordon's plan, and to secure the tools, until Colonel Montgomery comes up, submitting it then to Colonel Bouquet's opinion to bring or leave them.

Your chimney at this place is finished. I shall take care to put up one at the next post.*

I shall use every necessary precaution to get timely notice of the enemy's approach, so that I flatter myself you need be under no apprehensions on that head. A scouting party is just returned, and reports, that, five miles advanced, thay discovered the tracks of about forty persons making towards Kiskemanetas. The tracks appear to have been made to-day, or yesterday.

I am, with very great respect, your most obedient, &c.

TO GOVERNOR FAUQUIER.

Camp, at Fort Duquesne, 28 November, 1758.

SIR,

I have the pleasure to inform you, that Fort Duquesne, or the ground rather on which it stood, was possessed by his Majesty's troops on the 25th instant. The enemy, after letting us get within a day's march of

---

* The General had ordered a chimney to be built for his use at each of the entrenched camps.

the place, burned the fort, and ran away by the light of it, at night, going down the Ohio by water, to the number of about five hundred men, according to our best information. This possession of the fort has been matter of surprise to the whole army, and we cannot attribute it to more probable causes, than the weakness of the enemy, want of provisions, and the defection of their Indians. Of these circumstances we were luckily informed by three prisoners, who providentially fell into our hands at Loyal Hanna, when we despaired of proceeding further. A council of war had determined, that it was not advisable to advance this season beyond that place; but the above information caused us to march on without tents or baggage, and with only a light train of artillery. We have thus happily succeeded. It would be tedious, and I think unnecessary, to relate every trivial circumstance, that has happened since my last. To do this, if needful, shall be the employment of a leisure hour, when I shall have the pleasure to pay my respects to your Honor.

The General intends to wait here a few days to settle matters with the Indians, and then all the troops, except a sufficient garrison to secure the place, will march to their respective governments. I give your Honor this early notice, that your directions relative to the troops of Virginia may meet me on the road. I cannot help reminding you, in this place, of the hardships they have undergone, and of their present naked condition, that you may judge if it is not essential for them to have some little recess from fatigue, and time to provide themselves with necessaries. At present they are destitute of every comfort of life. If I do not get your orders to the contrary, I shall march the troops under my command directly to Winchester. They may then be disposed of, as you shall afterwards direct.

General Forbes desires me to inform you, that he is prevented, by a multiplicity of affairs, from writing to you so fully now, as he would otherwise have done. He has written to the commanding officers stationed on the communication from hence to Winchester, relative to the conduct of the Little Carpenter, a chief of the Cherokees, the purport of which was to desire, that they would escort him from one place to another, to prevent his doing any mischief to the inhabitants.

This fortunate, and, indeed, unexpected success of our arms will be attended with happy effects. The Delawares are suing for peace, and I doubt not that other tribes on the Ohio will follow their example. A trade, free, open, and on equitable terms, is what they seem much to desire, and I do not know so effectual a way of riveting them to our interest, as by sending out goods immediately to this place for that purpose. It will, at the same time, be a means of supplying the garrision with such necessaries as may be wanted; and, I think, the other colonies, which are as greatly interested in the support of this place as Virginia, should neglect no means in their power to establish and maintain a strong garrison here. Our business, without this precaution, will be but half finished; while, on the other hand, we shall obtain a firm and lasting peace with the Indians, if this end is once accomplished.

General Forbes is very assiduous in getting these matters settled upon a solid basis, and has great merit for the happy issue to which he has brought our affairs, infirm and worn down as he is.* At present I have nothing further to add, but the strongest assurances of my being your Honor's most obedient and most humble servant.

---

* General Forbes died a few weeks afterwards in Philadelphia.

TO GOVERNOR FAUQUIER.

Loyal Hanna, 2 December, 1758.

SIR,

The enclosed was written with the intention of sending it by the General's express, but his indisposition prevented that express from setting out for three days afterwards; and the General thought, that my waiting upon your Honor would be more eligible, as I could represent the situation of our affairs in this quarter more fully, than could well be done by letter. This I accordingly attempted; but, upon trial, I found it impracticable to proceed with despatch, for want of horses, having now nearly two hundred miles to march before I can get a supply, and those at present in use being entirely disabled. I shall, notwithstanding, endeavour to comply with the General's request, but I cannot possibly be down till towards the 1st of next month, and the bearer may arrive much sooner.

The General has, in his letters, told you what garrison he proposed to leave at Fort Duquesne, but the want of provisions rendered it impossible to leave more than two hundred men in all; and these, without great exertions, must, I fear, abandon the place or perish. To prevent, as far as possible, either of these events, I have by this conveyance written a circular letter to the back inhabitants of Virginia, setting forth the great advantages of keeping that place, the improbability of doing it without their immediate assistance, that they may travel safely out while we hold that post, and that they will be allowed good prices for such provisions as they may carry. Unless the most effectual means shall be taken early in the spring to reinforce the garrison, the place will inevitably be lost, and then our frontiers will fall into the same distressed condition as heretofore. I can very confidently assert, that we never can secure them properly, if we again lose our footing on the Ohio, since we shall thereby lose the interest of the Indians. I therefore think, that every necessary preparation should be made, and not a moment lost in adopting the most speedy and efficacious measures, for securing the advantages to be derived from our holding possession of that important country.

The preparatory steps should immediately be taken for preserving the communication from Virginia, by constructing a post at Red-stone Creek, which would greatly facilitate the supplying of our troops on the Ohio, where a formidable garrison should be sent, as soon as the season will admit. A trade with the Indians should be established upon such terms, and transacted by men of such principle, as would at the same time redound to the reciprocal advantage of the colony and the Indians, and effectually remove the bad impressions, which the Indians have received from the conduct of a set of villains, divested of all faith and honor, and give us such an early opportunity of establishing an interest with them, as would ensure to us a large share of the fur-trade, not only of the Ohio Indians, but, in time, of the numerous nations possessing the back country westward. To prevent this advantageous commerce from suffering in its infancy, by the sinister views of designing, selfish men in the different provinces, I humbly conceive it advisable, that commissioners from each of the colonies should be appointed to regulate the mode of that trade, and fix it on such a basis, that all the attempts of one colony to undermine another, and thereby weaken and diminish the general system, might be frustrated.

Although no one can entertain a higher sense of the great importance of maintaining a post on the Ohio than myself, yet, considering the present circumstances of my regiment, I would by no means have agreed to leave any part of it there, had not the General given an express order. I endeavoured to show, that the King's troops ought to garrison it; but he told me, that, as he had no instructions from the ministry relative to this point, he could not order it. Our men, left there, are in such a miserable condition, having hardly rags to cover their nakedness, and exposed to the inclemency of the weather in this rigorous season, that, unless provision is made by the country for supplying them immediately, they must perish. If the first Virginia regiment is to be kept up any longer, or any services are expected from it, the men should forthwith be clothed. By their present nakedness, the advanced season, and the inconceivable fatigues of an uncommonly long and laborious campaign, they are rendered totally incapable of any kind of service; and sickness, death, and desertion must, if they are not speedily supplied, greatly reduce their numbers. To replace them with equally good men will, perhaps, be found impossible.

With the highest respect, I am, &c.

TO GOVERNOR FAUQUIER.

Winchester, 9 December, 1758.

SIR,

I arrived at this place last night, and was just setting out (though very much indisposed), for my own house, when I was honored with your obliging favor of the 3d instant.

My last letters would fully inform your Honor of the success of his Majesty's arms under General Forbes, of the march of the Virginia troops to Winchester, and the condition, the very distressed condition, of the first regiment. It is needless, therefore, to recapitulate facts, or to trouble you further on this head.

Reason, nay, common humanity itself points out, that some respite should be granted to troops returning from every toil and hardship, that cold, hunger, and fatigue can inflict, and I hope your sentiments correspond with mine.

If I easily get the better of my present disorder, I shall hope for the honor of seeing you about the 25th instant. The want of almost every necessary for the journey, and the want of my papers requisite to a full and final settlement with the country, oblige me to take my own house in the way down.

Those matters, which your Honor has glanced at in your letters, have been fully communicated to me. That you had not the least share in causing them, I am equally well persuaded, and I shall think myself honored with your esteem; being, with the greatest respect, your most obedient and most obliged humble servant.

TO GENERAL FORBES.

Williamsburg, 30 December, 1758.

SIR,

As the Governor writes fully to you, respecting the posture of affairs here, and the present system of management, I have little to add. I hoped a General Assembly would be called immediately; but the Council were of opinion, that, as they had met so lately, and were summoned to attend some time in February, it would be inconvenient to convene them sooner; so that no measures for securing the communication between Fort Cumberland and Fort Duquesne, or, in short, any thing else, can be effected, or even attempted, until that time.

Captain McNeil, who commanded the first Virginia regiment in my absence, committed an error, I am informed, at Raystown, in confining Mr. Hoops, the commissary. I am not thoroughly acquainted with the particulars, but I believe, from the accounts received, that Mr. Hoops was equally culpable in detaining the provisions from half-starved men. This piece of rashness, I am told, is likely to bring McNeil into trouble. I therefore beg the favor of you, Sir, as I am well convinced McNeil had nothing in view but the welfare of his men, to interpose your kind offices to settle the difference. This will be doing a favor to Captain McNeil, as well as to myself.

I should be extremely glad to hear of your safe arrival at head-quarters, after a fatiguing campaign, and that a perfect return of health has contributed to crown your successes. I am, Sir, your most obedient and most humble servant.*

---

* As Colonel Washington had determined at the beginning of the season to remain in the army no longer, than till the conclusion of this campaign, he resigned his commission immediately after his arrival in Williamsburg. On this occasion his officers presented to him an address, deeply expressive of their affection, their respect, and their ardent wishes for his future prosperity and welfare. — See APPENDIX, No. V.

He was married on the 6th of January, 1759, to Martha Custis, widow of Daniel Parke Custis, and daughter of John Dandridge.

Being now a member of the House of Burgesses, he joined that Assembly when it was next convened. The House resolved to return their thanks to him, in a public manner, for the distinguished services, which he had rendered to his country, and this duty devolved on his friend the Speaker. Mr. Wirt relates the anecdote in the following words, on the authority of Edmund Randolph.

"As soon as Colonel Washington took his seat [in the Assembly], Mr. Robinson, in obedience to this order, and following the impulse of his own generous and grateful heart, discharged the duty with great dignity, but with such warmth of coloring, and strength of expression, as entirely to confound the young hero. He rose to express his acknowledgments

TO ROBERT CARY, MERCHANT, LONDON.

Williamsburg, 1 May, 1759.

SIR,

The enclosed is the clergyman's certificate of my marriage with Mrs. Martha Custis, properly, as I am told, authenticated. You will, therefore, for the future please to address all your letters, which relate to the affairs of the late Daniel Parke Custis, to me, as by marriage I am entitled to a third part of that estate, and am invested likewise with the care of the other two thirds by a decree of our General Court, which I obtained in order to strengthen the power I before had in consequence of my wife's administration.

I have many letters of yours in my possession unanswered; but at present this serves only to advise you of the above change, and at the same time to acquaint you, that I shall continue to make you the same consignments of tobacco as usual, and will endeavour to increase them in proportion as I find myself and the estate benefited thereby.

The scarcity of the last year's crop, and the consequent high prices of tobacco, would, in any other case, have induced me to sell the estate's crop in this country; but, for a present, and I hope small advantage only, I did not care to break the chain of correspondence, that has so long subsisted.

On the other side is an invoice of some goods, which I beg you to send me by the first ship, bound either to

---

for the honor; but such was his trepidation and confusion, that he could not give distinct utterance to a syllable. He blushed, stammered, and trembled, for a second; when the Speaker relieved him, by a stroke of address, that would have done honor to Louis the Fourteenth, in his proudest and happiest moment. 'Sit down, Mr. Washington,' said he, with a conciliating smile, 'your modesty is equal to your valor, and that surpasses the power of any language that I possess.'" — *Life of Patrick Henry*, p. 45.

the Potomac or Rappahannoc, as I am in immediate want of them. Let them be insured, and, in case of accident, re-shipped without delay. Direct for me at Mount Vernon, Potomac River, Virginia; the former is the name of my seat, the other of the river on which it is situated.* I am, &c.

---

* The product of Washington's plantations was at this period almost exclusively tobacco. This he usually exported to London for a market, making the shipments in his own name, and putting the tobacco on board the vessels, which came up the river to his mansion at Mount Vernon, or to such other point as was most convenient. In those days, also, it was the practice of the Virginia planters to send to London for all the articles of common use. Twice a year Washington forwarded a list of such articles to his agent, comprising not only all the necessaries and conveniences for household purposes, but likewise every article of wearing apparel for himself and each member of his family, specifying the names of each, and the ages of Mrs. Washington's two children, as also the size, description, and quality of the articles. He then required his agent to send him, in addition to a general bill of the whole, the original voucher of each one of the persons from whom purchases were made. So minute and particular was he in these concerns, that for many years he entered with his own hand, in books prepared for the purpose, all the long lists of orders, and copies of the multifarious receipts from the different tradesmen, merchants, and mechanics in London, who had supplied the goods. In this way he kept a perfect oversight of the business, and could tell when any advantage was taken of him even in the smallest matter, of which he did not fail to remind his agent the next time he wrote. As the price obtained for his tobacco depended on the judgment, fidelity, and efforts of the agent in effecting sales, he would sometimes divide the agency, sending part to one person, and part to another, and, by comparing the results, he could detect any inattention or mismanagement, which had been unfavorable to his interest.

The following extracts from letters, written in the year 1760, will afford hints of some of his habits.

"By this conveyance you will receive invoices of such goods as are wanting, which please to send, as there directed, by Captain Johnston in the spring; and let me beseech you to give the necessary directions for purchasing them upon the best terms. It is needless for me to particularize the sorts, qualities, or taste I would choose to have them in, unless it is observed; and you may believe me when I tell you, that, instead of getting things good and fashionable in their several kinds, we often have articles sent us, that could only have been used by our forefathers in days of yore. It is a custom, I have some reason to believe, with many of the shopkeepers and tradesmen in London, when they know goods are bespoken for

TO ROBERT CARY, LONDON.

Virginia, 12 June, 1759

SIR,

In a letter which I wrote you the 1st of last month, was enclosed an invoice of sundries, which I then was and still am much in need of. If those goods should not be shipped before this letter gets to hand, pray add to your purchase the things, which you will find on the other side, and send them as there directed.

I shall find occasion to write you fully by the fleet, and shall enclose a list of sundries, that will be wanted for the estate's use. Till then I shall forbear to trouble you with particulars, as I shall expect also by that time to receive some account of the sales of the estate's tobacco sent you, and an account current. As this last is necessary for me to compare with my own account, in order to a satisfactory settlement with our General Court, I entreat you to be punctual in sending me one every spring and fall yearly.

I shall keep the estate under the same direction as formerly, neither altering the managers, the kind of tobacco, nor the manner of treating it, unless you advise otherwise

---

exportation, to palm sometimes old and sometimes very slight and indifferent ones upon us, taking care at the same time to advance ten, fifteen, or perhaps twenty per cent upon them."

"And here I cannot forbear ushering in a complaint of the exorbitant prices of my goods this year. For many years I have imported goods from London, as well as other ports of Britain, and can truly say I never had such a pennyworth before. It would be a needless task to enumerate every article that I have cause to except against. Let it suffice to say, that the woollens, linens, nails, &c., are mean in quality, but not in price, for in this they excel. Indeed they are far above any I ever had. It has always been a custom with me, when I make out my invoices, to estimate the charge of them. This I do for my own satisfaction, to know whether I am too fast or not, and I seldom vary much from the real prices; but the amount of your invoice exceeds my calculation about twenty-five per cent, and many articles not sent that were ordered."

for our interest. And, while I continue to pursue this method, I hope you will be able to render such sales, as will not only justify the present consignments to you, but encourage my enlarging them; for I shall be candid in telling you, that duty to the charge with which I am entrusted, as well as self-interest, will incline me to abide by those, who give the greatest proof of their abilities in selling my own and the estate's tobacco, and purchasing our goods, of which I can no otherwise judge, than by the accounts that will be rendered. And here permit me to ask, if it would be advisable to change the marks of any of the tobacco, or had I best ship it all under the usual marks? If so, my part may be known by some small distinction, such as you can best advise.

In my last, among other things, I desired you would send me, besides a small octavo volume, the best system now extant of agriculture. Since then, I have been told, that there is one, lately published, done by various hands, but chiefly collected from the papers of Mr. Hale. If this is known to be the best, pray send it, but not if any other is in higher esteem. I am, &c.

TO RICHARD WASHINGTON, LONDON.

Mount Vernon, 20 September, 1759.

DEAR SIR,

Enclosed you will receive a bill, which please to accept, and place to my credit. Since my last, your agreeable favor, covering an invoice of sundries, has come to hand, as have the goods also, in good order; which is more than most of the importers by that ship can boast, great part of her cargo being damaged, through the negligence, it is said, of the captain.

My brother is safely arrived, and but little benefited

in point of health by his trip to England. The longing desire, which for many years I have had, of visiting the great metropolis of that kingdom, is not in the least abated by his prejudices, because I think the small share of health he enjoyed, while there, must have given a check to any pleasures he might anticipate, and would render any place irksome; but I am now tied, and must set inclination aside.

The scale of fortune in America is turned greatly in our favor, and success has become the companion of our fortunate generals. It would be folly in me to attempt particularizing their actions, since you receive accounts in a channel so much more direct than from hence.*

I am now, I believe, fixed at this seat with an agreeable partner for life, and I hope to find more happiness in retirement, than I ever experienced amidst the wide and bustling world. I thank you heartily for your affectionate wishes. Why will you not give me an occasion of congratulating you in the same manner? None would do it more cordially than, dear Sir, your most obedient and obliged servant.

TO RICHARD WASHINGTON.

Mount Vernon, 10 August, 1760.

Dear Sir,

The French are so well drubbed, and seem so much humbled in America, that I apprehend our generals will find it no difficult matter to reduce Canada to our obedience this summer. But what may be Montgomery's fate in the Cherokee country I cannot so readily deter-

---

* During this year Ticonderoga had been taken by General Amherst, Niagara by Sir William Johnson, and Quebec had fallen in consequence of the splendid victory of Wolfe on the Plains of Abraham.

mine. It seems he has made a prosperous beginning, having penetrated into the heart of the country, and he is now advancing his troops in high health and spirits to the relief of Fort Loudoun. But let him be wary. He has a crafty, subtle enemy to deal with, that may give him most trouble when he least expects it.* We are in pain here for the king of Prussia, and wish Hanover safe, these being events in which we are much interested.

My indulging myself in a trip to England depends upon so many contingencies, which, in all probability, may never occur, that I dare not even think of such a gratification. Nothing, however, is more ardently desired. But Mrs. Washington and myself would both think ourselves very happy in the opportunity of showing you the Virginia hospitality, which is the most agreeable entertainment we can give, or a stranger expect to find, in an infant, woody country, like ours.

I am, dear Sir, yours, &c.

---

* Such proved in fact to be the fate of Colonel Montgomery. He marched from South Carolina with a party of regular troops and militia, and was at first successful in destroying several Indian towns, but fell at length into an ambuscade, where the Indians defeated him, with the loss of twenty of his men killed, and seventy-six wounded. He was obliged to retreat, and return to South Carolina, without making any farther progress. Fort Loudoun, situate on the borders of the Cherokee country, was reduced to the greatest extremity by hunger, and the garrison forced to capitulate to the Indians, who agreed to escort the officers and men in safety to another fort. They were, however, made the victims of treachery; for the day after their departure a body of savages waylaid them, killed some, and captured the others, whom they took back to Fort Loudoun. — Ramsay's *History of South Carolina*, Vol. I. p. 177.

TO CAPTAIN ROBERT MACKENZIE, AT VENANGO.

Mount Vernon, 20 November, 1760.

DEAR SIR,

Had your favor of the 17th of August come to my hands before the 18th instant, I should not have given you the trouble of perusing my answer to it at this late season. I am sorry, that you should think it necessary to introduce a request to me, which is founded on reason and equity, with an apology. Had you claimed that as a right, which you seem to ask as a favor, I should have thought myself wanting in that justice, which is the distinguishing characteristic of an honest man, to have withheld it from you.

But how to answer your purposes, and at the same time to avoid the imputation of impertinence, I am, I confess, more at a loss to determine. That General Amherst may have heard of such a person as I am, is probable, and this I dare venture to say is the chief knowledge he has of me. How then should I appear to him in an epistolary way? And to sit down and write a certificate of your behaviour carries with it an air of formality, that seems more adapted to the case of a soldier than that of an officer. I must, therefore, beg the favor of you to make what use you please of this letter.

For, Sir, with not more pleasure than truth, I can declare to you and the world, that while I had the honor of commanding the regiment, your conduct, both as an officer and a gentleman, was unexceptionable, and in every instance, as far as I was capable of discerning, such as to merit applause from better judges. Since my time, Colonel Byrd has been witness to your behaviour, and his letter recommendatory must, I am persuaded, do you more service than my sanguine endeavours. Although neither he, nor any other person, is more sensible of your worth, or more inclined to contribute his best offices to the completion of your wishes, than, Sir, your obedient servant.

TO RICHARD WASHINGTON.

Mount Vernon, 14 July, 1761.

DEAR SIR,

Since my last, I have had the pleasure of receiving your obliging favors of the 16th of October and 1st of January. A mixture of bad health and indolence has kept me, till this time, from paying that due respect to your letters, which they merited at my hands; and now, having nothing to relate that could in any wise claim your attention, I was still inclined to a further delay.

The entire conquest of Canada, and of the French in most parts of North America, being a story too stale to relate in these days, we are often at a loss for something with which to fill our letters. True it is, the Cherokee nation, by a perfidious conduct, has caused Colonel Grant to be sent once more into their country with an armed force; but I believe supplies from the French on Mobile River come in so slowly, that they are more sincerely disposed to peace now than ever they were before. This pacific turn may be caused in some measure, too, by another regiment in the pay of this colony, which is ordered to penetrate into their country by a different passage. But it is generally thought, that their submission will put a stop to any further progress of our arms.*

* Colonel Grant had an engagement with the Cherokees, near the place of Colonel Montgomery's ambuscade, which lasted for several hours, but

We have received the account of the reduction of Belle Isle, and we hear of another fleet destined for some service, of which we are ignorant. But that, which most engrosses our attention at this time, is the congress at Augsburg, as I believe nothing is more sincerely desired in this part of the world, than an honorable peace. I am, &c.

TO RICHARD WASHINGTON.

Mount Vernon, 20 October, 1761.

DEAR SIR,

Since my last, of the 14th of July, I have in appearance been very near my last breath. My indisposition increased upon me, and I fell into a very low and dangerous state. I once thought the grim king would certainly master my utmost efforts, and that I must sink, in spite of a resolute struggle; but, thank God, I have now got the better of the disorder, and shall soon be restored, I hope, to perfect health again.

I do not know, that I can muster up one tittle of news to communicate. In short, the occurrences of this part of the world are at present scarce worth reciting; for, as we live in a state of peaceful tranquility ourselves, so we are at very little trouble to inquire after the operations against the Cherokees, who are the only people that disturb the repose of this great continent, and who, I believe, would gladly accommodate differences upon almost any terms; not, I conceive, from any apprehen-

---

the Indians were repulsed. He then destroyed all the villages and provisions, that came in his way, and took post for some time in Fort Prince George. Here the Cherokees, through their Chief, Attakullakulla, sued for peace, which was conceded to them, and which continued till the breaking out of the revolutionary war.

sions they are under, on account of our arms, but because they want the supplies, with which we and we only can furnish them. We catch the reports of peace with gaping mouths, and every person seems anxious for a confirmation of that desirable event, provided it comes, as no doubt it will, upon honorable terms.

On the other side is an invoice of clothes, which I beg the favor of you to purchase for me, and to send them by the first ship bound to this river. As they are designed for wearing-apparel for myself, I have committed the choice of them to your fancy, having the best opinion of your taste. I want neither lace nor embroidery. Plain clothes, with gold or silver buttons, if worn in genteel dress, are all that I desire. I have hitherto had my clothes made by one Charles Lawrence. Whether it be the fault of the tailor, or of the measure sent, I cannot say, but, certain it is, my clothes have never fitted me well. I therefore leave the choice of the workman to you. I enclose a measure, and, for a further direction, I think it not amiss to add, that my stature is six feet; otherwise rather slender than corpulent. I am very sincerely, dear Sir, your most affectionate humble servant.

TO ROBERT CARY.

Williamsburg, 3 November, 1761.

SIR,

I came to this place last night, and find, that the articles mentioned in the enclosed invoice are wanted for the plantations on York River. Please to send them as there directed.

We have little or no news. Our Assembly is at present convened to grant supplies for carrying on the war against the Cherokee Indians, should they choose to continue it; but this I am persuaded they are by no means inclined to do, nor are they prepared for it, as they have been soliciting peace for some time past. I wish the powers of Europe were as well disposed to an accommodation as these poor wretches. A stop would then soon be put to the effusion of blood, and peace and plenty would resume their empire again, to the joy and content, I believe, of most ranks and degrees of people. I am, &c.

TO ROBERT STEWART.

Williamsburg, 2 May, 1763.

DEAR STEWART,

With some difficulty I have at last procured the enclosed, which you will please to make use of as occasion may require. I was upon the point of forwarding these, and my letters to London, when Colonel Hunter arrived, and informed me that he left you at New York, and that your embarkation for England seemed to be a matter of doubt. I have, therefore, changed the route of these letters, now sending them to New York, to the care of Mr. Beverley Robinson.

Signing the definitive treaty seems to be the only piece of news, which prevails here at present, and diffuses general joy. Our Assembly is suddenly called, in consequence of a memorial of the British merchants to the Board of Trade, representing the evil consequences of our paper emission, and their Lordships' report and orders thereupon, which, I suppose, will set the whole country in flames. This stir of the merchants seems to be ill-timed, and cannot be attended with any good effects, but, I fear, the contrary. However, on the 19th instant the Assembly will meet; and till then I will suspend my further opinion of the matter.

I am, with the most unalterable regard, your most affectionate friend and servant.

TO ROBERT STEWART.

Mount Vernon, 13 August, 1763.

MY DEAR STEWART,

By Captain Walter Stewart I am favored with an opportunity of acknowledging the receipt of your letter of the 6th of June, and at the same time of forwarding the copy of my former one, which was in readiness before that came to hand, and which I incline to send, notwithstanding the original has reached you, because it contains the second bills, and other matters entire as they ought to have been sent, and as I dare say Mr. Stewart will be so good as to deliver them.

Another tempest has arisen upon our frontiers, and the alarm spread wider than ever. In short, the inhabitants are so apprehensive of danger, that no families remain above the Conococheague road, and many are gone below it. Their harvests are in a manner lost, and the distresses of the settlement are evident and manifold. In Augusta many people have been killed, and numbers fled. Confusion and despair prevail in every quarter. At this instant a calm is taking place, which forebodes some mischief to Colonel Bouquet. At least those, who wish well to the convoy, are apprehensive for him; since it is not unlikely, that the retreat of all the Indian parties at one and the same time from our frontiers, is a proof of their assembling a force somewhere, and for some particular purpose, and none more likely than to oppose his march.*

It was expected, that our Assembly would have been called, in such exigences as these; but it is concluded, as I have been informed, that an Assembly without money would be no eligible plan. To comprehend the meaning of this expression you must know, that the Board of Trade, at the instance of the British merchants, have undertaken to rebuke us in the most ample manner for our paper emissions; and therefore the Governor and Council have directed one thousand militia to be employed for the protection of the frontiers, five hundred of whom are to be drafted from Hampshire and other counties, and to be under the command of Colonel Stephen, whose military courage and capacity, says the Governor, are well established. The other five hundred, from the southern frontier counties, are to be conducted by Major Lewis; so that you may readily conceive what an enormous expense must attend these measures. Stephen, immediately upon the Indians' retiring, advanced to Fort Cumberland with two

* The Shawanees, Delawares, and other Ohio tribes of Indians, had made a general and almost simultaneous attack upon all the remote frontier settlements and posts. They had committed many murders, and taken the forts at Le Bœuf, Venango, Presqu'Isle, and others on Lake Michigan, the Miami River, the Wabash, at Sandusky, and Michilimackinac. Fort Pitt (formerly Duquesne) was in imminent danger of falling into their hands. In July, Colonel Bouquet was despatched by General Amherst with five hundred men and a supply of military stores for the relief of that fort. He marched through Pennsylvania, following the same route, that had been pursued by General Forbes's army. The Indians, who were then besieging Fort Pitt, heard of his march, and came out to meet him. They attacked his army on the 5th of August, in a defile near the head waters of Turtle Creek, and the contest was kept up during the whole day, with considerable loss on both sides. Colonel Bouquet maintained his ground through the night, and the next day routed the Indians, and marched without further molestation to Fort Pitt. The news of this action seems not to have reached Washington, when he wrote the above letter.

hundred or two hundred and fifty militia, and will doubtless achieve some signal advantage, of which the public will soon be informed.

I think I have now communicated the only news, which these parts afford. It is of a melancholy nature, indeed, and we cannot tell how or when the affair will end. I hope you may have got matters settled to your liking before this time. I should rejoice to hear it, as I should at every thing that gives you pleasure or profit.

Mrs. Washington makes a tender of her compliments, and you may be assured that I am, with great sincerity, dear Sir, your most obedient and affectionate servant.

TO ROBERT CARY.

Mount Vernon, 13 February, 1764.

SIR,

The enclosed is a copy of my last. We have been curiously entertained, of late, with the description of an engine lately constructed, I believe, in Switzerland, and which has undergone some improvements in England, for taking up trees by the roots. It is related, that trees of a considerable diameter are forced up by this engine; that six hands, in working one of them, will raise two or three hundred trees in the space of a day; and that an acre of ground may be eased of the trees, and laid fit for ploughing, in the same time. How far these assertions have been realized by repeated experiment, it is impossible for me at this distance to determine; but, if the accounts are not greatly exaggerated, such powerful assistance must be of vast utility in many parts of this woody country, where it is impossible for our force (and laborers are not to be hired here), between the finishing of one crop and the preparation for another, to clear ground fast enough to afford the proper changes, either in the planting or farming business.

The chief purport of this letter, therefore, is to beg the favor of you to make minute inquiries into the trials, that have been made by order of the Society, and, if they have proved satisfactory, to send me one of these engines by the first ship bound to the Potomac River. If they are made of different sizes, I should prefer one of a middle size, capable of raising a tree of fifteen or eighteen inches diameter. The cost I am a stranger to. Fifteen, twenty, and twenty-five guineas have been mentioned; but the price, were it double these sums, I should totally disregard, provided the engine is capable of performing what is related of it, and not of that complicated nature, which would cause it to be easily disordered, and rendered unfit for use, but constructed upon so plain, simple, and durable a plan, that the common artificers of this country may be able to repair it, if any accidents should happen. Should you send me one, be so good as to let me have with it the most ample directions for its use, together with a model of its manner of operating. I am, &c.

TO FRANCIS DANDRIDGE, LONDON.

Mount Vernon, 20 September, 1765.

SIR,

You will permit me, after six years' silence (the time I have been married to your niece), to pay my respects to you in this epistolary way. I shall think myself happy in beginning a correspondence, which cannot but be attended with pleasure on my side.

I should hardly have taken the liberty, Sir, of introducing myself to your acquaintance in this manner, had not a letter from Mr. Robert Cary given me reasons to believe, that such an advance on my part would not be altogether disagreeable to you. If I could flatter myself, that you would in anywise be entertained with the few occurrences, that it may be in my power to relate, I should endeavour to atone for my past remissness, in this respect, by future punctuality.

At present there are few things among us, that can be interesting to you. The Stamp Act, imposed on the colonies by the Parliament of Great Britain, engrosses the conversation of the speculative part of the colonists, who look upon this unconstitutional method of taxation, as a direful attack upon their liberties, and loudly exclaim against the violation. What may be the result of this, and of some other (I think I may add ill-judged) measures, I will not undertake to determine; but this I may venture to affirm, that the advantage accruing to the mother country will fall greatly short of the expectations of the ministry; for certain it is, that our whole substance already in a manner flows to Great Britain, and that whatsoever contributes to lessen our importations must be hurtful to her manufacturers. The eyes of our people already begin to be opened; and they will perceive, that many luxuries, for which we lavish our substance in Great Britain, can well be dispensed with, whilst the necessaries of life are mostly to be had within ourselves. This, consequently, will introduce frugality, and be a necessary incitement to industry. If Great Britain, therefore, loads her manufactures with heavy taxes, will it not facilitate such results? They will not compel us, I think, to give our money for their exports, whether we will or not; and I am certain, that none of their traders will part with them without a valuable consideration. Where, then, is the utility of these restrictions?

As to the Stamp Act, regarded in a single view, one and the first bad consequence attending it, is, that our courts of judicature must inevitably be shut up; for it is impossible, or next to impossible, under our present circumstances, that the act of Parliament can be complied with, were we ever so willing to enforce its execution. And, not to say (which alone would be sufficient) that we have not money to pay for the stamps, there are many other cogent reasons, which prove that it would be ineffectual. If a stop be put to our judicial proceedings, I fancy the merchants of Great Britain, trading to the colonies, will not be among the last to wish for a repeal of the act.

I live on the Potomac River in Fairfax county, about ten miles below Alexandria, and many miles distant from any of my wife's relations, who all reside upon York River, and whom we seldom see more than once a year, and not always so often. My wife, who is very well, and Master and Miss Custis, children of her former marriage, all join in making a tender of their duty and best respects to yourself and your lady. My compliments to her, also, I beg may be made acceptable, and that you will do me the justice to believe that I am, dear Sir, your most obedient humble servant.

TO CAPEL HANBURY, LONDON.

Mount Vernon, 25 July, 1767.

SIR,

Unseasonable as it may be, to take any notice of the repeal of the Stamp Act at this time, yet I cannot help observing, that a contrary measure would have introduced very unhappy consequences. Those, therefore, who wisely foresaw such an event, and were instrumental in procuring the repeal of the act, are, in my opinion, deservedly entitled to the thanks of the well-wishers to Britain and her colonies, and must reflect with pleasure, that, through their means, many scenes of confusion and distress have been prevented. Mine they accordingly have, and always shall have, for their opposition to any act of oppression; and that act could be looked upon in no other light by every person, who would view it in its proper colors.

I could wish it were in my power to congratulate you on the success of having the commercial system of these colonies put upon a more enlarged and extensive footing, than it is; because I am well satisfied, that it would ultimately redound to the advantage of the mother country, so long as the colonies pursue trade and agriculture, and would be an effectual let to manufacturing among them. The money, which they raise, would centre in Great Britain, as certainly as the needle will settle to the pole. I am, &c.*

---

* In writing to another correspondent in England, some months before, he expressed himself on this subject as follows.

"The repeal of the Stamp Act, to whatever cause owing, ought much to be rejoiced at; for had the Parliament of Great Britain resolved upon enforcing it, the consequences, I conceive, would have been more direful than is generally apprehended, both to the mother country and her colonies. All, therefore, who were instrumental in procuring the repeal, are entitled to the thanks of every British subject, and have mine cordially."

TO WILLIAM CRAWFORD.*

Mount Vernon, 21 September, 1767.

DEAR SIR,

From a sudden hint of your brother's, I wrote to you a few days ago in a hurry. Having since had more time for reflection, I now write deliberately, and with greater precision, on the subject of my last letter.

I then desired the favor of you (as I understood rights might now be had for the lands, which have fallen within the Pennsylvania line,) to look me out a tract of about fifteen hundred, two thousand, or more acres somewhere in your neighbourhood, meaning only by this, that it may be as contiguous to your own settlement, as such a body of good land can be found. It will be easy for you to conceive, that ordinary or even middling lands would never answer my purpose or expectation, so far from navigation, and under such a load of expenses, as these lands are encumbered with. No; a tract to please me must be rich, of which no person can be a better judge than yourself, and, if possible, level. Could such a piece of land be found, you would do me a singular favor in falling upon some method of securing it immediately from the attempts of others, as nothing is more certain, than that the lands cannot remain long un-

* Mr. Crawford had been a captain in General Forbes's campaign, and was now settled on Youghiogany River. He was afterwards a colonel in the Revolutionary war, and served on the frontiers. In the summer of 1782, he commanded an expedition into the Ohio country against the Indians, where, after a hard fought battle, he was taken prisoner, and tortured to death in a most cruel and shocking manner. He had approved himself an officer of merit, judicious, intrepid, and possessing much skill in Indian warfare. In May, 1778, he took command of the regiment at Pittsburg. General Washington, in writing at that time to the Board of War, said, — "I know him to be a brave and active officer, and of considerable influence upon the western frontier of Virginia."

granted, when once it is known, that rights are to be had.

The mode of proceeding I am at a loss to point out to you; but, as your own lands are under the same circumstances, self-interest will naturally lead you to an inquiry. I am told, that the land or surveyor's office is kept at Carlisle. If so, I am of opinion that Colonel Armstrong, an acquaintance of mine, has something to do in the direction of it, and I am persuaded he would readily serve me. I will write to him by the first opportunity on that subject, that the way may be prepared for your application to him, if you find it necessary. For your trouble and expense you may depend on being repaid. It is possible, but I do not know that it really is the case, that the custom in Pennsylvania will not admit so large a quantity of land, as I require, to be entered together; if so, this may perhaps be arranged by making several entries to the same amount, if the expense of doing it is not too heavy. This I only drop as a hint, leaving the whole to your discretion and good management. If the land can only be secured from others, it is all I want at present. The surveying I would choose to postpone, at least till the spring, when, if you can give me any satisfactory account of this matter, and of what I am next going to propose, I expect to pay you a visit about the last of April.

I offered in my last to join you, in attempting to secure some of the most valuable lands in the King's part, which I think may be accomplished after a while, notwithstanding the proclamation, that restrains it at present, and prohibits the settling of them at all; for I can never look upon that proclamation in any other light (but this I say between ourselves), than as a temporary expedient to quiet the minds of the Indians. It must fall, of course, in a few years, especially when those Indians consent to our occupying the lands.* Any person, therefore, who neglects the present opportunity of hunting out good lands, and in some measure marking and distinguishing them for his own, in order to keep others from settling them, will never regain it. If you will be at the trouble of seeking out the lands, I will take upon me the part of securing them, as soon as there is a possibility of doing it, and will moreover be at all the cost and charges of surveying and patenting the same. You shall then have such a reasonable proportion of the whole, as we may fix upon at our first meeting; as I shall find it necessary, for the better furthering of the design, to let some of my friends be concerned in the scheme, who must also partake of the advantages.

By this time it may be easy for you to discover, that my plan is to secure a good deal of land. You will consequently come in for a very handsome quantity; and as

---

* The above alludes to the King's proclamation in 1763, which prohibited all governors from granting warrants for lands to the westward of the sources of the rivers, which run into the Atlantic ocean, and forbade all persons purchasing such lands, or settling on them, without special license from the King first obtained. The proclamation seems never to have been heeded in this sense by the governors, who continued to grant warrants for lands known to be within the charter limits of their respective colonies, although beyond the head-waters of such streams. Washington's idea, as expressed in this letter, was, that the restriction would soon be taken off in regard to the territory beyond the charter boundaries, and then the persons, who were best acquainted with the lands, would have a good opportunity of making the most favorable selections and purchases.

Similar views seem to have been generally entertained. Chancellor Livingston, in a letter to Dr. Franklin, respecting the conditions of peace, previous to the treaty of 1782, says; — "Virginia, even after the Proclamation of 1763, patented considerable tracts on the Ohio, far beyond the Appalachian mountains. It is true, the several governments were prohibited at different times from granting lands beyond certain limits; but these were clearly temporary restrictions, which the policy of maintaining a good understanding with the natives dictated, and were always broken through after a short period, as is evinced by the grants above mentioned, made subsequent to the proclamation of 1763." — *Diplomatic Correspondence of the American Revolution*, Vol. III. p. 270.

you will obtain it without any costs, or expenses, I hope you will be encouraged to begin the search in time. I would choose, if it were practicable, to get large tracts together; and it might be desirable to have them as near your settlement, or Fort Pitt, as they can be obtained of good quality, but not to neglect others at a greater distance, if fine bodies of it lie in one place. It may be worthy of your inquiry, to find out how the Maryland back line will run, and what is said about laying off Neale's grant. I will inquire particularly concerning the Ohio Company, that we may know what to apprehend from them.* For my own part, I should have no objection to a grant of land upon the Ohio, a good way below Pittsburg, but would first willingly secure some valuable tracts nearer at hand.

I recommend, that you keep this whole matter a secret, or trust it only to those, in whom you can confide, and who can assist you in bringing it to bear by their discoveries of land. This advice proceeds from several very good reasons, and, in the first place, because I might be censured for the opinion I have given in respect to the King's proclamation, and then, if the scheme I am now proposing to you were known, it might give the alarm to others, and, by putting them upon a plan of the same nature, before we could lay a proper foundation for success ourselves, set the different interests clashing, and, probably, in the end, overturn the whole. All this may be avoided by a silent management, and the operation carried on by you under the guise of hunting game, which you may, I presume, effectually do, at the same time you are in pursuit of land. When this is fully discovered, advise me of it, and if there appears but a possibility of succeeding at any time hence, I will

* See APPENDIX, No. VI.

have the lands immediately surveyed, to keep others off, and leave the rest to time and my own assiduity.

If this letter should reach your hands before you set out, I should be glad to have your thoughts fully expressed on the plan here proposed, or as soon afterwards as convenient; for I am desirous of knowing in due time how you approve of the scheme. I am, &c.

TO WILLIAM RAMSAY.

Mount Vernon, 29 January, 1769.

DEAR SIR,

Having once or twice of late heard you speak highly of the New Jersey College, as if you had a desire of sending your son William there (who, I am told, is a youth fond of study and instruction, and disposed to a studious life, in following which he may not only promote his own happiness, but the future welfare of others), I should be glad, if you have no other objection to it than the expense, if you would send him to that college, as soon as convenient, and depend on me for twenty-five pounds a year for his support, so long as it may be necessary for the completion of his education. If I live to see the accomplishment of this term, the sum here stipulated shall be annually paid; and if I die in the mean time, this letter shall be obligatory upon my heirs, or executors, to do it according to the true intent and meaning hereof.

No other return is expected, or wished, for this offer, than that you will accept it with the same freedom and good will, with which it is made, and that you may not even consider it in the light of an obligation, or mention it as such; for, be assured, that from me it will never be known. I am, &c.

TO GEORGE MASON.*

Mount Vernon, 5 April, 1769.

DEAR SIR,

Herewith you will receive a letter and sundry papers,† which were forwarded to me a day or two ago by Dr. Ross of Bladensburg. I transmit them with the greater pleasure, as my own desire of knowing your sentiments upon a matter of this importance exactly coincides with the Doctor's inclinations.

At a time, when our lordly masters in Great Britain will be satisfied with nothing less than the deprivation of American freedom, it seems highly necessary that something should be done to avert the stroke, and maintain the liberty, which we have derived from our ancestors. But the manner of doing it, to answer the purpose effectually, is the point in question.

That no man should scruple, or hesitate a moment, to use arms in defence of so valuable a blessing, is clearly my opinion. Yet arms, I would beg leave to add, should be the last resource, the *dernier resort.* We have already, it is said, proved the inefficacy of addresses to the throne, and remonstrances to Parliament. How far, then, their attention to our rights and privileges is to be awakened or alarmed, by starving their trade and manufactures, remains to be tried.

The northern colonies, it appears, are endeavouring to

---

* A neighbour and intimate friend of Washington, who afterwards distinguished himself by drafting the first constitution of Virginia, and by the ability he displayed in the Convention for forming the Constitution of the United States, and also in the Virginia Convention for adopting that instrument. He was opposed to the Constitution, as encroaching too much on State rights, and containing the principles of a consolidated government.

† Containing resolves of the merchants of Philadelphia, respecting the non-importation of articles of British manufacture.

adopt this scheme. In my opinion it is a good one, and must be attended with salutary effects, provided it can be carried pretty generally into execution. But to what extent it is practicable to do so, I will not take upon me to determine. That there will be a difficulty attending the execution of it every where, from clashing interests, and selfish, designing men, ever attentive to their own gain, and watchful of every turn, that can assist their lucrative views, cannot be denied; and in the tobacco colonies, where the trade is so diffused, and in a manner wholly conducted by factors for their principals at home [in England], these difficulties are certainly enhanced, but I think not insurmountably increased, if the gentlemen in their several counties will be at some pains to explain matters to the people, and stimulate them to cordial agreements to purchase none but certain enumerated articles out of any of the stores after a definite period, and neither import nor purchase any themselves. This, if it should not effectually withdraw the factors from their importations, would at least make them extremely cautious in doing it, as the prohibited goods could be vended to none but the non-associators, or those who would pay no regard to their association; both of whom ought to be stigmatized, and made the objects of public reproach.

The more I consider a scheme of this sort, the more ardently I wish success to it, because I think there are private as well as public advantages to result from it, — the former certain, however precarious the other may prove. In respect to the latter, I have always thought, that by virtue of the same power, which assumes the right of taxation, the Parliament may attempt at least to restrain our manufactures, especially those of a public nature, the same equity and justice prevailing in the one case as the other, it being no greater hardship to forbid my manufacturing, than it is to order me to buy goods loaded with duties, for the express purpose of raising a revenue. But as a measure of this sort would be an additional exertion of arbitrary power, we cannot be placed in a worse condition, I think, by putting it to the test.

On the other hand, that the colonies are considerably indebted to Great Britain, is a truth universally acknowledged. That many families are reduced almost, if not quite, to penury and want by the low ebb of their fortunes, and that estates are daily selling for the discharge of debts, the public papers furnish too many melancholy proofs. That a scheme of this sort will contribute more effectually than any other that can be devised to extricate the country from the distress it at present labors under, I most firmly believe, if it can be generally adopted. And I can see but one class of people, the merchants excepted, who will not, or ought not, to wish well to the scheme, namely, they who live genteelly and hospitably on clear estates. Such as these, were they not to consider the valuable object in view, and the good of others, might think it hard to be curtailed in their living and enjoyments. As to the penurious man, he would thereby save his money and his credit, having the best plea for doing that, which before, perhaps, he had the most violent struggles to refrain from doing. The extravagant and expensive man has the same good plea to retrench his expenses. He would be furnished with a pretext to live within bounds, and embrace it. Prudence dictated economy before, but his resolution was too weak to put it in practice; "For how can I," says he, "who have lived in such and such a manner, change my method? I am ashamed to do it, and, besides, such an alteration in the system of my living will create suspicions of the decay of my fortune, and such a thought the world must not harbour." He continues his course, till at last his estate comes to an end, a sale of it being the consequence of his perseverance in error. This I am satisfied is the way, that many, who have set out in the wrong track, have reasoned, till ruin has stared them in the face. And in respect to the needy man, he is only left in the same situation that he was found in, — better, I may say, because, as he judges from comparison, his condition is amended in proportion as it approaches nearer to those above him.

Upon the whole, therefore, I think the scheme a good one, and that it ought to be tried here, with such alterations as our circumstances render absolutely necessary. But in what manner to begin the work, is a matter worthy of consideration. Whether it can be attempted with propriety or efficacy, further than a communication of sentiments to one another, before May, when the Court and Assembly will meet at Williamsburg, and a uniform plan can be concerted, and sent into the different counties to operate at the same time and in the same manner everywhere, is a thing upon which I am somewhat in doubt, and I should be glad to know your opinion.* I am, &c.

---

* The following is an extract from Mr. Mason's reply to this letter, dated the same day.

"I entirely agree with you, that no regular plan of the sort proposed can be entered into here, before the meeting of the General Court at least, if not of the Assembly. In the mean time it may be necessary to publish something preparatory to it in our gazettes, to warn the people of the impending danger, and induce them the more readily and cheerfully to concur in the proper measures to avert it; and something of this sort I had begun, but am unluckily stopped by a disorder, which affects my head and eyes. As soon as I am able, I shall resume it, and then write you more fully, or endeavour to see you. In the mean time pray commit to writing such hints as may occur.

"Our all is at stake, and the little conveniences and comforts of life,

TO LORD BOTETOURT, GOVERNOR OF VIRGINIA.

Mount Vernon, 15 April, 1770.

MY LORD,

Being fully persuaded of your Excellency's inclination to render every just and reasonable service to the people you govern, or to any body or society of them, that shall ask it, and being encouraged in a more particu-

---

when set in competition with our liberty, ought to be rejected, not with reluctance, but with pleasure. Yet it is plain, that in the tobacco colonies we cannot at present confine our importations within such narrow bounds, as the northern colonies. A plan of this kind, to be practicable, must be adapted to our circumstances; for if not steadily executed, it had better have remained unattempted. We may retrench all manner of superfluities, finery of all descriptions, and confine ourselves to linens, woollens, &c. not exceeding a certain price. It is amazing how much this practice, if adopted in all the colonies, would lessen the American imports, and distress the various traders and manufacturers in Great Britain.

"This would awaken their attention. They would see, they would feel, the oppressions we groan under, and exert themselves to procure us redress. This once obtained, we should no longer discontinue our importations, confining ourselves still not to import any article, that should hereafter be taxed by act of Parliament for raising a revenue in America; for, however singular I may be in my opinion, I am thoroughly convinced, that, justice and harmony happily restored, it is not the interest of these colonies to refuse British manufactures. Our supplying our mother country with gross materials, and taking her manufactures in return, is the true chain of connexion between us. These are the bands, which, if not broken by oppression, must long hold us together, by maintaining a constant reciprocation of interest. Proper caution should, therefore, be used in drawing up the proposed plan of association. It may not be amiss to let the ministry understand, that, until we obtain a redress of grievances, we will withhold from them our commodities, and particularly refrain from making tobacco, by which the revenue would lose fifty times more than all their oppressions could raise here.

"Had the hint, which I have given with regard to taxation of goods imported into America, been thought of by our merchants before the repeal of the Stamp Act, the late American revenue acts would probably never have been attempted."

The Assembly in May was the first that met after the arrival of Lord Botetourt as Governor. The Burgesses had been together but a few days, when they passed a series of very strong resolves respecting the rights

lar manner by a letter, which I have just received from Mr. Blair, clerk of the Council, to believe, that your Lordship is desirous of being fully informed how far the grant of land solicited by Mr. Walpole and others will affect the interest of this country in general, or individuals in particular, I shall take the liberty (as I am pretty intimately acquainted with the situation of the frontiers of this dominion) to inform your Lordship, that the bounds of that grant, if obtained upon the extensive plan

---

of the colonies. The Governor took the alarm, and immediately dissolved the Assembly. As soon as the Burgesses left the public hall, they all met again at a private house in Williamsburg (May 18th, 1769), appointed a moderator, and assented unanimously to a non-importation agreement, otherwise called an *Association*, consisting of a preamble and eight resolves. It was signed by every member present, and sent throughout the country for the signatures of the people. Washington was a member of the Assembly at that time.

The *Association* is printed at large in Burk's *History of Virginia*, Vol. III. p. 345. On comparing it with Mr. Mason's manuscript draft, retained by Washington, I find it precisely the same, except the addition of two short articles, and the omission of another. The following article, contained in Mr. Mason's draft, was left out by the Burgesses.

"If the measures already entered into should prove ineffectual, and our grievances and oppressions should notwithstanding be continued, then, and in that case, the subscribers will put a stop to their exports to Europe of tar, pitch, turpentine, timber, lumber, and skins and furs of all sorts, and will endeavour to find some other employment for their slaves and other hands than cultivating tobacco, which they will entirely leave off making, and will enter into such regulations, as may be necessary with regard to the rents and other tobacco debts."

As Mr. Mason was not then a member of the House of Burgesses, and as Washington left home for Williamsburg shortly after receiving the draft, he must have taken it with him to the Assembly, and of course have been a principal agent in procuring its adoption.

He wrote afterwards as follows to his correspondent in London, on sending out his customary orders; — "You will perceive, in looking over the several invoices, that some of the goods there required, are upon condition, that the act of Parliament imposing a duty on tea, paper, &c. for the purpose of raising a revenue in America, is totally repealed; and I beg the favor of you to be governed strictly thereby, as it will not be in my power to receive any articles contrary to our non-importation agreement, which I have subscribed, and shall religiously adhere to, and should, if it were, as I could wish it to be, ten times as strict."

proposed, will comprehend at least four fifths of the land, for the purchase and survey of which this government has lately voted two thousand five hundred pounds sterling. It must, therefore, destroy the well grounded hopes of those, (if no reservation is made in their favor,) who have had the strongest assurances, that the government could give, of enjoying a certain portion of the lands, which have cost this country so much blood and treasure to secure.

By the extracts, which your Excellency did me the honor to enclose, I perceive, that the petitioners propose to begin opposite to the mouth of the Scioto River, which is at least seventy or seventy-five miles below the Great Kenhawa, and more than three hundred from Pittsburg, and to extend from thence in a southwardly direction through the pass of the Ouasioto Mountain, which, by Evans's map, and the best accounts I have been able to get from persons, who have explored that country, will bring them near the latitude of North Carolina. Thence they proceed northeastwardly to the Kenhawa, at the junction of New River and Green Briar, upon both of which waters we have many settlers upon lands actually patented. From that point they go up the Green Briar to the head of its northeasterly branch, thence easterly to the Allegany Mountains, thence along these mountains to the line of Lord Fairfax, and thence with his line, and the lines of Maryland and Pennsylvania, till the west boundary of the latter intersects the Ohio, and finally down that river to the place of beginning.*

These, my Lord, are the bounds of a grant prayed for, and which, if obtained, will give a fatal blow, in my humble opinion, to the interests of this country. But

---

* See APPENDIX, No. VII.

these are my sentiments as a member of the community at large. I now beg leave to offer myself to your Excellency's notice, in a more interested point of view, as an individual, and as a person, who considers himself in some degree the representative of the officers and soldiers, who claim a right to two hundred thousand acres of this very land, under a solemn act of government, adopted at a period very important and critical to his Majesty's affairs in this part of the world. I shall, therefore, rely on your Lordship's accustomed goodness and candor, whilst I add a few words in support of the equity of our pretensions, although, in truth, I have very little to say on this subject now, which I have not heretofore taken the liberty of observing to your Excellency.

The first letter I ever did myself the honor of writing to you, on the subject of this land, and to which I beg leave to refer, contained a kind of historical account of our claim; but as there requires nothing more to elucidate a right, than to offer a candid exhibition of the case, supported by facts, I shall beg leave to refer your Lordship to an order of Council, of the 18th of February, 1754, and to Governor Dinwiddie's proclamation, which issued in consequence of that order, both of which are enclosed. I will next add, that these troops not only enlisted agreeably to the proclamation, but behaved so much to the satisfaction of the country, as to be honored with the most public acknowledgments of it by the Assembly. Would it not be hard, then, my Lord, to deprive men under these circumstances, or their representatives, of the just reward of their toils? Was not this act of the Governor and Council offered to the soldiers, and accepted by them, as an absolute compact? And though the exigency of affairs, or the policy of government, made it necessary to continue these lands in a dormant state for some time, ought not their claim to be considered, in preference to all others? When the causes cease, we fain would hope so. We flatter ourselves, that it will also appear to your Lordship in this point of view, and that, by your kind interposition, and favorable representation of the case, his Majesty will be graciously pleased to confirm this land to us, agreeably to a petition presented to your Excellency in Council on the 15th of last December; with this difference only, that, instead of Sandy Creek (one of the places allotted for the location of our grant, and which we now certainly know will not be comprehended within the ministerial line, as it is called), we may be allowed to lay a part of our grant between the west boundary of Pennsylvania and the river Ohio, which will be expressly agreeable to the words of Governor Dinwiddie's proclamation, inasmuch as it is contiguous to the Fork of the Monongahela. This favor, my Lord, would be conferring a singular obligation on soldiers, most of whom, either in their persons or fortunes, have suffered in the cause of their country; and it cannot fail to receive the thanks of a grateful body of men, but of none more warmly than of your Lordship's most obedient and humble servant.

TO LORD DUNMORE, GOVERNOR OF VIRGINIA.

Mount Vernon, 15 June, 1771.

MY LORD,

The very obliging offer your Lordship was pleased to make, the day I left Williamsburg, in behalf of the officers and soldiers, who, under the faith of government, lay claim to two hundred thousand acres of land, on the waters of the Ohio, promised them by proclamation in 1754, I did not embrace, because it is evident to me, who am in some degree acquainted with the situation of that country, and the rapid progress now making in the settlement of it, that delay at this time in the prosecution of our plan would amount to the loss of the land, inasmuch as emigrants are daily and hourly settling on the choice spots, and waiting a favorable opportunity to solicit legal titles, on the ground of preoccupancy, when the office shall be opened. I therefore hoped, and the officers and soldiers, who have suffered in the cause of their country, still hope, that, although your Lordship was of opinion you could not at that time vest them with an absolute and *bonâ fide* grant of the land, yet that you will permit them to take such steps, at their own expense and risk, as others do, to secure their lands agreeably to proclamation, especially as their claim is prior to any other, and better founded, they having a solemn act of government and the general voice of the country in their favor.

This is the light, my Lord, in which the matter appeared to me, and in this light it is also considered by the officers with whom I have lately had a meeting. The report gains ground, that a large tract of country on the Ohio, including every foot of land to the westward of the Allegany Mountains, is granted to a company of gentlemen in England, to be formed into a separate government. If this report is really well founded, there can be no doubt of your Lordship's having the earliest and most authentic accounts of it, since it so essentially interferes with the interests and expectations of this country.

To request the favor of your Lordship to inform me whether this report be true, and, if true, whether any attention has been or probably will be paid to the order of Council and proclamation of 1754, may be presumptuous; but, as the officers and soldiers confide in me to transact this business for them, and as it would be a real advantage to them to know the truth of this report, and how it is likely to affect them, there needs no other apology for my taking the liberty of addressing to you this request, in the hope that your Lordship will condescend to do me the honor of writing a line on the subject by the next post to Alexandria, which will be acknowledged as a peculiar obligation conferred on, my Lord, your Lordship's most obedient servant.

TO THE REVEREND JONATHAN BOUCHER.*

Mount Vernon, 9 July, 1771.

DEAR SIR,

From several concurring causes, which exist at this moment, at the eve of my departure for Williamsburg, I have both my head and hands too full of business to allow me time to write more than a hasty letter. This, however, I shall attempt to do, in answer to yours of the 4th instant.

In my last I informed you, that the friends (I do not by this confine myself to the relations only) of Mr. Custis were divided in opinion, as to the propriety of his travelling, not because they thought advantages would not result from it, but on account of the expense, as he would commence his tour with the heavy charge, which you thought requisite to induce you to accompany him, and which would at once anticipate half his income. His estate is of that kind, which rather comes under the denomination of a large than a profitable one. This di-

* Mr. Boucher was an Episcopal clergyman residing in Annapolis. He was tutor to John Parke Custis, the son of Mrs. Washington by her former marriage. Mr. Boucher went to England when the Revolution broke out, and never returned. He published a volume of sermons, which he had preached in America, and some other writings.

vided opinion was a sufficient cause, I observed in my last, for me to be circumspect in my conduct, as I am accountable to another tribunal, besides that in my own breast, for the part I am to act on this occasion. You cannot but know, that every farthing, expended in behalf of this young gentleman, must undergo the inspection of the General Court, in their examination of my guardianship accounts, and that it would be imprudent in me to permit him to launch into any uncommon or extravagant course, especially at a time when a heavy and expensive chancery suit is instituted against his estate, without first knowing whether such a charge would be approved by those, who have a constitutional right to judge of the expediency or propriety of the measure.

These are the reasons why I said in my last letter, that my own inclinations were still as strong as ever for Mr. Custis's pursuing his travelling scheme, provided the Court should approve of the expense, and provided, also, that it should appear, when his judgment was a little more matured, that he was desirous of undertaking this tour upon a plan of improvement, rather than a vague desire of gratifying an idle curiosity, or spending his money. If his mother does not speak her own sentiments, rather than his, he is lukewarm in the scheme; and I cannot help giving it as my opinion, that his education, from what I have understood of his improvement, however advanced it may be for a youth of his age, is by no means ripe enough for a travelling tour. Not that I think his becoming a mere scholar is a desirable education for a gentleman, but I conceive a knowledge of books is the basis upon which other knowledge is to be built, and in travelling he is to become acquainted with men and things rather than books. At present, however well versed he may be in the principles of the Latin language (which is not to be wondered at, as he began the study of it as soon as he could speak), he is unacquainted with several of the classical authors, that might be useful to him. He is ignorant of Greek, the advantages of learning which I do not pretend to judge of, and he knows nothing of French, which is absolutely necessary to him as a traveller. He has little or no acquaintance with arithmetic, and is totally ignorant of the mathematics, than which, at least so much of them as relates to surveying, nothing can be more essentially necessary to any man possessed of a large landed estate, the bounds of some part or other of which are always in controversy.

Now, whether he has time between this and next spring to acquire a sufficient knowledge of these studies, or so much of them as is requisite, I leave you to judge; as also whether a boy of seventeen years old, which will be his age next November, can have any just notions of the end and design of travelling. I have already given it as my opinion, that it would be precipitating this event, unless he were to go immediately to the university for a couple of years, in which case he could see nothing of America; which might be a disadvantage to him, as it is to be expected that every man, who travels with a view of observing the laws and customs of other countries, should be able to give some description of the situation and government of his own.

Upon the whole, it is impossible for me at this time to give a more decisive answer, however strongly inclined I may be to put you upon a certainty in this affair, than I have done; and I should think myself wanting in candor, if I concealed any circumstance from you, which leads me to fear, that there is a possibility, if not a probability, that the whole design may be totally defeated. Before I ever thought myself at liberty to encourage this plan, I judged it highly reasonable and necessary, that his mother should be consulted. I laid your first letter and proposals before her, and desired that she would reflect well, before she resolved, as an unsteady behaviour might be a disadvantage to you. Her determination was, that, if it appeared to be his inclination to undertake this tour, and it should be judged for his benefit, she would not oppose it, whatever pangs it might give her to part with him. To this declaration she still adheres, but in so faint a manner, that I think, with her fears and his indifference, it will soon be declared he has no inclination to go. I do not say that this will be the case. I cannot speak positively; but as this is the result of my own reflections upon the matter, I thought it but fair to communicate it to you.

Several causes, I believe, have concurred to make her view his departure, as the time approaches, with more reluctance than she expected. The unhappy situation of her daughter has in some degree fixed her eyes upon him as her only hope. To what I have already said, I can only add, that my warmest wishes are to see him prosecute a plan, at a proper period, which I may be sure will redound to his advantage, and that nothing shall be wanting on my part to aid and assist him. In the event of his going, I should think myself highly favored, and him much honored, by Governor Eden's letters of introduction. Such letters, with others that might be procured, could not fail of having their advantages.

You will please to make my compliments to Mr. Dulany, and assure him, that I have not the vestige of a house at the Frederic Springs, otherwise it should have been, if unengaged, much at his service. The two seasons I spent there I occupied a house of Mr. Mercer's.

I am, &c.

TO GEORGE MERCER, LONDON.

Williamsburg, 7 November, 1771.

DEAR SIR,

Since you first left this country, I have been favored with two letters from you; one of them serving to enter your own, and the claims of Captains Stobo and Vanbraam, to part of the two hundred thousand acres of land, granted under Governor Dinwiddie's proclamation; and the other, of the 18th of December, which did not come to my hands till about the first of last month, urging the expediency of prosecuting our right to those lands with spirit.

In respect to the first, I have only to inform you, that your own claim, as well that for your brother as yourself, was entered before the receipt of your letter, and that Stobo's and Vanbraam's are also entered. In answer to the second, I can only add, that the same backwardness, which has ever appeared in our Honorable Board to recognise our right to these lands, seems still to prevail, and that our business in this affair is by no means in that forwardness, which I could wish, owing, I believe I may say, to other causes, as well as to a lukewarmness in those from whom we seek redress. The unequal interest and dispersed situation of the claimants make a regular coöperation difficult. An undertaking of this kind cannot be conducted without a good deal of expense and trouble; and the doubt of obtaining the lands, after the utmost efforts, is such, as to discourage the larger part of the claimants from lending assistance, whilst a few are obliged to wade through every difficulty, or relinquish every hope.

In this state of things, and in behalf of those, who had contributed to the expense of exploring and surveying the lands, I petitioned the Governor and Council, that the amount of each man's share, according to his rank, should be ascertained, and each claimant suffered to designate and survey his portion separately, by which means every man would stand upon his own footing. This petition I thought so reasonable, and so consistent with every principle of common justice, to say nothing of the disadvantage of being forced into large tracts, and the manifest inconvenience of dividing them afterwards, that I conceived it could not possibly be rejected; but to my great astonishment it was so, and we are now compelled to be at the expense of surveying our whole quantity in twenty surveys, and then each individual subjected to the charge of surveying his own separately. In this way we are doubly taxed, while the whole is held as a kind of joint interest, and no man knows his property, or can tell how or in what manner to dispose of it. In short, so many glaring obstacles opposed their mode of proceeding, that they did not even attempt to remove them, but contented themselves with putting the soldiers upon a worse footing, than the meanest individual in the community, rather than be thought to give a license for the pillaging of his Majesty's or the Proprietary lands, when it is a fact well known, and every age evinces it, that no country ever was or ever will be settled without some indulgence. What inducements have men to explore uninhabited wilds, but the prospect of getting good lands? Would any man waste his time, expose his fortune, nay, life, in such a search, if he was to share the good and the bad with those that come after him? Surely not. We have surveyed ten of the largest tracts we can find in the district allowed us, and have been able to get sixty thousand acres, and for this tract we have been obliged to go between two and three hundred miles below Fort Pitt, as the lands thereabouts are thought to be within the Pennsylvania government; at least, they are surveyed under those rights, and held by such a number of individuals, that it was thought to be impolitic to engage in private disputes, whilst there appeared a gloomy prospect of getting any land at all.

The claims, which have been presented to me, are now all given in, and the Governor and Council have determined, that each officer shall share according to the rank in which he entered the service, and that the land shall be distributed in the following manner, namely, to each field-officer fifteen thousand acres, to each captain nine thousand, to each subaltern six thousand, to the cadets two thousand five hundred each, six hundred to a sergeant, five hundred to a corporal, and four hundred to each private soldier. They have made a reserve of thirty thousand acres, as well to provide for any claims, which may hereafter come in, as to compensate those, who have been and must necessarily continue to be saddled with the expense, which we find will not be very inconsiderable, as we have already expended near two hundred pounds, and the surveyor not yet paid.*

---

* The Major in the expedition had been accused of cowardice at the affair of the Great Meadows, and his name was omitted in the vote of thanks to the officers by the legislature. It was decided, however, that this person should have his share of the land, and the following extract from a letter to him on this subject will show with what spirit and tone Washington could retort upon rudeness, when there was occasion.

"SIR,

"Your impertinent letter was delivered to me yesterday. As I am not accustomed to receive such from any man, nor would have taken the same language from you personally, without letting you feel some marks of my resentment, I would advise you to be cautious in writing me a second of the same tenor. But for your stupidity and sottishness you might have known, by attending to the public gazette, that you had your full quantity of ten thousand acres of land allowed you, that is, nine thousand and seventy-three acres in the great tract, and the remainder in the small tract.

"But suppose you had really fallen short, do you think your superlative merit entitles you to greater indulgence than others? Or, if it did, that I

This expense must now be greatly augmented, as we shall be exposed to a considerable charge in exploring the lands, before we can proceed to survey any more. From every thing we know at present, it appears impossible to get two hundred thousand acres in twenty surveys, without including mountains and inhospitable hills to the amount of near one half, which will render the grant of little value, and be the source of much discontent at a division. It behooves us, therefore, to examine the lands well before we survey. And allow me to add, that it will be very proper for you to give Messrs. Stobo and Vanbraam a hint, that something more than entering their claims is necessary. I dare say they will hardly think it reasonable to profit by the labor and purse of others. It is highly incumbent on them, therefore, to appoint an agent in this country to transact their business and advance their proportion of the expense, if they expect to share in the lands.

To give you a minute detail of the proceedings, respecting this grant, would be a work of time, and afford you little entertainment. What I have here said will serve as a general outline, and that is all I have aimed at in this letter. I should not have delayed answering your first letter till this time, had you not mentioned your intention of embarking soon on your return. This

---

was to make it good to you, when it was at the option of the Governor and Council to allow but five hundred acres in the whole, if they had been so inclined? If either of these should happen to be your opinion, I am very well convinced, that you will be singular in it; and all my concern is, that I ever engaged in behalf of so ungrateful a fellow as you are. But you may still be in need of my assistance, as I can inform you, that your affairs, in respect to these lands, do not stand upon so solid a basis as you may imagine, and this you may take by way of hint.

"I wrote to you a few days ago concerning the other distribution, proposing an easy method of dividing our lands; but since I find in what temper you are, I am sorry I took the trouble of mentioning the land or your name in a letter, as I do not think you merit the least assistance from me."

account having been frequently corroborated by your brother, of whom I often inquired after you, I thought a letter could have little chance of finding you in England. I have just been told by Mr. Mercer, that you are to remain in London for some advices from him, respecting the affairs of the Ohio Company.* Mrs. Washington makes a tender of her compliments to you, and I am, with very sincere regard, dear Sir, your most obedient humble servant.

TO WILLIAM EDWARDS, GOVERNOR OF WEST FLORIDA.

Virginia, 25 March, 1773.

SIR,

Mr. Wood, the bearer of this, is a gentleman of Virginia, going upon a tour to Florida. He proposes, before his return, to explore some of the ungranted lands in your government; and, as I have never yet been able to designate the lands to which I am entitled under his Majesty's proclamation of October, 1763, he has promised, if he meets with such lands as he thinks will answer my purpose, to have ten thousand acres surveyed for me. To five thousand acres I am entitled in my own right, by virtue of that proclamation; to the residue by purchase, certificates of which will be presented to your Excellency by Mr. Wood, under the hand and seal of Lord Dunmore, our present governor.†

* See APPENDIX, No. VI.

† By this proclamation, three new colonies were established in America, namely, Quebec, or Canada, East Florida, and West Florida. Lands were also granted to the officers and soldiers, who had served in the late war, and who resided in America, on their personal application for the same, in the following quantities and proportions. To every field-officer five thousand acres, to every captain three thousand, to every subaltern or staff-officer two thousand, to every non-commissioned officer two hundred, and

My entire ignorance of the climate and soil, the advantages and disadvantages, of the country of West Florida, is the reason why his Lordship's certificates are couched in such general terms; and of my giving Mr. Wood a discretionary power to select the lands, or not, as he may be influenced by these appearances. Should he meet with a spot favorable to my wishes, I have no doubt of your Excellency's granting the land, with such indulgences as have been practised in similar cases, agreeably to his Majesty's gracious intention, with the terms of which I shall endeavour strictly to comply.

Could I, Sir, a stranger, take it upon me with propriety to recommend Mr. Wood, I should briefly add, that he is a gentleman well esteemed in Virginia, and I am persuaded will duly appreciate any little civilities you may be pleased to bestow on him. I have the honor to be, Sir, with very great respect, &c.

TO BENEDICT CALVERT.

Mount Vernon, 3 April, 1773.

Dear Sir,

I am now set down to write to you on a subject of importance, and of no small embarrassment to me. My son-in-law and ward, Mr. Custis, has, as I have been informed, paid his addresses to your second daughter, and, having made some progress in her affections, has solicited her in marriage. How far a union of this sort may be agreeable to you, you best can tell; but I should think myself wanting in candor, were I not to confess, that Miss Nelly's amiable qualities are acknowledg-

---

to every private fifty, and all to be free of quitrents for ten years. The lands could be chosen, however, only in one of the above three new colonies.

ed on all hands, and that an alliance with your family will be pleasing to his.

This acknowledgment being made, you must permit me to add, Sir, that at this, or in any short time, his youth, inexperience, and unripened education, are, and will be, insuperable obstacles, in my opinion, to the completion of the marriage. As his guardian, I conceive it my indispensable duty to endeavour to carry him through a regular course of education (many branches of which, I am sorry to add, he is totally deficient in), and to guard his youth to a more advanced age before an event, on which his own peace and the happiness of another are to depend, takes place. Not that I have any doubt of the warmth of his affections, nor, I hope I may add, any fears of a change in them; but at present I do not conceive that he is capable of bestowing that attention to the important consequences of the married state, which is necessary to be given by those, who are about to enter into it, and of course I am unwilling he should do it till he is. If the affection, which they have avowed for each other, is fixed upon a solid basis, it will receive no diminution in the course of two or three years, in which time he may prosecute his studies, and thereby render himself more deserving of the lady and useful to society. If, unfortunately, as they are both young, there should be an abatement of affection on either side, or both, it had better precede than follow marriage.

Delivering my sentiments thus freely will not, I hope, lead you into a belief, that I am desirous of breaking off the match. To postpone it is all I have in view; for I shall recommend to the young gentleman, with the warmth that becomes a man of honor, (notwithstanding he did not vouchsafe to consult either his mother or me on the occasion,) to consider himself as much engaged to your daughter, as if the indissoluble knot were tied;

and, as the surest means of effecting this, to apply himself closely to his studies, (and in this advice I flatter myself you will join me,) by which he will, in a great measure, avoid those little flirtations with other young ladies, that may, by dividing the attention, contribute not a little to divide the affection.

It may be expected of me, perhaps, to say something of property; but, to descend to particulars, at this time, must seem rather premature. In general, therefore, I shall inform you, that Mr. Custis's estate consists of about fifteen thousand acres of land, a good part of it adjoining the city of Williamsburg, and none of it forty miles from that place; several lots in the said city; between two and three hundred negroes; and about eight or ten thousand pounds upon bond, and in the hands of his merchants. This estate he now holds independent of his mother's dower, which will be an addition to it at her death; and, upon the whole, it is such an estate as you will readily acknowledge ought to entitle him to a handsome portion with a wife. But as I should never require a child of my own to make a sacrifice of himself to interest, so neither do I think it incumbent on me to recommend it as a guardian.

At all times when you, Mrs. Calvert, or the young ladies, can make it convenient to favor us with a visit, we should be happy in seeing you at this place. Mrs. Washington and Miss Custis join me in respectful compliments, and

I am, dear Sir, your most obedient servant.

TO LORD DUNMORE, GOVERNOR OF VIRGINIA.

Mount Vernon, 13 April, 1773.

MY LORD,

In obedience to your Lordship's request, I do myself the honor to inform you, that, by letters this day received from Dr. Cooper of King's College in New York, I find it will be about the first of next month before I shall set off for that place, and that it will perhaps be the middle of June before I return. Harvest then coming on, and seldom ending till after the middle of July, I could almost wish to see it accomplished; but if the delay in doing it is attended with any kind of inconvenience to your Lordship, I will, at all events, be ready by the first of July to accompany you through any and every part of the western country, which you may think proper to visit.

I beg the favor of your Lordship to inform me, therefore, as nearly as you can, of the precise time you will do me the honor of calling here, that I may get ready accordingly, and give notice of it to Mr. Crawford (if your Lordship purposes to take the route of Pittsburg), whom I took the liberty of recommending as a good woods-man, and well acquainted with the lands in that quarter, that he may be disengaged when we get to his house, which is directly on that communication. I am persuaded, that such a person will be found very necessary in an excursion of this sort, from his superior knowledge of the country, and of the inhabitants, who are thinly scattered over it.

No person can be better acquainted with the equipage and simple conveniences necessary in an undertaking of this sort, than your Lordship, and, therefore, it would be impertinent in me to mention them; but if your Lordship should find it convenient to have any thing provided in this part of the country, and will please to honor me with your commands, they shall be punctually obeyed. As, also, if your Lordship chooses to have an Indian engaged, I will write to Colonel Croghan, Deputy Indian Agent, who lives near Pittsburg, to have one provided.

The design of my journey to New York is to take my son-in-law, Mr. Custis, to King's College. If your Lordship, therefore, has any letters or commands, either to that place or Philadelphia, I shall think myself honored in being the bearer of them, as well as benefited by means of the introduction.

I am, with the greatest respect, your Lordship's most obedient and most humble servant.

TO THE REVEREND DR. COOPER, PRESIDENT OF KING'S COLLEGE, NEW YORK.

New York, 31 May, 1773.

REVEREND SIR,

Enclosed you have a set of bills for one hundred pounds sterling, which please to set at the prevailing exchange, and retain the money in your own hands to answer Mr. Custis's expenses at college, and such calls as he may have for cash to defray the incident expenses of his abode in this city.

In respect to the first article of charge, I submit the matter wholly to your better judgment, under a firm belief of your adopting such measures, as will most contribute to promote the principal end of Mr. Custis's coming here, not regarding the extra charge incurred in the accomplishment of it. In regard to the second, as I do not know what sum he ought, with propriety, to expend in such a place as New York, I shall not undertake to determine it; but hope, if, contrary to my expectation, you should find him inclined to run into any kind of extravagance, you will be so good, by your friendly admonition, as to check its progress.

As Mr. Custis may probably want clothing and other necessaries, you will please to establish a credit in his behalf with such merchants as you can recommend; and when the deposit now lodged with you is expended in this and other payments, be so good as to transmit me a copy of the disbursements, and I shall furnish you with other bills whereby to lay in a new fund.

I have nothing further to add at present, except that at the next vacation, or at any other time, I shall think myself very happy in seeing you in Virginia, and that I am, with very great respect and esteem, your most obedient humble servant.

TO WILLIAM CRAWFORD.

Mount Vernon, 25 September, 1773.

DEAR SIR,

I have heard, (the truth of which, if you saw Lord Dunmore in his way to or from Pittsburg you possibly are better acquainted with than I am,) that his Lordship will grant patents for lands lying below the Scioto, to the officers and soldiers, who claim under the proclamation of October, 1763. If so, I think no time should be lost in having them surveyed, lest some new revolution should happen in our political system. I have, therefore, by this conveyance, written to Captain Bullitt, to desire he will have ten thousand acres surveyed for me; five thousand of which I am entitled to in my own right, the other five thousand by purchase from a captain and lieutenant.

I have desired him to get this quantity of land in one tract, if to be had of the first quality; if not, then in two, or even in three, agreeably to the several rights under which I hold, rather than survey bad land for me, or even that which is middling. I have also desired him to get it as near the mouth of the Scioto, that is, to the western bounds of the new colony* as may be; but for the sake of better lands, I would go quite down to the Falls, or even below, meaning thereby to get richer and wider bottoms, as it is my desire to have my lands run out upon the banks of the Ohio. If you should go down the river this fall, in order to look out your own quantity under the proclamation, I shall be much obliged to you for your assistance to Captain Bullitt, in getting these ten thousand acres for me, of the most valuable land you can, and I will endeavour to make you ample amends for your trouble; but I by no means wish or desire you to go down on my account, unless you find it expedient on your own. Of this I have written to Captain Bullitt, under cover to you, desiring, if you should be with him, that he will ask your assistance.

As I have understood that Captain Thompson (by what authority I know not) has been surveying a good deal of land for the Pennsylvania officers, and that Dr. Connolly has a promise from our Governor of two thousand acres at the Falls, I have desired Captain Bullitt by no means to involve me in disputes with any person, who has an equal claim to land with myself, under the proclamation of 1763. As to the pretensions of other people, it is not very essential; as I am told that the Governor has declared he will grant patents to none but the officers and soldiers, who are comprehended within

* This *new colony* was "Walpole's Grant," mentioned above in the letter to Lord Botetourt, April 15th, 1770.

the proclamation aforementioned; but even of these claims, if I could get lands equally as good, as convenient, and as valuable in every respect, elsewhere, I should choose to steer clear.

Old David Wilper, who was an officer in our regiment, and has been with Bullitt running out land for himself and others, tells me, that they have already discovered four salt springs in that country, three of which Captain Thompson has included within some surveys he has made; and the other, an exceedingly valuable one, upon the River Kentucky, is in some kind of dispute. I wish I could establish one of my surveys there; I would immediately turn it to an extensive public benefit, as well as private advantage. However, as four are already discovered, it is more than probable there are many others, and if you could come at the knowledge of them by means of the Indians, or otherwise, I would join you in taking them up in the name or names of some persons, who have a right under the proclamation, and whose right we can be sure of buying, as it seems there is no other method of having lands granted; but this should be done with a good deal of circumspection and caution, till patents are obtained.

I did not choose to forego the opportunity of writing to you by the gentlemen, who are going to divide their land at the mouth of the great Kenhawa, though I could wish to have delayed it till I could hear from the Governor, to whom I have written, to know certainly whether he will grant patents for the land which Captain Bullitt is surveying, that one may proceed with safety; as also whether a discretionary power, which I had given Mr. Wood to select my land in West Florida, under an information, even from his Lordship himself, that lands could not be had here, would be any bar to my surveying on the Ohio; especially as I have heard since

Mr. Wood's departure, that all the lands on that part of the Mississippi, to which he was restricted by me, are already engaged by the emigrants, who have resorted to that country. Should I, however, receive any discouraging account from his Lordship on these heads, I shall embrace the first opportunity that offers afterwards to acquaint you with it.

By Mr. Leet I informed you of the unhappy cause, which prevented my going out this fall. But I hope nothing will prevent my seeing you in that country in the spring.* The precise time, as yet, it is not in my power to fix; but I should be glad if you would let me know how soon it may be attended with safety, ease, and comfort, after which I will fix upon a time to be at your house.

I am in the mean while, with sincere good wishes for you, Mrs. Crawford, and family, your friend, &c.

TO LORD DUNMORE, GOVERNOR OF VIRGINIA.†

Williamsburg, 2 November, 1773.

My Lord,

Urged by repeated applications from a number of officers, whom I have had the honor to command in the

---

* It had been his purpose to accompany Lord Dunmore on a tour to the western country, but his design was frustrated by the death of Miss Custis, the daughter of Mrs. Washington by her former marriage. She died on the 19th of June, 1773, after a long and very painful illness.

† Colonel Washington had previously written to Lord Dunmore on the subject of granting lands for the officers and soldiers. The letter has not been preserved, but the following is Lord Dunmore's answer.

"Williamsburg, 24 September, 1773.

"Dear Sir,

"I last post received yours of the 12th instant, wherein you beg to be informed whether I propose granting patents on the Ohio to such officers and soldiers, as claim under his Majesty's proclamation in October, 1763.

service of this colony, I take the liberty of addressing your Excellency on the subject of the lands, which the gentlemen conceive themselves entitled to under his Majesty's bounty of October, 1763.

The exception in favor of the officers and soldiers, contained in his Majesty's order in Council, of the 6th of April last, they humbly conceive is so strong an implication of your Lordship's right to grant them these lands, as to remove every restraint you were under before; and as there are no waste lands to be had in this colony, but such as lie upon the western waters, they humbly pray for leave to survey on the river Ohio, and its waters, below the mouth of Scioto (the western boundary of the new colony, should it ever take place), apprehending that your Excellency has an undoubted right to grant patents for these lands, since they have ever been considered as appertaining to Virginia, warranted, as they have been informed, by the Colony Charter, and sold by the Six Nations at the treaty of Fort Stanwix, in 1768. Nor is the right thereto, it is humbly presumed, by any means diminished by the nominal line, commonly called the *Ministerial Line;* since that transaction seems to have been considered by government as a temporary expedient, at the instigation of the Indian Agent, to satisfy the southern Indians, who, as it is said, have disclaimed any right to the very

---

I do not mean to grant any patents on the western waters, as I do not think I am at present empowered so to do. I did, indeed, tell a poor old German lieutenant, who was with me, and informed me he was very poor, and had ten children, that I might possibly grant him a patent contiguous to that, which he had under Mr. Dinwiddie's proclamation, which I suppose is what may have given rise to the report you have heard. As to Captain Bullitt, I know nothing about his surveying any lands, and did, when I was at Fort Pitt, write to him and advise him to return again immediately.

"I beg my best respects to Mrs. Washington, and am, dear Sir, your most obedient and very humble servant.

"DUNMORE."

lands in contest; and no further regard has been paid to it by the ministers themselves.

The officers of the Virginia troops, impressed with these sentiments, and having undoubted reason to believe, that there is no other chance left them to obtain their lands, but on the Ohio, and knowing at the same time, that the officers of Pennsylvania, under a belief that these lands appertain to Virginia, and that patents will be granted for them, have surveyed two hundred thousand acres, — would fain hope, that they may be allowed to proceed by authority to make their surveys also, anywhere upon the Ohio, or its waters, below the Scioto; humbly representing to your Lordship, that a delay in this case is, in effect, equal to a refusal, as the country is becoming spread over with emigrants, and experience has convinced all those, who have had occasion to attend to the matter, that these people when once fixed are not to be dispossessed, were it politic to attempt it.

The officers have an entire confidence in your Lordship's disposition to promote their just rights. They have no other dependence, and they hope to be put on an equal footing with those other officers, whose pretensions are not better founded than their own.

The part I take in bringing this matter to a hearing will, I hope, meet with your Lordship's excuse, as I am, with the greatest respect, my Lord, your Lordship's most obedient and most humble servant.

TO THE REVEREND DR. COOPER, PRESIDENT OF KING'S COLLEGE, NEW YORK.

Mount Vernon, 15 December, 1773.

REVEREND SIR,

The favorable account, which you were pleased to transmit to me, of Mr. Custis's conduct at college, gave me very great satisfaction. I hoped to have felt an increase of it by his continuance at that place, under a gentleman so capable of instructing him in every branch of useful knowledge. But this hope is at an end; and it has been against my wishes, that he should quit college, in order that he may enter soon into a new scene of life, which I think he would be much fitter for some years hence, than now.* But having his own inclination, the desires of his mother, and the acquiescence of almost all his relatives to encounter, I did not care, as he is the last of the family, to push my opposition too far, and I have therefore submitted to a kind of necessity.

Not knowing how his expenses at college may stand, I shall be much obliged to you if you will render me an account of them. You will please to charge liberally for your own particular attention to Mr. Custis, and sufficiently reward the other gentlemen, who were engaged in the same good offices. If the money I left with you is insufficient to answer these purposes, please to advise me thereof, and I will remit the deficiency.

I am very sorry it was not in my power to see you whilst in these parts. I thank you very sincerely, Sir, for your polite regard to Mr. Custis, during his abode at college, and through you beg leave to offer my ac-

* His marriage with the daughter of Mr. Benedict Calvert, which took place on the 3d of February, 1774.

knowledgments in like manner to the professors. With very great esteem and regard, Reverend Sir,

I am, your most obedient humble servant.

TO JAMES TILGHMAN, PHILADELPHIA.

Mount Vernon, February, 1774.

Dear Sir,

I am going to give you a little trouble, because I am persuaded you will excuse it. No good reason, you will say; but it is the best I can offer for such a liberty.

Interested as well as political motives render it necessary for me to seat the lands, which I have patented on the Ohio, in the cheapest, most expeditious, and effectual manner. Many expedients have been proposed to accomplish this, but none, in my judgment, so likely to succeed as the importing of Palatines. But how to do this upon the best terms, is a question I wish to have answered. Few of this kind of people ever come to Virginia, whether because it is out of the common course of its trade, or because they object to it, I am unable to determine. I shall take it very kind in you, therefore, to resolve the following questions, which I am persuaded you can do with precision, by inquiring of such gentlemen, as have been engaged in this business.

Whether there is any difficulty in procuring these people in Holland? If so, from whence does it proceed? Whether they are to be had at all times, or at particular seasons only, and when? Whether they are engaged previously to sending for them, and in what manner? Or do ships take their chance after getting there? Upon what terms are they generally engaged? And how much for each person do they commonly stand the importer landed at Philadelphia.? Is it customary to send an intelligent German in the ship, that is to bring them? Do vessels ever go immediately to Holland for them, and, if they do, what cargoes do they carry? Or are they to go round, and where? In short, what plan would be recommended to me, by the knowing ones, as best for importing a full freight, say two or three hundred or more, to Alexandria? In case of full freight, how are the numbers generally proportioned to the tonnage of a vessel?

Your favor in answering these several queries, with any other information, which you may think necessary for me to be possessed of, I shall gratefully receive, as I am totally unacquainted with every thing of the kind.

I hope, though you have removed from this part of the world, that you do not mean to forsake us altogether, and that it is unnecessary to add, that I shall at all times be happy in seeing you at this place. My best respects attend your good father, sisters, and brothers; and, with very sincere regard, I remain, dear Sir, &c.

TO HENRY RIDDELL.

Mount Vernon, 22 February, 1774.

SIR,

Mr. Young, hearing me express a desire of importing Palatines to settle on my lands on the Ohio, tells me, that, in discoursing of this matter in your company, you suggested an expedient, which might probably be attended with success; and that if I inclined to adopt it, you wished to be informed before the sailing of your ship.

The desire of seating and improving my lands on the Ohio, is founded on interested as well as political views. But the intention of importing Palatines for the purpose was more the effect of sudden thought, than mature consideration, because I am totally unacquainted with the manner, as well as the expense of doing it; and I was led into the notion principally from a report of either this or some other ship of yours being blamed, for not taking an offered freight of these Germans at forty shillings sterling. I was thus induced to think if this charge was not much accumulated by other expenses, that I could fall on no better expedient to settle my lands with industrious people, than by such an importation.

The terms upon which I have thought of importing Palatines, or people from Ireland, or Scotland, are these; to import them at my expense, where they are unable to transport themselves, into the Potomac River, and from hence to the Ohio; to have them, in the first case, engaged to me under indenture; in the second, by some other contract equally valid, to become tenants upon the terms hereafter mentioned; as without these securities, I would not encounter the expense, trouble, and hazard of such an importation.

But to make matters as easy and agreeable as possible to these emigrants, I will engage, on my part, that the indentures shall be considered in no other light, than as a security for reimbursing to me every expense I am under, with interest, in importing them, removing them to the land, and supporting them there, till they can raise a crop for their own subsistence; giving up the said indentures, and considering them altogether as freemen and tenants, so soon as this shall happen; not to each person or family respectively, but when the whole accumulated expense shall be discharged; as I must, for my own safety, consider them as jointly bound for this payment, till the expiration of the indented terms, otherwise I must be an inevitable loser by every death or other accident; whilst they cannot, in the worst light, be considered as more than servants at large during the indented term. I can also engage to set them down upon as good land as any in that country; and, where there is neither house built, nor land cleared, I will allow them an exemption of rent four years; and, where there is a house erected, and five acres of land cleared and fit for cultivation, two years.

They shall have the land upon lease for twenty-one years, under the usual covenants; and also at an annual rent, after the first becomes due, of four pounds sterling for each hundred acres, allowing each family to take more or less, as inclination and convenience may prompt. And I will, moreover, engage to renew the leases at the expiration of the above twenty-one years; and, in like manner, at the end of every seven years afterwards, upon an increased rent, to be agreed on between the landlord and tenant; or, in order to fix the matter absolutely, if this should be more agreeable, the rent may be increased at these periods in proportion to the increased value of that, or the adjoining lands possessed of equal advantages of soil and situation.

These are the terms on which I thought to import and plant people on my Ohio lands, which are, for the quantity, equal if not superior to any in that country; situate altogether upon the Ohio, or Great Kenhawa, two fine inland navigable rivers, abounding in fish and wild fowl of all sorts, as the lands do in wild meats of the best kind.

From Alexandria to the navigable waters of the Ohio, along a much frequented road used by wagons, is, according to the computed distance, two hundred miles. This land-carriage, if the inland navigation of the Potomac should be effected, than which I think nothing easier, will be reduced to sixty miles as matters now stand; some say to forty, and others to twenty. But, call it the greatest distance, any commodity made upon any part of these lands of mine may be transported along a very easy water-communication to the settlement of Red-stone, where the land-carriage at this time begins. To say nothing, therefore, of the advantages of raising stock of all kinds, and horses, which will carry themselves to market, and are now and will, from the nature of things, continue to be in great demand in the interior parts of this great continent, hemp, flax, potashes, indigo, and the like, will well afford the expense of this land-carriage, admitting it never may be reduced, and can be cultivated to advantage on the river bottoms in that country.

Having thus exhibited a general view of my design, I shall now be obliged to you, Sir, to inform me with as much precision as you can, what certainty there is that your ship will go to Holland; what probability there is of her getting Palatines, if she does go; when they may be expected in this country; what would be the freight; and, as near as you can judge, the whole incidental expense attending each person delivered at Alexandria; and, moreover, whether it would be expected, that the whole of these charges, including freight, should be paid down immediately on the arrival of the ship here, as it must appear rather hard to make a certain provision for an uncertain event.

It may not be amiss further to observe, that I see no prospect of these people being restrained in the smallest degree, either in their civil or religious principles; which I take notice of, because these are privileges, which mankind are solicitous to enjoy, and upon which emigrants must be anxious to be informed.

I wrote to Philadelphia by the last post for full information of the manner and charge of importing these people from Holland; and, if your account in answer to this letter should prove agreeable to my wishes, I will send a more particular description of the lands, which I wish to settle, as well as copies of the plots, and do any other matter which may be judged necessary to further the design. I am, &c.*

TO EDWARD SNICKERS.

Williamsburg, 16 June, 1774.

SIR,

Enclosed you will receive Mr. Hughes's warrant in his own right, for two thousand acres of land, the getting of which, at this time, he must look upon as a very great favor, as the Governor has dispensed with two positive instructions to oblige him. He would not grant a warrant for the other claims under Johnston. Hughes was very negligent in not sending the former certificates granted him.

I got a gentleman of my acquaintance in Maryland to mention his case to Governor Eden, who promised to have the matter inquired into, and do what he could for his relief. Why it has not been done, I cannot tell; but if my contributing twenty or twenty-five pounds to his relief will procure his liberty, you may set me down for that sum, and I will pay it at any time when the subscription is full. But how he is to get over the other matter, of giving Maryland security for his good behaviour, I know not. You are best acquainted with the circumstances of the case. I am, &c.†

---

* The approaching crisis of the revolutionary war, as well as some other obstacles, prevented this scheme for settling his western lands from being carried into effect.

† See APPENDIX, No. VIII.

TO BRYAN FAIRFAX.*

Mount Vernon, 4 July, 1774.

DEAR SIR,

John has just delivered to me your favor of yesterday, which I shall be obliged to answer in a more concise manner, than I could wish, as I am very much engaged in raising one of the additions to my house, which I think (perhaps it is fancy) goes on better whilst I am present, than in my absence from the workmen.

I own to you, Sir, I wished much to hear of your making an open declaration of taking a poll for this county, upon Colonel West's publicly declining last Sunday; and I should have written to you on the subject, but for information then received from several gentlemen in the churchyard, of your having refused to do so, for the reasons assigned in your letter;† upon which, as I think the country never stood more in need of men of abilities and liberal sentiments than now, I entreated several gentlemen at our church yesterday to press Colonel Mason to take a poll, as I really think Major Broadwater, though a good man, might do as well in the discharge of his domestic concerns, as in the capacity

---

* Afterwards Lord Fairfax. See the notes in the present volume (pp. 51, 182,) respecting the Fairfax family in America.

† The poll here mentioned was for the election of delegates to the House of Burgesses. Mr. Fairfax declined, as he said, chiefly because he thought he could not give satisfaction at that time; for he should think himself bound to oppose strong measures, and was in favor of petitioning, and giving Parliament a fair opportunity of repealing their obnoxious acts. "There are scarce any at Alexandria," he adds, "of my opinion; and though the few I have elsewhere conversed with on the subject are so, yet from them I could learn, that many thought otherwise; so that I believe I should at this time give general dissatisfaction, and therefore it would be more proper to decline, even upon this account, as well as because it would necessarily lead me into great expenses, which my circumstances will not allow."

of a legislator. And therefore I again express my wish, that either you or Colonel Mason would offer. I can be of little assistance to either, because I early laid it down as a maxim not to propose myself, and solicit for a second.

As to your political sentiments, I would heartily join you in them, so far as relates to a humble and dutiful petition to the throne, provided there was the most distant hope of success. But have we not tried this already? Have we not addressed the Lords, and remonstrated to the Commons? And to what end? Did they deign to look at our petitions? Does it not appear, as clear as the sun in its meridian brightness, that there is a regular, systematic plan formed to fix the right and practice of taxation upon us? Does not the uniform conduct of Parliament for some years past confirm this? Do not all the debates, especially those just brought to us, in the House of Commons on the side of government, expressly declare that America must be taxed in aid of the British funds, and that she has no longer resources within herself? Is there any thing to be expected from petitioning after this? Is not the attack upon the liberty and property of the people of Boston, before restitution of the loss to the India Company was demanded, a plain and self-evident proof of what they are aiming at? Do not the subsequent bills (now I dare say acts), for depriving the Massachusetts Bay of its charter, and for transporting offenders into other colonies or to Great Britain for trial, where it is impossible from the nature of the thing that justice can be obtained, convince us that the administration is determined to stick at nothing to carry its point? Ought we not, then, to put our virtue and fortitude to the severest test?

With you I think it a folly to attempt more than we can execute, as that will not only bring disgrace upon us, but weaken our cause; yet I think we may do more than is generally believed, in respect to the non-importation scheme. As to the withholding of our remittances, that is another point, in which I own I have my doubts on several accounts, but principally on that of justice; for I think, whilst we are accusing others of injustice, we should be just ourselves; and how this can be, whilst we owe a considerable debt, and refuse payment of it to Great Britain, is to me inconceivable. Nothing but the last extremity, I think, can justify it. Whether this is now come, is the question.

I began with telling you, that I was to write a short letter. My paper informs me I have done otherwise. I shall hope to see you to-morrow, at the meeting of the county in Alexandria, when these points are to be considered. I am, dear Sir, your most obedient and humble servant.

TO BRYAN FAIRFAX.

Mount Vernon, 20 July, 1774.

DEAR SIR,

Your letter of the 17th was not presented to me till after the resolutions, which were judged advisable for this county to adopt, had been revised, altered, and corrected in the committee; nor till we had gone into a general meeting in the court-house, and my attention was necessarily called every moment to the business before us.* I did, however, upon the receipt of it, in

* In conformity with the spirit and practice, which now began to prevail in different parts of the colonies, the inhabitants of Fairfax county had assembled, and appointed a committee for drawing up resolutions expressive of their sentiments on the great topics, which agitated the country. Washington was chairman of this committee, and moderator of the meetings held by the people. An able report was prepared by the committee,

that hurry and bustle, hastily run it over, and I handed it round to the gentlemen on the bench, of whom there were many; but, as no person present seemed in the least disposed to adopt your sentiments, as there appeared a perfect satisfaction and acquiescence in the measures proposed (except from Mr. Williamson, who was for adopting your advice literally, without obtaining a second voice on his side), and as the gentlemen, to whom the letter was shown, advised me not to have it read, as it was not likely to make a convert, and was repugnant, some of them thought, to every principle we were contending for, I forbore to offer it otherwise than in the manner abovementioned; which I shall be sorry for, if it gives you any dissatisfaction that your sentiments were not read to the county at large, instead of being communicated to the first people in it, by offering them the letter in the manner I did.

That I differ very widely from you, in respect to the mode of obtaining a repeal of the acts so much and so justly complained of, I shall not hesitate to acknowledge; and that this difference in opinion probably proceeds from the different constructions we put upon the conduct and intention of the ministry may also be true; but, as I see nothing, on the one hand, to induce a belief, that the Parliament would embrace a favorable opportunity of repealing acts, which they go on with great rapidity to pass, in order to enforce their tyrannical system; and, on the other, I observe, or think I observe, that government is pursuing a regular plan at the ex-

---

containing a series of resolutions, which were presented at a general meeting of the inhabitants at the court-house in Fairfax county on the 18th of July. See APPENDIX, No. IX.

Mr. Bryan Fairfax, who had been present on former occasions, not approving all the resolutions, absented himself from this meeting, and wrote a long letter to the chairman, stating his views and objections, with the request that it should be publicly read.

pense of law and justice to overthrow our constitutional rights and liberties, how can I expect any redress from a measure, which has been ineffectually tried already? For, Sir, what is it we are contending against? Is it against paying the duty of three pence per pound on tea because burthensome? No, it is the right only, that we have all along disputed; and to this end we have already petitioned his Majesty in as humble and dutiful a manner, as subjects could do. Nay, more, we applied to the House of Lords and House of Commons in their different legislative capacities, setting forth, that, as Englishmen, we could not be deprived of this essential and valuable part of our constitution. If, then, as the fact really is, it is against the right of taxation that we now do, and, as I before said, all along have contended, why should they suppose an exertion of this power would be less obnoxious now than formerly? And what reason have we to believe, that they would make a second attempt, whilst the same sentiments fill the breast of every American, if they did not intend to enforce it if possible? *

---

* Mr. Fairfax had written; — "I come now to consider a resolve, which ought to be the most objected to, as tending more to widen the breach, and prevent a reconciliation than any other. I mean that, wherein the authority of Parliament is almost in every instance denied. Something similar to this, though more imprudent, is the most exceptionable part of the conduct of some in New England. It has been asserted in the House of Commons, that America has been gradually encroaching; that, as they have given up points, we have insisted on more. The fact is true, as to encroachment, but the reason assigned is wrong. It is not because they have given up points, but because they have not given them up, that we out of resentment demand more than we at first thought of. But however natural it is for people incensed to increase their claims, and whatever our anger may induce us to say, in calm deliberations we should not insist on any thing unreasonable. We have all along submitted to the authority of Parliament. From the first settlement of the colonies I believe there never was an act of Parliament disputed, till the famous Stamp Act. It is a maxim in law, that all the acts made since the settlement of the colonies

The conduct of the Boston people could not justify the rigor of their measures, unless there had been a requisition of payment and refusal of it; nor did that conduct require an act to deprive the government of Massachusetts Bay of their charter, or to exempt offenders from trial in the places where offences were committed, as there was not, nor could there be, a single instance produced to manifest the necessity of it. Are not all these things evident proofs of a fixed and uniform plan to tax us? If we want further proofs, do not all the debates in the House of Commons serve to confirm this? And has not General Gage's conduct since his arrival, in stopping the address of his Council, and publishing a proclamation more becoming a Turkish bashaw, than an English governor, declaring it treason to associate in any manner by which the commerce of Great Britain is to be affected,—has not this exhibited an unexampled testimony of the most despotic system of

do not extend here, unless the colonies are particularly named; therefore all acts wherein they are included do extend here.

"When the Stamp Act was repealed, it was said, and I did not hear it contradicted, that the Americans objected to internal taxes, but not to external duties. When the duty on tea was laid, as an external duty, we objected to it, and with some reason, because it was not for the regulation of trade, but for the express purpose of raising a revenue. This was deemed a small encroachment on our first demands. Some now object to the authority, which has established and regulated the post-office, a very useful regulation. Others deny their authority in regard to our internal affairs. If we go on at this rate, it is impossible that the troubles of America should ever have an end. Whatever we may wish to be the case, it becomes good subjects to submit to the constitution of their country. Whenever a political establishment has been settled, it ought to be considered what that is, and not what it ought to be. To fix a contrary principle is to lay the foundation of continual broils and revolutions.

"The Parliament from prescription have a right to make laws binding on the colonies, except those imposing taxes. From prescription the Americans are exempt from taxation. Let us stand upon good ground in our opposition, otherwise many upon reflection may desert the cause. Therefore I hope some alteration will be made in the second resolve, or that nothing under this head will be mentioned."

tyranny, that ever was practised in a free government? In short, what further proofs are wanting to satisfy any one of the designs of the ministry, than their own acts, which are uniform and plainly tending to the same point, nay, if I mistake not, avowedly to fix the right of taxation? What hope have we then from petitioning, when they tell us, that now or never is the time to fix the matter? Shall we, after this, whine and cry for relief, when we have already tried it in vain? Or shall we supinely sit and see one province after another fall a sacrifice to despotism?

If I were in any doubt, as to the right which the Parliament of Great Britain had to tax us without our consent, I should most heartily coincide with you in opinion, that to petition, and petition only, is the proper method to apply for relief; because we should then be asking a favor, and not claiming a right, which, by the law of nature and by our constitution, we are, in my opinion, indubitably entitled to. I should even think it criminal to go further than this, under such an idea; but I have none such. I think the Parliament of Great Britain have no more right to put their hands into my pocket, without my consent, than I have to put my hands into yours; and this being already urged to them in a firm, but decent manner, by all the colonies, what reason is there to expect any thing from their justice?

As to the resolution for addressing the throne, I own to you, Sir, I think the whole might as well have been expunged. I expect nothing from the measure, nor should my voice have sanctioned it, if the non-importation scheme was intended to be retarded by it;* for I

---

* Among the Alexandria resolves, which were the subject of Mr. Fairfax's letter, there was one for petitioning the King. In relation to this, he wrote; — "I hope it will be recommended, that, if a petition should be agreed upon, and sent home by the general Congress, no conditional reso-

am convinced, as much as I am of my existence, that there is no relief for us but in their distress; and I think, at least I hope, that there is public virtue enough left among us to deny ourselves every thing but the bare necessaries of life to accomplish this end. This we have a right to do, and no power upon earth can compel us to do otherwise, till it has first reduced us to the most abject state of slavery. The stopping of our exports would, no doubt, be a shorter method than the other to effect this purpose; but if we owe money to Great Britain, nothing but the last necessity can justify the non-payment of it; and, therefore, I have great doubts upon this head, and wish to see the other method first tried, which is legal and will facilitate these payments.

I cannot conclude without expressing some concern, that I should differ so widely in sentiments from you, on a matter of such great moment and general import; and I should much distrust my own judgment upon the occasion, if my nature did not recoil at the thought of submitting to measures, which I think subversive of every thing that I ought to hold dear and valuable, and did I not find, at the same time, that the voice of mankind is with me. I must apologize for sending you so rough a

---

lution, which may be formed at the time, should be published until it is known, that the petition has had no effect. For we should otherwise destroy the very intention of it. To petition and to threaten at the same time seems to be inconsistent. It might be of service with the ministry, if they have evil designs, to know the dispositions of the people here. I am sure that sufficiently appears from what has already been published. And if that appears, no threatenings ought to accompany the petition. It ought to be as modest as possible, without descending to meanness. There is one expression, then, in one of our resolves, which I much object to; that is, a hint to the King, that, if his Majesty will not comply, there lies but one appeal. This ought surely to be erased. There are two methods proposed to effect a repeal; the one by petition, the other by compulsion. They ought then to be kept separate and distinct, and we shall find few for joining them together, who are not rather against the former."

sketch of my thoughts upon your letter. When I look back, and see the length of my own, I cannot, as I am a good deal hurried at this time, think of taking off a fair copy.

I am, dear Sir, your most obedient humble servant.

TO BRYAN FAIRFAX.

Mount Vernon, 24 August, 1774.

DEAR SIR,

Your letter of the 5th instant came to this place, forwarded by Mr. Ramsay, a few days after my return from Williamsburg,* and I delayed acknowledging it sooner, in the hope that I should find time, before I began my journey to Philadelphia, to answer it fully, if not satisfactorily; but, as much of my time has been

---

* In compliance with the recommendation of the deputies, who sent out a circular from Williamsburg on the 31st of May, town and county meetings had been held in all parts of the colony, and delegates chosen to assemble in convention at Williamsburg on the 1st of August. Washington was elected for Fairfax county, and was present at the Convention. By this body were appointed delegates to meet those from other colonies in a general congress at Philadelphia, in the September following. The persons selected were Peyton Randolph, Richard Henry Lee, George Washington, Patrick Henry, Richard Bland, Benjamin Harrison, and Edmund Pendleton. The other important acts of the Convention were the instructions to these deputies (Wirt's *Life of Patrick Henry*, p. 101), and a series of resolves put forth in the form of an *Association*. — Burk's *History of Virginia*, Vol. III. p. 382. These resolves are nearly the same in substance and temper as those, which had been adopted two weeks before in Fairfax county. After sitting six days the Convention broke up, having authorized the moderator, Peyton Randolph, to call the deputies together again on any occasion, which he might deem expedient.

According to Governor Hutchinson, the idea of a General Congress originated with Dr. Franklin, and was first suggested by him in a letter to the Massachusetts Assembly. — *History of Massachusetts*, Vol. III. p. 393. The date of this suggestion is not mentioned; but in the early part of the year 1774, the necessity of such a congress began to be a popular sentiment throughout all the colonies.

engrossed since I came home by company, by your brother's sale and the business consequent thereupon, in writing letters to England, and now in attending to my own domestic affairs previous to my departure, I find it impossible to bestow as much attention on the subject of your letter as I could wish, and, therefore, I must rely upon your good nature and candor in excuse for not attempting it.* In truth, persuaded as I am, that you have read all the political pieces, which compose a large share of the gazettes at this time, I should think it, but for your request, a piece of inexcusable arrogance in me, to make the least essay towards a change in your political opinions; for I am sure I have no new light to throw upon the subject, nor any other arguments to offer in support of my own doctrine, than what you have seen; and I could only in general add, that an innate spirit of freedom first told me, that the measures, which the administration have for some time been, and now are most violently pursuing, are opposed to every principle of natural justice; whilst much abler heads than my own have fully convinced me, that they are not only repugnant to natural right, but subversive of the laws and constitution of Great Britain itself, in the establishment of which some of the best blood in the kingdom has been spilt.

* In his last letter, Mr. Fairfax had taken a wide view of the subject, and requested a full reply. "I am uneasy to find," he says, "that any one should look upon the letter sent down, as repugnant to the principle we are contending for; and, therefore, when you have leisure, I shall take it as a favor if you will let me know wherein it was thought so. I beg leave to look upon you as a friend, and it is a great relief to unbosom one's thoughts to a friend. Besides, the information, and the correction of my errors, which I may obtain from a correspondence, are great inducements to it. For I am convinced, that no man in the colony wishes its prosperity more, would go greater lengths to serve it, or is at the same time a better subject to the crown. Pray excuse these compliments; they may be tolerable from a friend."

Satisfied, then, that the acts of the British Parliament are no longer governed by the principles of justice, that they are trampling upon the valuable rights of Americans, confirmed to them by charter and by the constitution they themselves boast of, and convinced beyond the smallest doubt, that these measures are the result of deliberation, and attempted to be carried into execution by the hand of power, is it a time to trifle, or risk our cause upon petitions, which with difficulty obtain access, and afterwards are thrown by with the utmost contempt? Or should we, because heretofore unsuspicious of design, and then unwilling to enter into disputes with the mother country, go on to bear more, and forbear to enumerate our just causes of complaint? For my own part, I shall not undertake to say where the line between Great Britain and the colonies should be drawn; but I am clearly of opinion, that one ought to be drawn, and our rights clearly ascertained. I could wish, I own, that the dispute had been left to posterity to determine, but the crisis is arrived when we must assert our rights, or submit to every imposition, that can be heaped upon us, till custom and use shall make us tame and abject slaves.

I intended to write no more than an apology for not writing; but I find I am insensibly running into a length I did not expect, and therefore shall conclude with remarking, that, if you disavow the right of Parliament to tax us, unrepresented as we are, we only differ in respect to the mode of opposition, and this difference principally arises from your belief, that they (the Parliament, I mean,) want a decent opportunity to repeal the acts; whilst I am fully convinced, that there has been a regular, systematic plan formed to enforce them, and that nothing but unanimity and firmness in the colonies, which they did not expect, can prevent it. By the best advices from Boston it seems, that General Gage is exceedingly disconcerted at the quiet and steady conduct of the people of the Massachusetts Bay, and at the measures pursuing by the other governments. I dare say he expected to force those oppressed people into compliance, or irritate them to acts of violence before this, for a more colorable pretence of ruling that and the other colonies with a high hand.

I shall set off on Wednesday next for Philadelphia, where, if you have any commands, I shall be glad to oblige you in them; being, dear Sir, with real regard,

Your most obedient servant.

P. S. Pray what do you think of the Canada Bill?

TO CAPTAIN ROBERT MACKENZIE.*

Philadelphia, 9 October, 1774.

DEAR SIR,

Your letter of the 13th ultimo from Boston gave me pleasure, as I learnt thereby, that you were well, and might be expected at Mount Vernon in your way to or from James River, in the course of the winter.

When I have said this, permit me with the freedom of a friend (for you know I always esteemed you) to

---

* Captain Mackenzie had been a captain of the Virginia regiment, commanded by Washington in the French War, and a friendly intimacy seems always to have subsisted between them. Mackenzie had obtained a commission in the regular army, and was now attached to the forty-third regiment of foot. He was wounded at the battle of Bunker's Hill, while fighting in that regiment. He wrote as follows to Washington from Boston, September 13th, 1774.

"Mr. Atcheson can sufficiently inform you of the state of this unhappy province, of their tyrannical oppression over one another, of their fixed aim at total independence, of the weakness and temper of the mainsprings that set the whole in motion, and how necessary it is, that abler heads and bet-

express my sorrow, that fortune should place you in a service, that must fix curses to the latest posterity upon the contrivers, and, if success (which, by the by, is impossible) accompanies it, execrations upon all those, who have been instrumental in the execution.

I do not mean by this to insinuate, that an officer is not to discharge his duty, even when chance, not choice, has placed him in a disagreeable situation; but I conceive, when you condemn the conduct of the Massachusetts people, you reason from effects, not causes; otherwise you would not wonder at a people, who are every day receiving fresh proofs of a systematic assertion of an arbitrary power, deeply planned to overturn the laws and constitution of their country, and to violate the most essential and valuable rights of mankind, being irritated, and with difficulty restrained from acts of the greatest violence and intemperance. For my own part, I confess to you candidly, that I view things in a very different point of light from the one in which you seem to consider them; and though you are led to believe by venal men,—for such I must take the liberty of calling those new-fangled counsellors, who fly to and surround you, and all others, who, for honors or pecuniary gratifications, will lend their aid to overturn the constitution, and introduce a system of arbitrary government,—although you are taught, I say, by discoursing with such

---

ter hearts should draw a line for their guidance. Even when this is done, it is much to be feared, that they will follow it no further, than it coincides with their present sentiments.

"Amidst all these jarrings we have until lately lived in a camp of pleasure; but the rebellious and numerous meetings of men in arms, their scandalous and ungenerous attacks upon the best characters in the province, obliging them to save themselves by flight, and their repeated but feeble threats to dispossess the troops, have furnished sufficient reasons to General Gage to put the town in a formidable state of defence, about which we are now fully employed, and which will be shortly accomplished to their great mortification."

men, to believe, that the people of Massachusetts are rebellious, setting up for independency, and what not, give me leave, my good friend, to tell you, that you are abused, grossly abused. This I advance with a degree of confidence and boldness, which may claim your belief, having better opportunities of knowing the real sentiments of the people you are among, from the leaders of them, in opposition to the present measures of the administration, than you have from those whose business it is, not to disclose truths, but to misrepresent facts in order to justify as much as possible to the world their own conduct.* Give me leave to add, and I think I can announce it as a fact, that it is not the wish or interest of that government, or any other upon this continent, separately or collectively, to set up for independence; but this you may at the same time rely on, that none of them will ever submit to the loss of those valuable rights and privileges, which are essential to the happiness of every free state, and without which, life, liberty, and property are rendered totally insecure.

These, Sir, being certain consequences, which must naturally result from the late acts of Parliament relative to America in general, and the government of Massachusetts Bay in particular, is it to be wondered at, I repeat, that men, who wish to avert the impending blow, should attempt to oppose it in its progress, or prepare for their defence, if it cannot be averted? Surely I may be allowed to answer in the negative; and again give me leave to add as my opinion, that more

* The writer being now at Philadelphia attending the first meeting of the Continental Congress, he alludes to his intercourse with the members from Massachusetts, and to his information derived from them. He seems to have taken pains to ascertain the impressions existing in different parts of the country, and to have cultivated an acquaintance with the delegates for that purpose. In his Diary, on the 28th of September, there is this entry; — "Spent the afternoon with the Boston gentlemen."

blood will be spilled on this occasion, if the ministry are determined to push matters to extremity, than history has ever yet furnished instances of in the annals of North America, and such a vital wound will be given to the peace of this great country, as time itself cannot cure, or eradicate the remembrance of.

But I have done. I was involuntarily led into a short discussion of this subject by your remarks on the conduct of the Boston people, and your opinion of their wishes to set up for independency. I am well satisfied, that no such thing is desired by any thinking man in all North America; on the contrary, that it is the ardent wish of the warmest advocates for liberty, that peace and tranquillity, upon constitutional grounds, may be restored, and the horrors of civil discord prevented.

I am very glad to learn, that my friend Stewart was well when you left London. I have not had a letter from him these five years, nor heard of him I think for two. I wish you had mentioned his employment.

I remain, dear Sir, your most obedient servant. *

TO JOHN WEST.

Mount Vernon, 13 January, 1775.

SIR,

Your letter of the 8th, which is just handed to me, could not have given you more pain in writing, than it has given me in reading, because I never deny or even hesitate in granting any request, that is made to me, especially by persons I esteem, and in matters of moment, without feeling inexpressible uneasiness. I do not wonder at your solicitude on account of your only son. The

---

* See APPENDIX, Nos. X. XI.

nurturing and bringing him up in a proper course is, no doubt, an object of great concern to you, as well as importance to him; but two things are essentially necessary in the man to whom this charge is committed, a capacity of judging with propriety of measures proper to be taken in the government of a youth, and leisure sufficient to attend to the execution of these measures. That you are pleased to think favorably of me, in respect to the first, I shall take for granted, from the request you have made; but to show my incapacity of attending to the latter, with that good faith, which I think every man ought to use, who undertakes a trust of this interesting nature, I can solemnly declare to you, that, for a year or two past, there has been scarce a moment, that I could properly call my own. What with my own business, my present ward's, my mother's, which is wholly in my hands, Colonel Colvill's, Mrs. Savage's, Colonel Fairfax's, Colonel Mercer's, and the little assistance I have undertaken to give in the management of my brother Augustine's concerns (for I have absolutely refused to qualify as an executor), together with the share I take in public affairs, I have been kept constantly engaged in writing letters, settling accounts, and negotiating one piece of business or another; by which means I have really been deprived of every kind of enjoyment, and had almost fully resolved to engage in no fresh matter, till I had entirely wound up the old.

Thus much, Sir, candor, indeed the principle of common honesty, obliged me to relate to you, as it is not my wish to deceive any person by promising what I do not think it in my power to perform with that punctuality and rectitude, which I conceive the nature of the trust would require. I do not, however, give a flat refusal to your request. I rather wish you to be fully informed of my situation, that you may think with me, or as I do, that, if it should please the Almighty to take you to himself so soon as you apprehend (but I hope without just cause), your son may be placed in better hands than mine. If you think otherwise, I will do the best I can, merely as a guardian.

You will act very prudently in having your will revised by some person skilled in the law, as a testator's intentions are often defeated by different interpretations of statutes, which require the whole business of a man's life to be perfectly conversant with them. I shall not, after what I have here said, add any thing more than my wishes, which are sincerely offered, for your recovery, and that you may live to see the accomplishment of your son's education. With very great esteem, Sir,

I am your most obedient humble servant.

TO JOHN AUGUSTINE WASHINGTON.

Richmond, 25 March, 1775.

Dear Brother,

Mr. Smith delivered me your letter of the 16th instant, but as one is generally in a hurry and bustle in such places, and at such times, as these, I have only time to acknowledge it, and add, that it would have given me pleasure to meet you here. I shall refer you to Mr. Smith for an account of our proceedings up to this day, and you cannot fail of learning the rest from the 'Squire, who delights in the minutiæ of a tale. I am in doubt whether we shall finish here this week; but as I shall delay little time on the road in returning, I shall hope to see you on your way up, or down, from Berkeley. I am much obliged to you for the holly-berries and cotton-seed. My love to my sister and the children.*

I had like to have forgotten to express my entire approbation of the laudable pursuit you are engaged in, of training an independent company. I have promised to review the independent company of Richmond some time this summer, they having made me a tender of the command of it. At the same time I could review yours, and shall very cheerfully accept the honor of commanding it, if occasion require it to be drawn out, as it is my full intention to devote my life and fortune in the cause we are engaged in, if needful.†

I remain, dear Sir, your most affectionate brother.

---

* Washington was now attending the second Virginia Convention, which met at Richmond on the 20th of March. At this Convention Patrick Henry introduced resolutions for putting the colony in a state of defence, and embodying, arming, and disciplining a sufficient number of men for that purpose. This was considered a bold measure, and was opposed by some of the ablest patriots in the Assembly. It was on this occasion, and in defence of his resolutions, that Mr. Henry uttered his memorable declaration;—"We must fight! I repeat it, Sir, we must fight! An appeal to arms and to the God of Hosts is all that is left to us!" The resolutions were carried, and a plan adopted for putting them in execution. Washington was one of the committee for drafting and reporting this plan.

The former deputies were reappointed to the next Continental Congress, Mr. Jefferson being substituted for Peyton Randolph, in case the latter should not be able to attend.

In connexion with the above declaration of Patrick Henry, it is proper to state, that the expression, "*We must fight*," was used four months previously by the ardent patriot Major Hawley of Massachusetts, in a letter to Mr. John Adams, which Mr. Adams showed to Mr. Henry while they were together in the first Congress.—Tudor's *Life of Otis*, p. 256.

† Soon after the war broke out, spurious letters were circulated in the name of Washington, tending to show, that he did not engage heartily in the cause of his country at the beginning of her complaints. These assertions were repeated and believed; they crept into history; they were revived by his political opponents, for no good purpose, near the close of his life. They do not require confutation. If they did, we need only refer to his letter to George Mason, dated April 5th, 1769; the Fairfax county resolves; his letters to Bryan Fairfax and Captain Mackenzie in 1774;

TO GEORGE WILLIAM FAIRFAX, ENGLAND.

Philadelphia, 31 May, 1775.*

DEAR SIR,

Before this letter will come to hand, you must undoubtedly have received an account of the engagement in the Massachusetts Bay, between the ministerial troops (for we do not, nor can we yet prevail upon ourselves to call them the King's troops), and the provincials of that government. But as you may not have heard how that affair began, I enclose you the several affidavits, which were taken after the action.

General Gage acknowledges, that the detachment under Lieutenant-Colonel Smith was sent out to destroy private property; or, in other words, to destroy a magazine, which self-preservation obliged the inhabitants to establish. And he also confesses, in effect at least, that his men made a very precipitate retreat from Concord, notwithstanding the reinforcement under Lord Percy; the last of which may serve to convince Lord Sandwich, and others of the same sentiment, that the Americans will fight for their liberties and property, however pusillanimous in his Lordship's eye they may appear in other respects.

From the best accounts I have been able to collect of that affair, indeed from every one, I believe the fact, stripped of all coloring, to be plainly this, that, if the retreat had not been as precipitate as it was, and God knows it could not well have been more so, the ministerial troops must have surrendered, or been totally cut off. For they had not arrived in Charlestown (under

---

the above letter to his brother; and the uniform tenor of his conduct. See APPENDIX, No. XII.

* Washington was now attending the second Continental Congress, which assembled in Philadelphia on the 10th of May.

cover of their ships) half an hour, before a powerful body of men from Marblehead and Salem was at their heels, and must, if they had happened to be up one hour sooner, inevitably have intercepted their retreat to Charlestown. Unhappy it is, though, to reflect, that a brother's sword has been sheathed in a brother's breast, and that the once happy and peaceful plains of America are either to be drenched with blood, or inhabited by slaves. Sad alternative! But can a virtuous man hesitate in his choice?

I am with sincere regard, and affectionate compliments to Mrs. Fairfax, dear Sir, your &c.

APPENDIX.

APPENDIX.

No. I. p. 1.

WASHINGTON'S EARLY PAPERS.

Among the earliest papers, found in the archives at Mount Vernon, were the fragments of manuscripts written by Washington during his boyhood and youth. These are chiefly confined to his school exercises in arithmetic and geometry, and are of little value. They are remarkable only for the neatness of the handwriting, a beautiful method, accuracy in drawing the geometrical figures, and as indicating the strong bent of his inclination to mathematical studies. Some of his original field-books, and a brief journal of one of his expeditions as a surveyor of lands, are also preserved. A few short extracts from these papers may not be amiss, as showing the turn of his mind in early youth, and other traits in some degree characteristic.

The first manuscript in the order of dates was written when he was thirteen years old, filling thirty folio pages, and entitled "*Forms of Writing*." It consists for the most part of forms used in the various transactions of business, such as a note of hand, bill of exchange, bond, indenture, lease, and will, copied out with much exactness and care. Then follow two or three poetical selections, among which are lines on *True Happiness*, abounding more in sentiment than poetry. But the most curious piece in the manuscript is a series of maxims, under the head of "*Rules of Civility and Decent Behaviour in Company and Conversation*." One hundred and ten rules are here written out and numbered. The source from which they were derived is not mentioned. They form a minute code of regulations for building up the habits of morals, manners, and good conduct in a very young person. A few specimens will be enough to show their general complexion; and whoever has studied the character of Washington will be persuaded, that some of its most prominent features took their shape from these rules thus early selected and adopted as his guide.

"1. Every action in company ought to be with some sign of respect to those present.

"2. In the presence of others sing not to yourself with a humming noise, nor drum with your fingers or feet.

"3. Sleep not when others speak, sit not when others stand, speak not when you should hold your peace, walk not when others stop.

"4. Turn not your back to others, especially in speaking; jog not the table or desk on which another reads or writes; lean not on any one.

"5. Be no flatterer; neither play with any one, that delights not to be played with.

"6. Read no letters, books, or papers in company; but when there is a necessity for doing it, you must ask leave. Come not near the books or writings of any one so as to read them, unless desired, nor give your opinion of them unasked; also, look not nigh when another is writing a letter.

"7. Let your countenance be pleasant, but in serious matters somewhat grave.

"8. Show not yourself glad at the misfortune of another, though he were your enemy.

"9. When you meet with one of greater quality than yourself, stop and retire, especially if it be at a door or any strait place, to give way for him to pass.

"10. They that are in dignity, or in office, have in all places precedency; but whilst they are young they ought to respect those that are their equals in birth, or other qualities, though they have no public charge.

"11. It is good manners to prefer them to whom we speak before ourselves, especially if they be above us, with whom in no sort we ought to begin.

"12. Let your discourse with men of business be short and comprehensive.

"13. In visiting the sick, do not presently play the physician, if you be not knowing therein.

"14. In writing, or speaking, give to every person his due title, according to his degree and the custom of the place.

"15. Strive not with your superiors in argument, but always submit your judgment to others with modesty.

"16. Undertake not to teach your equal in the art himself professes; it savours of arrogancy.

"17. When a man does all he can, though it succeeds not well, blame not him that did it.

"18. Being to advise, or reprehend any one, consider whether it ought to be in public or in private, presently or at some other time, in what terms to do it; and in reproving show no signs of choler, but do it with sweetness and mildness.

"19. Take all admonitions thankfully, in what time or place soever given; but afterwards, not being culpable, take a time or place convenient to let him know it that gave them.

"20. Mock not, nor jest at any thing of importance; break no jests that are sharp-biting, and if you deliver any thing witty, and pleasant, abstain from laughing thereat yourself.

"21. Wherein you reprove another be unblamable yourself; for example is more prevalent than precepts.

"22. Use no reproachful language against any one, neither curse, nor revile.

"23. Be not hasty to believe flying reports to the disparagement of any.

"24. In your apparel, be modest, and endeavour to accommodate nature, rather than to procure admiration; keep to the fashion of your equals, such as are civil and orderly with respect to times and places.

"25. Play not the peacock, looking every where about you to see if you be well decked, if your shoes fit well, if your stockings sit neatly, and clothes handsomely.

"26. Associate yourself with men of good quality, if you esteem your own reputation, for it is better to be alone, than in bad company.

"27. Let your conversation be without malice or envy, for it is a sign of a tractable and commendable nature; and in all causes of passion, admit reason to govern.

"28. Be not immodest in urging your friend to discover a secret.

"29. Utter not base and frivolous things amongst grave and learned men; nor very difficult questions or subjects among the ignorant; nor things hard to be believed.

"30. Speak not of doleful things in time of mirth, nor at the table; speak not of melancholy things, as death, and wounds, and if others mention them, change, if you can, the discourse. Tell not your dreams, but to your intimate friend.

"31. Break not a jest where none takes pleasure in mirth; laugh not aloud, nor at all without occasion. Deride no man's misfortune, though there seem to be some cause.

"32. Speak not injurious words neither in jest nor earnest; scoff at none, although they give occasion.

"33. Be not forward, but friendly and courteous; the first to salute, hear, and answer; and be not pensive when it is a time to converse.

"34. Detract not from others, neither be excessive in commending.

"35. Go not thither, where you know not whether you shall be welcome or not. Give not advice without being asked, and when desired, do it briefly.

"36. If two contend together take not the part of either unconstrained, and be not obstinate in your own opinion; in things indifferent be of the major side.

"37. Reprehend not the imperfections of others, for that belongs to parents, masters, and superiors.

"38. Gaze not on the marks or blemishes of others, and ask not how they came. What you may speak in secret to your friend, deliver not before others.

"39. Speak not in an unknown tongue in company, but in your own language, and that as those of quality do, and not as the vulgar; sublime matters treat seriously.

"40. Think before you speak, pronounce not imperfectly, nor bring out your words too hastily, but orderly and distinctly.

"41. When another speaks, be attentive yourself, and disturb not the audience. If any hesitate in his words, help him not, nor prompt him without being desired; interrupt him not, nor answer him, till his speech be ended.

"42. Treat with men at fit times about business, and whisper not in the company of others.

"43. Make no comparisons, and if any of the company be commended for any brave act of virtue, commend not another for the same.

"44. Be not apt to relate news, if you know not the truth thereof. In discoursing of things you have heard, name not your author always. A secret discover not.

"45. Be not curious to know the affairs of others, neither approach to those that speak in private.

"46. Undertake not what you cannot perform, but be careful to keep your promise.

"47. When you deliver a matter, do it without passion, and with discretion, however mean the person be you do it to.

"48. When your superiors talk to any body, hearken not, neither speak, nor laugh.

"49. In disputes be not so desirous to overcome, as not to give liberty to each one to deliver his opinion, and submit to the judgment of the major part, especially if they are judges of the dispute.

"50. Be not tedious in discourse; make not many digressions, nor repeat often the same manner of discourse.

"51. Speak not evil of the absent, for it is unjust.

"52. Make no show of taking great delight in your victuals; feed not with greediness; cut your bread with a knife; lean not on the table; neither find fault with what you eat.

"53. Be not angry at table, whatever happens, and if you have reason to be so, show it not; put on a cheerful countenance, especially if there be strangers, for good humor makes one dish of meat a feast.

"54. Set not yourself at the upper end of the table; but if it be your due, or that the master of the house will have it so, contend not, lest you should trouble the company.

"55. When you speak of God, or his attributes, let it be seriously in reverence. Honor and obey your natural parents, although they be poor.

"56. Let your recreations be manful, not sinful.

"57. Labor to keep alive in your breast that little spark of celestial fire, called conscience."

The list might be extended, but these specimens will answer the purpose here designed, which is to indicate the sources of some of the impressions, that contributed to form the character of Washington.

His military propensities early discovered themselves, and at the age of fourteen he was seized with a desire to enter the navy. His brother Lawrence, who was himself a military man, approved this choice, and procured for him a midshipman's warrant. At first his mother seemed to consent, though reluctantly, to this project; but as the time of separation approached, her maternal feelings, and more mature reflection, caused her to waver in her decision, and finally to oppose the wishes of her son and his friends. The following is an extract from a letter written to Lawrence Washington by his father-in-law, William Fairfax, and dated September 10th, 1746.

"George has been with us, and says he will be steady, and thankfully follow your advice as his best friend. I gave him his mother's letter to deliver, with a caution not to show his. I have spoken to

Dr. Spencer, who I find is often at the widow's [Mrs. Washington's], and has some influence, to persuade her to think better of your advice in putting George to sea with good recommendations."

The following extract, on the same subject, was written by Mr. Robert Jackson to Lawrence Washington, and dated at Fredericksburg, October 18th, 1746.

"I am afraid Mrs. Washington will not keep up to her first resolution. She seems to intimate a dislike to George's going to sea, and says several persons have told her it was a bad scheme. She offers several trifling objections, such as fond, unthinking mothers habitually suggest; and I find that one word against his going has more weight than ten for it. Colonel Fairfax seems desirous he should go, and wished me to acquaint you with Mrs. Washington's sentiments. I intend shortly to take an opportunity to talk with her, and will let you know the result."

These are the only written facts, which I have found, relating to this incident in the life of Washington. It is known, that his mother's opposition continued, and that on this account the plan of his going to sea was abandoned. The feelings of the mother will not be thought unnatural, or unreasonable, when it is remembered, that he was her eldest son, that his father had been dead three years and a half, and that she was left with four younger children.

His predilection for mathematical studies made him soon acquainted with the art of surveying lands, and he became a practical surveyor at the age of sixteen. He went into the woods upon a surveying tour among the Allegany mountains, accompanied by Mr. George Fairfax, in March, 1748, being then but just sixteen years old. He kept a rough journal, or diary, from which the following extracts are taken.

"*March 13th.* — Rode to his Lordship's [Lord Fairfax's] quarter. About four miles higher up the river Shenandoah we went through most beautiful groves of sugar trees, and spent the best part of the day in admiring the trees and richness of the land.

"*14th.* — We sent our baggage to Captain Hite's, near Fredericktown [afterwards Winchester], and went ourselves down the river about sixteen miles, (the land exceedingly rich all the way, producing abundance of grain, hemp, and tobacco,) in order to lay off some land on Cate's Marsh and Long Marsh.

"*15th.* — Worked hard till night, and then returned. After supper we were lighted into a room, and I, not being so good a woodsman as the rest, stripped myself very orderly, and went into the bed, as they called it, when to my surprise I found it to be nothing but a little straw matted together, without sheet or any thing else but only one threadbare blanket, with double its weight of vermin. I was glad to get up, and put on my clothes, and lie as my companions did. Had we not been very tired, I am sure we should not have slept much that night. I made a promise to sleep so no more, choosing rather to sleep in the open air before a fire.

"*18th.*—We travelled to Thomas Berwick's on the Potomac, where we found the river exceedingly high, by reason of the great rains that had fallen among the Alleganies. They told us it would not be fordable for several days, it being now six feet higher than usual, and rising. We agreed to stay till Monday. We this day called to see the famed Warm Springs.* We camped out in the field this night.

"*20th.*—Finding the river not much abated, we in the evening swam our horses over to the Maryland side.

"*21st.*—We went over in a canoe, and travelled up the Maryland side all day in a continued rain to Colonel Cresap's, over against the mouth of the South Branch, about forty miles from our place of starting in the morning, and over the worst road I believe that ever was trod by man or beast.

"*23d.*—Rained till about two o'clock, and then cleared up, when we were agreeably surprised at the sight of more than thirty Indians coming from war with only one scalp. We had some liquor with us, of which we gave them a part. This, elevating their spirits, put them in the humor of dancing. We then had a war-dance. After clearing a large space and making a great fire in the middle, the men seated themselves around it, and the speaker made a grand speech, telling them in what manner they were to dance. After he had finished, the best dancer jumped up, as one awaked from sleep, and ran and jumped about the ring in a most comical manner. He was followed by the rest. Then began their music, which was performed with a pot half full of water and a deerskin stretched tight over it, and a gourd with some shot in it to rattle, and a piece of horse's tail tied to it to make it look fine. One person kept rattling and another drumming all the while they were dancing.

"*25th.*—Left Cresap's, and went up to the mouth of Patterson's Creek. There we swam our horses over the Potomac, and went over ourselves in a canoe, and travelled fifteen miles where we camped.

---

* The mineral springs at Bath, in Virginia, afterwards and at the present day the resort of many visiters in the summer season.

"*26th.*—Travelled up to Solomon Hedge's, *Esquire*, one of *his Majesty's justices of the peace* in the county of Frederic, where we camped. When we came to supper, there was neither a knife on the table, nor a fork to eat with; but, as good luck would have it, we had knives of our own.

"*28th.*—Travelled up the South Branch (having come to that river yesterday), about thirty miles to Mr. J. R.'s (horse-jockey), and about seventy miles from the mouth of the river.

"*29th.*—This morning went out and surveyed five hundred acres of land. Shot two wild turkeys.

"*30th.*—Began our intended business of laying off lots.

"*April 2d.*—A blowing, rainy night. Our straw, upon which we were lying, took fire, but I was luckily preserved by one of our men awaking when it was in a flame. We have run off four lots this day.

"*4th.*—This morning Mr. Fairfax left us, with the intention to go down to the mouth of the river. We surveyed two lots, and were attended with a great company of people, men, women, and children, who followed us through the woods, showing their antic tricks. They seem to be as ignorant a set of people as the Indians. They would never speak English; but when spoken to they all spoke Dutch. This day our tent was blown down by the violence of the wind.

"*6th.*—The last night was so intolerably smoky, that we were obliged to leave our tent to the mercy of the wind and fire. Attended this day by the aforesaid company.

"*7th.*—This morning one of our men killed a wild turkey, that weighed twenty pounds. We surveyed fifteen hundred acres of land, and returned to Vanmeter's about one o'clock. I took my horse and went up to see Mr. Fairfax. We slept in Cassey's house, which was the first night I had slept in a house since we came to the Branch.

"*8th.*—We breakfasted at Cassey's, and rode down to Vanmeter's to get our company together, which when we had accomplished, we rode down below the *Trough* to lay off lots there. The *Trough* is a couple of ledges of mountains impassable, running side by side for seven or eight miles, and the river between them. You must ride round the back of the mountains to get below them. We camped in the woods, and after we had pitched our tent, and made a large fire, we pulled out our knapsack to recruit ourselves. Every one was his own cook. Our spits were forked sticks; our plates were large chips. As for dishes we had none.

"*10th.*—We took our farewell of the Branch and travelled over hills and mountains to Coddy's on Great Cacapehon about forty miles.

"12*th*. — Mr. Fairfax got safe home, and I to my brother's house at Mount Vernon, which concludes my journal."

In the little volume, which contains this journal, are the rough drafts of letters written during the same period. They are imperfect, and of very little importance. One of them is descriptive of his adventures.

"DEAR RICHARD,

"The receipt of your kind favor of the 2d instant afforded me unspeakable pleasure, as it convinces me that I am still in the memory of so worthy a friend, — a friendship I shall ever be proud of increasing. Yours gave me the more pleasure, as I received it among barbarians and an uncouth set of people. Since you received my letter of October last, I have not slept above three or four nights in a bed, but, after walking a good deal all the day, I have lain down before the fire upon a little hay, straw, fodder, or a bearskin, whichever was to be had, with man, wife, and children, like dogs and cats; and happy is he, who gets the berth nearest the fire. Nothing would make it pass off tolerably but a good reward. A doubloon is my constant gain every day, that the weather will permit of my going out, and sometimes six pistoles. The coldness of the weather will not allow of my making a long stay, as the lodging is rather too cold for the time of year. I have never had my clothes off, but have lain and slept in them, except the few nights I have been in Frederictown."

From the tenor of two or three of the letters it would appear, that the charms of some beauty among his acquaintances had made an early assault upon the heart of the young hero.

"DEAR FRIEND ROBIN,

"As it is the greatest mark of friendship and esteem, which absent friends can show each other, to write and often communicate their thoughts, I shall endeavour from time to time, and at all times, to acquaint you with my situation and employments in life, and I could wish you would take half the pains to send me a letter by any opportunity, as you may be well assured of its meeting with a very welcome reception.

"My place of residence at present is at his Lordship's [Lord Fairfax's], where I might, were my heart disengaged, pass my time very pleasantly, as there is a very agreeable young lady in the same house, Colonel George Fairfax's wife's sister. But that only adds fuel to the fire, as being often and unavoidably in company with her revives my former passion for your Lowland beauty; whereas, were I to live more retired from young women, I might in some measure alleviate my sorrow, by burying that chaste and troublesome passion in oblivion; and I am very well assured, that this will be the only antidote or remedy."

The desponding tone of this letter is reiterated in others. How long the tender sentiment had possession of his heart, or whether he ever had the courage to explain himself to the young lady, is not ascertained. For three years he was occupied nearly all the time, when the season would permit, in surveying wild lands among the Allegany mountains in Virginia, and on the various southern branches of the Potomac River. His mode of life in this occupation may be understood from the above extracts from his journal. It was exposed to peculiar hardships and privations, with none of the refinements or comforts of civilization. The country was an entire wilderness. The fatigue and endurance were such, that he was rarely out but a few weeks at a time. His home was with his brother, Lawrence Washington, at Mount Vernon, though he passed portions of his time with his mother at Fredericksburg.

The following letter, dated the 5th of May, 1749, was written to his brother Lawrence, then in Williamsburg, probably attending as a member of the House of Burgesses, as it is known, that he was a delegate for that year.

"DEAR BROTHER,

"I hope your cough is much mended since I saw you last. If so, I trust you have given over all thoughts of leaving Virginia. As there is not an absolute occasion of my coming down, I hope you will get the deeds acknowledged without me. My horse is in very poor order to undertake such a journey, and is in no likelihood of mending, for want of corn sufficient to support him; though if there be any certainty of the Assembly's not rising until the latter end of May, I will, if I can, be down by that time.

"As my mother's term of years is out at the place at Bridge Creek, she designs to settle a quarter * on the piece at Deep Run, but seems backward in doing it, till the right is made good, for fear of accident. It is reported here, that Mr. Spotswood intends to put down the ferry at the wharf where he now lives, and that Major Francis Taliaferro intends to petition the Assembly to have it kept from his house over against my mother's quarter, and through the very heart and best of the land. Whereas he can have no other view in it, than for the

* Place of residence for the families of negro laborers.

convenience of a small mill, which he has on the water-side, that will not grind above three months in the twelve, and on account of the great inconvenience and prejudice it will be to us, I hope it will not be granted. Besides, I do not see where he can possibly have a landing-place on his side, that will ever be sufficient for a lawful landing, by reason of the steepness of the banks. I think we suffer enough from the free ferry, without being troubled with such an unjust and iniquitous petition as that; but I hope, as it is only a flying report, that he will consider better of it, and drop his pretensions.

"I shall be glad, if it is not too much trouble, to hear from you. In the mean time I remain, with my love to my sister, dear Sir, your affectionate brother."

George was so much indebted on many accounts to his brother Lawrence, that it is proper in this place to bestow upon this brother the tribute of a passing notice. The father, whose name was Augustine Washington, was twice married, first to Jane Butler, and afterwards to Mary Ball. The fruit of the first marriage was three sons and a daughter; and, of the second, four sons and two daughters. The eldest son by the first marriage was called Butler, who died young. Lawrence was the second son, and was born about the year 1718. George was the eldest son by the second marriage. Dr. Burnaby, in the appendix to the third edition of his *Travels in America*, says that Lawrence was educated in England. However this may be, it is evident from several of his manuscript letters, which I have seen, that he was a gentleman of a good education and of highly respectable parts. He joined the army, and received a captain's commission, dated June 9th, 1740. He was assigned to a company in a regiment to be raised in America, under the command of Colonel Alexander Spotswood, designed for the West India service, and to act in the Spanish war. The regiment was transported to Jamaica early in 1741, where it was united with the British forces in time to take a part in the unsuccessful siege of Carthagena, conducted by Admiral Vernon and General Wentworth, in March of that year. After the failure of the expedition the fleet sailed back to Jamaica, where the land forces were stationed, except during a few months in the summer season, when for reasons not known they were taken to Cuba. Captain Washington returned to Virginia near the close of the year 1742, having been absent about two years.

At this time he had an intention of joining his regiment in England, with the view of seeking promotion in the army, where he had good hopes of success under the friendly auspices of General Wentworth. But as he soon afterwards married Anne Fairfax, daughter of William Fairfax, and a relative of Lord Fairfax, he changed his mind, and resolved to abandon the army. Meantime his father died, April 12th, 1743, leaving him, as the eldest son then living, in charge of his estate and family. He had already obtained the post of adjutant, a colonial appointment of some consideration, from which he derived the rank of major, and the more substantial remuneration of one hundred and fifty pounds a year. When the officers of his regiment obtained a grant of half-pay in England, he declined receiving it, on the ground that he could not conscientiously take the oath required, while he held the adjutancy in Virginia. He inherited an estate on the banks of the Potomac, which he called Mount Vernon, in honor of Admiral Vernon, and here he resided during the remainder of his life. His time was chiefly devoted to his private affairs, as the duties of his adjutancy were only occasional and at stated periods. He was a member of the Virginia House of Burgesses, and likewise a principal agent in forming the Ohio Company.

Naturally of a delicate constitution, his health began to decline soon after his return from the military expedition to the West Indies, till at length it was assailed by a consumption, which made rapid and fatal ravages. By the advice of his physicians he went to England, hoping to derive benefit from the voyage, but he returned in a few months without essential relief. For the same object he passed a summer, but with little advantage, at the Bath Springs, in Virginia, then surrounded by a wilderness. A voyage to the West Indies was the last remedy, and he sailed for Barbadoes on the 28th of September, 1751, and arrived there about the 3d of November. His brother George, to whom he was much attached, accompanied him on this voyage. A few weeks after his arrival in Barbadoes, he wrote as follows to Lord Fairfax.

"This climate has not afforded the relief I expected from it, so that I have almost determined to try the Bermudas on my return, and, if it does not do, the dry air of Frederic. This is the finest island of the West Indies, but I own no place can please me without a change of seasons. We soon tire of the same prospect. Our bodies are too much relaxed, and require a winter to brace them up. However, some of the country gentlemen look well, and live to a reasonable age. We have no kind of bodily diversions but dancing, which frequently produces yellow fever. I am obliged to ride out by the first dawn of the day, for by the time the sun is half an hour high, it is as hot as at any time of the day. The gentlemen are very polite and hospitable."

Having spent the winter at Barbadoes, he went to Bermuda in

March, 1752, his brother George in the mean time having sailed for Virginia. On the 6th of April he wrote from Bermuda to a friend;

"I have now got to my last refuge, where I must receive my final sentence, which at present Dr. Forbes will not pronounce. He leaves me, however, I think, like a criminal condemned, though not without hopes of a reprieve. But this I am to obtain by meritoriously abstaining from flesh of every sort, all strong liquors, and by riding as much as I can bear through several parts of the island. These are the only terms on which I am to hope for life. My doctor is an excellent guide for me to follow, who, by a perseverance in a milk diet, has restored his constitution from a most desperate state. These are hard terms, but what he further adds is still worse, that, let me receive what benefit I may from this climate, the next winter in Virginia will not only render it of no service, but will most certainly destroy me, the truth of which assertion I am too well convinced of, by coming here too soon; for though I was much mended and had lost some of the worst symptoms of my disorder, yet the air being very keen brought all on again in a worse degree than ever, and so they yet continue. As my endeavour to overcome this cruel disorder has already cost me much money and fatigue, I should unwillingly give over the pursuit whilst any just foundation for hope remains. Six weeks will determine me what to resolve on. Forbes advises the south of France, or else Barbadoes."

In the same letter he expressed a strong wish, that his wife would come to him, as he thought, in any event, that he should remain there at least a year. He proposed, that George should accompany her to Bermuda, but he did not insist on her undertaking this voyage, leaving it to the decision of herself and her friends. It would seem, however, that his health was not restored, in the degree he had anticipated. He soon wrote again,—"The unhappy state of health, which I labor under, makes me uncertain as to my return. If I grow worse, I shall hurry home to my grave; if better, I shall be induced to stay longer here to complete a cure." All his hopes were fallacious. Although his disorder sometimes put on a more flattering aspect, and inspired a momentary confidence, yet it was gradually making its encroachments with a sure and deadly progress. He hastened back to Virginia, and arrived only in time to receive the last melancholy greetings of his friends. He died in his own house at Mount Vernon, July 26th, 1752, at the age of thirty-four, and his remains were deposited in the same vault, in which were afterwards entombed those of his illustrious brother.

George kept a journal of his voyage to Barbadoes and back, and during his short residence on the island; but time and accident have made such breaches in the manuscript, that little can now be gathered from it. Among other particulars he entered each day an exact copy of the log-book, with his own remarks on the weather, winds, and nautical occurrences. A few extracts from his journal, while he was at Barbadoes, may not be uninteresting.

"*November 4th*, 1751.—This morning received a card from Major Clarke, welcoming us to Barbadoes, with an invitation to breakfast and dine with him. We went,—myself with some reluctance, as the smallpox was in his family. We were received in the most kind and friendly manner by him. Mrs. Clarke was much indisposed, insomuch that we had not the pleasure of her company, but in her place officiated Miss Roberts, her niece, and an agreeable young lady. After drinking tea we were again invited to Mr. Carter's, and desired to make his house ours till we could provide lodgings agreeable to our wishes, which offer we accepted.

"*5th.*—Early this morning came Dr. Hilary, an eminent physician recommended by Major Clarke, to pass his opinion on my brother's disorder, which he did in a favorable light, giving great assurances that it was not so fixed but that a cure might be effectually made. In the cool of the evening we rode out accompanied by Mr. Carter to seek lodgings in the country, as the Doctor advised, and were perfectly enraptured with the beautiful prospects, which every side presented to our view,—the fields of cane, corn, fruit-trees, &c. in a delightful green. We returned without accomplishing our intentions.

"*7th.*—Dined with Major Clarke, and by him was introduced to the Surveyor-General and the Judges, who likewise dined there. In the evening they complaisantly accompanied us in another excursion into the country to choose lodgings. We pitched on the house of Captain Croftan, commander of James's Fort. He was desired to come to town next day to propose his terms. We returned by the way of Needham's Fort.

"*8th.*—Came Captain Croftan with his proposals, which, though extravagantly dear, my brother was obliged to accept. Fifteen pounds a month were his terms, exclusive of liquor and washing, which we find. In the evening we removed some of our things up, and went ourselves. It is very pleasantly situated near the sea, and about a mile from town. The prospect is extensive by land and pleasant by sea, as we command a view of Carlyle Bay and the shipping.

"*9th.*—Received a card from Major Clarke, inviting us to dine with him at Judge Maynard's to-morrow. He had a right to ask, being a member of a club called the *Beef-steak and Tripe*, instituted by himself.

"*10th.* — We were genteelly received by Judge Maynard and his lady, and agreeably entertained by the company. They have a meeting every Saturday, this being Judge Maynard's day. After dinner there was the greatest collection of fruits set on the table, that I have yet seen, — the granadilla, sapadilla, pomegranate, sweet orange, water-lemon, forbidden fruit, apples, guavas, &c. &c. We received invitations from every gentleman there. Mr. Warren desired Major Clarke to show us the way to his house. Mr. Hacket insisted on our coming Saturday next to his, it being his day to treat with beef-steak and tripe. But, above all, the invitation of Mr. Maynard was most kind and friendly. He desired, and even insisted, as well as his lady, on our coming to spend some weeks with him, and promised nothing should be wanting to render our stay agreeable. My brother promised he would accept the invitation, as soon as he should be a little disengaged from the doctors.

"*15th.* — Was treated with a ticket to see the play of *George Barnwell* acted. The character of Barnwell and several others were said to be well performed. There was music adapted and regularly conducted.

"*17th.* — Was strongly attacked with the smallpox. Sent for Dr Lanahan, whose attendance was very constant till my recovery and going out, which were not till Thursday the 12th of December.

"*December 12th.* — Went to town and called on Major Clarke's family, who had kindly visited me in my illness, and contributed all they could in sending me the necessaries, which the disorder required. On Monday last began the grand session, and this day was brought on the trial of Colonel C., a man of opulent fortune and infamous character. He was brought in guiltless, and saved by a single evidence, who was generally reckoned to have been suborned.

"*22d.* — Took leave of my brother, Major Clarke, and others, and embarked on board the *Industry* for Virginia. Weighed anchor and got out of Carlyle Bay about twelve o'clock.

"The Governor of Barbadoes seems to keep a proper state, lives very retired and at little expense, and is a gentleman of good sense. As he avoids the errors of his predecessor, he gives no handle for complaint; but, at the same time, by declining much familiarity, he is not over-zealously beloved.

"There are several singular risings in this island one above another, so that scarcely any part is deprived of a beautiful prospect, both of sea and land; and, what is contrary to observation in other countries, each elevation is better than the next below. There are many delicious fruits, but as they are particularly described by Mr. Hughes, in his Natural History of the Island, I shall say nothing further, than that the China orange is good. The avagavo pear is generally most admired, though none pleases my taste so well as the pine. The earth in most parts is extremely rich, and as black as our richest marsh meadows. The common produce of the cane is from forty to seventy polls of sugar, each poll valued at twenty shillings, out of which a third is deducted for expenses. Many acres last year produced in value from one hundred and forty to one hundred and seventy pounds, as I was informed by credible authority, though that was in ginger, and a very extraordinary year for the sale of that article. How wonderful that such people should be in debt, and not be able to indulge themselves in all the luxuries as well as necessaries of life. Yet so it happens. Estates are often alienated for debts. How persons coming to estates of two, three, and four hundred acres (which are the largest), can want, is to me most wonderful. One third of their land, or nearly that portion, is generally in train for harvest. The rest is in young cane, Guinea corn (which greatly supports their negroes), yams, plantains, potatoes, and the like, and some small part left waste for stock. Provisions are generally very indifferent, but much better than the same quantity of pasturage would afford in Virginia. The very grass, that grows among their corn, is not lost, but carefully gathered for provender for their stock.

"Hospitality and a genteel behaviour are shown to every gentleman stranger by the gentlemen inhabitants. Taverns they have none, except in the towns; so that travellers are obliged to go to private houses. The people are said to live to a great age where they are not intemperate. They are, however, very unhappy in regard to their officers' fees, which are not paid by any law. They complain particularly of the provost-marshal, or sheriff-general, of the island, patented at home and rented at eight hundred pounds a year. Every other officer is exorbitant in his demands. There are few, who may be called middling people. They are very rich or very poor; for by a law of the island every gentleman is obliged to keep a white person for every ten acres, capable of acting in the militia, and consequently the persons so kept cannot but be very poor. They are well disciplined, and appointed to their several stations; so that in any alarm every man may be at his post in less than two hours. They have large intrenchments cast up wherever it is possible to land, and, as nature has greatly assisted, the island may not improperly be said to be one entire fortification."

These remarks were made on his departure from Barbadoes. He arrived in Virginia about the 1st of February, 1752, after a tempestuous passage of more than five weeks. At the time of his brother's death he was at Mount Vernon, and the care and immediate affairs of the family devolved on him. That place continued to be his residence, till he was called from home by public duties. Lawrence Washington left an only child, a daughter, who deceased at an early age, having been sickly from her birth. The widow married George Lee, and the estate at Mount Vernon became the property of George Washington, as an inheritance from his brother, who, from the time of his father's death, had shown for him a parental as well as fraternal attachment, and rendered him many services of kindness and affection. Mrs. Lee died on the 19th of November, 1761. Judge Marshall says, that George received an appointment as one of the adjutants-general of Virginia, in the year 1751, with the rank of major, when he was yet only nineteen years old. This post was probably obtained through the influence of his brother. After Governor Dinwiddie came to Virginia, the colony was divided into four military districts, and an adjutant assigned to each. George Washington's appointment was then renewed (November, 1753), and he was stationed over the northern district. The duties consisted in exercising the officers, and inspecting the militia at stated times, in the manner prescribed by law.

Intelligence had been received, from time to time, that the French were making encroachments on what was deemed British territory beyond the Allegany mountains. Messengers were sent out for observation and inquiry, who had brought back various reports, and particularly that a French army was approaching from Canada, with a view to erect fortifications on the Ohio River, and take possession of the whole country, in the name of the French King. As this region was supposed to be within the limits of Virginia, Governor Dinwiddie regarded it as his duty, in conformity with his instructions, to watch the motions of the French, and make preparations for defending the British claims. He resolved to send a commissioner duly authorized to demand of the principal French officer his designs, to ascertain facts, and to make such observations as his opportunities would allow. Major Washington was selected for this arduous undertaking. His knowledge of the Indians, his practical acquaintance with the modes of living and travelling in the woods, acquired in his surveying expeditions, and the marked traits of character, which he had already displayed, were doubtless the qualities that recommended him for this delicate and important mission, although he was not yet twenty-two years of age. The following instructions from Governor Dinwiddie, and extracts from letters written by him to the Board of Trade in London, will indicate the objects and nature of this service.

INSTRUCTIONS FOR GEORGE WASHINGTON.

"Whereas I have received information of a body of French forces being assembled in a hostile manner on the river Ohio, intending by force of arms to erect certain forts on the said river within this territory, and contrary to the dignity and peace of our sovereign the King of Great Britain;

"These are, therefore, to require and direct you, the said George Washington, forthwith to repair to Logstown on the said river Ohio; and, having there informed yourself where the said French forces have posted themselves, thereupon to proceed to such place; and, being there arrived, to present your credentials, together with my letter to the chief commanding officer, and in the name of his Britannic Majesty to demand an answer thereto.

"On your arrival at Logstown you are to address yourself to the Half-King, to Monacatoocha, and other the sachems of the Six Nations, acquainting them with your orders to visit and deliver my letter to the French commanding officer, and desiring the said chiefs to appoint you a sufficient number of their warriors to be your safeguard, as near the French as you may desire, and to wait your further direction.

"You are diligently to inquire into the numbers and force of the French on the Ohio, and the adjacent country; how they are likely to be assisted from Canada; and what are the difficulties and conveniences of that communication, and the time required for it.

"You are to take care to be truly informed what forts the French have erected, and where; how they are garrisoned, and appointed, and what is their distance from each other, and from Logstown; and from the best intelligence you can procure, you are to learn what gave occasion to this expedition of the French; how they are likely to be supported, and what their pretensions are.

"When the French commandant has given you the required and necessary despatches, you are to desire of him a proper guard to protect you as far on your return, as you may judge for your safety, against any straggling Indians or hunters, that may be ignorant of your character, and molest you.

"Wishing you good success in your negotiation, and a safe and speedy return, I am, &c.

"ROBERT DINWIDDIE."

"Williamsburg, 30 October, 1753."

TO GEORGE WASHINGTON, ESQUIRE, ONE OF THE ADJUTANTS-GENERAL OF THE TROOPS AND FORCES IN THE COLONY OF VIRGINIA.

"I, reposing especial trust and confidence in the ability, conduct, and fidelity of you, the said George Washington, have appointed you my express messenger; and you are hereby authorized and empowered to proceed hence, with all convenient and possible despatch, to that part or place, on the river Ohio, where the French have lately erected a fort or forts, or where the commandant of the French forces resides, in order to deliver my letter and message to him; and after waiting not exceeding one week for an answer, you are to take your leave and return immediately back.

"To this commission I have set my hand, and caused the great seal of this Dominion to be affixed, at the city of Williamsburg, the seat of my government, this 30th day of October, in the twenty-seventh year of the reign of his Majesty George the Second, King of Great Britain, &c. &c. annoque Domini, 1753.

"ROBERT DINWIDDIE."

TO ALL TO WHOM THESE PRESENTS MAY COME OR CONCERN, GREETING.

"Whereas I have appointed George Washington, Esquire, by commission under the great seal, my express messenger to the commandant of the French forces on the river Ohio, and as he is charged with business of great importance to his Majesty and this Dominion;

"I do hereby command all his Majesty's subjects, and particularly require all in alliance and amity with the crown of Great Britain, and all others to whom this passport may come, agreeably to the law of nations, to be aiding and assisting as a safeguard to the said George Washington and his attendants, in his present passage to and from the river Ohio as aforesaid.

"ROBERT DINWIDDIE."

TO THE LORDS OF THE BOARD OF TRADE.

"Williamsburg, Virginia, 17 November, 1753.

"RIGHT HONORABLE,

"My last to you was on the 16th of June, to which I beg you to be referred. In that I acquainted you of the accounts we have had of the French, with the Indians in their interest, invading his Majesty's lands on the river Ohio.

"The person sent as a commissioner to the commandant of the French forces neglected his duty, and went no further than Logstown on the Ohio. He reports the French were then one hundred and fifty miles further up that river, and I believe was afraid to go to them. On the application of the Indians in friendship with us on the Ohio, I sent Mr. William Trent, with guns, powder, and shot, to them, with some clothing; and enclosed I send you his report and conferences with these people, on his delivering them the present.*

"I have received, by a man-of-war sloop, orders from the Right Honorable Earl of Holdernesse, and instructions from his Majesty. In consequence thereof I have sent one of the adjutants of the militia out to the commander of the French forces, to know their intentions and by what authority they presume to invade his Majesty's dominions in the time of tranquil peace. When he returns I shall transmit you an account of his proceedings, and the French commander's answer. Your Lordships' &c.

"ROBERT DINWIDDIE."

---

* A copy of Trent's journal is preserved among the papers in the office of the Board of Trade. Trent reports his having been informed by an Indian, that "the French say they took possession of all the lands on the other side of the Allegany Hill for the King of France three years ago, by sinking iron plates at the mouth of several of the creeks, and putting up tin plates on the trees."—*MS. Journal.* This circumstance is also mentioned in Smith's *History of Canada*, Vol. I. p. 209.

Within a few years one of these plates has been found near the mouth of the Muskingum. It was a leaden and not an iron plate, eight inches by ten in size, and three eighths of an inch thick, with an inscription dated August 16th, 1749. In addition to the names and words of form, the inscription affirms,—"We have deposited this plate as a monument and memorial of the reëstablishment of our power in the territory, which we claim near that river [Ohio], and near all those which empty into it, and in all that country on both sides, and in the neighbourhood of the sources of those rivers, and which we have gained to our empire by a long line of wise and prudent princes, maintained by our arms and solemn treaties, especially by those of Ryswick, Utrecht, and Aix-la-Chapelle." The name of the officer, who deposited the plates, was Celeron.—*Communicated by Mr. William Smith, of Quebec, author of the History of Canada.*

TO THE LORDS OF THE BOARD OF TRADE.

"Williamsburg, Virginia, 29 January, 1754.

"RIGHT HONORABLE,

"This is to acquaint you, that Mr. Washington, the gentleman I sent to the commandant of the French forces on the river Ohio, returned here the 16th current.

"I enclose to your Lordships copies of my commission to him, his instructions, a letter of protection for his safe passing and repassing to the French camp, and my letter to the French commander. You also have enclosed a copy of Mr. Washington's journal, and the French commander's letter in answer to mine, which you may observe is written in a very loose style. He would have been glad if this messenger had been directed to proceed to Canada, which is a journey of eight hundred miles from the fort they have erected on a creek that runs into the Ohio, in order to prolong time. He complains that I did not write particulars of the ill treatment they had done to the British subjects, contrary to treaties subsisting between the crowns of Britain and France, which I could not properly do, when Mr. Washington left this, as it was only from reports.

"Mr. Washington had my orders to make what observations he could on his journey, and to take a plan of their fort, which I now enclose to you, and from these directions his journal becomes so large. He assures me, that they had begun another fort at the mouth of the creek, which he thinks will be finished by the month of March.

"There were in the fort where the commander resided about three hundred regular forces, and nine hundred more were gone to winter-quarters, in order to save their provisions, to some forts on Lake Erie, but were to return by the month of March. Then they fully determined, with all the forces they could collect, which he understood would be fifteen hundred regulars, besides Indians, to go down the river Ohio, and proposed building many other forts, and that their chief residence would be at Logstown; and that they had near three hundred canoes to transport their soldiers, provisions, and ammunition.

"They cannot offer any reasons for this extraordinary conduct, but their general's orders, nor can they set up any just claim to these lands, but their determined resolution to possess themselves of them by force of arms, and the ill treatment of the British subjects in the time of peace, inconsistent with treaties, and I humbly think, contrary to the law of nations. I am, &c.

"ROBERT DINWIDDIE."

Major Washington's Journal, mentioned above, was published in England, and has been several times reprinted in this country. It is curious, not only as a narrative, but as indicating some of the strong traits of the writer's character.

MAJOR WASHINGTON'S JOURNAL OF A TOUR OVER THE ALLEGANY MOUNTAINS.

"I was commissioned and appointed by the Honorable Robert Dinwiddie, Esquire, Governor of Virginia, to visit and deliver a letter to the commandant of the French forces on the Ohio, and set out on the intended journey on the same day; the next, I arrived at Fredericksburg, and engaged Mr. Jacob Vanbraam to be my French interpreter, and proceeded with him to Alexandria, where we provided necessaries. From thence we went to Winchester, and got baggage, horses, &c., and from thence we pursued the new road to Will's Creek, where we arrived on the 14th of November.

"Here I engaged Mr. Gist to pilot us out, and also hired four others as servitors, Barnaby Currin and John McQuire, Indian traders, Henry Steward, and William Jenkins; and in company with those persons left the inhabitants the next day.

"The excessive rains and vast quantity of snow, which had fallen, prevented our reaching Mr. Frazier's, an Indian trader, at the mouth of Turtle Creek, on Monongahela River, until Thursday the 22d. We were informed here, that expresses had been sent a few days before to the traders down the river, to acquaint them with the French general's death, and the return of the major part of the French army into winter-quarters.

"The waters were quite impassable without swimming our horses, which obliged us to get the loan of a canoe from Frazier, and to send Barnaby Currin and Henry Steward down the Monongahela, with our baggage, to meet us at the Fork of the Ohio, about ten miles; there to cross the Allegany.

"As I got down before the canoe, I spent some time in viewing the rivers, and the land in the Fork, which I think extremely well situated for a fort, as it has the absolute command of both rivers. The land at the point is twenty, or twenty-five feet above the common surface of the water; and a considerable bottom of flat, well-timbered land all around it, very convenient for building. The rivers are each a quarter of a mile or more across, and run here very nearly at right angles; Allegany bearing northeast; and Monongahela southeast. The former of these two is a very rapid and swift running water, the other deep and still, without any perceptible fall.

"About two miles from this, on the southeast side of the river, at the place where the Ohio Company intended to erect a fort, lives Shingiss, King of the Delawares. We called upon him, to invite him to council at the Logstown.

"As I had taken a good deal of notice yesterday of the situation at the Fork, my curiosity led me to examine this more particularly, and I think it greatly inferior, either for defence or advantages; especially the latter. For a fort at the Fork would be equally well situated on the Ohio, and have the entire command of the Monongahela, which runs up our settlement, and is extremely well designed for water-carriage, as it is of a deep, still nature. Besides, a fort at the Fork might be built at much less expense than at the other places.

"Nature has well contrived this lower place for water defence; but the hill whereon it must stand being about a quarter of a mile in length, and then descending gradually on the land side, will render it difficult and very expensive to make a sufficient fortification there. The whole flat upon the hill must be taken in, the side next the descent made extremely high, or else the hill itself cut away; otherwise the enemy may raise batteries within that distance without being exposed to a single shot from the fort.

"Shingiss attended us to the Logstown, where we arrived between sun-setting and dark, the twenty-fifth day after I left Williamsburg. We travelled over some extremely good and bad land to get to this place.

"As soon as I came into town, I went to Monacatoocha (as the Half-King was out at his hunting cabin on Little Beaver Creek, about fifteen miles off), and informed him by John Davidson, my Indian interpreter, that I was sent a messenger to the French general; and was ordered to call upon the Sachems of the Six Nations to acquaint them with it. I gave him a string of wampum and a twist of tobacco, and desired him to send for the Half-King, which he promised to do by a runner in the morning, and for other sachems. I invited him and the other great men present to my tent, where they stayed about an hour and returned.

"According to the best observations I could make, Mr. Gist's new settlement (which we passed by) bears about west northwest seventy miles from Will's Creek; Shannopins, or the Fork, north by west, or north northwest, about fifty miles from that; and from thence to the Logstown, the course is nearly west about eighteen or twenty miles:

so that the whole distance, as we went and computed it, is at least one hundred and thirty-five or one hundred and forty miles from our back inhabitants.

"*25th.*—Came to town four of ten Frenchmen, who had deserted from a company at the Kuskuskas, which lies at the mouth of this river. I got the following account from them. They were sent from New Orleans with a hundred men and eight canoe-loads of provisions to this place, where they expected to have met the same number of men, from the forts on this side of Lake Erie, to convoy them and the stores up, who were not arrived when they ran off.

"I inquired into the situation of the French on the Mississippi, their numbers, and what forts they had built. They informed me, that there were four small forts between New Orleans and the Black Islands, garrisoned with about thirty or forty men, and a few small pieces in each. That at New Orleans, which is near the mouth of the Mississippi, there are thirty-five companies of forty men each, with a pretty strong fort mounting eight carriage-guns; and at the Black Islands there are several companies and a fort with six guns. The Black Islands are about a hundred and thirty leagues above the mouth of the Ohio, which is about three hundred and fifty above New Orleans. They also acquainted me, that there was a small palisadoed fort on the Ohio, at the mouth of the Obaish, about sixty leagues from the Mississippi. The Obaish heads near the west end of Lake Erie, and affords the communication between the French on the Mississippi and those on the lakes. These deserters came up from the lower Shannoah town with one Brown, an Indian trader, and were going to Philadelphia.

"About three o'clock this evening the Half-King came to town. I went up and invited him with Davidson, privately, to my tent, and desired him to relate some of the particulars of his journey to the French commandant, and of his reception there; also, to give me an account of the ways and distance. He told me, that the nearest and levelest way was now impassable, by reason of many large, miry savannas; that we must be obliged to go by Venango, and should not get to the near fort in less than five or six nights' sleep, good travelling. When he went to the fort, he said he was received in a very stern manner by the late commander, who asked him very abruptly what he had come about, and to declare his business, which he said he did in the following speech.

"'Fathers, I am come to tell you your own speeches, what your own mouths have declared. Fathers, you, in former days, set a silver basin before us, wherein there was the leg of a beaver, and desired all the nations to come and eat of it, to eat in peace and plenty, and not to be churlish to one another; and that if any such person should be found to be a disturber, I here lay down by the edge of the dish a rod, which you must scourge them with; and if your father should get foolish, in my old days, I desire you may use it upon me as well as others.

" 'Now, fathers, it is you who are the disturbers in this land, by coming and building your towns, and taking it away unknown to us, and by force.

" 'Fathers, we kindled a fire a long time ago, at a place called Montreal, where we desired you to stay, and not to come and intrude upon our land. I now desire you may despatch to that place; for be it known to you, fathers, that this is our land and not yours.

" 'Fathers, I desire you may hear me in civilness; if not, we must handle that rod which was laid down for the use of the obstreperous. If you had come in a peaceable manner, like our brothers the English, we would not have been against your trading with us as they do; but to come, fathers, and build houses upon our land, and to take it by force, is what we cannot submit to.

" 'Fathers, both you and the English are white, we live in a country between; therefore, the land belongs to neither one nor the other. But the Great Being above allowed it to be a place of residence for us; so, fathers, I desire you to withdraw, as I have done our brothers the English; for I will keep you at arm's length. I lay this down as a trial for both, to see which will have the greatest regard to it, and that side we will stand by, and make equal sharers with us. Our brothers, the English, have heard this, and I come now to tell it to you; for I am not afraid to discharge you off this land.'

"This he said was the substance of what he spoke to the general, who made this reply.

" 'Now, my child, I have heard your speech; you spoke first, but it is my time to speak now. Where is my wampum that you took away, with the marks of towns on it? This wampum I do not know, which you have discharged me off the land with; but you need not put yourself to the trouble of speaking, for I will not hear you. I am not afraid of flies or musquitoes, for Indians are such as those; I tell you down that river I will go, and build upon it, according to my command. If the river was blocked up, I have forces sufficient to burst it open, and tread under my feet all that stand in opposition, together with their alliances; for my force is as the sand upon the sea-shore; therefore here is your wampum; I sling it at you. Child, you talk foolish; you say this land belongs to you, but there is not the black of my nail yours. I saw that land sooner than you did, before the Shannoahs and you were at war; Lead was the man who went down and took possession of that river. It is my land, and I will have it, let who will stand up for, or say against it. I will buy and sell with the English (mockingly). If people will be ruled by me, they may expect kindness, but not else.'

"The Half-King told me he had inquired of the general after two Englishmen, who were made prisoners, and received this answer.

"'Child, you think it a very great hardship that I made prisoners of those two people at Venango. Don't you concern yourself with it; we took and carried them to Canada, to get intelligence of what the English were doing in Virginia.'

"He informed me, that they had built two forts, one on Lake Erie, and another on French Creek, near a small lake, about fifteen miles asunder, and a large wagon-road between. They are both built after the same model, but different in size; that on the lake the largest. He gave me a plan of them of his own drawing.

"The Indians inquired very particularly after their brothers in Carolina gaol.

"They also asked what sort of a boy it was, who was taken from the South Branch; for they were told by some Indians, that a party of French Indians had carried a white boy by Kuskuska Town, towards the lakes.

"*26th.*—We met in council at the long-house about nine o'clock, where I spoke to them as follows.

"'Brothers, I have called you together in council, by order of your brother, the Governor of Virginia, to acquaint you, that I am sent with all possible despatch, to visit and deliver a letter to the French commandant, of very great importance to your brothers, the English; and I dare say to you, their friends and allies.

"'I was desired, brothers, by your brother, the Governor, to call upon you, the sachems of the nations, to inform you of it, and to ask your advice and assistance to proceed the nearest and best road to the French. You see, brothers, I have gotten thus far on my journey.

"'His Honor likewise desired me to apply to you for some of your young men to conduct and provide provisions for us on our way, and be a safeguard against those French Indians, who have taken up the hatchet against us. I have spoken thus particularly to you, brothers, because his Honor our Governor treats you as good friends and allies, and holds you in great esteem. To confirm what I have said, I give you this string of wampum.'

"After they had considered for some time on the above discourse, the Half-King got up and spoke.

"'Now, my brother, in regard to what my brother, the Governor, had desired of me, I return you this answer.

"'I rely upon you as a brother ought to do, as you say we are brothers, and one people. We shall put heart in hand and speak to our fathers, the French, concerning the speech they made to me; and you may depend that we will endeavour to be your guard.

"'Brother, as you have asked my advice, I hope you will be ruled by it, and stay until I can provide a company to go with you. The French speech-belt is not here; I have to go for it to my hunting-cabin. Likewise, the people whom I have ordered in are not yet come, and cannot until the third night from this; until which time, brother, I must beg you to stay.

"'I intend to send the guard of Mingoes, Shannoahs, and Delawares, that our brothers may see the love and loyalty we bear them.'

"As I had orders to make all possible despatch, and waiting here was very contrary to my inclination, I thanked him in the most suitable manner I could, and told him that my business required the greatest expedition, and would not admit of that delay. He was not well pleased that I should offer to go before the time he had appointed, and told me, that he could not consent to our going without a guard, for fear some accident should befall us, and draw a reflection upon him. Besides, said he, this is a matter of no small moment, and must not be entered into without due consideration; for I intend to deliver up the French speech-belt, and make the Shannoahs and Delawares do the same. And accordingly he gave orders to King Shingiss, who was present, to attend on Wednesday night with the wampum; and two men of their nation to be in readiness to set out with us the next morning. As I found it was impossible to get off without affronting them in the most egregious manner, I consented to stay.

"I gave them back a string of wampum, which I met with at Mr. Frazier's, and which they sent with a speech to his Honor the Governor, to inform him, that three nations of French Indians, namely, Chippewas, Ottowas, and Orundaks, had taken up the hatchet against the English; and desired them to repeat it over again. But this they postponed doing until they met in full council with the Shannoah and Delaware chiefs.

"*27th.*—Runners were despatched very early for the Shannoah chiefs. The Half-King set out himself to fetch the French speech-belt from his hunting-cabin.

KK *

"28*th.* — He returned this evening, and came with Monacatoocha, and two other sachems to my tent; and begged (as they had complied with his Honor the Governor's request, in providing men, &c.) to know on what business we were going to the French. This was a question I had all along expected, and had provided as satisfactory answers as I could; which allayed their curiosity a little.

"Monacatoocha informed me, that an Indian from Venango brought news, a few days ago, that the French had called all the Mingoes, Delawares, &c. together at that place; and told them, that they intended to have been down the river this fall, but the waters were growing cold, and the winter advancing, which obliged them to go into quarters; but that they might assuredly expect them in the spring, with a far greater number; and desired that they might be quite passive, and not intermeddle unless they had a mind to draw all their force upon them; for that they expected to fight the English three years (as they supposed there would be some attempts made to stop them), in which time they should conquer. But that if they should prove equally strong, they and the English would join to cut them all off, and divide the land between them; that though they had lost their general, and some few of their soldiers, yet there were men enough to reinforce them, and make them masters of the Ohio.

"This speech, he said, was delivered to them by one Captain Joncaire, their interpreter in chief, living at Venango, and a man of note in the army.

"29*th.* — The Half-King and Monacatoocha came very early, and begged me to stay one day more; for notwithstanding they had used all the diligence in their power, the Shannoah chiefs had not brought the wampum they ordered, but would certainly be in to-night; if not, they would delay me no longer, but would send it after us as soon as they arrived. When I found them so pressing in their request, and knew that the returning of wampum was the abolishing of agreements, and giving this up was shaking off all dependence upon the French, I consented to stay, as I believed an offence offered at this crisis might be attended with greater ill consequence, than another day's delay. They also informed me, that Shingiss could not get in his men, and was prevented from coming himself by his wife's sickness, (I believe by fear of the French), but that the wampum of that nation was lodged with Kustalogo, one of their chiefs, at Venango.

"In the evening, late, they came again, and acquainted me that the Shannoahs were not yet arrived, but that it should not retard the prosecution of our journey. He delivered in my hearing the speech that was to be made to the French by Jeskakake, one of their old chiefs, which was giving up the belt the late commandant had asked for, and repeating nearly the same speech he himself had done before.

"He also delivered a string of wampum to this chief, which was sent by King Shingiss, to be given to Kustalogo, with orders to repair to the French, and deliver up the wampum.

"He likewise gave a very large string of black and white wampum, which was to be sent up immediately to the Six Nations, if the French refused to quit the land at this warning; which was the third and last time, and was the right of this Jeskakake to deliver.

"*30th.*—Last night, the great men assembled at their council house, to consult further about this journey, and who were to go; the result of which was, that only three of their chiefs, with one of their best hunters, should be our convoy. The reason they gave for not sending more, after what had been proposed at council the 26th, was, that a greater number might give the French suspicions of some bad design, and cause them to be treated rudely; but I rather think they could not get their hunters in.

"We set out about nine o'clock with the Half-King, Jeskakake, White Thunder, and the Hunter; and travelled on the road to Venango, where we arrived the 4th of December, without any thing remarkable happening but a continued series of bad weather.

"This is an old Indian town, situated at the mouth of French Creek, on the Ohio; and lies near north about sixty miles from the Logstown, but more than seventy the way we were obliged to go.

"We found the French colors hoisted at a house from which they had driven Mr. John Frazier, an English subject. I immediately repaired to it, to know where the commander resided. There were three officers, one of whom, Captain Joncaire, informed me that he had the command of the Ohio; but that there was a general officer at the near fort, where he advised me to apply for an answer. He invited us to sup with them, and treated us with the greatest complaisance.

"The wine, as they dosed themselves pretty plentifully with it, soon banished the restraint which at first appeared in their conversation, and gave a license to their tongues to reveal their sentiments more freely.

"They told me, that it was their absolute design to take possession of the Ohio, and by G— they would do it; for that, although they were sensible the English could raise two men for their one, yet they knew their motions were too slow and dilatory to prevent any undertaking of theirs. They pretend to have an undoubted right to the river from a discovery made by one La Salle, sixty years ago; and the rise of this expedition is, to prevent our settling on the river or waters of it, as they heard of some families moving out in order thereto. From the best intelligence I could get, there have been fifteen hundred men on this side Ontario Lake. But upon the death of the general, all were recalled to about six or seven hundred, who were left to garrison four forts, one hundred and fifty or thereabout in each. The first of them is on French Creek, near a small lake, about sixty miles from Venango, near north northwest; the next lies on Lake Erie, where the greater part of their stores are kept, about fifteen miles from the other; from this it is one hundred and twenty miles to the carrying-place, at the Falls of Lake Erie, where there is a small fort, at which they lodge their goods in bringing them from Montreal, the place from whence all their stores are brought. The next fort lies about twenty miles from this, on Ontario Lake. Between this fort and Montreal, there are three others, the first of which is nearly opposite to the English fort Oswego. From the fort on Lake Erie to Montreal is about six hundred miles, which, they say, requires no more (if good weather) than four weeks' voyage, if they go in barks or large vessels, so that they may cross the lake; but if they come in canoes, it will require five or six weeks, for they are obliged to keep under the shore.

"*December 5th.* — Rained excessively all day, which prevented our travelling. Captain Joncaire sent for the Half-King, as he had but just heard that he came with me. He affected to be much concerned that I did not make free to bring them in before. I excused it in the best manner of which I was capable, and told him, I did not think their company agreeable, as I had heard him say a good deal in dispraise of Indians in general; but another motive prevented me from bringing them into his company; I knew that he was an interpreter, and a person of very great influence among the Indians, and had lately used all possible means to draw them over to his interest; therefore I was desirous of giving him no opportunity that could be avoided.

"When they came in, there was great pleasure expressed at seeing them. He wondered how they could be so near without coming to visit him, made several trifling presents, and applied liquor so fast, that they were soon rendered incapable of the business they came about, notwithstanding the caution which was given.

"*6th.* — The Half-King came to my tent, quite sober, and insisted very much that I should stay and hear what he had to say to the

French. I fain would have prevented him from speaking any thing until he came to the commandant, but could not prevail. He told me, that at this place a council-fire was kindled, where all their business with these people was to be transacted, and that the management of the Indian affairs was left solely to Monsieur Joncaire. As I was desirous of knowing the issue of this, I agreed to stay; but sent our horses a little way up French Creek, to raft over and encamp; which I knew would make it near night.

"About ten o'clock they met in council. The King spoke much the same as he had before done to the general; and offered the French speech-belt which had before been demanded, with the marks of four towns on it, which Monsieur Joncaire refused to receive, but desired him to carry it to the fort to the commander.

"*7th.* — Monsieur La Force, commissary of the French stores, and three other soldiers, came over to accompany us up. We found it extremely difficult to get the Indians off to-day, as every stratagem had been used to prevent their going up with me. I had last night left John Davidson (the Indian interpreter), whom I brought with me from town, and strictly charged him not to be out of their company, as I could not get them over to my tent; for they had some business with Kustalogo, chiefly to know why he did not deliver up the French speech-belt which he had in keeping; but I was obliged to send Mr. Gist over to-day to fetch them, which he did with great persuasion.

"At twelve o'clock, we set out for the fort, and were prevented arriving there until the 11th by excessive rains, snows, and bad travelling through many mires and swamps; these we were obliged to pass to avoid crossing the creek, which was impassable, either by fording or rafting, the water was so high and rapid.

"We passed over much good land since we left Venango, and through several extensive and very rich meadows, one of which, I believe, was nearly four miles in length, and considerably wide in some places.

"*12th.* — I prepared early to wait upon the commander, and was received and conducted to him by the second officer in command. I acquainted him with my business, and offered my commission and letter; both of which he desired me to keep until the arrival of Monsieur Reparti, captain at the next fort, who was sent for and expected every hour.

"This commander is a knight of the military order of St. Louis, and named Legardeur de St. Pierre. He is an elderly gentleman, and has much the air of a soldier. He was sent over to take the command immediately upon the death of the late general, and arrived here about seven days before me.

"At two o'clock, the gentleman who was sent for arrived, when I offered the letter, &c. again, which they received, and adjourned into a private apartment for the captain to translate, who understood a little English. After he had done it, the commander desired I would walk in and bring my interpreter to peruse and correct it; which I did.

"13*th.* — The chief officers retired to hold a council of war, which gave me an opportunity of taking the dimensions of the fort, and making what observations I could.

"It is situated on the south or west fork of French Creek, near the water; and is almost surrounded by the creek, and a small branch of it, which form a kind of island. Four houses compose the sides. The bastions are made of piles driven into the ground, standing more than twelve feet above it, and sharp at top, with port-holes cut for cannon, and loop-holes for the small arms to fire through. There are eight six-pounds pieces mounted in each bastion, and one piece of four pounds before the gate. In the bastions are a guard-house, chapel, doctor's lodging, and the commander's private store; round which are laid platforms for the cannon and men to stand on. There are several barracks without the fort, for the soldiers' dwellings, covered, some with bark, and some with boards, made chiefly of logs. There are also several other houses, such as stables, smith's shop, &c.

"I could get no certain account of the number of men here; but, according to the best judgment I could form, there are a hundred, exclusive of officers, of whom there are many. I also gave orders to the people who were with me, to take an exact account of the canoes, which were hauled up to convey their forces down in the spring. This they did, and told fifty of birch bark, and a hundred and seventy of pine; besides many others, which were blocked out, in readiness for being made.

"14*th.* — As the snow increased very fast, and our horses daily became weaker, I sent them off unloaded, under the care of Barnaby Currin and two others, to make all convenient despatch to Venango, and there to wait our arrival, if there was a prospect of the river's freezing; if not, then to continue down to Shannopin's Town, at the Fork of the Ohio, and there to wait until we came to cross the Allegany; intending myself to go down by water, as I had the offer of a canoe or two.

"As I found many plots concerted to retard the Indians' business, and prevent their returning with me, I endeavoured all that lay in my power to frustrate their schemes, and hurried them on to execute their intended design. They accordingly pressed for admittance this evening, which at length was granted them, privately, to the commander and one or two other officers. The Half-King told me, that he offered the wampum to the commander, who evaded taking it, and made many fair promises of love and friendship; said he wanted to live in peace and trade amicably with them, as a proof of which, he would send some goods immediately down to the Logs-town for them. But I rather think the design of that is to bring away all our straggling traders they meet with, as I privately understood they intended to carry an officer, with them. And what rather confirms this opinion, I was inquiring of the commander by what authority he had made prisoners of several of our English subjects. He told me that the country belonged to them; that no Englishman had a right to trade upon those waters; and that he had orders to make every person prisoner, who attempted it on the Ohio, or the waters of it.

"I inquired of Captain Reparti about the boy, that was carried by this place, as it was done while the command devolved on him, between the death of the late general, and the arrival of the present. He acknowledged, that a boy had been carried past; and that the Indians had two or three white men's scalps (I was told by some of the Indians at Venango, eight), but pretended to have forgotten the name of the place where the boy came from, and all the particular facts, though he had questioned him for some hours, as they were carrying him past. I likewise inquired what they had done with John Trotter and James McClocklan, two Pennsylvania traders, whom they had taken with all their goods. They told me, that they had been sent to Canada, but were now returned home.

"This evening I received an answer to his Honor the Governor's letter from the commandant.

"*15th.* — The commandant ordered a plentiful store of liquor, and provision to be put on board our canoes, and appeared to be extremely complaisant, though he was exerting every artifice, which he could invent, to set our Indians at variance with us, to prevent their going until after our departure; presents, rewards, and every thing, which could be suggested by him or his officers. I cannot say that ever in my life I suffered so much anxiety, as I did in this affair. I saw that every stratagem, which the most fruitful brain could invent, was practised to win the Half-King to their interest; and that leaving him there was giving them the opportunity they aimed at. I went to the Half-King and pressed him in the strongest terms to go; he told me that the commandant would not discharge him until the morning. I then went to the commandant, and desired him to do their business, and complained of ill treatment; for keeping them, as they were part of my company, was detaining me. This he promised not to do, but to forward my journey as much as he could. He protested he did not keep them, but was ignorant of the cause of their stay; though I soon found it out. He had promised them a present of guns, if they would wait until the morning. As I was very much pressed by the Indians to wait this day for them, I consented, on a promise that nothing should hinder them in the morning.

"16*th.* — The French were not slack in their inventions to keep the Indians this day also. But as they were obliged, according to promise, to give the present, they then endeavoured to try the power of liquor, which I doubt not would have prevailed at any other time than this; but I urged and insisted with the King so closely upon his word, that he refrained, and set off with us as he had engaged.

"We had a tedious and very fatiguing passage down the creek. Several times we had like to have been staved against rocks; and many times were obliged all hands to get out and remain in the water half an hour or more, getting over the shoals. At one place, the ice had lodged, and made it impassable by water; we were, therefore, obliged to carry our canoe across the neck of land, a quarter of a mile over. We did not reach Venango until the 22d, where we met with our horses.

"This creek is extremely crooked. I dare say the distance between the fort and Venango cannot be less than one hundred and thirty miles, to follow the meanders.

"23*d.* — When I got things ready to set off, I sent for the Half-King, to know whether he intended to go with us or by water. He told me that White Thunder had hurt himself much, and was sick, and unable to walk; therefore he was obliged to carry him down in a canoe. As I found he intended to stay here a day or two, and knew that Monsieur Joncaire would employ every scheme to set him against the English, as he had before done, I told him, I hoped he would guard against his flattery, and let no fine speeches influence him in their favor. He desired I might not be concerned, for he knew the French too well, for any thing to engage him in their favor; and that though he could not go down with us, he yet would endeavour to meet at the Fork with Joseph Campbell, to deliver a speech for me to carry to his Honor the Governor. He told me he would order the Young Hunter to attend us, and get provisions, &c if wanted.

"Our horses were now so weak and feeble, and the baggage so heavy (as we were obliged to provide all the necessaries which the journey would require), that we doubted much their performing it. Therefore, myself and others, except the drivers, who were obliged to ride, gave up our horses for packs, to assist along with the baggage. I put myself in an Indian walking-dress, and continued with them three days, until I found there was no probability of their getting home in any reasonable time. The horses became less able to travel every day; the cold increased very fast; and the roads were becoming much worse by a deep snow, continually freezing; therefore, as I was uneasy to get back, to make report of my proceedings to his Honor the Governor, I determined to prosecute my journey, the nearest way through the woods, on foot.

"Accordingly, I left Mr. Vanbraam in charge of our baggage, with money and directions to provide necessaries from place to place for themselves and horses, and to make the most convenient despatch in travelling.

"I took my necessary papers, pulled off my clothes, and tied myself up in a match-coat. Then, with gun in hand, and pack on my back, in which were my papers and provisions, I set out with Mr. Gist, fitted in the same manner, on Wednesday the 26th. The day following, just after we had passed a place called Murdering Town (where we intended to quit the path and steer across the country for Shannopin's Town), we fell in with a party of French Indians, who had lain in wait for us. One of them fired at Mr. Gist or me, not fifteen steps off, but fortunately missed. We took this fellow into custody, and kept him until about nine o'clock at night, then let him go, and walked all the remaining part of the night without making any stop, that we might get the start so far, as to be out of the reach of their pursuit the next day, since we were well assured they would follow our track as soon as it was light. The next day we continued travelling until quite dark, and got to the river about two miles above Shannopin's. We expected to have found the river frozen, but it was not, only about fifty yards from each shore. The ice, I suppose, had broken up above, for it was driving in vast quantities.

"There was no way for getting over but on a raft, which we set about, with but one poor hatchet, and finished just after sun-setting. This was a whole day's work; we next got it launched, then went on board of it, and set off; but before we were half way over, we were jammed in the ice in such a manner, that we expected every moment our raft to sink, and ourselves to perish. I put out my setting-pole to try to stop the raft, that the ice might pass by, when the rapidity of the stream threw it with so much violence against the pole, that it jerked me out into ten feet water; but I fortunately saved myself by catching hold of one of the raft-logs. Notwithstanding all our efforts, we could not get to either shore, but were obliged, as we were near an island, to quit our raft and make to it.

"The cold was so extremely severe, that Mr. Gist had all his fingers and some of his toes frozen, and the water was shut up so hard, that we found no difficulty in getting off the island on the ice in the morning, and went to Mr. Frazier's. We met here with twenty warriors, who were going to the southward to war; but coming to a place on the head of the Great Kenhawa, where they found seven people killed and scalped (all but one woman with very light hair), they turned about and ran back, for fear the inhabitants should rise and take them as the authors of the murder. They report that the bodies were lying about the house, and some of them much torn and eaten by the hogs. By the marks which were left, they say they were French Indians of the Ottoway nation, who did it.

"As we intended to take horses here, and it required some time to find them, I went up about three miles to the mouth of Youghiogany, to visit Queen Aliquippa, who had expressed great concern that we passed her in going to the fort. I made her a present of a watch-coat and a bottle of rum, which latter was thought much the better present of the two.

"Tuesday, the 1st of January, we left Mr. Frazier's house, and arrived at Mr. Gist's, at Monongahela, the 2d, where I bought a horse and saddle. The 6th, we met seventeen horses loaded with materials and stores for a fort at the Fork of the Ohio, and the day after, some families going out to settle. This day, we arrived at Will's Creek, after as fatiguing a journey as it is possible to conceive, rendered so by excessive bad weather. From the 1st day of December to the 15th, there was but one day on which it did not rain or snow incessantly; and throughout the whole journey, we met with nothing but one continued series of cold, wet weather, which occasioned very uncomfortable lodgings, especially after we had quitted our tent, which was some screen from the inclemency of it.

"On the 11th, I got to Belvoir, where I stopped one day to take necessary rest; and then set out and arrived in Williamsburg the 16th, when I waited upon his Honor the Governor, with the letter I had brought from the French commandant, and to give an account of the success of my proceedings. This I beg leave to do by offering the foregoing narrative, as it contains the most remarkable occurrences, which happened in my journey.

"I hope what has been said will be sufficient to make your Honor satisfied with my conduct; for that was my aim in undertaking the journey, and chief study throughout the prosecution of it."

No. II. p. 39.

DEATH OF JUMONVILLE.

The circumstances attending the death of Jumonville have been so remarkably misunderstood and perverted by the French historians, and the character of Washington, in regard to this event, has suffered so much in their hands, that the subject demands a further consideration. The following extracts, from three of the most recent and accredited French writers, will show in what light this point of history is still viewed by that nation. The first extract is from Flassan, whose history holds a high rank in French literature, and was written with the approbation of Napoleon, if not in consequence of his suggestion.

"M. de Jumonville," says Flassan, "setting off with an escort of thirty men, found himself surrounded in the morning by a body of English and savages. The former fired twice in rapid succession, and killed several Frenchmen. Jumonville made a sign, that he was the bearer of a letter from his commandant. The fire ceased, and they gathered around him to hear the letter. He caused the summons to be read, but the reading was not finished when the English reiterated their fire and killed him. The remaining Frenchmen of his escort were immediately made prisoners of war." *

The next extract is from Lacretelle, whose history likewise enjoys a distinguished reputation in his native country.

"An officer, by the name of Jumonville, was sent with an escort of thirty men. The English, ranged in a circle around him, listened to the representations, which he came to make. Had they premeditated so atrocious a crime? Were they moved by a sudden impulse of hatred and ferocity? This cannot now be known; but they disgraced the New World by an outrage never before heard of among civilized

---

* *Histoire de la Diplomatie Française, ou de la Politique de la France,* &c Par M. DE FLASSAN. Paris, 1811. Tom. VI. p. 28.

people, and which excited the savages to a transport of indignation. They assassinated Jumonville, and immolated eight soldiers, who fell bleeding by the side of their chief. They made prisoners of the rest of the escort."

To this passage M. Lacretelle adds the following note.

"It is painful to state, that the detachment of the English, who committed this atrocity, was commanded by Washington. This officer, who afterwards displayed the purest virtues of the warrior, the citizen, and the sage, was then no more than twenty-two years old. He could not restrain the wild and undisciplined troops, who marched under his orders." *

Montgaillard, another French historian, who has sketched with great ability and eloquence, in the form of annals, the events of the French Revolution, thus speaks of Washington, after quoting the elegant tribute to his memory by Mallet-Dupan.

"This great man, the only person with whom no other in modern history can be compared, would have enjoyed a renown without reproach, his public career would have been without fault, his glory would have shone with an unsullied lustre, had it not been for the fatal event of the death of Jumonville, a young officer sent to him with a summons by the commandant of the French establishments on the Ohio. Washington, then a major in the forces of the King of England, commanded the post, which assassinated Jumonville. He was then twenty-three [twenty-two] years of age. Far from offering any reparation, himself attacked by the brother of Jumonville, and made prisoner with his troops, he received his life and liberty on the condition of sending back the Frenchmen, who escaped from the massacre; yet he violated his promise. The French could never efface the remembrance of this deplorable circumstance, whatever veneration the political life of this illustrious citizen might have merited." †

Many other French historians might be cited, who make the same statements, in almost the same words; and even very recently the writer of a life of Washington in the *Biographie Universelle*, who aims apparently to be accurate and impartial, and who has done justice for the most part to Washington's character, repeats this story of the assassination of Jumonville, adding, like Lacretelle, as the only extenuating circumstances, the youth of Washington, and the ungovernable ferocity of his soldiers.

---

* *Histoire de France, pendant le Dix-Huitième Siècle.* Par M. LACRETELLE LE JEUNE. Paris, 1809. Tom. II. p. 234.

† *Histoire de France, depuis la Fin du Règne de Louis XVI*, &c. Par L'ABBÉ DE MONTGAILLARD. Paris, 1828. Tom. V. p. 297.

It will be seen, by comparing the above extracts, that they are in substance precisely the same, and must unquestionably have been derived from a common source. Every thing will depend on the degree of credit, that is due to this single authority, upon which alone all the accounts of subsequent writers are founded. A supposed fact is not strengthened by the repetition of one historian from another, whatever merit each writer may have on the score of talents and honest intentions. All history is built on evidence, and if this is fallacious, or partial, or dubious, the deductions from it must be equally uncertain and deceptive. Of this obvious position the present instance affords a remarkable illustration.

The authority, from which all the French historians have drawn their intelligence, is a letter written by M. de Contrecœur to the Marquis Duquesne, at that time governor of Canada. This letter is dated June 2d, 1754. The following is a literal translation of the part, which relates to the subject in question.

"Since the letter, which I had the honor of writing to you on the 30th ultimo, in which I informed you, that I expected the return of M. de Jumonville in four days, it has been reported by the savages, that his party has been taken, and eight men killed, among whom is M. de Jumonville. A Canadian belonging to the party, named Mouceau, made his escape, who relates, that they had built cabins in a low bottom, where they lay during a heavy rain. At seven o'clock in the morning, they saw themselves encircled on one side by the English, and by savages on the other. Two discharges of musketry were fired upon them by the English, but none by the savages. M. de Jumonville called to them by an interpreter to desist, as he had something to say to them. The firing ceased. M. de Jumonville caused the summons to be read, which I had sent, admonishing them to retire, a copy of which I have the honor to enclose. Whilst this was reading, the said Mouceau saw the French gathered close around M. de Jumonville, in the midst of the English and the savages. At that time Mouceau escaped through the woods, making his way hither partly by land, and partly in a small canoe on the river Monongahela.

"This, Sir, is all that I have been able to learn from Mouceau. The misfortune is, that our people were taken by surprise. The English had surrounded and come upon them before they were seen.

"I have this moment received a letter from M. de Chauvignerie, which I have the honor to send you herewith, from which you will see, that we have certainly lost eight men, of whom M. de Jumonville is one. The savages, who were present, say, that M. de Jumonville was killed by a musket-shot in the head, while he was listening to the reading of the summons, and that the English would immediately have destroyed the whole party, if the savages had not rushed in before them and prevented their attempt. M. Drouillon and M. de la Force were made prisoners. We are not informed whether M. de Boucherville and M. du Sablé, two cadets, are among the slain. Such is the account, which we have received from the savages." *

Here we have all the particulars, as they appear in the citations from the French historians, and almost in the same language. And this is the original and sole authority, from which have been derived all the succeeding French accounts of the conflict between the forces of Washington and Jumonville, which terminated so fatally to the latter. By what testimony is this statement of M. de Contrecœur sustained? First, by the report of a Canadian, who fled affrighted at the beginning of the action; and, next, by the vague rumors of the savages, who were said to have been on the spot. These savages, if any there were, who returned to M. de Contrecœur, must have come out with the French party. No such savages are mentioned as being seen by the English; and consequently, if there were any originally with the party, they escaped, like the Canadian, at the beginning of the action, and could have had no knowledge of the manner in which it was conducted. In any other case would such testimony be taken as evidence of facts? It can certainly have no claim to be made the basis of a historical narrative. Much less can it warrant severe censures upon the character of an officer, who was in reality discharging his duty in the execution of his orders.

In the year 1759, five years after these events, M. Thomas published his epic in four cantos, entitled "JUMONVILLE," founded on the incidents real and imaginary of the skirmish, in which his hero fell, and of the attack of M. de Villiers upon Fort Necessity, which soon followed. He states the subject of his poem to be, "*L'Assassinat de M. de Jumonville en Amérique, et la Vengeance de ce Meurtre.*" It is written with extreme warmth of patriotic passion throughout, and Zimmerman, in his treatise on NATIONAL PRIDE, cites the "*Jumonville*" of Thomas, as a remarkable instance of the effect of national antipathy. The preface contains an exaggerated paraphrase of M. de Contrecœur's letter, as the groundwork of the author's poetical fabric. With the materials thus furnished, and with the machinery of the deep and wild forests, the savages, the demon of

* See the whole letter in the *Mémoire contenant le Précis des Faits, &c.* p. 106.

battles, and the ghost of Jumonville, his epic speedily assumes a tragic garb, and the scenes of horror and cries of vengeance cease not till the poem closes. The general merits of this piece, as a poetical composition, and the high character of M. Thomas as a man of letters, gave it a currency in the literary world, which had the effect of perpetuating the impressions then received, and so far of biasing prevalent opinions, as to prevent that cautious examination into facts, which is the first duty of a faithful historian.

The official letters of Washington, now for the first time published, and also the manuscript letters of Governor Dinwiddie, throw much additional light upon this subject, and afford the means for drawing up the following accurate statement of all the essential particulars.

When the news of the capitulation of Ensign Ward to the French on the Ohio, in consequence of a military summons, reached Will's Creek, where the Virginia troops were encamped, Colonel Washington considered the frontiers to be actually invaded, and that, in compliance with the tenor of his orders, it was his duty to march forward and be prepared to meet the invading forces wherever they should present themselves. A council of war was immediately held, by which this opinion was confirmed, and it was resolved to proceed to the junction of Red-stone Creek with the Monongahela, thirty-seven miles from the fort captured by the French, construct such a fortification there, as circumstances would permit, and wait for reinforcements. On the 1st of May the little army, amounting to one hundred and fifty men, set off from Will's Creek, and advanced by slow and tedious marches into the wilderness. The Indians brought in frequent reports of their having seen French scouts in the woods, and on the 24th of May the Half-King sent a message to Washington, apprizing him, that a French force, in what numbers he could not tell, was on its march to attack the English wherever they should be found, and warning him to be on his guard. He was now a few miles beyond the Great Meadows, and on receiving this intelligence he hastened back to that place, and threw up an entrenchment, determined to wait there the approach of the enemy, whom he supposed to be coming out with a hostile intention.

Early in the morning of the 27th, Mr. Gist arrived in camp from his residence, which was about thirteen miles distant, and informed Colonel Washington, that M. La Force with fifty men had been at his plantation the day before, and that on his way he had seen the tracks of the same party five miles from the encampment at the Great Meadows. Seventy-five men were immediately despatched in pursuit of this party, but they returned without having discovered it.

Between eight and nine o'clock the same night an express arrived from the Half-King, who was then six miles off, with intelligence that he had seen the tracks of two Frenchmen, which had been traced to an obscure retreat, and that he imagined the whole party to be concealed within a short distance. Fearing this might be a stratagem of the French for attacking his camp, Colonel Washington put his ammunition in a place of safety, and, leaving a strong guard to protect it, he set out with forty men, and reached the Indians' camp a little before sunrise, having marched through a rainy and exceedingly dark night.

On counselling with the Half-King, and the other Indians of his party, it was agreed, that they should march together and make the attack in concert on the French. They then proceeded in single file through the woods, after the manner of the Indians, till they came upon the tracks of the two Frenchmen, when the Half-King sent two Indians forward to retrace these tracks, and discover the position of the main body. This was found to be in a very retired place surrounded by rocks, and half a mile from the road. A disposition for attack was then formed, in which the English occupied the right wing and the Indians the left. In this manner they advanced, till they came so near as to be discovered by the French, who instantly ran to their arms. Washington then ordered his men to fire, and a skirmish ensued. The firing continued on both sides about fifteen minutes, till the French were defeated, with the loss of their whole party, ten men being killed, including their commander, M. de Jumonville, one wounded, and twenty-one taken prisoners. Colonel Washington's loss was one man killed, and two or three wounded. The Indians escaped without injury, as the firing of the French was directed chiefly against the right wing, where Washington and his men were stationed.

This is a brief and simple narrative of facts, drawn from Washington's official letters written at the time, and from the account transmitted by Governor Dinwiddie to the British ministry, which are both confirmed by the extracts from Washington's private journal published by the French government. It is worthy of remark, that this journal, kept for his own private use, and captured the year following by the French at Braddock's defeat, accords in every essential point with his public communications to Governor Dinwiddie. Is not this accordance an irrefragable proof of the fidelity of his statement, even if his character permitted us to demand any other proof, than his single declaration? Were it possible for him to give a deceptive coloring to his public despatches, yet there could be no conceivable inducement for recording such deceptions among the broken minutes of his daily transactions, which were intended for no eye but his own.

Let it now be asked, what ground there can be for calling the death of Jumonville in this skirmish an *assassination*, or affixing to it the stigma of a crime, with which it has been marked by the French historians? Is this charge authorized either by the act itself, or by the nature of the causes, which led to it?

As to the act itself, it differs in no respect from that of any other commander, who leads his men into an engagement, in which some of the enemy are slain. It was a conflict into which both parties entered, with such means of annoyance as they could command. One of Washington's men was killed by the French, and others were wounded. There would be just as much justice in calling the death of this man an assassination, as that of M. de Jumonville. It is true, as M. de Contrecœur wrote to the Marquis Duquesne, that Washington came upon the French by surprise; but this circumstance, so far from being a matter of censure, is not only considered allowable among the stratagems of honorable warfare, but an object of praise in the commander who effects it with success. The report of the Canadian, that the reading of the summons was begun by M. de Jumonville's order, and of the savages, that he was killed while the interpreter was reading it, are manifestly fictions, as these incidents are nowhere else mentioned. Some of the prisoners said, after they were taken, that, when the firing commenced, the French called out to the English, with the design to make known the object of their mission, and the purport of the summons brought by M. de Jumonville. This was not told to Washington by the prisoners, nor was he informed of it till after their departure. He wrote to the Governor, however, stating that he had heard such a report, and affirming it to be false. The same particulars and the same affirmation were entered in his journal. As he was at the head of his men, and the first person seen by the French, he believed it impossible that any such call should have been made without his hearing it, which was not the case, but, on the contrary, he saw them run to their arms and they immediately commenced firing.

In regard to the causes, which led to the attack, it has been presumed by the French writers, that hostilities had not been committed, and that war did not in reality exist. Without discussing the abstract merits of the question, it is certain that the Governor and people of Virginia looked upon the frontiers as at that time in a state of war, and supposed it lawful to repel by force the French, and Indians in league with them, wherever found. M. de Contrecœur had appeared with an army before the fort on the Ohio, which was held by a party of Virginia troops, had drawn up his cannon in a menacing attitude, demanded a surrender, and threatened to take forcible possession in case his demand was disregarded. Compelled by this threat, the chief officer of the fort had capitulated. This act, on the part of the French commander, was considered as the beginning of an open war. Governor Dinwiddie, alluding to this subject in writing to the Governor of South Carolina, says, "I think there can be no greater act of hostility, than taking a fort begun to be built by his Majesty's immediate commands, and this must be esteemed the first breach from the French; and what followed in taking some of their people prisoners, and killing others, was in consequence thereof." In his message to the House of Burgesses of Virginia, August 23d, 1754, the Governor also says, "In open contempt and violation of the treaties now subsisting between the crowns of Great Britain and France, they have unjustly invaded his Majesty's lands on the river Ohio, and with an armed force taken a fort, that by his Majesty's orders I had directed to be built on that river." It is moreover certain, that Colonel Washington acted in strict conformity with the orders he had received; for the Governor approved his conduct both in writing to the ministry in England, and to M. Drouillon, one of the prisoners, who complained of his detention. It must be inferred, therefore, that, whatever may be the political aspect of this question, as concerning the relations between France and England, Washington was in no degree censurable for the course he pursued, but on the contrary was engaged in the discharge of his duty, by acting in strict obedience to the will and directions of the government of Virginia, under whose authority he held his commission.

The representations of the French prisoners, that Jumonville's detachment did not come out in a military capacity, but merely to bring a civil message, or summons, is well answered in Washington's letters to the Governor of Virginia. The same reasoning is used by the Governor himself in his reply to M. Drouillon, who made to him similar representations after he reached Winchester.

"The protection due to messengers of peace," says Governor Dinwiddie, "is so universally acknowledged, and the sacredness of their character so inviolably preserved, that even among the most barbarous nations their persons are safe and unhurt. You cannot be ignorant how much all the various tribes of Indians revere the calumet, and you must know, that a flag of truce would sooner have induced our protection and regard, than a body of men armed with the instruments of destruction. Thus I think the inconsistency of your appearance with your pretensions obliges me to consider you in no other light, than that in which you presented yourselves. You remained several days about our camp without telling your message, nor would you do it till you were prepared for our destruction. You had neither a right to demand, nor Colonel Washington to discuss, the King my master's title to the land on the Ohio River. Such a disquisition lay only with your superiors. But it was his duty to preserve his Majesty's dominions in peace, and protect his subjects; and they, who attempt the violation of either, must acknowledge the justice of their fate, if they meet with destruction. Colonel Washington assures me of the contrary to what you represent, regarding the circumstances of the action; and after it, the papers of summons and instructions to the Sieur Jumonville are incontestable proofs and justifications of his conduct, and laid him under the necessity of continuing to act as he afterwards did."

Again, alluding to this subject, Governor Dinwiddie writes to Lord Albemarle; — "The prisoners said they were come on an embassy from their fort; but your Lordship knows, that ambassadors do not come with such an armed force, without a trumpet, or any other sign of friendship; nor can it be thought they were on an embassy, by staying so long reconnoitring our small camp, but more probably, that they expected a reinforcement from their fort to cut them all off."

It may not be possible to ascertain at this time the precise object, for which the party under Jumonville was sent out. The tenor of his instructions, and the manner in which he approached Colonel Washington's camp, make it evident enough that he deviated widely from the mode usually adopted in conveying a summons; and his conduct was unquestionably such, as to create just suspicions, if not to afford a demonstration, of his hostile designs. His appearance on the route at the head of an armed force, his subsequent concealment at a distance from the road, his remaining there for nearly two days, his sending off messengers to M. de Contrecœur, were all circumstances unfavorable to a pacific purpose. If he came really as a peaceful messenger, and if any fault was committed by the attack upon him, it must be ascribed to his own imprudence and injudicious mode of conducting his enterprise, and not to any deviation from strict military rules on the part of Colonel Washington, who did no more than execute the duty of a vigilant officer, for which he received the unqualified approbation of his superiors and of the public.

No. III. p. 51.

BATTLE OF THE GREAT MEADOWS.

When the council of war was held at Gist's plantation, on the intelligence being received that the French at Fort Duquesne were reinforced, and would speedily march against the English, it was resolved to send an express to Captain Mackay, then at the Great Meadows, desiring him to join Colonel Washington with his Independent Company of South Carolinians, and also to call in Captain Lewis and Captain Polson, who were out with separate detachments. Captain Mackay arrived at camp in the evening, and the two detachments the next morning, when another council of war was convened, and it was unanimously resolved to retreat. A good deal of labor had been expended at Gist's in throwing up intrenchments, with the intention of waiting the approach of the French at that place, but the news of their increased numbers rendered this an inexpedient measure.

Preparations for a retreat commenced immediately. The horses were few, and Colonel Washington set a noble example to the officers by lading his own horse with ammunition and other public stores, leaving his baggage behind, and giving the soldiers four pistoles to carry it forward. The other officers followed this example. There were nine swivels, which were drawn by the soldiers of the Virginia regiment over a very broken road, unassisted by the men belonging to the Independent Company, who refused to perform any service of this kind. Nor would they act as pioneers, nor aid in transporting the public stores, considering this a duty not incumbent on them as King's soldiers. This conduct had a discouraging effect upon the soldiers of the Virginia regiment, by damping their ardor, and making them more dissatisfied with their extreme fatigue; but the whole party reached the Great Meadows on the 1st of July.

It was not the intention of Colonel Washington at first to halt at this place, but his men had become so much fatigued from great labor, and a deficiency of provisions, that they could draw the swivels no further, nor carry the baggage on their backs. They had been eight days without bread, and at the Great Meadows they found only a few bags of flour. It was thought advisable to wait here, therefore, and fortify themselves in the best manner they could, till they should receive supplies and reinforcements. They had heard of the arrival at Alexandria of two Independent Companies from New York twenty days before, and it was presumed they must by this time have reached Will's Creek. An express was sent to hasten them on, with as much despatch as possible.

Meantime Colonel Washington set his men to felling trees, and carrying logs to the fort, with a view to raise a breastwork, and enlarge and strengthen the fortification in the best manner, that circumstances would permit. The space of ground, called the Great Meadows, is a level bottom, through which passes a small creek, and is surrounded by hills of a moderate and gradual ascent. This bottom, or glade, is entirely level, covered with long grass and small bushes, and varies in width. At the point where the fort stood, it is about two hundred and fifty yards wide, from the base of one hill to that of the opposite. The position of the fort was well chosen, being about one hundred yards from the upland, or wooded ground, on the one side, and one hundred and fifty on the other, and so situated on the margin of the creek, as to afford an easy access to water. At one point the high ground comes within sixty yards of the fort, and this was the nearest distance to which an enemy could approach under the shelter of trees. The outlines of the fort were still visible, when the spot was visited by the writer in 1830, occupying an irregular square, the dimensions of which were about one hundred feet on each side. One of the angles was prolonged further than the others, for the purpose of reaching the water in the creek. On the west side, next to the nearest wood, were three entrances, protected by short breastworks, or bastions. The remains of a ditch, stretching round the south and west sides, were also distinctly seen. The site of this fort, named *Fort Necessity* from the circumstances attending its erection and original use, is three or four hundred yards south of what is now called the National Road, four miles from the foot of Laurel Hill, and fifty miles from Cumberland at Will's Creek.

On the 3d of July early in the morning an alarm was received from a sentinel, who had been wounded by the enemy; and at nine o'clock intelligence came, that the whole body of the enemy, amounting, as was reported, to nine hundred men, was only four miles off. At eleven o'clock they approached the fort, and began to fire, at the distance of six hundred yards, but without effect. Colonel Washington had drawn up his men on the open and level ground outside of the trenches, waiting for the attack, which he presumed would be made as soon as the enemy's forces emerged from the woods; and he ordered his men to reserve their fire, till they should be near enough to do execution. The distant firing was supposed to be a stratagem to draw Washington's men into the woods, and thus to take them at a disadvantage. He suspected the design, and maintained his post till he found the French did not incline to leave the woods, and attack the fort by an assault, as he supposed they would, considering their superiority of numbers. He then drew his men back within the trenches, and gave them orders to fire according to their discretion, as suitable opportunities might present themselves. The French and Indians remained on the side of the rising ground, which was nearest to the fort, and, sheltered by the trees, kept up a brisk fire of musketry, but never appeared in the open plain below. The rain fell heavily through the day, the trenches were filled with water, and many of the arms of Colonel Washington's men were out of order, and used with difficulty.

In this way the battle continued from eleven o'clock in the morning till eight at night, when the French called and requested a parley. Suspecting this to be a feint to procure the admission of an officer into the fort, that he might discover their condition, Colonel Washington at first declined listening to the proposal, but when the call was repeated, with the additional request that an officer might be sent to them, engaging at the same time their parole for his safety, he sent out Captain Vanbraam, the only person under his command, that could speak French, except the Chevalier de Peyrouny, an ensign in the Virginia regiment, who was dangerously wounded, and disabled from rendering any service on this occasion. Vanbraam returned, and brought with him from M. de Villiers, the French commander, proposed articles of capitulation. These he read and pretended to interpret, and, some changes having been made by mutual agreement, both parties signed them about midnight.

By the terms of the capitulation, the whole garrison was to retire, and return without molestation to the inhabited parts of the country, and the French commander promised, that no embarrassment should be interposed, either by his own men or the savages. The English were to take away every thing in their possession, except their artillery, and to march out of the fort the next morning with the honors of war, their drums beating and colors flying. As the French had killed all the horses and cattle, Colonel Washington had no means of transporting his heavy baggage and stores; and it was conceded to him, that his men might conceal their effects, and that a guard might be left to protect them, till horses could be sent up to take them away. Colonel Washington agreed to restore the prisoners, who had been taken at the skirmish with Jumonville; and as a surety for this article two hostages, Captain Vanbraam and Captain Stobo, were delivered up to the French, and were to be retained till the prisoners should return. It was moreover agreed, that the party capitulating should not attempt to build any more establishments at that place, or beyond the mountains, for the space of a year.

Early the next morning Colonel Washington began to march from the fort in good order, but he had proceeded only a short distance, when a body of one hundred Indians, being a reinforcement to the French, came upon him, and could hardly be restrained from attacking his men. They pilfered the baggage and did other mischief. He marched forward, however, with as much speed as possible, in the weakened and encumbered condition of his army, there being no other mode of conveying the wounded men and the baggage, than on the soldiers' backs. As the provisions were nearly exhausted, no time was to be lost; and, leaving much of the baggage behind, he hastened to Will's Creek, where all the necessary supplies were in store. Thence Colonel Washington and Captain Mackay proceeded to Williamsburg, and communicated in person to the Governor the events of the campaign. *

A good deal of dissatisfaction was expressed with some of the articles of capitulation, when they came to be made public. The truth

---

* The following are the articles of capitulation, as published at the time from the duplicate copy retained by Colonel Washington.

"ARTICLE I. Nous accordons au commandant Anglais de se retirer avec toute sa garnison, pour s'en retourner paisiblement dans son pays, et lui promettons d'empêcher qu'il lui soit fait aucune insulte par nos Français, et de maintenir, autant qu'il sera en notre pouvoir, tous les sauvages qui sont avec nous.

"ART. II. Il lui sera permis de sortir, et d'emporter tout ce qui leur appartiendra, *à l'exception de l'artillerie, que nous nous réservons.*

"ART. III. Que nous leur accordons les honneurs de la guerre; qu'ils sortiront tambour battant avec une petite pièce de canon, voulant bien par-là leur prouver que nous les traitons en amis.

"ART. IV. Que si-tôt les articles signés de part et d'autre, ils amèneront le pavillon Anglais.

"ART. V. Que demain à la pointe du jour, un détachement Français ira faire defiler la garnison et prendre possession du dit fort.

"ART. VI. Que comme les Anglais n'ont presque plus de chevaux ni bœufs, ils seront libres de mettre leurs effets en cache pour venir chercher lorsqu'ils auront rejoint des chevaux; ils pourront à cette fin laisser des gardiens, en tel nombre qu'ils voudront, *aux conditions qu'ils donneront parole d'honneur de ne plus travailler à aucun établissement dans ce lieu-ci, ni deça de la hauteur des terres, pendant une année à compter de ce jour.*

"ART. VII. Que comme les Anglais ont en leur pouvoir un officier, deux cadets, et généralement les prisonniers qu'ils nous ont faits *dans l'assassinat du Sieur de Jumonville*, et qu'ils promettent de les envoyer avec sauvegarde jusqu'au Fort Duquesne, situé sur la Belle-Rivière; et que pour sureté de cet

is, Colonel Washington had been grossly deceived by the interpreter, either through ignorance or design. An officer of his regiment, who was present at the reading and signing of the articles, wrote as follows on this point five weeks afterwards in a letter to a friend.

"When Mr. Vanbraam returned with the French proposals, we were obliged to take the sense of them from his mouth; it rained so hard, that he could not give us a written translation of them; we could scarcely keep the candle lighted to read them by; and every officer there is ready to declare, that there was no such word as *assassination* mentioned. The terms expressed were, *the death of Jumonville.* If it had been mentioned, we would by all means have had it altered, as the French, during the course of the interview, seemed very condescending, and desirous to bring things to a conclusion; and, upon our insisting, altered the articles relating to stores and ammunition, which they wanted to detain; and that of the cannon, which they agreed to have *destroyed,* instead of *reserved for their use.*

"Another article, which appears to our disadvantage, is that whereby we oblige ourselves not to attempt an establishment beyond the mountains. This was translated to us, *not to attempt buildings or improvements on the lands of his Most Christian Majesty.* This we never intended, as we denied he had any there, and therefore thought it needless to dispute the point.

"The last article, which relates to the hostages, is quite different from the translation of it given to us. It is mentioned *for the security of the performance of this treaty*, as well as for the return of the prisoners. There was never such an intention on our side, or mention of it made on theirs by our interpreter. Thus by the evil intention or negligence of Vanbraam, our conduct is scrutinized by a busy world, fond of criticizing the proceedings of others, without considering circumstances, or giving just attention to reasons, which might be offered to obviate their censures."

Vanbraam was a Dutchman, and had but an imperfect knowledge of either the French or English language. How far his ignorance

article, *ainsi que de ce traité*, Messrs. Jacob Vanbraam et Robert Stobo, tous deux capitaines, nous seront remis en ôtage jusqu'à l'arrivée de nos Français et Canadiens ci-dessus mentionnés."

The parts here marked in italics were misrepresented by the interpreter, or at least the meaning of them was so imperfectly and obscurely expressed by him, as to be misunderstood by Colonel Washington and his officers. The words, *pendant une année à compter de ce jour*, which occur at the end of the sixth article in the copy retained by Colonel Washington, are not found in the copy of the articles printed by the French government.

should be taken as an apology for his blunders is uncertain. Although he had approved himself a good officer, yet there were other circumstances, which brought his fidelity in question. Governor Dinwiddie, in giving an account of this affair to Lord Albemarle, says, "In the capitulation they made use of the word *assassination*, but Washington, not knowing French, was deceived by the interpreter, who was a poltroon, and though an officer with us, they say he has joined the French." How long Vanbraam was detained as a hostage is not known, but he never returned to Virginia, and it was the general belief, that he practised an intentional deception in his attempts to interpret the articles of capitulation. But whether this be true or not, the consequence was unfortunate, as the articles in their written form implied an acknowledgment of the charge of assassinating Jumonville. The French writers, regarding this as an authentic public document, were confirmed by it in their false impressions derived from M. de Contrecœur's letter concerning the fate of Jumonville; and thus a grave historical error, inflicting a deep injustice on the character of Washington, has been sanctioned by eminent names, and perpetuated in the belief of the reading portion of the French people.

M. de Villiers, the commander of the French forces, was the brother of Jumonville. His account of the march from Fort Duquesne, and the transactions at the Great Meadows, was published by the French government, in connexion with what purported to be extracts from Colonel Washington's journal taken at Braddock's defeat. Many years afterwards, some person sent to Washington a translation of these papers, upon which he made a brief comment, which it is proper to introduce in this place, after inserting an extract from that part of M. de Villiers' narrative, which relates to the affair of the Great Meadows.

"As we had no knowledge of the place," says M. de Villiers, "we presented our flank to the fort, when they began to fire on us with their cannon. Almost at the same instant, that I saw the English on the right coming towards us, the Indians as well as ourselves set up a loud cry, and we advanced upon them; but they did not give us time to fire before they retreated behind an intrenchment adjoining the fort. We then prepared ourselves to invest the fort. It was advantageously situated in a meadow, and within musket-shot of the wood. We approached as near to them as possible, and not uselessly expose his Majesty's subjects. The fire was spirited on both sides, and I placed myself in the position where it seemed to me most likely a sortie would be attempted. If the expression may be allowed, we almost extinguished the fire of their cannon by our musketry.

"About six o'clock in the evening the fire of the enemy increased with renewed vigor, and continued till eight. We returned it briskly. We had taken effectual measures to secure our posts, and keep the enemy in the fort all night; and, after having put ourselves in the best position possible, we called out to the English, that, if they desired a parley with us, we would cease firing. They accepted the proposal. A captain came out, and I sent M. de Mercier to receive him, and went to the Meadow myself, where we told him, that not being at war, we were willing to save them from the cruelties to which they would expose themselves on the part of the savages by an obstinate resistance, that we could take from them all the hope of escape during the night, that we consented nevertheless to show them favor, as we had come only to avenge the assassination, which they had inflicted upon my brother, in violation of the most sacred laws, and to oblige them to depart from the territories of the King. We then agreed to accord to them the capitulation, a copy of which is hereunto annexed.

"We considered that nothing could be more advantageous to the nation than this capitulation, as it was unnatural in the time of peace to make prisoners. We made the English consent to sign, that they had assassinated my brother in his camp. We took hostages for the French, who were in their power; we caused them to abandon the lands belonging to the King; we obliged them to leave their cannon, which consisted of nine pieces; we had destroyed all their horses and cattle, and made them sign, that the favor we granted them was only to prove how much we desired to treat them as friends. That very night the articles were signed, and I received in camp the hostages, whom I had demanded.

"On the 4th, at the dawn of day, I sent a detachment to take possession of the fort. The garrison defiled, and the number of their dead and wounded excited my pity, in spite of the resentment, which I felt for the manner in which they had taken away the life of my brother.

"The savages, who in every thing had adhered to my wishes, claimed the right of plunder, but I prevented them. The English, struck with a panic, took to flight, and left their flag and one of their colors. I demolished the fort, and M. de Mercier caused the cannon to be broken, as also the one granted by the capitulation, the English not being able to take it away. I hastened my departure, after having burst open the casks of liquor, to prevent the disorders which would otherwise infallibly have followed. One of my Indians took ten Englishmen, whom he brought to me, and whom I sent back by another." — *Mémoire contenant le Précis des Faits*, &c. p. 147.

Such is the statement of M. de Villiers. The incident, mentioned at the close, of an Indian taking ten Englishmen, is so ludicrous, that it must necessarily cast a shade of doubt over the whole, and cause us to suspect the writer's accuracy of facts and soundness of judgment, whatever we may think of the fertility of his imagination, and his exuberant self-complacency. Washington's remarks on this extract were communicated in the following letter to a gentleman, who had previously written to him on the subject.

"SIR,

"I am really sorry, that I have it not in my power to answer your request in a more satisfactory manner. If you had favored me with the journal a few days sooner, I would have examined it carefully, and endeavoured to point out such errors as might conduce to your use, my advantage, and the public satisfaction; but now it is out of my power.

"I had no time to make any remarks upon that piece, which is called my journal. The enclosed are observations on the French notes. They are of no use to me separated, nor will they, I believe, be of any to you; yet I send them unconnected and incoherent as they were taken, for I have no opportunity to correct them.

"In regard to the journal, I can only observe in general, that I kept no regular one during that expedition; rough minutes of occurrences I certainly took, and find them as certainly and strangely metamorphosed; some parts left out, which I remember were entered, and many things added that never were thought of; the names of men and things egregiously miscalled; and the whole of what I saw Englished is very incorrect and nonsensical; yet, I will not pretend to say that the little body, who brought it to me, has not made a literal translation, and a good one.

"Short as my time is, I cannot help remarking on Villiers' account of the battle of, and transactions at, the Meadows, as it is very extraordinary, and not less erroneous than inconsistent. He says the French received the first fire. It is well known, that we received it at six hundred paces' distance. He also says, our fears obliged us to retreat in a most disorderly manner after the capitulation. How is this consistent with his other account? He acknowledges, that we sustained the attack warmly from ten in the morning until dark, and that he called first to parley, which strongly indicates that we were not totally absorbed in fear. If the gentleman in his account had adhered to the truth, he must have confessed, that we looked upon his offer to parley as an artifice to get into and examine our trenches, and refused on this account, until they desired an officer might be sent to them, and gave their parole for his safe return. He might also, if he had been as great a lover of the truth as he was of vainglory, have said, that we absolutely refused their first and second proposals, and would consent to capitulate on no other terms than such as we obtained. That we were wilfully, or ignorantly, deceived by our interpreter in regard to the word *assassination*, I do aver, and will to my dying moment; so will every officer that was present. The interpreter was a Dutchman, little acquainted with the English tongue, therefore might not advert to the tone and meaning of the word in English; but, whatever his motives were for so doing, certain it is, he called it the *death*, or the *loss*, of the Sieur Jumonville. So we received and so we understood it, until, to our great surprise and mortification, we found it otherwise in a literal translation.

"That we left our baggage and horses at the Meadows is certain; that there was not even a possibility to bring them away is equally certain, as we had every horse belonging to the camp killed or taken away during the action; so that it was impracticable to bring any thing off, that our shoulders were not able to bear; and to wait there was impossible, for we had scarce three days' provisions, and were seventy miles from a supply; yet, to say we came off precipitately is absolutely false; notwithstanding they did, contrary to articles, suffer their Indians to pillage our baggage, and commit all kinds of irregularity, we were with them until ten o'clock the next day; we destroyed our powder and other stores, nay, even our private baggage, to prevent its falling into their hands, as we could not bring it off. When we had got about a mile from the place of action, we missed two or three of the wounded, and sent a party back to bring them up; this is the party he speaks of. We brought them all safe off, and encamped within three miles of the Meadows. These are circumstances, I think, that make it evidently clear, that we were not very apprehensive of danger. The colors he speaks of as left were a large flag of immense size and weight; our regimental colors were brought off and are now in my possession. Their gasconades, and boasted clemency, must appear in the most ludicrous light to every considerate person, who reads Villiers' journal; such preparations for an attack, such vigor and intrepidity as he pretends to have conducted his march with, such revenge as by his own account appeared in his attack, considered, it will hardly be thought that compassion was his motive for calling a parley. But to sum up the whole,

Mr. Villiers pays himself no great compliment in saying, we were struck with a panic when matters were adjusted. We surely could not be afraid without cause, and if we had cause after capitulation, it was a reflection upon himself.

"I do not doubt, but your good nature will excuse the badness of my paper, and the incoherence of my writing; think you see me in a public house in a crowd, surrounded with noise, and you hit my case. You do me particular honor in offering your friendship; I wish I may be so happy as always to merit it, and deserve your correspondence, which I should be glad to cultivate."

In September, somewhat more than two months after the capitulation, Captain Mackay wrote to Washington from Will's Creek, stating that he had recently returned from Philadelphia, and adding,— "I had several disputes about our capitulation, but I satisfied every person, that mentioned the subject, as to the articles in question, that they were owing to a bad interpreter, and contrary to the translation made to us when we signed them."

No more needs be said to show the true light, in which the articles of capitulation were understood by Washington and his officers. It is not to be inferred, however, that M. de Villiers was knowingly guilty of an imposition, in regard to the clause relating to the death of his brother. On the contrary, it seems more than probable, that he really believed the report of the assassination, for he had received no other intelligence, or explanation, than the rumor brought to M. de Contrecœur by the Canadian and the savages. This fact, however, does not lessen the injury done to Washington, in seriously using the articles of capitulation as a historical document to sanction a charge, equally untrue in all its essential particulars, and unjust in its application.

When the Virginia House of Burgesses met in August, they requested the Governor to lay before them a copy of the capitulation, and, upon a due consideration of the subject, passed a vote of thanks to Colonel Washington and his officers "for their bravery and gallant defence of their country." The names of all the officers were enumerated, except those of the major of the regiment, and of Captain Vanbraam, the former of whom was charged with cowardice, and the latter of having acted a treacherous part in his interpretation of the articles. The Burgesses, also, in an address to the Governor, expressed their approbation of the instructions he had given to the officers and forces sent on the Ohio expedition. In short, all the proceedings of the campaign were not only approved, but applauded, by the representatives of the people, and by the public generally. A pistole was granted to each of the soldiers, who had been in the engagement. To the vote of thanks Washington replied as follows.

TO THE SPEAKER OF THE HOUSE OF BURGESSES.

"Williamsburg, 23 October, 1754.

"SIR,

"Nothing could give me, and the officers under my command, greater satisfaction, than to receive the thanks of the House of Burgesses, in so particular and public a manner, for our behaviour in the late unsuccessful engagement with the French; and we unanimously hope, that our future proceedings in the service of our country will entitle us to a continuance of your approbation. I assure you, Sir, I shall always look upon it as my indispensable duty to endeavour to deserve it.

"I was desired by the officers of the Virginia regiment to make their suitable acknowledgments for the honor they have received in your thanks; I therefore hope the enclosed will be agreeable, and answer their, and the intended purpose of, Sir, your most obedient humble servant,

"GEORGE WASHINGTON."

TO THE WORSHIPFUL THE SPEAKER, AND THE GENTLEMEN OF THE HOUSE OF BURGESSES.

"We, the officers of the Virginia regiment, are highly sensible of the particular mark of distinction, with which you have honored us, in returning your thanks for our behaviour in the late action, and cannot help testifying our grateful acknowledgments for your high sense of what we shall always esteem a duty to our country and the best of kings.

"Favored with your regard, we shall zealously endeavour to deserve your applause, and by our future actions strive to convince the worshipful House of Burgesses, how much we esteem their approbation, and, as it ought to be, regard it as the voice of our country.

"Signed for the whole corps,

"GEORGE WASHINGTON."

The exact number of men engaged in the action of the Great Meadows cannot be ascertained. The Virginia regiment consisted of three hundred and five, including officers, of whom twelve were killed and forty-three wounded. These numbers are stated in a return made out by Colonel Washington himself. Captain Mackay's

Independent Company was supposed to contain about one hundred, but the number of killed and wounded is not known. The two Independent Companies from New York, which arrived at Alexandria, never joined the Virginia regiment, although former writers, in describing this event, have said they were present. The amount of the French force is also uncertain. It was believed by Colonel Washington, from such information as he could get, to consist of nine hundred men. M. de Villiers says, that he left Fort Duquesne with five hundred Frenchmen and eleven Indians. The number of French is perhaps correct, but the Indians were much more numerous, when they arrived at the scene of action; and there is good reason for believing, that the French and Indians together made a body of at least nine hundred.

It was a subject of mortification to Colonel Washington, that Governor Dinwiddie refused to ratify the capitulation, in regard to the French prisoners. The Governor thus explained his conduct in a letter to the Board of Trade. — "The French, after the capitulation entered into with Colonel Washington, took eight of our people, and exposed them to sale, and, missing thereof, sent them prisoners to Canada. On hearing of this, I detained the seventeen prisoners, the officer, and two cadets, as I am of opinion, after they were in my custody, Washington could not engage for their being returned. I have ordered a flag of truce to be sent to the French, offering the return of their officer and the two cadets for the two hostages they have of ours." This course of proceeding was not suitable to the principles of honor and sense of equity entertained by Colonel Washington, but he had no further control of the affair.

The hostages were not returned, as requested by the Governor's flag of truce, and the French prisoners were detained in Virginia, and supported and clothed at the public charge, having a weekly allowance for that purpose. The private men were kept in confinement, but Drouillon and the two cadets were allowed to go at large, first in Williamsburg, then at Winchester, and last at Alexandria, where they resided when General Braddock arrived. It was then deemed improper for them to go at large, observing the motions of the General's army, and the Governor applied to Commodore Keppel to take them on board his ships; but he declined, on the ground that he had no instructions about prisoners. By the advice of General Braddock, the privates were put on board the transports, and sent to England. M. Drouillon and the cadets went passengers in another ship at the charge of the colony. La Force, having been only a volunteer in the skirmish, and not in a military capacity, and having previously committed acts of depredation on the frontiers, was kept in prison at Williamsburg. Being a person of ready resources, and an enterprising spirit, he broke from prison and made his way several miles into the country, when his foreign accent betrayed him, and he was taken up, and remanded to close confinement.

Vanbraam and Stobo were conveyed to Quebec, and retained there as prisoners; they were both ultimately released, and after the war they went to England.

No. IV. p. 91.

BRADDOCK'S DEFEAT.

The defeat of General Braddock, on the banks of the Monongahela, is one of the most remarkable events in American history. Great preparations had been made for the expedition under that experienced officer, and there was the most sanguine anticipation, both in England and America, of its entire success. Such was the confidence in the prowess of Braddock's army, according to Dr. Franklin, that, while he was on his march to Fort Duquesne, a subscription paper was handed about in Philadelphia to raise money to celebrate his victory by bonfires and illuminations, as soon as the intelligence should arrive. When, therefore, the news of his total defeat and overthrow went abroad, the effect produced on the public mind was like the shock of an earthquake, unexpected and astounding. Of the possibility of such an issue no one had dreamed, and the expressions of surprise, as well as of disappointment, were loud and universal. The consequences were alarming to the middle colonies, as their frontiers were left exposed to the ravages of the French and Indians, in which situation they continued till Fort Duquesne was taken by General Forbes, more than three years afterwards.

General Braddock landed in Virginia on the 20th of February, 1755, with two regiments of the British army from Ireland, the forty-fourth and forty-eighth, each consisting of five hundred men, one of them commanded by Sir Peter Halket, and the other by Colonel Dunbar. To these was joined a suitable train of artillery, with military supplies and provisions. The General's first head-quarters were at Alexandria, and the troops were stationed in that place and its vicinity, till they marched for Will's Creek, where they arrived about the middle of May. It took four weeks to effect that march. In letters written at Will's Creek, General Braddock, with much severity of censure, complained of the lukewarmness of the colonial governments and tardiness of the people in facilitating his enterprise, the dishonesty of agents, and the faithlessness of contractors. The forces, which he brought together at Will's Creek, however, amounted to somewhat more than two thousand effective men, of whom about one thousand belonged to the royal regiments, and the remainder were furnished by the colonies. In this number were embraced the fragments of two Independent Companies from New York, one of which was commanded by Captain Gates, afterwards a major-general in the Revolutionary war. Thirty sailors had also been granted for the expedition by Admiral Keppel, who commanded the squadron, that brought over the two regiments.

At this post the army was detained three weeks, nor could it then have moved, had it not been for the energetic personal services of Franklin, among the Pennsylvania farmers, in procuring horses and wagons to transport the artillery, provisions, and baggage. The details of the march are well described in Colonel Washington's letters. The army was separated into two divisions. The advanced division, under General Braddock, consisted of twelve hundred men besides officers. The other, under Colonel Dunbar, was left in the rear to proceed by slower marches. On the 8th of July the General arrived with his division, all in excellent health and spirits, at the junction of the Youghiogany and Monongahela Rivers. At this place Colonel Washington joined the advanced division, being but partially recovered from a severe attack of fever, which had been the cause of his remaining behind. The officers and soldiers were now in the highest spirits, and firm in the conviction, that they should within a few hours victoriously enter the walls of Fort Duquesne.

The steep and rugged grounds, on the north side of the Monongahela, prevented the army from marching in that direction, and it was necessary in approaching the fort, now about fifteen miles distant, to ford the river twice, and march a part of the way on the south side. Early on the morning of the 9th all things were in readiness, and the whole train passed through the river a little below the mouth of the Youghiogany, and proceeded in perfect order along the southern margin of the Monongahela. Washington was often heard to say during his lifetime, that the most beautiful spectacle he had ever beheld was the display of the British troops on this eventful morning. Every man was neatly dressed in full uniform, the soldiers were arranged in columns and marched in exact order, the sun gleamed from their burnished arms, the river flowed tranquilly on their right, and the deep forest overshadowed them with solemn grandeur on their left. Officers and men were equally inspirited with cheering hopes and confident anticipations.

In this manner they marched forward till about noon, when they arrived at the second crossing-place, ten miles from Fort Duquesne. They halted but a little time, and then began to ford the river and regain its northern bank. As soon as they had crossed, they came upon a level plain, elevated but a few feet above the surface of the river, and extending northward nearly half a mile from its margin. Then commenced a gradual ascent at an angle of about three degrees, which terminated in hills of a considerable height at no great distance beyond. The road from the fording-place to Fort Duquesne led across the plain and up this ascent, and thence proceeded through an uneven country, at that time covered with wood.

By the order of march, a body of three hundred men, under Colonel Gage, made the advanced party, which was immediately followed by another of two hundred. Next came the General with the columns of artillery, the main body of the army, and the baggage. At one o'clock the whole had crossed the river, and almost at this moment a sharp firing was heard upon the advanced parties, who were now ascending the hill, and had got forward about a hundred yards from the termination of the plain. A heavy discharge of musketry was poured in upon their front, which was the first intelligence they had of the proximity of an enemy, and this was suddenly followed by another on their right flank. They were filled with the greater consternation, as no enemy was in sight, and the firing seemed to proceed from an invisible foe. They fired in their turn, however, but quite at random and obviously without effect, as the enemy kept up a discharge in quick and continued succession.

The General advanced speedily to the relief of these detachments; but before he could reach the spot, which they occupied, they gave way and fell back upon the artillery and the other columns of the army, causing extreme confusion, and striking the whole mass with such a panic, that no order could afterwards be restored. The General and the officers behaved with the utmost courage, and used every effort to rally the men, and bring them to order, but all in vain. In this state they continued nearly three hours, huddling together in confused bodies, firing irregularly, shooting down their own officers and men, and doing no perceptible harm to the enemy. The Virginia provincials were the only troops, who seemed to retain their senses, and they behaved with a bravery and resolution worthy of a better fate. They adopted the Indian mode, and fought each man for himself behind a tree. This was prohibited by the General, who endeavoured to form his men into platoons and columns, as if they had been manœuvring on the plains of Flanders. Meantime the French and Indians, concealed in the ravines and behind trees, kept up a deadly and unceasing discharge of musketry, singling out their objects, taking deliberate aim, and producing a carnage almost unparalleled in the annals of modern warfare. More than half of the whole army, which had crossed the river in so proud an array only three hours before, were killed or wounded, the General himself had received a mortal wound, and many of his best officers had fallen by his side.

In describing the action a few days afterwards, Colonel Orme wrote to the Governor of Pennsylvania; — "The men were so extremely deaf to the exhortation of the General and the officers, that they fired away in the most irregular manner all their ammunition, and then ran off, leaving to the enemy the artillery, ammunition, provision, and baggage; nor could they be persuaded to stop till they got as far as Gist's plantation, nor there only in part, many of them proceeding as far as Colonel Dunbar's party, who lay six miles on this side. The officers were absolutely sacrificed by their good behaviour, advancing sometimes in bodies, sometimes separately, hoping by such example to engage the soldiers to follow them, but to no purpose. The General had five horses shot under him, and at last received a wound through his right arm into his lungs, of which he died the 13th instant. Secretary Shirley was shot through the head; Captain Morris, wounded. Colonel Washington had two horses shot under him, and his clothes shot through in several places, behaving the whole time with the greatest courage and resolution. Sir Peter Halket was killed upon the spot. Colonel Burton and Sir John St. Clair were wounded." In addition to these, the other field-officers wounded were Lieutenant-Colonel Gage (afterwards so well known as the commander of the British forces in Boston, at the beginning of the Revolution), Colonel Orme, Major Sparks, and Brigade-Major Halket. Ten captains were killed, and five wounded; fifteen lieutenants killed, and twenty-two wounded; the whole number of officers in the engagement was eighty-six, of whom twenty-six were killed, and thirty-seven wounded. The killed and wounded of the privates amounted to seven hundred and fourteen. Of these at least one half were supposed to be killed. Their bodies, left on the field of action, were stripped and scalped by the Indians. All the artillery, ammunition, provisions, and baggage, every thing in the train of the army, fell into the enemy's hands, and were given up to be pillaged by the savages. General Braddock's papers were also taken, among which were his instructions and correspondence with the ministry after his arrival in Virginia. The same fate befell the papers of Colonel Washington, including a private journal and his official correspondence during his campaign of the preceding year.

No circumstantial account of this affair has ever been published by the French, nor has it hitherto been known from any authentic source what numbers were engaged on their side. Washington conjectured, as stated in his letters, that there were no more than three hundred, and Dr. Franklin, in his account of the battle, considers them at most as not exceeding four hundred. The truth is, there was no accurate information on the subject, and writers have been obliged to rely on conjecture.

In the archives of the *War Department*, at Paris, I found three separate narratives of this event written at the time, all brief and imperfect, but one of them apparently drawn up by a person on the spot. From these I have collected the following particulars.

M. de Contrecœur, the commandant of Fort Duquesne, received early intelligence of the arrival of General Braddock and the British regiments in Virginia. After his remove from Will's Creek, French and Indian scouts were constantly abroad, who watched his motions, reported the progress of his march, and the route he was pursuing. His army was represented to consist of three thousand men. M. de Contrecœur was hesitating what measures to take, believing his small force wholly inadequate to encounter so formidable an army, when M. de Beaujeu, a captain in the French service, proposed to head a detachment of French and Indians, and meet the enemy in their march. The consent of the Indians was first to be obtained. A large body of them was then encamped in the vicinity of the Fort, and M. de Beaujeu opened to them his plan, and requested their aid. This they at first declined, giving as a reason the superior force of the enemy, and the impossibility of success. But at the pressing solicitation of M. de Beaujeu, they agreed to hold a council on the subject, and to talk with him again the next morning. They still adhered to their first decision, and when M. de Beaujeu went out among them to inquire the result of their deliberation, they told him a second time that they could not go. This was a severe disappointment to M. de Beaujeu, who had set his heart upon the enterprise, and was resolved to prosecute it. Being a man of great good nature, affability, and ardor, and much beloved by the savages, he said to them; "I am determined to go out and meet the enemy. What! will you suffer your Father to go out alone? I am sure we shall conquer." With this spirited harangue, delivered in a manner that pleased the Indians, and won upon their confidence, he subdued their unwillingness, and they agreed to accompany him.

It was now the 7th of July, and news came that the English were within six leagues of the Fort. This day and the next were spent in making preparations, and reconnoitring the ground for attack. Two other captains, Dumas and Liguery were joined with M. de Beaujeu, and also four lieutenants, six ensigns, and two cadets. On the morning of the 9th they were all in readiness, and began their march at an early hour. It seems to have been their first intention to make a stand at the ford, and annoy the English while crossing the river, and then retreat to the ambuscade on the side of the hill where the contest actually commenced. The trees on the bank of the river afforded a good opportunity to effect this manœuvre, in the Indian mode of warfare, since the artillery could be of little avail against an enemy, where every man was protected by a tree, and at the same time the English would be exposed to a point-blank musket-shot in fording the river. As it happened, however, M. de Beaujeu and his party did not arrive in time to execute this part of the plan.

The English were preparing to cross the river, when the French and Indians reached the defiles on the rising ground, where they posted themselves, and waited till Braddock's advanced columns came up. This was a signal for the attack, which was made at first in front, and repelled by so heavy a discharge from the British, that the Indians believed it proceeded from artillery, and showed symptoms of wavering and retreat. At this moment M. de Beaujeu was killed, and the command devolving on M. Dumas, he showed great presence of mind in rallying the Indians, and ordered his officers to lead them to the wings and attack the enemy in flank, while he with the French troops would maintain the position in front. This order was promptly obeyed, and the attack became general. The action was warm and severely contested for a short time; but the English fought in the European method, firing at random, which had little effect in the woods, while the Indians fired from concealed places, took aim, and almost every shot brought down a man. The English columns soon got into confusion; the yell of the savages, with which the woods resounded, struck terror into the hearts of the soldiers, till at length they took to flight, and resisted all the endeavours of their officers to restore any degree of order in their escape. The rout was complete, and the field of battle was left covered with the dead and wounded, and all the artillery, ammunition, provisions, and baggage of the English army. The Indians gave themselves up to pillage, which prevented them from pursuing the English in their flight.

Such is the substance of the accounts written at the time by the French officers, and sent home to their government. In regard to the numbers engaged, there are some slight variations in the three statements. The largest number reported is two hundred and fifty French and Canadians, and six hundred and forty-one Indians; and the smallest, two hundred and thirty-three French and Canadians, and six hundred Indians. If we take a medium, it will make the whole number led out by M. de Beaujeu at least eight hundred and fifty. In an imperfect return, three officers were stated to be killed, and four wounded; about thirty soldiers and Indians killed, and as many wounded.

When these facts are taken into view, the result of the action will appear much less wonderful, than has generally been supposed. And this wonder will be still diminished, when another circumstance is recurred to, worthy of particular consideration, and that is, the shape of the ground on which the battle was fought. This part of the description, so essential to the understanding of military operations, and above all in the present instance, has never been touched upon, it is believed, by any writer. We have seen that Braddock's advanced columns, after crossing the valley extending for nearly half a mile from the margin of the river, began to move up a hill, so uniform in its ascent, that it was little else than an inclined plane of a somewhat crowning form. Down this inclined surface extended two ravines, beginning near together, at about one hundred and fifty yards from the bottom of the hill, and proceeding in different directions till they terminated in the valley below. In these ravines the French and Indians were concealed and protected. At this day they are from eight to ten feet deep, and sufficient in extent to contain at least a thousand men. At the time of the battle, the ground was covered with trees and long grass, so that the ravines were entirely hidden from view, till they were approached within a few feet. Indeed, at the present day, although the place is cleared from trees, and converted into pasture, they are perceptible only at a very short distance. By this knowledge of the local peculiarities of the battle-ground, the mystery, that the British conceived themselves to be contending with an invisible foe, is solved. Such was literally the fact. They were so paraded between the ravines, that their whole front and right flank were exposed to the incessant fire of the enemy, who discharged their muskets over the edge of the ravines, concealed during that operation by the grass and bushes, and protected by an invincible barrier below the surface of the earth. William Butler, a veteran soldier still living (1832), who was in this action, and afterwards at the Plains of Abraham, said to me, "We could only tell where the enemy were by the smoke of their muskets." A few scattering Indians were behind trees, and some were killed in venturing out to take scalps, but much the larger portion fought wholly in the ravines.

It is not probable, that either General Braddock or any one of his officers suspected the actual situation of the enemy, during the whole bloody contest. It was a fault in the General, for which no apology can be offered, that he did not keep scouts and guards in advance and on the wings of his army, who would have made all proper discoveries before the whole had been brought into a snare. This neglect was the primary cause of his defeat, which might have been avoided. Had he charged with the bayonet, the ravines would have been cleared instantly; or had he brought his artillery to the points where the ravines terminated in the valley, and scoured them with grape-shot, the same consequence would have followed. But the total insubordination of his troops would have prevented both these movements, even if he had become acquainted with the ground in the early part of the action. The disasters of this day, and the fate of the commander, brave and resolute as he undoubtedly was, are to be ascribed to his contempt of Indian warfare, his overweening confidence in the prowess of veteran troops, his obstinate self-complacency, his disregard of prudent counsel, and his negligence in leaving his army exposed to a surprise on their march. He freely consulted Colonel Washington, whose experience and judgment, notwithstanding his youth, claimed the highest respect for his opinions; but the General gave little heed to his advice. While on his march, George Croghan, the Indian interpreter, joined him with one hundred friendly Indians, who offered their services. These were accepted in so cold a manner, and the Indians themselves treated with so much neglect, that they deserted him one after another. Washington pressed upon him the importance of these men, and the necessity of conciliating and retaining them, but without effect.

A report has long been current in Pennsylvania, that Braddock was shot by one of his own men, founded on the declaration of a provincial soldier, who was in the action. There is another tradition, also, worthy of notice, which rests on the authority of Dr. Craik, the intimate friend of Washington from his boyhood to his death, and who was with him at the battle of the Monongahela. Fifteen years after that event, they travelled together on an expedition to the western country, with a party of woodsmen, for the purpose of exploring wild lands. While near the junction of the Great Kenhawa and Ohio Rivers, a company of Indians came to them with an interpreter, at the head of whom was an aged and venerable chief. This personage made known to them by the interpreter, that, hearing Colonel Washington was in that region, he had come a long way to visit him, adding that during the battle of the Monongahela, he had singled him out as a conspicuous object, fired his rifle at him many times, and directed his young warriors to do the same, but to his utter astonishment none of their balls took effect. He was then persuaded, that the youthful hero was under the special guardianship of the Great Spirit, and ceased to fire at him any longer. He was now come to pay homage to the man, who was the particular favorite of Heaven, and who could never die in battle. Mr. Custis, of Arlington, to whom these incidents were related by Dr. Craik, has dramatized them in a piece called *The Indian Prophecy*.

When the battle was over, and the remnant of Braddock's army had gained, in their flight, the opposite bank of the river, Colonel Washington was despatched by the General to meet Colonel Dunbar and order forward wagons for the wounded with all possible speed. But it was not till the 11th, after they had reached Gist's plantation with great difficulty and much suffering from hunger, that any arrived. The General was at first brought off in a tumbril; he was next put on horseback, but, being unable to ride, was obliged to be carried by the soldiers. They all reached Dunbar's camp, to which the panic had already extended, and a day was passed there in the greatest confusion. The artillery was destroyed, and the public stores and heavy baggage were burnt, by whose order was never known. They moved forward on the 13th, and that night General Braddock died, and was buried in the road, for the purpose of concealing his body from the Indians. The spot is still pointed out, within a few yards of the present National Road, and about a mile west of the site of Fort Necessity at the Great Meadows. Captain Stewart, of the Virginia forces, had taken particular charge of him from the time he was wounded till his death. On the 17th the sick and wounded arrived at Fort Cumberland, and were soon after joined by Colonel Dunbar with the remaining fragments of the army. The French sent out a party as far as Dunbar's camp, and destroyed every thing that was left. Colonel Washington, being in very feeble health, proceeded in a few days to Mount Vernon.

No. V. p. 327.

ADDRESS OF THE OFFICERS TO COLONEL WASHINGTON, ON HIS RESIGNING THE COMMAND OF THE VIRGINIA FORCES.

Dated at Fort Loudoun, 31 December, 1758.

SIR,

We, your most obedient and affectionate officers, beg leave to express our great concern, at the disagreeable news we have received of your determination to resign the command of that corps, in which we have under you long served.

The happiness we have enjoyed, and the honor we have acquired together, with the mutual regard that has always subsisted between you and your officers, have implanted so sensible an affection in the minds of us all, that we cannot be silent on this critical occasion.

In our earliest infancy you took us under your tuition, trained us up in the practice of that discipline, which alone can constitute good troops, from the punctual observance of which you never suffered the least deviation.

Your steady adherence to impartial justice, your quick discernment, and invariable regard to merit, wisely intended to inculcate those genuine sentiments of true honor and passion for glory, from which the greatest military achievements have been derived, first heightened our natural emulation and our desire to excel. How much we improved by those regulations and your own example, with what alacrity we have hitherto discharged our duty, with what cheerfulness we have encountered the severest toils, especially while under your particular directions, we submit to yourself, and flatter ourselves that we have in a great measure answered your expectations.

Judge, then, how sensibly we must be affected with the loss of such an excellent commander, such a sincere friend, and so affable a companion. How rare is it to find these amiable qualities blended together in one man! How great the loss of such a man! Adieu to that superiority, which the enemy have granted us over other troops, and which even the regulars and provincials have done us the honor publicly to acknowledge! Adieu to that strict discipline and order, which you have always maintained! Adieu to that happy union and harmony, which have been our principal cement!

It gives us additional sorrow, when we reflect, to find our unhappy country will receive a loss no less irreparable than our own. Where will it meet a man so experienced in military affairs, one so renowned for patriotism, conduct, and courage? Who has so great a knowledge of the enemy we have to deal with? Who so well acquainted with their situation and strength? Who so much respected by the soldiery? Who, in short, so able to support the military character of Virginia?

Your approved love to your King and country, and your uncommon perseverance in promoting the honor and true interest of the service, convince us that the most cogent reasons only could induce you to quit it; yet we, with the greatest deference, presume to entreat you to suspend those thoughts for another year, and to lead us on to assist in the glorious work of extirpating our enemies, towards which so considerable advances have been already made. In you we place the most implicit confidence. Your presence only will cause a steady firmness and vigor to actuate every breast, despising the greatest dangers, and thinking light of toils and hardships, while led on by the man we know and love.

But if we must be so unhappy as to part, if the exigencies of your affairs force you to abandon us, we beg it as our last request, that you will recommend some person most capable to command, whose military knowledge, whose honor, whose conduct, and whose disinterested principles, we may depend on.

Frankness, sincerity, and a certain openness of soul, are the true characteristics of an officer, and we flatter ourselves that you do not think us capable of saying any thing contrary to the purest dictates of our minds. Fully persuaded of this, we beg leave to assure you, that, as you have hitherto been the actuating soul of our whole corps, we shall at all times pay the most invariable regard to your will and pleasure, and will always be happy to demonstrate by our actions with how much respect and esteem we are, &c.

No. VI. p. 349.

THE OHIO COMPANY.

As the Ohio Company is often mentioned in this volume, and as two of Washington's brothers were much concerned in it, a brief sketch of its history may not be unsuitable in this place.

In the year 1748, Thomas Lee, one of his Majesty's Council in Virginia, formed the design of effecting settlements on the wild lands west of the Allegany mountains, through the agency of an association of gentlemen. Before this date there were no English residents in those regions. A few traders wandered from tribe to tribe, and dwelt among the Indians, but they neither cultivated nor occupied the lands.

With the view of carrying his plan into operation, Mr. Lee associated himself with twelve other persons in Virginia and Maryland, and with Mr. Hanbury, a merchant in London, who formed what they called "*The Ohio Company.*" Lawrence Washington, and his brother Augustine Washington, were among the first, who engaged in this scheme. A petition was presented to the King in behalf of the Company, which was approved, and five hundred thousand acres of land were granted almost in the terms requested by the Company.

The object of the Company was to settle the lands, and to carry on the Indian trade upon a large scale. Hitherto the trade with the western Indians had been mostly in the hands of the Pennsylvanians. The Company conceived, that they might derive an important advantage over their competitors in this trade, from the water communication of the Potomac and the eastern branches of the Ohio, whose head waters approximated each other. The lands were to be chiefly taken on the south side of the Ohio, between the Monongahela and Kenhawa Rivers, and west of the Alleganies. The privilege was reserved, however, by the Company, of embracing a portion of the lands on the north side of the river, if it should be deemed expedient. Two hundred thousand acres were to be selected immediately, and to be held for ten years free from quitrent or any tax to the King, on condition that the Company should at their own expense seat one hundred families on the lands within seven years, and build a fort, and maintain a garrison sufficient to protect the settlement.

The first steps taken by the Company were to order Mr. Hanbury, their agent in London, to send over for their use two cargoes of goods suited to the Indian trade, amounting in the whole to four thousand pounds sterling, one cargo to arrive in November, 1749, the other in March following. They resolved, also, that such roads should be made and houses built, as would facilitate the communication from the head of navigation on the Potomac River across the mountains to some point on the Monongahela. And as no attempt at establishing settlements could safely be made without some previous arrangements with the Indians, the Company petitioned the government of Virginia to invite them to a treaty. As a preliminary to other proceedings, the Company also sent out Mr. Christopher Gist with instructions to explore the country, examine the quality of the lands, keep a journal of his adventures, draw as accurate a plan of the country as his observations would permit, and report the same to the board. On his first tour he was absent nearly seven months, penetrated the country for several hundred miles north of the Ohio, visited the Twigtwee Indians, and proceeded as far south as the falls of that river. In November following (1751), he passed down the south side of the river, as far as the Great Kenhawa, and spent the winter in exploring the lands on that route. Meantime the Indians had failed to assemble at Logstown, where they had been invited by the Governor of Virginia to hold a treaty. It was natural that the traders, who had already got possession of the ground, should endeavour to bias the Indians, and throw obstacles in the way of any interference from another quarter. The French were likewise tampering with them, and from political motives were using means to withdraw them from every kind of alliance or intimacy with the English. The Company found, that it would be in vain to expect much progress in their designs, till measures had been adopted for winning over the Indians; and accordingly the proposed treaty of Logstown took place the next year, when Mr. Gist attended as an agent from the Company, and the Indians agreed not to molest any settlements, that might be made on the south-east side of the Ohio. This treaty was concluded June 13th, 1752. Colonel Fry, and two other commissioners, were present on the part of Virginia.

It is remarkable, that, in the debates attending the negotiation of this treaty, the Indians took care to disclaim a recognition of the English title to any of these lands. In a speech to the Commissioners, one of the old chiefs said, "You acquainted us yesterday with the King's right to all the lands in Virginia, as far as it is settled, and back from thence to the sun-setting, whenever he shall think fit to extend his settlements. You produced also a copy of his deed from the Onondaga Council, at the Treaty of Lancaster [1744], and desired, that your brethren of the Ohio might likewise confirm the deed. We are well acquainted, that our Chief Council at the Treaty of Lancaster confirmed a deed to you for a quantity of land in Virginia, which you have a right to; but we never understood, before you told us yesterday, that the lands then sold were to extend farther to the sun-setting, than the hill on the other side of the Allegany Hill, so that we can give you no farther answer." — *MS. Journal of the Commissioners.* Hence it appears, that the Indians west of the Ohio, who inhabited the lands, had never consented to any treaty ceding them to the English, nor understood that this cession extended beyond the Allegany Mountains.

When the Company was first instituted, Mr. Lee, its projector, was its principal organ, and most efficient member. He died soon afterwards, and then the chief management fell on Lawrence Washington, who had engaged in the enterprise with an enthusiasm and energy peculiar to his character. His agency was short, however, as his rapidly declining health soon terminated in his death. Several of the Company's shares changed hands. Governor Dinwiddie and George Mason became proprietors. There were originally but twenty shares, and the Company never consisted of more than that number of members.

Mr. Lawrence Washington had a project for inducing German settlers to take up the lands. He wrote to Mr. Hanbury as follows.

"Whilst the unhappy state of my health called me back to our Springs [at Bath in Virginia], I conversed with all the Pennsylvanian Dutch, whom I met either there or elsewhere, and much recommended their settling on the Ohio. The chief reason against it was the paying of an English clergyman, when few understood, and none made use of him. It has been my opinion, and I hope ever will be, that restraints on conscience are cruel, in regard to those on whom they are imposed, and injurious to the country imposing them. England, Holland, and Prussia I may quote as examples, and much more Pennsylvania, which has flourished under that delightful liberty, so as to become the admiration of every man, who considers the short time it has been settled. As the Ministry have thus far shown the true spirit of patriotism, by encouraging the extending of our dominions in America, I doubt not by an application they would still go farther, and complete what they have begun, by procuring some kind of charter to prevent the residents on the Ohio and its branches from being subject to parish taxes. They all assured me, that they might have from Germany any number of settlers, could they but obtain their favorite exemption. I have promised to endeavour for it, and now do my utmost by this letter. I am well assured we shall never obtain it by a law here. This colony was greatly settled in the latter part of Charles the First's time, and during the usurpation, by the zealous churchmen; and that spirit, which was then brought in, has ever since continued, so that except a few Quakers we have no dissenters. But what has been the consequence? We have increased by slow degrees, except negroes and convicts, whilst our neighbouring colonies, whose natural advantages are greatly inferior to ours, have become populous."

A proposition was made by several Germans in Pennsylvania, that, if they could have the above exemption, they would take fifty thousand acres of the Company's land, and settle it with two hundred families. Mr. Washington wrote likewise on the subject to Governor Dinwiddie, then in England, who replied; "It gave me pleasure, that the Dutch wanted fifty thousand acres of the land granted to the Ohio Company, and I observe what you write about their own clergyman, and your endeavour to have them freed from paying the Church of England. I fear this will be a difficult task to get over; and at present the Parliament is so busy with public affairs, and the Ministry in course engaged, that we must wait some time before we can reply; but be assured of my utmost endeavours therein." No proof exists, that any other steps were taken in the affair.

Soon after the treaty at Logstown, Mr. Gist was appointed the Company's surveyor, and instructed to lay off a town and fort at Shurtees Creek, a little below the present site of Pittsburg, and on the east side of the Ohio. The Company assessed on themselves four hundred pounds towards constructing the fort. In the mean time Mr. Gist had fixed his residence on the other side of the Alleganies, in the valley of the Monongahela, and induced eleven families to settle around him on lands, which it was presumed would be within the Company's grant. The goods had come over from England, but had never been taken farther into the interior, than Will's Creek, where they were sold to traders and Indians, who received them at that post. Some progress had been made in constructing a road to the Monongahela, but the temper of the Indians was such, as to discourage an attempt to send the goods at the Company's risk to a more remote point.

Things were in this state, when the troubles on the frontiers broke out between the French and English, involving on one side or the other the various Indian tribes. All further operations were suspended till towards the close of the war, when hostilities had nearly ceased on the Virginia frontier from the capture of Fort Duquesne, and the weakened efforts of the French. In 1760 a state of the Company's case was drawn up by Mr. John Mercer, secretary to the board, and forwarded to Mr. Charlton Palmer, a solicitor in London, who was employed by the Company to apply to the King for such further orders and instructions to the government in Virginia, as might enable the Company to carry their grant into execution. The business was kept in a state of suspense for three years, when the Company resolved to send out an agent, with full powers to bring it as speedily as possible to a close. Colonel George Mercer was selected for this commission, and instructed to procure leave for the Company to take up their lands, according to the conditions of the original grant, or to obtain a reimbursement of the money, which had been paid on the faith of that grant. He repaired to London accordingly, and entered upon his charge. But at this time the counteracting interests of private individuals in Virginia, the claims of the officers and soldiers under Dinwiddie's proclamation, which extended to lands within the Ohio Company's grant, and moreover the schemes and application of the proprietors of *Walpole's Grant*, were obstacles not to be overcome. Colonel Mercer remained six years in London, without making any apparent progress in the object of his mission, and at last he agreed to merge the interests of the Ohio Company in those of Walpole's, or the *Grand Company*, as it was called, on condition of securing to the former two shares in the latter, amounting to one thirty-sixth part of the whole. These terms were not approved by the members of the Ohio Company in Virginia, nor was it clear, that Colonel Mercer's instructions authorized him to conclude such an arrangement. While the subject was still in agitation, the Revolutionary war came on, and put an end, not only to the controversy, but to the existence of the two companies. Thus the Ohio Company was in action only about four years, having never in reality revived after its first check, at the commencement of hostilities with the French and Indians on the frontiers. All persons concerned were losers to a considerable amount, though at its outset the scheme promised important advantages both to individuals, and to the country at large. The original records and papers of the Ohio Company are now in possession of Mr. Charles Fenton Mercer, of Virginia, by whose politeness I have been favored with the use of them in drawing up this brief outline.

No. VII. p. 357.

WALPOLE'S GRANT.

Immediately after the peace of 1763, a plan was suggested for settling the lands on the Ohio River. During that year a pamphlet was published in London, entitled "*The Advantages of a Settlement upon the Ohio in North America*," in which the subject was ably argued.

In the year 1766, William Franklin, governor of New Jersey, and Sir William Johnson, Indian agent for the northern colonies, proposed a scheme for establishing a new colony on the Ohio. They wrote to Dr. Franklin, who was then in London, requesting his agency in endeavouring to procure a grant for this purpose, including the territory described in Washington's letter. He pressed the application for more than a year; but the change of ministers, and the contending interests of individuals, prevented its success, and the project seems to have been suspended till 1770, when it was renewed. In April of that year, Mr. Thomas Pownall wrote to Sir William Johnson; —

"A society of us, in which some of the first people in England are engaged, and in which you and Colonel Croghan are made original partakers, have concluded a bargain with the Treasury for a large tract of land lying and fronting on the Ohio (part of the lands lately ceded by the Indians to Great Britain), large enough for a government. Having it suggested to us by Lord Hillsborough, that it would be right that we should have a charter of government, in consequence of this bargain so concluded, we are next to apply to the Council-Board, that the grant may issue. We expect to meet with opposition, and some objections arising from the impressions made by such opposition, yet have no doubt of carrying this point, as we have settled the main point. As soon as the grant has issued, we are to apply to the Lords of Trade on the subject of the charter. It will naturally occur to you, that on this matter I shall be a little referred to, and the plan I propose is, to take the charter of the province of Massachusetts Bay for the model of our government, making some few alterations therein, which practice and experience have shown to be necessary, but such only as every constituent of the proposed province would wish; such as every man, who desires to become a settler in it, would expect, be he of what denomination or description of religionist he may.

"From our peculiar situation, as a frontier province and as immediately connected with the Indian country, some peculiar additional department will be wanting in our form of government, and that is an *Indian Department*, formed for negotiation in matters of police, for a just and regular intercourse in trade, and so connected with the military branch, as to become a principal part in the time of war.

"On the subject of this department, and its several necessary offices and officers, as a department interwoven into the constitution of the government of this province, I most earnestly beg you to give me your plan and explanatory sentiments, such as will establish a proper federate connexion and intercommunion between our government and the Indians, founded on the one hand in justice and true policy towards those Indians, and on the other creative of the only security, which such a province so situated can or ought to confide in." — *MS. Letter.*

At the head of the Company was Mr. Thomas Walpole, an eminent banker in London, and from this circumstance the tract of land solicited was usually denominated "*Walpole's Grant.*" The stock of the Association was divided into seventy-two shares, and many persons of distinction were concerned in it, both in England and America. The proprietors, who had the management of the business in procuring the grant, were Thomas Walpole, Thomas Pownall, Dr. Franklin, and Samuel Wharton. They had a strenuous opponent in Lord Hillsborough, who wrote a report for the Board of Trade hostile to their petition; though it would seem from Mr. Pownall's letter, that his opposition did not show itself in the first stages of the application. This report was answered by Dr. Franklin, in one of the ablest tracts he ever penned. (Franklin's *Works*, Vol. IV. p. 250.) It was so conclusive and satisfactory, that the petition was granted by the King in Council, notwithstanding the opposition of the Board of Trade.

On the 18th of December, 1770, Colonel George Mercer, agent for the Ohio Company in England, wrote to Washington from Dublin; — "Before I left England, I mentioned my having agreed with, or I may rather say prevailed with, the great Land Company there, that the two hundred thousand acres, claimed by the officers of the Virginia troops, should be allowed out of their grant." This arrangement was of course not known to Washington, when he wrote on the subject to Lord Botetourt, and afterwards to Lord Dunmore.

Mr. Wharton wrote to Colonel Mercer, then in London, as follows, August 20th, 1772. — "I do myself the pleasure to inform you, that on the 14th instant his Majesty in Council was pleased to approve of, and order to be carried into execution, the report of the Committee of the Privy Council, in favor of the grant of land to Mr. Walpole and his Associates, and that a new government should be established thereon." The increasing troubles between the mother country and the colonies prevented the ultimate completion of the project. But it was not abandoned till the beginning of the year 1776. The Ohio Company had been merged in this Grand Association, by the consent of their agent, though not with the entire approbation of the Company. The grant covered a large part of the tract, which that Company claimed, as well as the two hundred thousand acres pledged to the officers and soldiers of Washington's first campaign by Governor Dinwiddie's proclamation. Other particulars relating to this subject are contained in Franklin's *Familiar Letters*, &c. pp. 275 - 285.

No. VIII. p. 387.

Colonel Washington was at this time (June, 1774) in Williamsburg, where he had been attending the regular sitting of the House of Burgesses. A few days after the members had assembled, news came of the act of Parliament for shutting up the port of Boston, which was to take effect on the 1st of June. Much excitement was produced by this intelligence; and when the Burgesses met on the 24th of May, they passed an order, that the 1st day of June "should be set apart by that House, as a day of fasting, humiliation, and prayer, devoutly to implore the divine interposition for averting the heavy calamity, which threatened destruction to their civil rights, and the evils of civil war, and to give them one heart and one mind firmly to oppose, by all just and proper means, every injury to American rights." Governor Dunmore was displeased at this order, and dissolved the House the next morning.

The members, however, were not driven from their purpose. They assembled, to the number of eighty-nine, at the Raleigh tavern, on the 25th of May, organized themselves, and drew up an Association, which they all signed, enumerating some of the grievances under which the colonies labored, assuming the cause of Boston as common to all, and recommending to the Committee of Correspondence in Virginia to correspond with the Committees of other colonies, on the expediency of appointing deputies to meet annually in a general Congress, at such place as should be thought most convenient. — Wirt's *Life of Patrick Henry*, 3d edit. p. 95.

Nor did the delegates disperse, till they had performed other acts of duty to their country, and even of complaisance to the Governor and his lady. They had made arrangements for honoring Lady Dunmore with a ball on the 27th of May, which were carried into execution with the same marks of attention and respect, as if nothing had occurred. The Burgesses also took care to observe with strictness their order for a fast. The following brief notes are from Washington's diary.

"*May 16th.* — Came to Williamsburg. Dined at the Governor's, and spent the evening at Mrs. Campbell's.

"*25th.* — Dined and spent the evening at the Governor's.

"*26th.* — Rode out with the Governor to his farm, and breakfasted with him there.

"*27th.* — Dined at the Treasurer's, and went to the ball given by the House of Burgesses to Lady Dunmore.

"*June 1st, Wednesday.* — Went to church, and fasted all day.

"*10th.* — Dined at the Raleigh, and went to the fireworks.

"*16th.* — Dined at the Governor's, and spent the evening at Anderson's.

"*20th.* — Set off on my return home."

On the 28th of May, as nothing more seemed necessary to be done, many of the delegates departed for their homes. But on Sunday morning, the 29th, letters were received in Williamsburg from Boston, giving an account of the proceedings of a town meeting, in which it was recommended to the colonies to enter into a general association, or agreement, neither to export nor import articles of any kind to or from Great Britain. Twenty-five of the late delegates only were then in Williamsburg, among whom was Washington. They assembled the next day, and took the subject into consideration; but, disagreeing on some points, they resolved to address a circular to the members of the different committees, and other gentlemen in the colony, which contained the following sentiments and recommendation. — "Most of the gentlemen present seemed to think it absolutely necessary for us to enlarge our late association, and that we ought to adopt the scheme of non-importation to a very large extent; but we were divided in our opinions as to stopping our exports. We could not, however, being so small a proportion of our late associates, presume to make any alteration in the terms of our general association, and we resolved to invite all the members of the late House of Burgesses to a general meeting in this city on the 1st day of August next. We fixed this distant day in the hopes of accommodating the meeting to every gentleman's private affairs, and that they might, in the mean time, have an opportunity of collecting the sense of their respective counties. The inhabitants of this city were convened yesterday afternoon, and most cheerfully acceded to the measures we had adopted."

This circular was signed by Peyton Randolph as moderator, and by the twenty-four other delegates then present. It was printed and distributed through the colony.

No. IX. p. 391.

FAIRFAX COUNTY RESOLVES.

The draft, from which the following resolves are printed, I find among Washington's papers in the handwriting of George Mason, by whom they were probably drawn up; yet as they were adopted by the committee of which Washington was chairman, and reported by him as moderator of the meeting, they may be presumed to express his opinions, formed on a perfect knowledge of the subject, and after cool deliberation. This may indeed be inferred from his letter to Mr. Bryan Fairfax, in which he intimates a doubt only as to the article favoring the idea of a further petition to the King. He was opposed to such a step, believing enough had been done in this way already; but he yielded the point in tenderness to the more wavering resolution of his associates.

These resolves are framed with much care and ability, and exhibit the question then at issue, and the state of public feeling, in a manner so clear and forcible, as to give them a special claim to a place in the present work, in addition to the circumstance of their being the matured views of Washington, at the outset of the great revolutionary struggle, in which he was to act so conspicuous a part.

"At a general Meeting of the Freeholders and Inhabitants of the County of Fairfax on Monday, the 18th day of July, 1774, at the Court-House; George Washington, Chairman, and Robert Harrison, Clerk of the said Meeting;

"1. *Resolved,* That this colony and dominion of Virginia cannot be considered as a conquered country; and if it was, that the present inhabitants are the descendants not of the conquered, but of the conquerors. That the same was not settled at the national expense of England, but at the private expense of the adventurers, our ancestors, by solemn compact with, and under the auspices and protection of, the British crown; upon which we are in every respect as dependent, as the people of Great Britain, and in the same manner subject to all his Majesty's just, legal, and constitutional prerogatives. That our ancestors, when they left their native land and settled in America, brought with them (even if the same had not been confirmed by charters) the civil constitution and form of government of the country they came from; and were, by the laws of nature and nations, entitled to all its privileges, immunities, and advantages; which have descended to us their posterity, and ought of right to be as fully enjoyed, as if we had still continued within the realm of England.

"2. *Resolved,* That the most important and valuable part of the British constitution, upon which its very existence depends, is the fundamental principle of the people's being governed by no laws, to which they have not given their consent by representatives freely chosen by themselves; who are affected by the laws they enact equally with their constituents; to whom they are accountable, and whose burthens they share; in which consists the safety and happiness of the community; for if this part of the constitution was taken away, or materially altered, the government must degenerate either into an absolute and despotic monarchy, or a tyrannical aristocracy, and the freedom of the people be annihilated.

"3. *Resolved,* Therefore, as the inhabitants of the American colonies are not, and, from their situation, cannot be represented in the British Parliament, that the legislative power here can of right be exercised only by our own provincial Assemblies or Parliaments, subject to the assent or negative of the British crown, to be declared within some proper limited time. But as it was thought just and reasonable, that the people of Great Britain should reap advantages from these colonies adequate to the protection they afforded them, the British Parliament have claimed and exercised the power of regulating our trade and commerce, so as to restrain our importing from foreign countries such articles as they could furnish us with, of their own growth or manufacture, or exporting to foreign countries such articles and portions of our produce, as Great Britain stood in need of, for her own consumption or manufactures. Such a power directed with wisdom and moderation, seems necessary for the general good of that great body politic, of which we are a part; although in some degree repugnant to the principles of the constitution. Under this idea our ancestors submitted to it; the experience of more than a century, during the government of his Majesty's royal prodecessors, has proved its utility, and the reciprocal benefits flowing from it produced mutual uninterrupted harmony and good will, between the inhabitants of Great Britain and her colonies, who, during that long period, always considered themselves as one and the same people; and though such a power is capable of abuse, and in some instances has been stretched beyond the original design and institution, yet to avoid strife and contention with our fellow-subjects, and strongly impressed with the experience of mutual benefits, we always cheerfully acquiesced in it, while the entire regulation of our internal policy, and giving and granting our own money, were preserved to our own provincial legislatures.

"4. *Resolved*, That it is the duty of these colonies, on all emergencies, to contribute, in proportion to their abilities, situation, and circumstances, to the necessary charge of supporting and defending the British empire, of which they are part; that while we are treated upon an equal footing with our fellow-subjects, the motives of self-interest and preservation will be a sufficient obligation, as was evident through the course of the last war; and that no argument can be fairly applied to the British Parliament's taxing us, upon a presumption that we should refuse a just and reasonable contribution, but will equally operate in justification of the executive power taxing the people of England, upon a supposition of their representatives refusing to grant the necessary supplies.

"5. *Resolved*, That the claim, lately assumed and exercised by the British Parliament, of making all such laws as they think fit, to govern the people of these colonies, and to extort from us our money without our consent, is not only diametrically contrary to the first principles of the constitution, and the original compacts by which we are dependent upon the British crown and government; but is totally incompatible with the privileges of a free people and the natural rights of mankind, will render our own legislatures merely nominal and nugatory, and is calculated to reduce us from a state of freedom and happiness to slavery and misery.

"6. *Resolved*, That taxation and representation are in their nature inseparable; that the right of withholding, or of giving and granting their own money, is the only effectual security to a free people, against the encroachments of despotism and tyranny; and that whenever they yield the one, they must quickly fall a prey to the other.

"7. *Resolved*, That the powers over the people of America now claimed by the British House of Commons, in whose election we have no share, on whose determinations we can have no influence, whose information must be always defective and often false, who in many instances may have a separate, and in some an opposite interest to ours, and who are removed from those impressions of tenderness and compassion arising from personal intercourse and connexions, which soften the rigors of the most despotic governments, must, if continued, establish the most grievous and intolerable species of tyranny and oppression, that ever was inflicted upon mankind.

"8. *Resolved*, That it is our greatest wish and inclination, as well as interest, to continue our connexion with, and dependence upon the British government; but though we are its subjects, we will use every means, which Heaven hath given us to prevent our becoming its slaves.

"9. *Resolved*, That there is a premeditated design and system, formed and pursued by the British ministry, to introduce an arbitrary government into his Majesty's American dominions; to which end they are artfully prejudicing our sovereign, and inflaming the minds of our fellow-subjects in Great Britain, by propagating the most malevolent falsehoods, particularly that there is an intention in the American colonies to set up for independent states; endeavouring at the same time, by various acts of violence and oppression, by sudden and repeated dissolutions of our Assemblies, whenever they presume to examine the illegality of ministerial mandates, or deliberate on the violated rights of their constituents, and by breaking in upon the American charters, to reduce us to a state of desperation, and dissolve the original compacts by which our ancestors bound themselves and their posterity to remain dependent upon the British crown; which measures, unless effectually counteracted, will end in the ruin both of Great Britain and her colonies.

"10. *Resolved*, That the several acts of Parliament for raising a revenue upon the people of America without their consent, the creating new and dangerous jurisdictions here, the taking away our trials by jury, the ordering persons, upon criminal accusations, to be tried in another country than that in which the fact is charged to have been committed, the act inflicting ministerial vengeance upon the town of Boston, and the two bills lately brought into Parliament for abrogating the charter of the province of Massachusetts Bay, and for the protection and encouragement of murderers in the said province, are part of the abovementioned iniquitous system. That the inhabitants of the town of Boston are now suffering in the common cause of all British America, and are justly entitled to its support and assistance; and therefore that a subscription ought immediately to be opened, and proper persons appointed in every county of this colony to purchase provisions, and consign them to some gentlemen of character in Boston, to be distributed among the poorer sort of people there.

"11. *Resolved*, That we will cordially join with our friends and brethren of this and the other colonies, in such measures as shall be judged most effectual for procuring redress of our grievances, and that upon obtaining such redress, if the destruction of the tea at Boston be regarded as an invasion of private property, we shall be willing to contribute towards paying the East India Company the value;

but as we consider the said Company as the tools and instruments of oppression in the hands of government, and the cause of our present distress, it is the opinion of this meeting, that the people of these colonies should forbear all further dealings with them, by refusing to purchase their merchandise, until that peace, safety, and good order, which they have disturbed, be perfectly restored. And that all tea now in this colony, or which shall be imported into it shipped before the 1st day of September next, should be deposited in some storehouse to be appointed by the respective committees of each county, until a sufficient sum of money be raised by subscription to reimburse the owners the value, and then to be publicly burned and destroyed; and if the same is not paid for and destroyed as aforesaid, that it remain in the custody of the said committees, at the risk of the owners, until the act of Parliament imposing a duty upon tea, for raising a revenue in America, be repealed; and immediately afterwards be delivered unto the several proprietors thereof, their agents, or attorneys.

"12. *Resolved,* That nothing will so much contribute to defeat the pernicious designs of the common enemies of Great Britain and her colonies, as a firm union of the latter, who ought to regard every act of violence or oppression inflicted upon any one of them, as aimed at all; and to effect this desirable purpose, that a Congress should be appointed, to consist of deputies from all the colonies, to concert a general and uniform plan for the defence and preservation of our common rights, and continuing the connexion and dependence of the said colonies upon Great Britain, under a just, lenient, permanent, and constitutional form of government.

"13. *Resolved,* That our most sincere and cordial thanks be given to the patrons and friends of liberty in Great Britain, for their spirited and patriotic conduct, in support of our constitutional rights and privileges, and their generous efforts to prevent the present distress and calamity of America.

"14. *Resolved,* That every little jarring interest and dispute, which has ever happened between these colonies, should be buried in eternal oblivion; that all manner of luxury and extravagance ought immediately to be laid aside, as totally inconsistent with the threatening and gloomy prospect before us; that it is the indispensable duty of all the gentlemen and men of fortune to set examples of temperance, fortitude, frugality, and industry, and give every encouragement in their power, particularly by subscriptions and premiums, to the improvement of arts and manufactures in America; that great care and attention should be had to the cultivation of flax, cotton, and other materials for manufactures; and we recommend it to such of the inhabitants, as have large stocks of sheep, to sell to their neighbours at a moderate price, as the most certain means of speedily increasing our breed of sheep, and quantity of wool.

"15. *Resolved*, That until American grievances be redressed, by restoration of our just rights and privileges, no goods or merchandise whatsoever ought to be imported into this colony, which shall be shipped from Great Britain or Ireland after the 1st day of September next, except linens not exceeding fifteen pence per yard, coarse woollen cloth, not exceeding two shillings sterling per yard, nails, wire and wire cards, needles and pins, paper, saltpetre, and medicines, which may be imported until the 1st day of September, 1776; and if any goods or merchandise, other than those hereby excepted, should be shipped from Great Britain, after the time aforesaid, to this colony, that the same, immediately upon their arrival, should either be sent back again, by the owners, their agents, or attorneys, or stored and deposited in some warehouse, to be appointed by the committee for each respective county, and there kept, at the risk and charge of the owners, to be delivered to them, when a free importation of goods hither shall again take place. And that the merchants and venders of goods and merchandise within this colony ought not to take advantage of our present distress, but continue to sell the goods and merchandise which they now have, or which may be shipped to them before the 1st day of September next, at the same rates and prices they have been accustomed to do, within one year last past; and if any person shall sell such goods on any other terms than above expressed, that no inhabitant of this colony should at any time, for ever thereafter, deal with him, his agent, factor, or storekeepers for any commodity whatsoever.

"16. *Resolved*, That it is the opinion of this meeting, that the merchants and venders of goods and merchandise within this colony should take an oath, not to sell or dispose of any goods or merchandise whatsoever, which may be shipped from Great Britain after the 1st day of September next as aforesaid, except the articles before excepted, and that they will, upon receipt of such prohibited goods, either send the same back again by the first opportunity, or deliver them to the committees in the respective counties, to be deposited in some warehouse, at the risk and charge of the owners, until they, their agents, or factors be permitted to take them away by the said committees; the names of those who refuse to take such oath to be advertised by the respective committees in the counties wherein they reside. And to the end that the inhabitants of this colony may know what merchants and venders of goods and merchandise have taken such oath, that the respective committees should grant a certificate thereof to every such person who shall take the same.

"17. *Resolved,* That it is the opinion of this meeting, that during our present difficulties and distress, no slaves ought to be imported into any of the British colonies on this continent; and we take this opportunity of declaring our most earnest wishes to see an entire stop for ever put to such a wicked, cruel, and unnatural trade.

"18. *Resolved,* That no kind of lumber should be exported from this colony to the West Indies, until America be restored to her constitutional rights and liberties, if the other colonies will accede to a like resolution; and that it be recommended to the general Congress to appoint as early a day as possible for stopping such export.

"19. *Resolved,* That it is the opinion of this meeting, if American grievances be not redressed before the 1st day of November, 1775, that all exports of produce from the several colonies to Great Britain should cease; and to carry the said resolution more effectually into execution, that we will not plant or cultivate any tobacco, after the crop now growing; provided the same measure shall be adopted by the other colonies on this continent, as well those who have heretofore made tobacco, as those who have not. And it is our opinion also, if the Congress of deputies from the several colonies shall adopt the measure of non-exportation to Great Britain, as the people will be thereby disabled from paying their debts, that no judgments should be rendered by the courts in the said colonies for any debt, after information of the said measure's being determined upon.

"20. *Resolved,* That it is the opinion of this meeting that a solemn covenant and association should be entered into by the inhabitants of all the colonies upon oath, that they will not, after the times which shall be respectively agreed on at the general Congress, export any manner of lumber to the West Indies, nor any of their produce to Great Britain, or sell or dispose of the same to any person who shall not have entered into the said covenant and association; and also that they will not import or receive any goods or merchandise which shall be shipped from Great Britain after the 1st day of September next, other than the before enumerated articles, nor buy or purchase any goods, except as before excepted, of any person whatsoever, who shall not have taken the oath herein before recommended to be taken by the merchants and venders of goods, nor buy or purchase any slaves hereafter imported into any part of this continent until a free exportation and importation be again resolved on by a majority of the representatives or deputies of the colonies. And that the respective committees of the counties in each colony, so soon as the covenant and association becomes general, publish by advertisements in their several counties, a list of the names of those (if any such there be) who will not accede thereto; that such traitors to their country may be publicly known and detested.

"21. *Resolved,* That it is the opinion of this meeting, that this and the other associating colonies should break off all trade, intercourse, and dealings, with that colony, province, or town, which shall decline or refuse to agree to the plan, which shall be adopted by the general Congress.

"22. *Resolved,* That should the town of Boston be forced to submit to the late cruel and oppressive measures of government, that we shall not hold the same to be binding upon us, but will, notwithstanding, religiously maintain and inviolably adhere to such measures as shall be concerted by the general Congress, for the preservation of our lives, liberties, and fortunes.

"23. *Resolved,* That it be recommended to the deputies of the general Congress to draw up and transmit an humble and dutiful petition and remonstrance to his Majesty, asserting with decent firmness our just and constitutional rights and privileges; lamenting the fatal necessity of being compelled to enter into measures disgusting to his Majesty and his Parliament, or injurious to our fellow-subjects in Great Britain; declaring, in the strongest terms, our duty and affection to his Majesty's person, family, and government, and our desire to continue our dependence upon great Britain; and most humbly conjuring and beseeching his Majesty not to reduce his faithful subjects of America to a state of desperation, and to reflect, that from our sovereign there can be but one appeal. And it is the opinion of this meeting, that after such petition, and remonstrance shall have been presented to his Majesty, the same should be printed in the public papers, in all the principal towns in Great Britain.

"24. *Resolved,* That George Washington and Charles Broadwater, lately elected our representatives to serve in the General Assembly, be appointed to attend the convention at Williamsburg on the 1st day of August next, and present these Resolves, as the sense of the people of this county, upon the measures proper to be taken in the present alarming and dangerous situation of America."

Such were the opinions of Washington, and his associates in Virginia, at the beginning of the revolutionary contest. The seventeenth resolve merits attention, from the pointed manner in which it condemns the slave-trade.

No X. p. 402.

AMERICAN INDEPENDENCE.

It is not easy to determine at what precise date the idea of independence was first entertained by the principal persons in America. English writers, arguing from the conduct of the colonists, have commonly charged them with secretly harbouring such designs at a very early period. This is not probable. The spirit and form of their institutions, it is true, led them to act frequently as an independent *people*, and to set up high claims in regard to their rights and privileges, but there is no sufficient evidence to prove, that any province, or any number of prominent individuals, entertained serious thoughts of separating entirely from the mother country, till very near the actual commencement of the war of the revolution.

Chalmers, who had ample means of research among the papers in the Board of Trade, and whose historical veracity claims respect, has spoken explicitly on this subject. In reference to the change, which took place in the affairs of the Board of Trade, in 1766, he observes; — "None of the statesmen of that period, nor those of the preceding or subsequent times, had any suspicion, that there lay among the documents in the Board of Trade, and Paper Office, the most satisfactory proofs, from the epoch of the revolution in 1688, throughout every reign, and during every administration, of the settled purpose of the revolted colonies to acquire *direct independence*." — *Opinions of Eminent Lawyers*, &c. *Preface*, p. xvi. But this statement, unsupported as it is by the citation of any examples, is too vague for history. It indicates the impression left on the mind of Chalmers, but affords nothing in the nature of testimony.

Gordon relates the following anecdote of a conversation, said to have taken place in the year 1759, between Mr. Pratt, afterwards Lord Camden, and Dr. Franklin, but he cites no authority. — "For all what you Americans say of your loyalty," observed Mr. Pratt, "I know you will one day throw off your dependence upon this country; and, notwithstanding your boasted affection to it, will set up for independence." Franklin answered, "No such idea is entertained in the mind of the Americans; and no such idea will ever enter their heads, unless you grossly abuse them." "Very true," replied Mr. Pratt, "that is one of the main causes I see will happen, and will produce the event." — Gordon's *Hist. of the Am. Revolution*, Vol. I. p. 136.

As early as the year 1774, Dr. Franklin began to talk of a "*total emancipation*," or independence.—*Memoir of Josiah Quincy, Jr.* p. 250. And Mr. Wirt represents Patrick Henry, as uttering the same sentiment anterior to the meeting of the first Continental Congress. Yet the manner in which it was received by his hearers indicates, that it was to them a novel and unexpected doctrine; "at the word *independence* the company appeared to be startled, for they had never heard any thing of the kind before even suggested."—*Life of Patrick Henry*, p. 94.

Washington, in his letter to Captain Mackenzie, denies, in very strong terms, that such was the design of any persons, so far as his knowledge extended. No man, perhaps, was better informed on the subject by mingling in the society of others; and it may hence be confidently inferred, that the topic of independence was not openly broached by the members of the first Congress, even in their private discourse among themselves. That he and his immediate friends had no such object in view is manifest, from a clause in the *Fairfax County Resolves*, passed on the 18th of July preceding, at a public meeting over which he presided. It is there stated as a cause of complaint, "that the British ministry are artfully prejudicing our sovereign, and inflaming the minds of our fellow-subjects in Great Britain, by propagating the most malevolent falsehoods, *particularly that there is an intention in the American colonies to set up for independent states*." It was the opinion of Washington, and of the framers of these resolves, that the colonies had the power, by withholding their support of British commerce, to inflict so much distress on the people of Great Britain, as to rouse the government to a sense of the colonial wrongs, and produce a speedy change in their measures. And it was moreover supposed, that spirited resolutions, showing the almost universal sense of the people, that the acts of the British Parliament in regard to them were oppressive and unjust, would tend to hasten so desirable a result. Such were no doubt the views entertained by all classes of people, and the motives actuating them in the primary movements of the revolution.

The subject being somewhat curious, as well as interesting in its historical aspect, I thought it not amiss to obtain the impressions of Mr. Madison, who could not fail to have a vivid recollection of the popular feeling and principal events in Virginia at the period in question, and to know the sentiments of the political leaders. The following is an extract from his letter, dated January 5th, 1828.

"You wish me to say whether I believe, 'that at the beginning of the revolution, or at the assembling of the first Congress, the leaders of that day were resolved on independence.' I readily express my entire belief, that they were not; though I must admit, that my means of information were more limited, than may have been the case with others still living to answer the inquiry. My first entrance on public life was in May, 1776, when I became a member of the Convention in Virginia, which instructed her delegates in Congress to propose the Declaration of Independence. Previous to that date I was not in sufficient communication with any under the denomination of leaders, to learn their sentiments, or views, on that cardinal subject.

"I can only say, therefore, that so far as ever came to my knowledge, no one of them ever avowed, or was understood to entertain a pursuit of independence, at the assembling of the first Congress, or for a considerable period thereafter. It has always been my impression, that a reëstablishment of the colonial relations to the parent country, as they were previous to the controversy, was the real object of every class of the people, till despair of obtaining it, and the exasperating effects of the war, and the manner of conducting it, prepared the minds of all for the event declared on the 4th of July, 1776, as preferable, with all its difficulties and perils, to the alternative of submission to a claim of power, at once external, unlimited, irresponsible, and under every temptation to abuse from interest, ambition, and revenge. If there were individuals, who aimed at independence, their views must have been confined to their own bosoms, or to a very confidential circle."

It was the belief, before the meeting of the Congress, particularly of the more cautious and moderate, that petitions to the King and Parliament by a body of representatives assembled from all parts of the colonies, would be respected, and in the end procure redress. They, on the contrary, who, like Washington, had no confidence in the success of this measure, looked forward to the probable issue of arms, but still without any other anticipations than, by a resolute vindication of their rights, to effect a change in the conduct and policy of the British government, and restore the colonies to their former condition. It was not till these petitions were rejected with a show of indifference, if not of contempt, that the eyes of all were opened to the necessity of unconditional submission, or united resistance. From that time the word *independence* was boldly pronounced, and soon became a familiar sound to the ears of the whole people.

On the 10th of November, 1775, Mr. Richard Penn, who had been governor of Pennsylvania, and had left Philadelphia in the preceding July, was examined before the House of Lords, while the petition from Congress, which had been brought over and presented by Mr. Penn, in conjunction with the agents for the colonies, was under discussion. The following questions and answers occur in the examination.

"*Question.* Are you personally acquainted with many of the members of Congress?

"*Answer.* I am acquainted with almost all the members of the Congress.

"*Quest.* Do you think they levy and carry on this war for the purpose of establishing an *independent empire?*

"*Ans.* I think they do not carry on the war for independency. I never heard them breathe sentiments of that nature.

"*Quest.* For what purpose do you believe they have taken up arms?

"*Ans.* In defence of their liberties." — *Parliamentary Debates, November*, 1775.

It is a curious fact, that the ministers had at this moment in their hands two intercepted letters, written by Mr. John Adams in Congress, which expressed sentiments quite at variance with the testimony of Mr. Penn. These letters were dated on the 24th of July, only two weeks later than the petition to the King, taken to England by Mr. Penn, which was approved in Congress on the 8th. They were intercepted in crossing the ferry at Newport, and sent on board Admiral Graves's fleet, whence they found their way to Lord Dartmouth. The originals are now in the State Paper Office. One of these letters was from Mr. Adams to his wife, in which he said;

"The business I have had on my mind has been as great and important, as can be entrusted to one man, and the difficulty and intricacy of it are prodigious. When fifty or sixty men have a constitution to form for a great empire, at the same time that they have a country of fifteen hundred miles in extent to fortify, millions to arm and train, a naval power to begin, an extensive commerce to regulate, numerous tribes of Indians to negotiate with, a standing army of twenty-seven thousand men to raise, pay, victual, and officer, I really shall pity those fifty or sixty men."

The other letter was to James Warren, at that time Speaker of the Massachusetts Assembly, and contained the following declarations.

"We ought to have had in our hands a month ago the whole legislative, executive, and judicial power of the whole continent, and have completely modelled a constitution; to have raised a naval power and opened all our ports wide; to have arrested every friend to government on the continent, and held them as hostages for the poor victims in Boston; and then opened the door as wide as possible for peace and reconciliation. After this, they might have petitioned, and negotiated, and addressed, if they would. Is all this extravagant? Is it wild? Is it not the soundest policy?"

With sentiments like these, coming from a prominent member of Congress, it is no wonder that the ministry should be puzzled to reconcile the doctrines and assertions of the petition to the King, in which that body express their loyalty, and desire an opportunity "of evincing the sincerity of their professions, by every testimony of devotion becoming the most dutiful subjects and the most affectionate colonists." No charge of insincerity, however, can attach to Mr. Adams. It is well known, that he had little sympathy with the party, who insisted on this last petition, and that he and others yielded to their associates, with the view of preserving peace and harmony within the walls of Congress, as the only means of ultimate union and success. At this stage of affairs they hoped nothing from petitions, and anticipated a remedy of evils from no other source, than strong and determined measures on the part of the representatives of the people. Whatever may have been the opinions or wishes of other members of Congress, it is hardly possible, that Mr. Adams could have written the above letters without looking forward at least to the possibility of a speedy separation, and an independent form of government. The fact of their being in the hands of the ministry, when the petition came under the notice of Parliament, may serve as a key to some of the proceedings on the subject.

In tracing this matter farther, we shall find the opinions of Washington, Madison, and Penn, in regard to a scheme of independence among the colonists anterior to the beginning of the revolution, confirmed by other testimony of the highest order. In a letter, which Dr. Franklin wrote to his son, dated March 22d, 1775, he relates a conversation he had held in the August preceding with Lord Chatham, in which that statesman spoke of the prevailing belief in England, that the colonies aimed at setting themselves up as an independent state. "I assured him," said Franklin, "that having more than once travelled almost from one end of the continent to the other, and kept a great variety of company, eating, drinking, and conversing with them freely, I never had heard in any conversation from any person, drunk or sober, the least expression of a wish for a separation, or a hint that such a thing would be advantageous to America." — *Franklin's Works*, Vol. I. p. 278.

Again, Mr Jay, remarking on certain parts of Botta's History of the American Revolution, in a letter to Mr. Otis, January 13th, 1821, thus expressed himself. "During the course of my life, and until after the second petition of Congress, in 1775, I never did hear an American of any class, or of any description, express a wish for the independence of the colonies." "It has always been, and still is my opinion and belief, that our country was prompted and impelled to independence by *necessity*, and not by *choice*. They, who know how we were then circumstanced, know from whence that necessity resulted." — *Life of John Jay*, Vol. II. p. 412.

We have likewise the opinions, uttered on the same occasion, of two other persons not less qualified to judge, than any that have been mentioned. "That there existed a general desire of independence of the crown," says Mr. John Adams, "in any part of America, before the revolution, is as far from the truth as the zenith from the nadir." "For my own part, there was not a moment during the revolution, when I would not have given every thing I possessed for a restoration to the state of things before the contest began, provided we could have had a sufficient security for its continuance." — *Ibid.* p. 416. And Mr. Jefferson affirmed, — "What, eastward of New York, might have been the dispositions towards England before the commencement of hostilities, I know not; before that I never had heard a whisper of a disposition to separate from Great Britain; and after that, its possibility was contemplated with affliction by all." — *Ibid.* p. 417.

This mass of testimony, derived from separate sources, coincident in every particular, vouched by the first names in American history, and the principal actors in producing a separation, is perfectly conclusive on this point. It is moreover established, as Mr. Jay has remarked, by all the public documents and proceedings of the colonial legislatures, in which assurances of loyalty and allegiance are uniform and cordial. Any opinion, therefore, that the spirit of independence had an early origin, and a progressive growth, with a direct aim to a separation, or the prospect of such an event, must be a mere inference, sanctioned only by the circumstances of the free institutions of the colonies, and the tendency of a people under such institutions to self-government and a system independent of foreign control.

The following curious and characteristic letter from John Adams to Richard Henry Lee was written in Congress, November 15th, 1775, nearly eight months before the declaration of independence. A copy was taken from the original by a merchant in Virginia, and forwarded to his friend in Glasgow, by whom it was transmitted to the British ministry. It is now in the State Paper Office.

"The course of events," says Mr. Adams, "naturally turns the thoughts of gentlemen in common to the subjects of legislation and jurisprudence; and it is a current problem, what form of government is most readily and easily adopted by a colony upon a sudden emergency. Nature and experience have already pointed out a solution of this problem in the choice of conventions and committees of safety. Nothing is wanting, in addition to these, to make a complete government, but the choice of magistrates for the administration of justice. Taking nature and experience for my guide, I have formed the following sketch, which may be varied in any one particular an infinite number of ways, so as to accommodate it to the genius, temper, principles, and even prejudices of different people.

"A legislative, executive, and judicial power comprehends the whole of what is meant and understood by government. It is by balancing each of these powers against the other two, that the effort in human nature towards tyranny can alone be checked and restrained, and any degree of freedom preserved in the constitution.

"Let a full and free representation be chosen for a house of commons. Let the house choose by ballot twelve, sixteen, twenty-four, or twenty-eight persons, either members of the house, or from the people at large, as the electors please, for a council. Let the house and council by joint ballot choose a governor annually, or septennially, as you like. Let the governor, council, and house be each a distinct and independent branch of legislation, and have a negative on all laws. Let the lieutenant-governor, secretary, commissary, attorney-general, and solicitor-general, be chosen annually by joint ballot of both houses. Let the governor, with seven counsellors, be a quorum. Let all officers and magistrates, civil and military, be nominated and appointed by the governor, by and with the advice and consent of his council. Let no officers be appointed but by a general council. Let the judges, at least of the superior court, be incapacitated by law from holding any share in the legislative or executive powers, and let their commissions be during good behaviour, and their salaries ascertained and established by law. Let the governor have the command of the army, militia, forts. Let the colony have a seal, and affix it to all commissions.

"In this way, a single month is sufficient, without the least convulsion or animosity, to accomplish a total revolution. If it is thought more beneficial, a law may be made by the new legislature, leaving to the people at large the privilege of choosing their governor and council annually, as soon as matters get into a more quiet course. Adopting a plan similar to this, human nature will appear in its proper glory, asserting its own real dignity, putting down tyrannies at a single exertion, and erecting such new fabrics, as it thinks best calculated to promote its happiness."

No. XI. p. 402.

BRIEF EXTRACTS FROM A DIARY.

Although Washington could hardly be considered a man of reading, or one who gathered knowledge from a deep study of books, yet few were better informed on all the practical topics of life, or had a more perfect understanding of the political principles on which the English government was founded, and of the true merits of the controversy between Great Britain and the colonies. No gentleman associated more constantly and intimately with men of the first talents and attainments, or was more eager or better qualified to profit by such an intercourse. At Mount Vernon he lived in the exercise of an open and generous hospitality, which drew to his house the best part of the society of Virginia and Maryland, as well as strangers from other colonies. He also spent a portion of every year at Williamsburg, as a member of the House of Burgesses, where he frequented the circles of wealth and fashion, at the same time that he was brought into contact with men of powerful minds in the transaction of public affairs. His manner of life was a school, in which every day increased his insight into human character, and sharpened his faculties of observation and judgment, always acute and always active.

The following meagre hints from his Diary, during the whole time of his attendance at the first Congress in Philadelphia, are of no other value, than as showing how he passed his time while not occupied with his public duties. It will be seen, that he was constantly abroad, in company with the most enlightened society, and thus in a condition to collect the sentiments of all parties on the great subjects, which then agitated the country. This trait in his habits is worth recording, and worth remembering, as it is a key to many incidents in his career, not easily explained without it. In the present instance, also, these entries in his Diary afford an evidence of the high consideration in which he was already held, if we may judge from the eagerness with which his company was sought.

Mr. Pendleton and Patrick Henry spent a day and night with him at Mount Vernon, on their way to Philadelphia, and they all set off together for that place on the 31st of August.

"*September 4th.* — Breakfasted at Christiana Ferry; dined at Chester; and lodged at Dr. Shippen's in Philadelphia, after supping at the New Tavern.

"*5th.* — Breakfasted and dined at Dr. Shippen's. Spent the evening at the Tavern.

"*6th.* — Dined at the New Tavern, after being in Congress all day.

"*7th.* — Dined at Mr. Pleasant's, and spent the evening with a club at the New Tavern.

"*8th.* — Dined at Mr. Andrew Allen's, and spent the evening at my own lodgings.

"*9th.* — Dined at Mr. Tilghman's, and spent the evening at home.

"*10th.* — Dined at Mr. Richard Penn's. — *11th.* At Mr. Griffin's *12th.* At Mr. James Allen's. — *13th.* At Mr. Thomas Mifflin's.

"*14th.* — Rode over the Province Island, and dined at Mr. William Hamilton's.

"*15th.* — Dined at my lodgings.

"*16th.* — Dined at the Stone House, at an entertainment given by the city to the members of Congress.

"*17th.* — Dined at Mr. Dickinson's, about two miles from town.

"*18th.* — Dined at Mr. Hill's, about six miles from town.

"*19th.* — Rode out in the morning, and dined at Mr. Ross's.

"*20th.* — Dined with Mr. Fisher, the mayor. — *21st.* With Mr. James Mease. — *22d.* With Mr. Chew, chief justice. — *23d.* With Mr. Joseph Pemberton. — *24th.* With Mr. Thomas Willing, and spent the evening at the City Tavern.

"*25th.* — Went to the Quaker meeting in the forenoon, and to St. Peter's in the afternoon; dined at my lodgings.

"*26th.* — Dined at old Dr. Shippen's, and went to the hospital.

"*27th.* — Dined at the tavern with the Virginia gentlemen.

"*28th.* — Dined at Mr. Edward Shippen's; spent the afternoon with the Boston gentlemen.

"*29th.* — Dined with Mr. Allen and went to the ball in the afternoon.

"*30th.* — Dined at Dr. Cadwalader's.

"*October 1st.* — At the Congress till three o'clock; dined with Mr. Hamilton at Bush Hill.

"*2d.* — Went to Christ's Church, and dined at the New Tavern.

"*3d.* — At Congress till three o'clock; dined at Mr. Reed's.

"*4th.* — At Congress till three o'clock; dined at young Dr. Shippen's.

"*5th.* — At Congress as above; dined at Dr. Bond's. — *6th.* At Congress; dined at Mr. Samuel Meredith's. — *7th.* At Congress; dined at Mr. Thomas Smith's. — *8th.* At Mr. John Cadwalader's.

"*9th.* — Went to the Presbyterian meeting in the forenoon, and the Romish church in the afternoon; dined at Bevans's.

"*10th.* — At Congress; dined at Mr. Morgan's.

"*11th.* —Dined at my lodgings, and spent the evening at Bevans's.

"*12th.* — At Congress all the forenoon; dined at Mr. Thomas Wharton's, and went to the Governor's club.

"*13th.* — At Congress till four o'clock; dined at my lodgings. — *14th.* Dined at Mr. Thomas Barclay's, and spent the evening at Smith's. — *15th.* Dined at Bevans's; spent the evening at home.

"*16th.* — Went to Christ's Church in the morning; after which rode to and dined at the Province Island; supped at Byrns's.

"*17th.* — After Congress, dined on board with Captain Hamilton; evening at Mr. Mifflin's.

"*18th.* — Dined at Dr. Rush's, and spent the evening at the New Tavern. — *19th.* Dined at Mr. Willing's; evening at my own lodgings.

"*20th.* — Dined at the New Tavern with the Pennsylvania Assembly; went to the ball afterwards.

"*21st.* — Dined and spent the evening at my lodgings. — *22d.* Dined at Mr. Griffin's, and drank tea with Mr. Roberdeau. — *23d.* Dined at my lodgings, and spent the evening there. — *24th.* Dined with Mr. Mease; evening at the New Tavern. — *25th.* Dined at my lodgings. — *26th.* Dined at Bevans's, and spent the evening at the New Tavern.

"*27th.* — Set out on my return home; dined at Chester and lodged at New Castle."

The Congress met at Carpenter's Hall, in Philadelphia, on the 5th of September, and was dissolved on the 26th of October. Washington took a deep interest in the transactions of this body, and gave his unremitted attendance during its sittings. It was his custom thoroughly to understand every important measure in which he engaged, to examine its grounds, and study and weigh its details. There is now among his papers a copy of the petition to the King, sent out by this Congress, carefully and handsomely written with his own hand. This was his habit through life. When he wished to possess himself perfectly of the contents of any paper, he would copy it in a fair hand, and apparently with deliberation, that no point might escape his notice, or fail of making its due impression. Another habit akin to this was to condense documents and papers, by writing down their substance in few words, and always in a distinct and clear method. Many papers of both these kinds have been preserved, particularly on political subjects after the revolution, to which we shall have occasion to recur hereafter.

The opinion entertained of him, by his associates in the first Congress, may perhaps be gathered from the following anecdote related by Mr. Wirt.

"Congress arose in October, and Mr. Henry returned to his native county. Here, as was natural, he was surrounded by his neighbours, who were eager to hear not only what had been done, but what kind of men had composed that illustrious body. He answered their inquiries with all his wonted kindness and candor; and, having been asked by one of them, 'whom he thought the greatest man in Congress,' he replied, — 'If you speak of eloquence, Mr. Rutledge of South Carolina is by far the greatest orator; but if you speak of solid information and sound judgment, Colonel Washington is, unquestionably, the greatest man on that floor.' Such was the penetration, which, at that early period of Washington's life, could pierce through his retiring modesty and habitual reserve, and estimate so correctly the unrivalled worth of his character." — *Life of Patrick Henry*, p. 113.

No. XII. p. 406.

INDEPENDENT COMPANIES.

It had been a custom, of several years' standing in Virginia, for persons in the different counties to form themselves into independent companies, for the purpose of military discipline. On the first prospect of hostilities, these companies were prepared to act, and became zealous in the cause of liberty. They chose their own officers, and, according to the plan of their original organization, they seem to have been under no other command, than that of their captains respectively. They adopted such uniforms, as they thought proper, and provided themselves with arms, colors, and drums. As soon as war was apprehended, many of these companies solicited Colonel Washington to take them under his command. The following are the resolutions of the *Independent Company of Cadets*, in Prince William county, dated November 11th, 1774, and signed by William Grayson, as captain.

"*Resolved*, That the motto of this company shall be, *Aut liber aut nullus.*

"*Resolved*, unanimously, that Thomas Blackburn, Richard Graham, and Philip Richard Francis Lee, gentlemen, do wait on Colonel

George Washington, and request him to take the command of this company, as their field-officer, and that he will be pleased to direct the fashion of their uniform; that they also acquaint him with the motto of their company, which is to be fixed on their colors."

He always acceded to these requests, and assisted as far as he could in procuring equipments. While attending the first Congress in Philadelphia, he made contracts for articles of this sort for the independent company of Fairfax county. He reviewed the companies in different places, and animated them by his counsel and example to become expert in military science and tactics.

On one occasion he was very near being brought into an active command of these companies. The hasty step of Governor Dunmore in causing the powder to be secretly removed from the magazine in Williamsburg, and placed on board one of his Majesty's ships in the river, roused the indignation, and kindled the martial spirit, of the whole colony. The independent companies flew instantly to their arms, and resolved to march to Williamsburg, and compel the Governor by force to restore the powder. The following letters will show the tone of feeling that prevailed.

TO COLONEL GEORGE WASHINGTON.

"Fredericksburg, 25 April, 1775.

"SIR,

"By intelligence from Williamsburg it appears, that Captain Collins of his Majesty's navy, at the head of fifteen marines, carried off the powder from the magazine in that city on the night of Thursday last, and conveyed it on board his vessel by order of the Governor. The gentlemen of the Independent Company of this town think this first public insult is not to be tamely submitted to, and determine, with your approbation, to join any other bodies of armed men, who are willing to appear in support of the honor of Virginia, as well as to secure the military stores yet remaining in the magazine. It is proposed to march from hence on Saturday next for Williamsburg, properly accoutred as light-horsemen.

"Expresses are sent off to inform the commanding officers of companies in the adjacent counties of this our resolution, and we shall wait prepared for your instructions and their assistance.

"We are, Sir, your humble servants,

"HUGH MERCER,
"G. WEEDON,
"ALEXANDER SPOTSWOOD,
"JOHN WILLIS.

"P. S. As we are not sufficiently supplied with powder, it may be proper to request of the gentlemen, who join us from Fairfax or Prince William, to come provided with an over proportion of that article."

TO COLONEL GEORGE WASHINGTON.

"Charlottesville, 29 April, 1775.

"SIR,

"The county of Albemarle in general, and the gentlemen volunteers in particular, are truly alarmed, and highly incensed with the unjustifiable proceedings of Lord Dunmore, who, we are informed, has clandestinely taken possession of our ammunition lodged in the magazine. We should have attended at Fredericksburg, in order to have proceeded to Williamsburg to demand a return of the powder, had the alarm reached us before an account of security being given for its delivery. However, to assure you and the world of our readiness and willingness to resent any encroachment of arbitrary power, we now declare to you, should it be necessary, that the first company of Independents for Albemarle will attend in Williamsburg, properly equipped, and prepared to enforce an immediate delivery of the powder (if not to be obtained otherwise), or die in the attempt. With respect we remain ready to obey your commands.

"CHARLES LEWIS, *Captain.*
"GEORGE GILMER, *Lieut.*
"JOHN MARKS, *2nd Lieut.*

"P. S. The company will stand under arms all day on Tuesday waiting your answer."

Three names, signed to the first letter above, were well known in the subsequent revolutionary history. Mercer and Weedon were generals, and Spotswood a colonel, in the Continental army. The first died of wounds received at the battle of Princeton; the two last were officers of approved ability and courage.

The excitement about the powder gradually subsided, on the promise of the Governor to arrange the affair to the satisfaction of the people. More than seven hundred men well armed had collected at Fredericksburg. (Wirt's *Life of Patrick Henry*, p. 135.) A council of deputies from the assembled multitude was held, in which, after much warmth of discussion, it was resolved, that they should all return home, but be ready to march at a moment's warning, on any future alarm. At the close of the following letter is an allusion to this meeting. The letter is moreover interesting as an indication of the public opinion at that time, both in regard to approaching events, and to the character and influence of Washington.

TO COLONEL GEORGE WASHINGTON.

"Fredericksburg, 30 April, 1775.

"SIR,

"It is imagined, that the first thing, which will come on the carpet at the meeting of the Congress, will be that of establishing regular armies throughout the continent on pay. If such a thing should take place, there is not the least doubt, that you will have the command of the whole forces in this colony. In that case, I shall ever esteem you as my best friend, if you will use your interest in procuring me a commission; or, should the power of choosing officers be vested in you, and you should think proper to confer so great an honor on me, as qualifying me to be one of your officers, you will find me, as I have always been, ready to serve my country gratis in the glorious cause of liberty, at the risk of my life and fortune.

"I am extremely glad to inform you, that, after a long debate, it was at last agreed we should not march to Williamsburg. I am with respect, &c.

"ALEXANDER SPOTSWOOD."

Four days after the date of this letter, Washington set out from Mount Vernon for the Continental Congress, and as he was chosen commander-in-chief of the American forces in June, he never had any further immediate connexion with the Independent Companies. On his way to Congress he stopped a day in Baltimore (May 6th), reviewed the militia companies of that city, and dined at an entertainment given by the citizens.

No. XIII.

EXTRACTS FROM WASHINGTON'S DIARY.

1760.

January 1*st.* — Visited my plantations, and received an instance of Mr. F.'s great love of money, in disappointing me of some pork because the price had risen to twenty-two shillings and sixpence, after he had engaged to let me have it at twenty. Found Mrs. Washington upon my arrival broke out with the measles.

2d. — Mrs. Barnes, who came to visit Mrs. Washington yesterday, returned home in my chariot, the weather being too bad to travel in an open carriage; which, together with Mrs. Washington's indisposition, confined me to the house, and gave me an opportunity of posting my books and putting them in good order.

3d. — Hauled the seine and got some fish, but was near being disappointed of my boat by means of an oysterman, who had lain at my landing, and plagued me a good deal by his disorderly behaviour.

4th. — The weather continued drizzling and warm, and I kept the house all day. Mrs. Washington seeming to be very ill, I wrote to Mr. Green this afternoon, desiring his company to visit her in the morning.

5th. — Mrs. Washington appeared to be something better. Mr. Green, however, came to see her about 11 o'clock, and in an hour Mrs. Fairfax arrived. Mr. Green prescribed, and just as we were going to dinner, Captain Walter Stuart appeared with Dr. Laurie. The evening being very cold, and the wind high, Mrs. Fairfax went home in the chariot.

6th. — The chariot not returning time enough from Colonel Fairfax's we were prevented from going to church. Mrs. Washington was a good deal better to-day; but the oysterman still continuing his disorderly behaviour at my landing, I was obliged in the most peremptory manner to order him and his company away, which he did not incline to obey till the next morning.

7th. — Accompanied Mrs. Bassett to Alexandria, and engaged a keg of butter of Mr. Kirkpatrick, being quite out of that article. Wrote from thence to Dr. Craik to endeavour if possible to engage me a gardener from the regiment, and returned in the dusk of the evening.

8th. — Directed an indictment to be formed by Mr. Johnston against J. B. for a fraud in some iron he sold me.

12th. — Set out with Mrs. Bassett on her journey to Port Royal. The morning was clear and fine, but soon clouded and threatened much rain or other falling weather, which is generally the case after a remarkable white frost, as it was to-day. We passed Occoquan without any great difficulty, notwithstanding the wind was something high, and lodged at Mr. McCrae's in Dumfries, sending the horses to the tavern. Here I was informed, that Colonel C. was disgusted at my house, and left it because he saw an old negro there resembling his own image.

16*th*.—I parted with Mr. Gisbourne, leaving Colonel Champe's before the family was stirring, and about ten o'clock reached my mother's, where I breakfasted, and then went to Fredericksburg with my brother Samuel, whom I found there. About noon it began snowing, the wind at north-west, but not cold. Was disappointed of seeing my sister Lewis, and getting a few things, which I wanted out of the stores. Returned in the evening to my mother's; all alone with her.

17*th*.—The snow had turned to rain, and occasioned a sleet, the wind at north-east, and the ground covered about an inch and a half with snow; the rain continued with but little intermission till noon, and then came on a mist which lasted till night. About noon I set out from my mother's, and just at dusk arrived at Dumfries.

18*th*.—Continued my journey home, the mist continuing till noon, when the wind got southerly, and being very warm occasioned a great thaw. I however found Potomac River quite covered with ice. Dr. Craik at my house.

28*th*.—Visited my plantation; severely reprimanded young Stephens for his indolence, and his father for suffering it. Found the new negro, Cupid, ill of a pleurisy at Dogue Run quarter, and had him brought home in a cart for better care of him.

29*th*.—White frost, and wind at south till three o'clock, then north-west, but not very cold; clear all day. Cupid was extremely ill all this day, and at night when I went to bed I thought him within a few hours of breathing his last.

February 1*st*.—Visited my plantations; found Foster had been absent from his charge since the 28th ultimo; left orders for him to come immediately to me upon his return; reprehended him severely.

5*th*.—Visited my plantations, and found, to my great surprise, Stephens constant at work. Grig and Lucy nothing better. Passing by my carpenters, that were hewing, I found that four of them, viz. George, Tom, Mike, and young Billy, had only hewed one hundred and twenty feet yesterday from ten o'clock. Sat down, therefore, and observed Tom and Mike, in a less space than thirty minutes, clear the bushes from about a poplar stock, line it ten feet long, and hew each his side twelve inches deep. Then letting them proceed their own way, they spent twenty-five minutes more in getting the cross-cut saw, standing to consider what to do, sawing the stock off in two places, putting it on the blocks for hewing it square, and lining it. From this time till they had finished the stock entirely required twenty minutes more, so that in the space of one hour and a quarter, they each of them, from the stump, finished twenty feet of hewing; from hence it appears very clear, that, allowing they work only from sun to sun, and require two hours at breakfast, they ought to yield each his one hundred and twenty-five feet, while the days are at their present length, and more in proportion as they increase.

While this was doing, George and Billy sawed thirty feet of plank, so that it appears, that making the same allowance as before (but not for the time required in piling the stock), they ought to saw one hundred and eighty feet of plank. It is to be observed, that this hewing and sawing likewise were of poplar; what may be the difference, therefore, between the working of this wood and other, some future observations must make known.

10*th.* — Ordered all the men from the different quarters to assemble at Williamson's quarter in the morning to move Petit's house.

11*th.* — Went out early myself, and continued with my people till one o'clock, in which time we got the house about two hundred and fifty yards; was informed then that Mr. Digges was at my house, upon which I returned finding him and Dr. Laurie there. The ground being soft and deep, we found it no easy matter with twenty hands, eight horses, and six oxen, to get this house along. Exceeding clear and fine; wind northwardly.

12*th.* — A small frost happening last night to crust the ground, caused the house to move much lighter, and by nine o'clock it was got to the spot on which it was intended to stand.

14*th.* — Mr. Clifton came here, and we conditioned for his land; namely, if he is not bound by some prior engagement, I am to have all his land in the Neck (five hundred acres about his house excepted), and the land commonly called Brent's, for one thousand six hundred pounds currency; he getting Messrs. Digges to join in making me a good and sufficient title. But note, I am not bound to ratify this bargain unless Colonel Carlyle will let me have his land adjoining Brent's at half a pistole an acre.

15*th.* — Went to a ball at Alexandria, where music and dancing were the chief entertainment; however, in a convenient room detached for the purpose abounded great plenty of bread and butter, some biscuits, with tea and coffee, which the drinkers of could not distinguish from hot water sweetened. Be it remembered, that pocket-handkerchiefs served the purposes of table-cloths and napkins, and that no apologies were made for either. I shall therefore distinguish this ball by the style and title of the bread and butter ball. The proprietors of this ball were Messrs. Carlyle, Laurie, and Robert

Wilson; but the Doctor, not getting it conducted agreeably to his own taste, would claim no share of the merit of it.

21st. — Visited at Mr. Clifton's, and rode over his lands, but in an especial manner viewed that tract called Brent's, which pleased me exceedingly at the price he offered it at, viz. half a pistole an acre, provided Colonel Carlyle's three hundred acres just below it could be annexed at the same price; and this but a few months ago he offered it at, but, now seeming to set a higher value upon it, and at the same time putting on an air of indifference, induced me to make Clifton another offer for his land, viz. one thousand seven hundred pounds currency for all his lands in the Neck, including his own plantation; which offer he readily accepted, upon condition of getting his wife to acknowledge her right of dower to it; and of his success in this he was to inform me in a few days.

22d. — Waited on Lord Fairfax at Belvoir, and engaged him to dine at Mount Vernon on Monday next.

26th. — Made an absolute agreement with Mr. Clifton for his land (so far as depended upon him) on the following terms, to wit, I am to give him one thousand one hundred and fifty pounds sterling for his Neck lands, containing one thousand eight hundred and six acres, and to allow him the use of this plantation he lives on till fall twelve months. He on his part is to procure the gentlemen of Maryland, to whom his lands are under mortgage, to join in a conveyance, and is to put me in possession of the land so soon as this can be done; he is not to cut down any timber, nor clear any ground, nor to use more wood, than shall be absolutely necesssary for fences and firing; neither is he to assent to any alterations of tenants, or transferring of leases; but, on the contrary, is to discourage every practice that has a tendency to lessen the value of the land. N. B. He is also to bring Mr. Mercer's opinion concerning the validity of a private sale made by himself. — Bottled thirty-five dozen of cider; the weather very warm and cloudy with some rain last night.

29th. — A very great circle round the moon.

March 2d. — Mr. Clifton came here to-day, and, under pretence of his wife's not consenting to acknowledge her right of dower, wanted to disengage himself from the bargain he had made with me for his land, on the 26th past.

6th. — Fitted a two-eyed plough, instead of a duck-bill plough, and with much difficulty made my chariot wheel-horses plough.

7th. — Put the pole-end horses into the plough in the morning, and put in the postilion and hind horse in the afternoon, but the ground being well swarded over, and very heavy ploughing, I repented putting them in at all, for fear it should give them a habit of stopping in the chariot.

11th. — Visited at Colonel Fairfax's, and was informed that Clifton had sold his land to Mr. Mason for one thousand two hundred pounds sterling, which fully unravelled his conduct on the 2d instant.

13th. — Mulatto Jack returned home with the mares he was sent for; but so poor were they, and so much abused had they been by my rascally overseer, that they were scarce able to go, much less to assist in the business of the plantations.

14th. — Mr. Carlyle and his wife still remained here. We talked a good deal of a scheme of setting up iron-works on Colonel Fairfax's land on Shenandoah. Mr. Chapman, who was proposed as a partner, being a perfect judge of these matters, was to go up and view the conveniences and determine the scheme.

17th. — Went to my mill and took a view of the ruins, which the fresh had caused; determined, however, to repair it with all expedition, and accordingly set my carpenters to making wheel and hand barrows.

18th. — Went to the court, partly on my own private business, and partly on Clifton's affair; but, the commissioners not meeting, nothing was done in regard to the latter. Much discourse happened between him and me concerning his ungenerous treatment of me; the whole turning to little account, it is not worth reciting here; the result of which was, that for fifty pounds more than Mr. Mason offered him, he undertook, if possible, to disengage himself from that gentleman, and to let me have his land. I did not think myself restrained by any rules of honor and conscience from making him this offer, as his lands were first engaged to me by the most solemn assurance, that any man could give.

19th. — Peter (my smith) and I, after several efforts to make a plough after a new model, partly of my own contriving, were fain to give it over, at least for the present.

26th. — Spent the greatest part of the day in making a new plough of my own invention.

April 4th. — Apprehending the herrings were come, hauled the seine, but caught only a few of them, though a good many of other sorts of fish.

8th. — Seven o'clock, a messenger came to inform me, that my mill was in great danger of being destroyed. I immediately hurried off all hands with shovels, &c. to its assistance, and got there myself just time enough to give it a reprieve for this time, by wheeling gravel into the place, which the water had washed. While I was there a very heavy thunder-shower came on, which lasted upwards of an hour. I tried what time the mill required to grind a bushel of corn, and to my surprise found it was within five minutes of an hour. Old Anthony attributed this to the low head of water, but whether it was so or not I cannot say. The works are all decayed, and out of order, which I rather take to be the cause. This bushel of corn, when ground, measured near a peck more of meal.

May 4th. — Warm and fine; set out for Frederic to see my negroes, that lay ill of the smallpox. Took Church in my way to Coleman's, where I arrived about sun-setting.

5th. — Reached Mr. Stephenson's in Frederic, about four o'clock, just time enough to see Richard Mounts interred. Here I was informed, that Harry and Kit, the two first of my negroes that took the smallpox, were dead, and Roger and Phillis, the only two down with it, were recovering. Lodged at Mr. Stephenson's.

7th. — After taking the doctor's directions in regard to my people, I set out for my quarters and got there about twelve o'clock, time enough to go over them and find every thing in the utmost confusion, disorder, and backwardness, my overseer lying upon his back with a broken leg, and not half a crop especially of corn-ground prepared. Engaged Valentine Crawford to go in pursuit of a nurse to be ready in case more of my people should be seized with the same disorder.

8th. — Got blankets and every other requisite from Winchester, and settled things upon the best footing I could to prevent the smallpox from spreading, and, in case of its spreading, for the care of the negroes; Mr. Crawford agreeing, in case any more of the people at the lower quarter should take it, to remove them home to his house, and if any of those at the upper quarter should get it, to have them removed into my room, and the nurse sent for.

17th. — Began weeding my trefoil below the hill. Got an account that the Assembly was to meet on Monday; resolved to set out tomorrow.

18th. — Set out in company with Mr. George Johnston; at Colchester was informed by Colonels Thornton and Chissel, that the Assembly would be broken up before I could get down; turned back, therefore, and found at my house Colonel Fairfax and his family. The lightning, which had been attended with a good deal of rain, had struck my quarter, and about ten negroes in it; some very badly injured, but with letting blood they recovered.

No. XIV.

JOURNAL OF A TOUR TO THE OHIO RIVER.

1770.

October 5th. — Began a journey to the Ohio, in company with Dr. Craik, his servant, and two of mine, with a led horse and baggage. Dined at Towlston, and lodged at Leesburg, distant from Mount Vernon about forty-five miles. Here my portmanteau horse failed.

6th. — Fed our horses on the top of the Ridge, and arrived at my brother Samuel's, on Worthington's Marsh, a little after they had dined, the distance being about thirty miles; from hence I despatched a messenger to Colonel Stephen apprising him of my arrival and intended journey.

7th. — My portmanteau horse being unable to proceed, I left him at my brother's, and got one of his, and proceeded to Samuel Pritchard's on Cacapehon. Pritchard's is a pretty good house, there being fine pasturage, good fences, and beds tolerably clean.

8th. — My servant being unable to travel, I left him at Pritchard's with Dr. Craik, and proceeded myself with Valentine Crawford to Colonel Cresap's, in order to learn from him (being just arrrived from England) the particulars of the grant said to be lately sold to Walpole and others, for a certain tract of country on the Ohio. The distance from Pritchard's to Cresap's according to computation is twenty-six miles.

9th. — Went up to Rumney in order to buy work-horses, and met Dr. Craik and my baggage; arrived there about twelve o'clock.

10th. — Having purchased two horses, and recovered another which had been gone from me near three years, I despatched my boy Silas with my two riding-horses home, and proceeded on my journey; arriving at one Wise's (now Turner's) mill about twenty-two miles, it being reckoned seven to the place where Cox's Fort formerly stood; ten to one Parker's; and five afterwards.

11th. — The morning being wet and heavy we did not set off till eleven o'clock, and arrived that night at one Killam's, on a branch of George's Creek, distant ten and a half measured miles from the north branch of the Potomac, where we crossed at the lower end of my deceased brother Augustine's land, known by the name of Pendergrass's. This crossing is two miles from the aforesaid mill and the road bad, as it likewise is to Killam's, the country being very hilly and stony. From Killam's to Fort Cumberland is the same distance, that it is to the crossing above mentioned, and the road from thence to Jolliff's by the Old Town much better.

12th. — We left Killam's early in the morning; breakfasted at the Little Meadows, ten miles off, and lodged at the Great Crossing twenty miles further; which we found a tolerably good day's work. The country we travelled over to-day was very mountainous and stony, with but very little good land, and that lying in spots.

13th. — Set out about sunrise; breakfasted at the Great Meadows thirteen miles, and reached Captain Crawford's about five o'clock. The land from Gist's to Crawford's is very broken though not mountainous; in spots exceedingly rich, and in general free from stones. Crawford's is very fine land; lying on the Youghiogany at a place commonly called Stewart's Crossing.

14th. — At Captain Crawford's all day. Went to see a coal-mine not far from his house on the banks of the river. The coal seemed to be of the very best kind, burning freely, and abundance of it.

15th. — Went to view some land, which Captain Crawford had taken up for me near the Youghiogany, distant about twelve miles. This tract, which contains about one thousand six hundred acres, includes some as fine land as ever I saw, and a great deal of rich meadow. It is well watered, and has a valuable mill-seat, except that the stream is rather too slight, and, it is said, not constant more than seven or eight months in the year; but on account of the fall, and other conveniences, no place can exceed it. In going to this land, I passed through two other tracts, which Captain Crawford had taken up for my brothers Samuel and John. I intended to have visited the land, which Crawford had procured for Lund Washington, this day also, but, time falling short, I was obliged to postpone it Night came on before I got back to Crawford's, where I found Colonel Stephen. The lands, which I passed over to-day, were generally hilly, and the growth chiefly white-oak, but very good notwithstanding; and what is extraordinary, and contrary to the property of all other lands I ever saw before, the hills are the richest land; the soil upon the sides and summits of them being as black as a coal, and the growth walnut and cherry. The flats are not so rich, and a good deal more mixed with stone.

16th. — At Captain Crawford's till the evening, when I went to Mr. John Stephenson's, on my way to Pittsburg and lodged. This day I was visited by one Mr. Ennis, who had travelled down the Little Kenhawa, almost from the head to the mouth, on which he says the lands are broken, the bottoms neither very wide nor rich, but covered with beach. At the mouth the lands are good, and continue so up the river. About Wheeling, and Fisher's Creek, there is, according to his account, a body of fine land. I also saw a son of Captain John Harden's, who said he had been from the mouth of Little Kenhawa to the Big; but his description of the lands seemed to be so vague and indeterminate, that it was much doubted whether he ever was there or not.

17th. — Dr. Craik and myself, with Captain Crawford and others, arrived at Fort Pitt, distant from the Crossing forty-three and a half measured miles. In riding this distance we passed over a great deal of exceedingly fine land, chiefly white-oak, especially from Sewickly Creek to Turtle Creek, but the whole broken; resembling, as I think all the lands in this country do, the Loudoun lands. We lodged in what is called the town, distant about three hundred yards from the fort, at one Mr. Semple's, who keeps a very good house of public entertainment. The houses, which are built of logs, and ranged in streets, are on the Monongahela, and I suppose may be about twenty in number, and inhabited by Indian traders. The fort is built on the point between the rivers Allegany and Monongahela, but not so near the pitch of it as Fort Duquesne stood. It is five-sided and regular, two of which near the land are of brick; the others stockade. A moat encompasses it. The garrison consists of two companies of Royal Irish, commanded by Captain Edmondson.

18th. — Dined in the Fort with Colonel Croghan and the officers of the garrison; supped there also, meeting with great civility from the gentlemen, and engaged to dine with Colonel Croghan the next day at his seat, about four miles up the Allegany.

19th. — Received a message from Colonel Croghan, that the White Mingo and other chiefs of the Six Nations had something to say to me, and desiring that I would be at his house about eleven, where they were to meet. I went up and received a speech, with a string of wampum from the White Mingo, to the following effect.

"That as I was a person whom some of them remember to have seen, when I was sent on an embassy to the French, and most of them had heard of, they were come to bid me welcome to this country, and to desire that the people of Virginia would consider them as friends and brothers, linked together in one chain; that I would inform the governor, that it was their wish to live in peace and harmony with the white people, and that though there had been some unhappy differences between them and the people upon our frontiers, they were all made up, and they hoped forgotten; and concluded with saying, that their brothers of Virginia did not come among them and trade as the inhabitants of the other provinces did, from whence they were afraid that we did not look upon them with so friendly an eye as they could wish."

To this I answered, after thanking them for their friendly welcome, "that all the injuries and affronts, that had passed on either side, were now totally forgotten, and that I was sure nothing was more wished and desired by the people of Virginia, than to live in the strictest friendship with them; that the Virginians were a people not so much engaged in trade as the Pennsylvanians, which was the reason of their not being so frequently among them; but that it was possible they might for the time to come have stricter connexions with them, and that I would acquaint the government with their desires."

After dining at Colonel Croghan's we returned to Pittsburg, Colonel Croghan with us, who intended to accompany us part of the way down the river, having engaged an Indian called the Pheasant, and one Joseph Nicholson an interpreter, to attend us the whole voyage; also a young Indian warrior.

20th.—We embarked in a large canoe, with sufficient store of provision and necessaries, and the following persons, besides Dr. Craik and myself, to wit, Captain Crawford, Joseph Nicholson, Robert Bell, William Harrison, Charles Morgan, and Daniel Rendon, a boy of Captain Crawford's, and the Indians, who were in a canoe by themselves. From Fort Pitt we sent our horses and boys back to Captain Crawford's, with orders to meet us there again on the 14th day of November. Colonel Croghan, Lieutenant Hamilton, and Mr. Magee, set out with us. At two we dined at Mr. Magee's, and encamped ten miles below, and four above Logstown. We passed several large islands, which appeared to be very good, as the bottoms also did on each side of the river alternately; the hills on one side being opposite to the bottoms on the other, which seem generally to be about three or four hundred yards wide, and so *vice versâ*.

21st.—Left our encampment about six o'clock, and breakfasted at Logstown, where we parted with Colonel Croghan and company about nine o'clock. At eleven we came to the mouth of the Big Beaver Creek, opposite to which is a good situation for a house, and above it, on the same side, that is the west, there appears to be a body of fine land. About five miles lower down, on the east side, comes in Raccoon Creek, at the mouth of which and up it appears to be a body of good land also. All the land between this creek and the Monongahela, and for fifteen miles back, is claimed by Colonel Croghan under a purchase from the Indians, which sale he says is confirmed by his Majesty. On this creek, where the branches thereof interlock with the waters of Shurtees Creek, there is, according to Colonel Croghan's account, a body of fine, rich, level land. This tract he wants to sell, and offers it at five pounds sterling per hundred acres, with an exemption of quitrents for twenty years; after which, to be subject to the payment of four shillings and two pence sterling per hundred acres; provided he can sell it in ten-thousand-acre lots. At present the unsettled state of this country renders any purchase dangerous. From Raccoon Creek to Little Beaver Creek appears to me to be little short of ten miles, and about three miles below this we encamped; after hiding a barrel of biscuit in an island to lighten our canoe.

22d. — As it began to snow about midnight, and continued pretty steadily, it was about half after seven before we left our encampment. At the distance of about eight miles we came to the mouth of Yellow Creek, opposite to, or rather below which, appears to be a long bottom of very good land, and the ascent to the hills apparently gradual. There is another pretty large bottom of very good land about two or three miles above this. About eleven or twelve miles from this, and just above what is called the Long Island (which though so distinguished is not very remarkable for length, breadth, or goodness), comes in on the east side of the river a small creek, or run, the name of which I could not learn; and a mile or two below the island, on the west side, comes in Big Stony Creek (not larger in appearance than the other), on neither of which does there seem to be any large bottoms or bodies of good land. About seven miles from the last mentioned creek, twenty-eight from our last encampment, and about seventy-five from Pittsburg, we came to the Mingo Town, situate on the west side the river, a little above the Cross Creeks. This place contains about twenty cabins, and seventy inhabitants of the Six Nations. Had we set off early, and kept constantly at it, we might have reached lower than this place to-day; as the water in many places ran pretty swift, in general more so than yesterday. The river from Fort Pitt to Logstown has some ugly rifts and shoals, which we found somewhat difficult to pass, whether from our inexperience of the channel, or not, I cannot undertake to say. From Logstown to the mouth of Little Beaver Creek is much the same kind of water; that is, rapid in some places, gliding gently along in others, and quite still in many. The water from Little Beaver Creek to the Mingo Town, in general, is swifter than we found it the preceding day, and without any shallows; there being some one part or another always deep, which is a natural consequence, as the river in all the distance from Fort Pitt to this town has not widened at all, nor do the bottoms appear to be any larger. The hills which come close to the river opposite to each bottom are steep; and on the side in view, in many places, rocky and cragged; but said to abound in good land on the tops. These are not a range of hills, but broken and cut in two, as if there were frequent watercourses running through, which however we did not perceive to be the case. The river abounds in wild geese, and several kinds of ducks, but in no great quantity. We killed five wild turkeys to-day. Upon our arrival at the Mingo Town, we received the disagreeable news of two traders being killed at a town called the Grape-Vine Town, thirty-eight miles below this; which caused us to hesitate whether we should proceed, or wait for further intelligence.

23d. — Several imperfect accounts coming in, agreeing that only one person was killed, and the Indians not supposing it to be done by their people, we resolved to pursue our passage, till we could get a more distinct account of this transaction. Accordingly about two o'clock we set out with the two Indians, who were to accompany us in our canoe, and after about four miles came to the mouth of a creek on the east side. The Cross Creeks, as they are called, are not large; that on the west side is biggest. At the Mingo Town we found and left more than sixty warriors of the Six Nations, going to the Cherokee country to proceed to war against the Catawbas. About ten miles below the town, we came to two other cross creeks; that on the west side is the larger, and called by Nicholson, French Creek. About three miles, or a little more below this, at the lower point of some islands, which stand contiguous to each other, we were told by the Indians, that three men from Virginia had marked the land from hence all the way to Red-stone; that there was a body of exceedingly fine land lying about this place, and up opposite to the Mingo Town, as also down to the mouth of Fishing Creek. At this place we encamped.

24th. — We left our encampment before sunrise, and about six miles below it we came to the mouth of a small creek, coming in from the eastward, called by the Indians Split-Island Creek, from its running in against an island. On this creek there is the appearance of good land. Six miles below this again we came to another creek on the west side, called by Nicholson, Wheeling; and about a mile lower down appears to be another small water coming in on the east side, which I remark, because of the scarcity of them, and to show

how badly furnished this country is with mill-seats. Two or three miles below this is another run on the west side, up which is a near way by land to the Mingo Town; and about four miles lower, comes in another on the east, at which place is a path leading to the settlement at Red-stone. About a mile and a half below this comes in the Pipe Creek, so called by the Indians from a stone, which is found here, out of which they make pipes. Opposite to this, that is, on the east side, is a bottom of exceedingly rich land; but as it seems to lie low, I am apprehensive that it is subject to be overflowed. This bottom ends where the effects of a hurricane appear, by the destruction and havoc among the trees. Two or three miles below the Pipe Creek is a pretty large creek on the west side, called by Nicholson, Fox-Grape-Vine, by others Captema, Creek, on which, eight miles up, is the town called the Grape-Vine Town; and at the mouth of it is the place where it was said the trader was killed. To this place we came about three o'clock in the afternoon, and finding nobody there, we agreed to encamp, that Nicholson and one of the Indians might go up to the town, and inquire into the truth of the report concerning the murder.

25th. — About seven o'clock, Nicholson and the Indian returned; they found nobody at the town but two old Indian women (the men being a hunting); from these they learned that the trader was not murdered, but drowned in attempting to cross the Ohio; and that only one boy, belonging to the traders, was in these parts; the trader, his father, being gone for horses to take home their skins. About half an hour after seven we set out from our encampment; around which and up the creek is a body of fine land. In our passage down to this place we saw innumerable quantities of turkeys, and many deer watering and browsing on the shore-side, some of which we killed. Neither yesterday nor the day before did we pass any rifts, or very rapid water, the river gliding gently along; nor did we perceive any alteration in the general face of the country, except that the bottoms seemed to be getting a little longer and wider, as the bends of the river grew larger.

About five miles from the Vine Creek comes in a very large creek to the eastward, called by the Indians Cut Creek, from a town or tribe of Indians, which they say was cut off entirely in a very bloody battle between them and the Six Nations. This creek empties just at the lower end of an island, and is seventy or eighty yards wide; and I fancy it is the creek commonly called Wheeling by the people of Red-stone. It extends, according to the Indians' account, a great way, and interlocks with the branches of Split-Island Creek; abounding in very fine bottoms, and exceeding good land. Just below this, on the west side, comes in a small run; and about five miles below it, on the west side also, another creek empties, called by the Indians Broken-Timber Creek; so named from the timber that is destroyed on it by a hurricane; on the head of this was a town of the Delawares, which is now deserted. Two miles lower down, on the same side, is another creek smaller than the last, and bearing, according to the Indians, the same name. Opposite to these two creeks, on the east side, appears to be a large bottom of good land. About two miles below the last mentioned creek, on the east side, and at the end of the bottom aforementioned, comes in a small creek. Seven miles from this is Muddy Creek, on the east side of the river, a pretty large creek which heads with some of the waters of Monongahela, according to the Indians' account, and is bordered by some bottoms of very good land; but in general the hills are steep, and the country broken. At the mouth of this creek is the largest flat I have seen upon the river; the bottom extending two or three miles up the river above it, and a mile below; though it does not seem to be of the richest kind. About half way in the Long Reach we encamped, opposite to the beginning of a large bottom on the east side of the river. At this place we threw out some lines at night and found a catfish, of the size of our largest river catfish, hooked to one of them in the morning, though it was of the smallest kind here. We found no rifts in this day's passage, but pretty swift water in some places, and still in others. We found the bottoms increased in size, both as to length and breadth, and the river more choked up with fallen trees, and the bottom of the river next the shores rather more muddy, but in general stony, as it has been all the way down.

26th.—Left our encampment at half an hour after six o'clock, and passed a small run on the west side about four miles lower. At the lower end of the Long Reach, and for some distance up it, on the east side, is a large bottom, but low, and covered with beech near the river-shore, which is no indication of good land. The Long Reach is a straight course of the river for about eighteen or twenty miles, which appears the more extraordinary as the Ohio in general is remarkably crooked. There are several islands in this reach, some containing an hundred or more acres of land; but all I apprehend liable to be overflowed.

At the end of this reach we found Martin and Lindsay, two traders, and from them learnt, that the person drowned was one Philips, attempting, in company with Rogers, another Indian trader, to swim the river with their horses at an improper place; Rogers himself narrowly escaping. Five miles lower down comes in a large creek from the east, right against an island of good land, at least a mile or two in length. At the mouth of this creek (the name of which I could not learn, except that it was called by some Ball's Creek, from one Ball that hunted on it) is a bottom of good land, though rather too much mixed with beech. Opposite to this island the Indians showed us a buffalo's path, the tracks of which we saw. Five or six miles below the last mentioned creek we came to the Three Islands. Below these islands is a large body of flat land, with a watercourse running through it on the east side, and the hills back neither so high nor steep in appearance, as they are up the river. On the other hand, the bottoms do not appear so rich, though much longer and wider. The bottom last mentioned is upon a straight reach of the river, I suppose six or eight miles in length. About twelve miles below the Three Islands we encamped, just above the mouth of the creek, which appears pretty large at the mouth, and just above an island. All the lands from a little below the creek, which I have distinguished by the name of Ball's Creek, appear to be level, with some small hillocks intermixed, as far as we could see into the country. We met with no rifts to-day, but some pretty strong water; upon the whole tolerably gentle. The sides of the river were a good deal incommoded with old trees, which impeded our passage a little. This day proved clear and pleasant; the only day since the 18th that it has not rained or snowed, or threatened the one or other.

27th.—Left our encampment a quarter before seven; and after passing the creek near which we lay, and another of much the same size and on the same side, also an island about two miles in length, but not wide, we came to the mouth of Muskingum, distant from our encampment about four miles. This river is about one hundred and fifty yards wide at the mouth; it runs out in a gentle current and clear stream, and is navigable a great way into the country for canoes. From Muskingum to the Little Kenhawa is about thirteen miles. This is about as wide at the mouth as the Muskingum, but the water much deeper. It runs up towards the inhabitants of Monongahela, and, according to the Indians' account, forks about forty or fifty miles from the mouth, and the ridge between the two prongs leads directly to the settlement. To this fork, and above, the water is navigable for canoes. On the upper side of this river there appears to be a bottom of exceedingly rich land, and the country from hence quite up to the Three Islands level and in appearance fine. The Ohio running round it in the form of a horse-shoe forms a neck of flat land, which, added to that running up the second Long Reach aforementioned, cannot contain less than fifty thousand acres in view.

About six or seven miles below the mouth of the Little Kenhawa, we came to a small creek on the west side, which the Indians called Little Hockhocking; but before we did this, we passed another small creek on the same side near the mouth of that river, and a cluster of islands afterwards. The lands for two or three miles below the mouth of the Little Kenhawa on both sides of the Ohio appear broken and indifferent; but opposite to the Little Hockhocking there is a bottom of good land, through which there runs a small watercourse. I suppose there may be, of this bottom and flat land together, two or three thousand acres. The lower end of this bottom is opposite to a small island, of which I dare say little is to be seen when the river is high. About eight miles below Little Hockhocking we encamped opposite to the mouth of the Great Hockhocking, which, though so called, is not a large water; though the Indians say canoes can go up it forty or fifty miles. Since we left the Little Kenhawa the lands appear neither so level nor so good. The bends of the river and bottoms are longer, but not so rich as in the upper part of the river.

28th. — Left our encampment about seven o'clock. Two miles below, a small run comes in, on the east side, through a piece of land that has a very good appearance, the bottom beginning above our encampment, and continuing in appearance wide for four miles down, where we found Kiashuta and his hunting party encamped. Here we were under a necessity of paying our compliments, as this person was one of the Six Nation chiefs, and the head of those upon this river. In the person of Kiashuta I found an old acquaintance, he being one of the Indians that went with me to the French in 1753. He expressed a satisfaction at seeing me, and treated us with great kindness, giving us a quarter of very fine buffalo. He insisted upon our spending that night with him, and, in order to retard us as little as possible, moved his camp down the river just below the mouth of a creek, the name of which I could not learn. At this place we all encamped. After much counselling over night, they all came to my fire the next morning with great formality; when Kiashuta, rehearsing what had passed between me and the Sachems at Colonel Croghan's, thanked me for saying, that peace and friendship with them were the wish of the people of Virginia, and for recommending it to the traders to deal with them upon a fair and equitable footing; and then again expressed their desire of having a trade opened with Virginia, and that the governor thereof might not only be made acquainted therewith, but with their friendly disposition towards the white people. This I promised to do.

29th. — The tedious ceremony, which the Indians observe in their counsellings and speeches, detained us till nine o'clock. Opposite to the creek, just below which we encamped, is a pretty long bottom, and I believe tolerably wide; but about eight or nine miles below the aforementioned creek, and just below a pavement of rocks on the west side, comes in a creek, with fallen timber at the mouth, on which the Indians say there are wide bottoms and good land. The river bottoms above, for some distance, are very good, and continue so for near half a mile below the creek. The pavement of rocks is only to be seen at low water. About a mile below the mouth of the creek there is another pavement of rocks on the east side, in a kind of sedgy ground. On this creek are many buffaloes, according to the Indians' account. Six miles below this comes in a small creek on the west side, at the end of a small, naked island, and just above another pavement of rocks. This creek comes through a bottom of fine land, and opposite to it, on the east side of the river, appears to be a large bottom of very fine land also. At this place begins what they call the Great Bend. Two miles below, on the east side, comes in another creek, just below an island, on the upper point of which are some dead standing trees, and a parcel of white-bodied sycamores; in the mouth of this creek lies a sycamore blown down by the wind. From hence an east line may be run three or four miles; thence a north line till it strikes the river, which I apprehend would include about three or four thousand acres of valuable land. At the mouth of this creek is the warriors' path to the Cherokee country. For two miles and a half below this the Ohio runs a north-east course, and finishes what they call the Great Bend. Two miles and a half below this we encamped.

30th. — We set out about fifty minutes past seven, the weather being windy and cloudy, after a night of rain. After about two miles we came to the head of a bottom, in the shape of a horse-shoe, which I judge to be about six miles round; the beginning of the bottom appeared to be very good land, but the lower part did not seem so friendly. The upper part of the bottom we encamped on was exceeding good, but the lower part rather thin land, covered with beech. In it is some clear meadow-land, and a pond or lake. This bottom begins just below the rapid at the point of the Great Bend. The river from this place narrows very considerably, and for five or six miles is scarcely more than one hundred and fifty or two hundred yards over. The water yesterday, except the rapid at the Great

Bend, and some swift places about the islands, was quite dead, and as easily passed one way as the other; the land in general appeared level and good.

About ten miles below our encampment, and a little lower down than the bottom described to lie in the shape of a horse-shoe, comes in a small creek on the west side, and opposite to this on the east begins a body of flat land, which the Indians tell us runs quite across the fork to the falls in the Kenhawa, and must at least be three days' walk across; if so, the flat land contained therein must be very considerable. A mile or two below this we landed, and after getting a little distance from the river, we came, without any rising, to a pretty lively kind of land grown up with hickory and oaks of different kinds, intermixed with walnut. We also found many shallow ponds, the sides of which, abounding with grass, invited innumerable quantities of wild fowl, among which I saw a couple of birds in size between a swan and a goose, and in color somewhat between the two, being darker than the young swan and of a more sooty color. The cry of these birds was as unusual as the birds themselves; I never heard any noise resembling it before. About five miles below this we encamped in a bottom of good land, which holds tolerably flat and rich for some distance out.

31*st.* — I sent the canoe down about five miles to the junction of the two rivers, that is, the Kenhawa with the Ohio, and set out upon a hunting party to view the land. We steered nearly east for about eight or nine miles, then bore southwardly and westwardly, till we came to our camp at the confluence of the rivers. The land from the rivers appeared but indifferent, and very broken; whether these ridges may not be those that divide the waters of the Ohio from the Kenhawa is not certain, but I believe they are; if so, the lands may yet be good; if not, that which lies beyond the river bottoms is worth little.

November 1*st.* — Before eight o'clock we set off with our canoe up the river, to discover what kind of lands lay upon the Kenhawa. The land on both sides this river just at the mouth is very fine; but on the east side, when you get towards the hills, which I judge to be about six or seven hundred yards from the river, it appears to be wet, and better adapted for meadow than tillage. This bottom continues up the east side for about two miles; and by going up the Ohio a good tract might be got of bottom land, including the old Shawnee Town, which is about three miles up the Ohio, just above the mouth of a creek. We judged we went up the Kenhawa about ten miles to-day. On the east side appear to be some good bottoms, but small, neither long nor wide, and the hills back of them rather steep and poor.

2d. — We proceeded up the river with the canoe about four miles farther, and then encamped, and went a hunting; killed five buffaloes and wounded some others, three deer, &c. This country abounds in buffaloes and wild game of all kinds; as also in all kinds of wild fowl, there being in the bottoms a great many small, grassy ponds, or lakes, which are full of swans, geese, and ducks of different kinds. Some of our people went up the river four or five miles higher, and found the same kind of bottom on the west side; and we were told by the Indians, that it continued to the falls, which they judged to be fifty or sixty miles higher up. This bottom next the water in most places is very rich; as you approach to the hills you come to a thin white-oak land and poor. The hills as far as we could judge were from half a mile to a mile from the river, poor and steep in the parts we saw, with pine growing on them. Whether they are generally so or not we cannot tell, but I fear they are.

3d. — We set off down the river, on our return homewards, and encamped at the mouth. At the beginning of the bottom above the junction of the rivers, and at the mouth of a branch on the east side, I marked two maples, an elm, and hoop-wood tree, as a corner of the soldiers' land (if we can get it), intending to take all the bottom from hence to the rapids in the Great Bend into one survey. I also marked at the mouth of another run lower down on the west side, at the lower end of the long bottom, an ash and hoop-wood for the beginning of another of the soldiers' surveys, to extend up so as to include all the bottom in a body on the west side. In coming from our last encampment up the Kenhawa, I endeavoured to take the courses and distances of the river by a pocket compass, and by guessing.

4th. — After passing these hills, which may run on the river near a mile, there appears to be another pretty good bottom on the east side. At this place we met a canoe going to the Illinois with sheep; and at this place also, that is, at the end of the bottom from the Kenhawa, just as we came to the hills, we met with a sycamore about sixty yards from the river of a most extraordinary size, it measuring, three feet from the ground, forty-five feet round, lacking two inches; and not fifty yards from it was another, thirty-one feet round. After passing this bottom, and about a mile of hills, we entered another bottom and encamped. This bottom reaches within about half a mile of the rapid at the point of the Great Bend.

5th. — I sent off the canoe with our baggage, and walked across the neck on foot, with Captain Crawford, the distance, according to our walking, about eight miles, as we kept a straight course under the foot of the hills, which run about south-east and were two hours and a half in walking it. This is a good neck of land, the soil being generally good, and in places very rich. There is a large proportion of meadow ground, and the land as high, dry, and level as one could wish; the growth in most places beech intermixed with walnut, but more especially with poplar, of which there are numbers very large. The land towards the upper end is black-oak, and very good. Upon the whole, a valuable tract might be had here, and I judge the quantity to be about four thousand acres. After passing this bottom and the rapid, as also some hills, which jut pretty close to the river, we came to that bottom before remarked the 29th ultimo. A little above this bottom we encamped, the afternoon being rainy, and night wet.

6th — We left our encampment a little after daylight, and after about five miles we came to Kiashuta's hunting camp, which was now removed to the mouth of that creek, noted October 29th for having fallen timber at the mouth of it, in a bottom of good land. By the kindness and idle ceremony of the Indians, I was detained at Kiashuta's camp all the remaining part of this day; and having a good deal of conversation with him on the subject of land, he informed me, that it was further from the mouth of the Great Kenhawa to the fall of that river, than it was between the two Kenhawas; that the bottom on the west side, which begins near the mouth of the Kenhawa, continues all the way to the falls without the interposition of hills, and widens as it goes, especially from a pretty large creek that comes in about ten or fifteen miles higher up than where we were; that in the fork there is a body of good land, and at a considerable distance above this, the river forks again at an island, and there begins the reed, or cane, to grow; that the bottoms on the east side of the river are also very good, but broken with hills, and that the river is easily passed with canoes to the falls, which cannot be less than one hundred miles, but further it is not possible to go with them; that there is but one ridge from thence to the settlements upon the river above, on which it is possible for a man to travel, the country between being so much broken with steep hills and precipices.*

* For the succeeding ten days the manuscript journal has been so much injured by accident, that it is impossible to transcribe it. The route, however continued up the Ohio River, which was very much swollen by the rains.

17th. — By this morning the river had fallen in the whole twenty-two or twenty-three feet, and was still lowering. About eight o'clock we set out, and passing the lower Cross Creeks we came to a pretty long and tolerably wide and good bottom on the east side of the river; then came in the hills, just above which is Buffalo Creek. About three o'clock we came to the Mingo Town without seeing our horses, the Indian, who was sent express for them, having passed through only the morning before; being detained by the creeks, which were too high to ford.

Here we resolved to wait their arrival, which was expected to-morrow; and here then will end our water voyage along a river, the general course of which from Beaver Creek to the Kenhawa is about south-west, as near as I could determine; but, in its windings through a narrow vale, extremely serpentine; forming on both sides of the river alternately necks of very good bottoms, some exceedingly fine, lying for the most part in the shape of a half-moon, and of various sizes. There is very little difference in the general width of the river from Fort Pitt to the Kenhawa; but in the depth I believe the odds are considerably in favor of the lower parts, as we found no shallows below the Mingo Town, except in one or two places where the river was broad, and there, I do not know but there might have been a deep channel in some parts of it. Every here and there are islands, some larger and some smaller, which, operating in the nature of locks, or steps, occasion pretty still water above, but for the most part strong and rapid water alongside of them. However none of these is so swift but that a vessel may be rowed or set up with poles. When the river is in its natural state, large canoes, that will carry five or six thousand weight or more, may be worked against the stream by four hands, twenty or twenty-five miles a day; and down, a good deal more. The Indians, who are very dexterous (even their women) in the management of canoes, have their hunting-camps and cabins all along the river, for the convenience of transporting their skins by water to market. In the fall, so soon as the hunting-season comes on, they set out with their families for this purpose; and in hunting will move their camps from place to place, till by the spring they get two or three hundred or more miles from their towns; then catch beaver in their way up, which frequently brings them into the month of May, when the women are employed in planting. The men are at market, and in idleness, till the autumn again, when they pursue the same course. During the summer months they live a poor and perishing life.

The Indians who reside upon the Ohio, the upper parts of it at least, are composed of Shawanees, Delawares, and some of the Mingoes, who, getting but little part of the consideration that was given for the lands eastward of the Ohio, view the settlements of the people upon this river with an uneasy and jealous eye, and do not scruple to say, that they must be compensated for their right if the people settle thereon, notwithstanding the cession of the Six Nations. On the other hand, the people of Virginia and elsewhere are exploring and marking all the lands that are valuable, not only on the Redstone and other waters of the Monongahela, but along the Ohio as low as the Little Kenhawa; and by next summer I suppose they will get to the Great Kenhawa at least. How difficult it may be to contend with these people afterwards is easy to be judged, from every day's experience of lands actually settled, supposing these settlements to be made; than which nothing is more probable, if the Indians permit them, from the disposition of the people at present. A few settlements in the midst of some of the large bottoms would render it impracticable to get any large quantity of land together; as the hills all the way down the river, as low as I went, come pretty close, are steep and broken, and incapable of settlements (though some of them are rich), and only fit to support the bottoms with timber and wood. The land back of the bottoms, as far as I have been able to judge, either from my own observations or from information, is nearly the same, that is, exceedingly uneven and hilly; and I presume there are no bodies of flat, rich land to be found, till one gets far enough from the river to head the little runs and drains, that come through the hills, and to the sources of the creeks and their branches. This, it seems, is the case with the lands upon the Monongahela and Youghiogany, and I fancy holds good upon this river, till you get into the flat lands below the falls. The bottom land differs a good deal in quality. That highest up the river in general is richest; though the bottoms are neither so wide nor so long, as those below. Walnut, cherry, and some other kinds of wood neither tall nor large, but covered with grape vines, with the fruit of which this country at this instant abounds, are the growth of the richest bottoms; but on the other hand, these bottoms appear to me to be the lowest and most subject to floods. The sugar-tree and ash, mixed with walnut, compose the growth of the next richest low grounds; beech, poplar, and oaks the last. The soil of this is also good, but inferior to either of the other kinds; and beech bottoms are objectionable on account of the difficulty of clearing them, as their roots spread over a large surface of ground and are hard to kill.

18*th.*—Agreed with two Delaware Indians to take up our canoe to Fort Pitt, for the doing of which I was to pay six dollars and give them a quart tin can.

19th. — The Delawares set off with the canoe, and, our horses not arriving, the day appeared exceedingly long and tedious. Upon conversing with Nicholson, I found he had been two or three times to Fort Chartres, on the Illinois, and I got from him an account of the lands between this place and that, and upon the Shawnee River, on which he had been a hunting.

20th. — About one o'clock our horses arrived, having been prevented from getting to Fort Pitt by the freshes. At two we set out and got about ten miles, the Indians travelling along with us.

21st. — Reached Fort Pitt in the afternoon, distant from our last encampment about twenty-five miles, and, as near as I can guess, thirty-five from the Mingo Town. The land between the Mingo Town and Pittsburg is of different kinds. For four or five miles after leaving the first mentioned place we passed over steep, hilly ground covered with white-oak, and a thin shallow soil. This was succeeded by a lively white-oak land, less broken; and this again by rich land, the growth of which was chiefly white and red-oak mixed; which lasted, with some intervals of indifferent ridges, all the way to Pittsburg. It was very observable, that, as we left the river, the land grew better, which is a confirmation of the accounts I had before received, that the good bodies of land lie upon the heads of the runs and creeks; but in all my travels through this country, I have seen no large body of level land. On the branches of Raccoon Creek there appears to be good meadow ground, and on Shurtees Creek, over both of which we passed, the land looks well. The country between the Mingo Town and Fort Pitt appears to be well supplied with springs.

22d. — Stayed at Pittsburg all day. Invited the officers and some other gentlemen to dinner with me at Semple's, among whom was one Dr. Connolly, nephew to Colonel Croghan, a very sensible, intelligent man, who had travelled over a good deal of this western country both by land and water, and who confirms Nicholson's account of the good land on the Shawnee River, up which he had been near four hundred miles. This country (I mean on the Shawnee River), according to Dr. Connolly's description, must be exceedingly desirable on many accounts. The climate is fine, the soil remarkably good; the lands well watered with good streams, and level enough for any kind of cultivation. Besides these advantages from nature, it has others not less important to a new settlement, particularly game, which is so plentiful as to render the transportation of provisions thither, bread only excepted, altogether unnecessary. Dr. Connolly is so much delighted with the lands and climate on that river, that he wishes for nothing more, than to induce one hundred families to go there and live, that he might be among them. A new and most desirable government might be established there, to be bounded, according to his account, by the Ohio northward and westward, by the ridge that divides the waters of the Tennessee or Cherokee River southward and westward, and a line to be run from the Falls of the Ohio, or above, so as to cross the Shawnee River above the fork of it. Dr. Connolly gives much the same account of the land between Fort Chartres in the Illinois country, and Post St. Vincent, that Nicholson does, except in the article of water, which the Doctor says is bad, and in the summer scarce, there being little else than stagnant water to be met with.

23*d.* — After settling with the Indians and people that attended me down the river, and defraying the sundry expenses accruing at Pittsburg, I set off on my return home; and, after dining at the widow Miers's, on Turtle Creek, reached Mr. John Stephenson's in the night.

24*th.* — When we came to Stewart's Crossing at Crawford's, the river was too high to ford, and his canoe gone adrift. However, after waiting there two or three hours, a canoe was got, in which we passed, and swam our horses. The remainder of this day I spent at Captain Crawford's, it either raining or snowing hard all day.

25*th.* — I set out early in order to see Lund Washington's land; but the ground and trees being covered with snow, I was able to form but an indistinct opinion of it; though, upon the whole, it appeared to be a good tract of land. From this I went to Mr. Thomas Gist's and dined, and then proceeded on to the Great Crossing at Hogland's, where I arrived about eight o'clock.

26*th.* — Reached Killam's, on George's Creek, where we met several families going over the mountains to live; some without having any places provided. The snow upon the Allegany Mountains was near knee deep.

27*th.* — We got to Colonel Cresap's at the Old Town, after calling at Fort Cumberland and breakfasting with one Mr. Innis at the new store opposite.

28*th.* — The Old Town Creek was so high as to wet us in crossing it, and when we came to Cox's the river was impassable; we were obliged therefore to cross in a canoe, and swim our horses. At Henry Enoch's, at the Forks of Cacapehon, we dined, and lodged at Rinker's

29th. — Set out early, and reached my brother's by one o'clock. Dr. Craik, having business at Winchester, went that way, and was to meet me at Snickers's the next norning by ten o'clock.

30th. — According to appointment the Doctor and I met, and after breakfasting at Snickers's we proceeded to West's, where we arrived at or about sunset.

December 1st. — Reached home, having been absent nine weeks and one day.

END OF VOL II.